Praise for
The Art of Natural Building

The Art of Natural Building is a beautifully thought-out and e
edited by a veritable Who's Who of the natural building comm
grounding of the overall considerations of natural building, the n
options available, each supported by extensive resource listings, a

it all matters so much. Whether entering newly into natural build..., or seeking to broaden
and deepen your knowledge, this book is a trustworthy symposium of natural building's most
admired and experienced practitioners offering years of collective experience and wisdom.

— JUDY KNOX AND MATTS MYHRMAN, Out On Bale, (un)Ltd., Tucson, Arizona

How rich here is the spirit of natural building! If you've been wondering what's up in
the burgeoning movement to build in earth and straw, you can learn about it in this book.
More than fifty leaders in the alternative construction field have contributed to this freshly
arranged compendium of articles. The three editors, pioneers themselves in ecological
construction and organizers of numerous Natural Building Colloquia — the forum for
exchanging natural building know-how — have captured the best of what has been written
in recent years. The chapters flow logically from philosophy to the practical, with a focused
bibliography at the end of each. What's documented here is more than a novel yet timeless
way of building, it's the heart and soul of a new culture. To our high-tech life of stress
and disconnection, *The Art of Natural Building* opens a world of barefoot wisdom.

— LYNNE ELIZABETH, co-editor of *Alternative Construction: Contemporary Natural
Building Methods* and editor of *New Village,* the journal of Architects/
Designers/Planners for Social Responsibility.

We are all victims of bad design, unhealthy buildings and unsustainable building materials
and practices. This delightful book provides a powerful antidote — natural building with
natural building materials. The full spectrum of alternative materials is covered, from
papercrete to straw clay, by an eclectic mix of experts and advocates. This makes for
entertaining reading, and looking, as the text is well supported with photos and sketches.
Highly recommended! Should be required reading for all students and builders,
and everyone who wants a safe, secure, comfortable, enjoyable and sustainable home.

— DAVID A. BAINBRIDGE, solar and straw bale pioneer, coauthor
The Straw Bale House, Village Homes' Solar House Designs,
and Associate Professor, Alliant International University, San Diego

We engineers like to harrumph and scoff at anything new or different, but in doing so often overlook the obvious need to try things out and see what works. This book gives us a refreshing and comprehensive look at what people are trying worldwide — some of it brand new, some of it a revival of building methods that were proven centuries ago. It reminds us that the artistry and fun of building need not be limited to architects, and makes the case that how a building feels is as important to people's well-being as how the windows are flashed, or the roof is nailed. Our buildings express us as individuals and cultures, and *The Art of Natural Building* portrays a warm, rich palette of possibilities unencumbered by the technology obsession of our times. Read it and enjoy it, then go try something for yourself.

— BRUCE KING, author of *Buildings of Earth and Straw* and Director of the Ecological Building Network

A natural building renaissance in the industrial world has being bubbling away for decades among scattered pockets of committed pioneers and social activists, people who recognize the urgency to improve the well being of all creatures, and habitat on our planet. The 1990s brought a virtual explosion and synthesis of ideas and talent which is having a profound affect on the way communities are built. *The Art of Natural Building* is a much needed anthology of current ideas from leading thinkers and activists of our time. It is a book that will appeal to both professionals and people exploring these approaches for the first time. As a builder and educator committed to Natural Building practices I have often wished to have access to the kind of conversation which is the soul of this book. The articles shared here are a tremendous vehicle to stimulate the flow of ideas and critical questions which will further the passion and knowledge needed to bring about great change. Thank you for its timely arrival!

— KIM THOMPSON, Straw Bale Projects, Ship Harbour NS

THE ART OF
Natural Building

DESIGN, CONSTRUCTION, RESOURCES

EDITORS:
JOSEPH F. KENNEDY, MICHAEL G. SMITH, CATHERINE WANEK
ILLUSTRATED BY JOSEPH F. KENNEDY

NEW SOCIETY PUBLISHERS

Cataloguing in Publication Data:

A catalog record for this publication is available from the National Library of Canada.

Cover design by Diane McIntosh; cover image: Catherine Wanek; book design: Greg Green & Nancy Page.

Printed in Canada by Friesens Inc.

New Society Publishers acknowledges the support of the Government of Canada through the Book Publishing Industry Development Program (BPIDP) for our publishing activities, and the assistance of

 the Province of British Columbia through the British Columbia Arts Council.

Paperback ISBN: 0-86571-433-9

Inquiries regarding requests to reprint all of part of *The Art of Natural Building* should be addressed to New Society Publishers at the address below.

To order directly from the publishers, please add $4.50 shipping to the price of the first copy, and $1.00 for each additional copy (plus GST in Canada). Send check or money order to:

New Society Publishers
P.O. Box 189, Gabriola Island, BC V0R 1X0, Canada
1-800-567-6772

New Society Publishers' mission is to publish books that contribute in fundamental ways to building an ecologically sustainable and just society, and to do so with the least possible impact on the environment, in a manner that models this vision. We are committed to doing this not just through education, but through action. We are acting on our commitment to the world's remaining ancient forests by phasing out our paper supply from ancient forests worldwide. This book is one step towards ending global deforestation and climate change. It is printed on acid-free paper that is **100% old growth forest-free** (100% post-consumer recycled), processed chlorine free, and printed with vegetable based, low VOC inks. For further information, or to browse our full list of books and purchase securely, visit our website at: www.newsociety.com

New Society Publishers   www.newsociety.com

TABLE OF CONTENTS

The Earth She Laughed x
  Robert Francis Johnson
Foreword xi
  Albert Bates
Acknowledgments xii
Introduction 1
  Michael G. Smith

THE CONTEXT FOR NATURAL BUILDING 5

The Case for Natural Building 6
  Michael G. Smith
The Importance of Housing Ourselves 11
  Ianto Evans
Natural Building and Social Justice 14
  Robert Bolman
Building As If the Future Matters 16
  Ted Butchart
Vernacular Architecture of the Desert 21
  Jean-Louis Bourgeois
Sustainability and the Building Codes 26
  David Eisenberg
Life Cycle Cost and Value of Four Houses 31
  David A. Bainbridge
A Case for Caring Craftsmanship 33
  Duncan MacMaster

Design and Planning 35

Designing for Vitality 36
  Carol Venolia
Intuitive Design 43
  Linda Smiley
The Healthy House 49
  Paula Baker-Laporte
Responsive Design: Integrating the Spirit of Place with the
Vision of Home 53
  Susie Harrington
Eighteen Design Principles to Make Square Feet Work Harder 59
  Robert Gay
Combining Natural Materials for Energy Efficiency 62
  Catherine Wanek
R-Value Comparison Chart 64
Designing with the Sun 66
  Susie Harrington
Siting a Natural Building 68
  Michael G. Smith
The Permaculture House 75
  Peter Bane
Regenerative Building: An Ecological Approach 83
  Michael G. Smith
Ecovillages and Sustainable Communities 87
  Joseph F. Kennedy

Natural Building Materials and Techniques 93

Natural Building Materials: An Overview 94
   Joseph F. Kennedy
Natural Insulation 102
   Joseph F. Kennedy and Michael G. Smith
Foundations for Natural Buildings 105
   Michael G. Smith
Rubble Trench Foundations 111
   Rob Tom
Earthen Floors 113
   Athena and Bill Steen
A Tamped Road Base Floor 118
   Frank Meyer
Adobe Building 120
   Paul G. McHenry
Bamboo Construction 125
   Darrel DeBoer
Cob Building, Ancient and Modern 132
   Michael G. Smith
Compressed Earth Blocks 138
   Wayne Nelson
Cordwood Masonry: An Overview 143
   Rob Roy
Building with Earthbags 149
   Joseph F. Kennedy
Earthships: An Ecocentric Model 154
   Jack Ehrhardt
Digging In for Comfort 158
   Kelly Hart

Building with Hemp 161
   Tom Woolley
Light-Clay: An Introduction to German Clay Building Techniques 165
   Frank Andresen
Mechanizing Straw-Clay Production 169
   Alfred von Bachmayr
Paper Houses: Papercrete and Fidobe 171
   Gordon Solberg
Rammed Earth: From Pisé to P.I.S.E. 177
   Scott Grometer
Stone Masonry 182
   Michael G. Smith
Straw Bale Building: Lessons Learned 189
   Catherine Wanek
Timber Framing: A Natural Building Form 197
   Steve Chappell
Wattle and Daub 204
   Joseph F. Kennedy
Roofs for Natural Building 206
   Joseph F. Kennedy
Green Roofs with Sod, Turf, or Straw 212
   Paul Lacinski and Michel Bergeron
Thatching Comes to America 214
   Deanne Bednar
Earth Plasters and Aliz 219
   Carole Crews
Working with Lime 225
   Barbara Jones
Natural Paints and Finishes 233
   Joseph F. Kennedy
Recovering from Waste: Using Recycled and Agricultural Materials 239
   Dan Imhoff

CASE STUDIES 243

Building with the Sun: The Real Goods Solar Living Center 244
  David Arkin
From the Nile to the Rio Grande 249
  Dick Doughty
Elegant Solutions: The Work of Hassan Fathy 250
  Simone Swan
An Earthbag-Papercrete House 254
  Kelly Hart
Clay, Straw, and Permaculture: Natural Building at P.I.N.C. 258
  Toby Hemenway
The Earth Sweet Home Institute 263
  Juliet Cuming and David Shaw
Evolving a Village Vernacular: The Earthaven Experiment 265
  Chuck Marsh
Building with the Earth at Auroville 268
  Satprem Maini
Natural Building — A European Tradition 269
  Catherine Wanek

RESOURCES
Desert Island Books 276
Selected Learning Centers 281
Permissions 284
Contributors 285
Index 287

The Earth She Laughed

Robert Francis Johnson

The Earth she laughed
    as we massaged
        her skin
           dancing and
              singing with
           our hands
           and feet.
Building a home
    woven of love,
        straw, clay,
    water and sand.
Not just building to
    live in,
        but building
           ever building
              a new way
                of living.
Being held in her
    embrace
      at peace at peace.
And the Earth she smiles
    in sensuous shimmering
        cobfulls of delight
           ever more thankful
              ever more thankful
                of the beauty
              of it all.

Foreword

Albert Bates

TIME IS MOST OFTEN thought of as a progression, a movement along an axis from past to present to future. We think of human progress in the same terms – today we are better or worse off than we were yesterday or collectively were a century ago. We feel trends afoot. Tomorrow will bring another step.

Some aboriginal societies and – by 'aboriginal' I mean any culture still grounded in its origins – look at time as a circle. The Earth spins on its axis and another day is born. The moon goes once around and a month has passed. We circle the sun as seasons come and go, then come again.

In a linear model of progress, the human population continues to expand until its ever-enlarging technical prowess enables it to cross space and colonize the solar system, even leaping out to the stars. In another version, our exhaustion of natural resources and incautious dismemberment of natural evolutionary barriers with glitzy nano-bio-robo abandon, devolves Earth's inhabitants into bubbling gray goo.

Here is a different view. This loop we are on is at its apogee and about to change not only its direction but also everything we think about in terms of human settlements and lifestyles. Instead of planned obsolescence, we will want planned evanescence. The focus is on quality, not quantity. We need comfort, privacy, and self-respect. We want warmth that transcends temperature. We want beauty. We want to be in touch with the eternal.

The chapters that follow are sublimely poised as a clue to our future.

The Thierry Dronet workshop/stable in France demonstrates a hybrid design that uses straw, lime, cordwood, and a living roof.

JOSEPH F. KENNEDY

Albert Bates is the author of ten books on law, energy, history, and the environment, including Climate in Crisis *(1990), and* Voices from The Farm *(1998) with Rupert Fike. He holds a number of design patents and was the inventor of the concentrating photovoltaic arrays and solar-powered automobile displayed at environmental and civil rights cases before the U.S. Supreme Court, and drafted a number of legislative Acts. He has been Director of the Institute for Appropriate Technology since 1984 and of the Ecovillage Training Center at The Farm since 1994, where he has taught sustainable design, natural building, agriculture, and technology to students from more than 60 Nations.*

Joseph F. Kennedy

Michael G. Smith

Catherine Wanek

CHRIS BLUM

JOSEPH F. KENNEDY

SUSAN VICTORIA

Acknowledgments

THE EDITORS WISH TO THANK the authors, all of whom selflessly offered their time, experience, and wisdom for the edification of others. Generosity of spirit is one of the greatest qualities of the natural building community.

Although all of the authors and many other colleagues have provided us with information, support, and inspiration, there are a few individuals in the natural building and permaculture communities who have served as personal mentors to one or more of us. We would especially like to thank Lynne Elizabeth, Judy Knox and Matts Myhrman, Carole Crews, and Athena and Bill Steen. Catherine and Joe would like to thank the Graham Foundation for Advanced Studies in the Fine Arts, the Foundation for Sustainability and Innovation, and the Lifebridge Foundation for support of their work. We would also like to thank Chris Plant, Audrey Keating, and Greg Green of New Society Publishers for their skilled and kind assistance in making this book a reality.

This book could not have been written without the love and support of our partners, our families, and our communities. To Rose, Taya, Pete, Kristen, all the Black Rangers, and everyone at Emerald Earth, our undying gratitude.

Introduction

Michael G. Smith

NATURAL BUILDING is nothing new. It is as old as the paper wasps who construct insulated hives out of chewed wood fiber, the aquatic caddis fly larvae who make protective shells by cementing together grains of sand, the prairie dogs who excavate enormous towns of interconnecting tunnels, and the chimpanzees who build temporary rain shelters out of sticks and leaves. For thousands of years, our own species followed this same path, building our shelters out of locally available materials. Each group to settle in a new area developed a unique culture with its own architectural style, which evolved through small improvements from generation to generation, becoming more and more suited to specific local needs and opportunities. But always the basic materials stayed the same: the earth and stones beneath our feet, the trees and grasses that grow nearby. Building was a necessary skill shared by most people, a part of the traditional knowledge passed down through the centuries.

Only in the last few generations has our relationship to building begun to change. The Industrial Revolution came like a big splash in a small pond. It started in Western Europe and is still spreading into less-developed parts of the globe. This wave has carried changes in nearly every aspect of our lives, not least the way we shelter ourselves. New materials appear on the market every year, promising more strength and speed than the traditional ones. The new building techniques are often more complicated than the old ones and require specialized training and equipment, so most people in industrialized cultures no longer build their own homes.

The industrialization of building has made possible an enormous increase in the amount of construction that takes place every year. But not all of the consequences are positive. The extraction, manufacture, and transportation of building materials are major contributors to global environmental problems. Manufactured products are often toxic to the workers in the factories where they are made, the builders on the construction sites where they are employed, and the families who live in houses where they end up; they also create enormous waste-disposal problems. Industrial building tends to be expensive. Manufactured materials are often transported great distances and specialized labor is often involved. What results is high-cost housing and increasing homelessness in industrialized countries.

Mixing cob at the Natural Building Colloquium.

Some individuals have always challenged the industrial building paradigm, preferring to build for themselves using local materials and traditional techniques. During the back-to-the-land movement of the 1960s and 1970s, thousands of people in the United States chose to build their own homes from available resources, without professional assistance, without much training or money. Some were inspired and aided by contemporary pioneers like Helen and Scott Nearing (authors of *Living the Good Life* and other classics) and Ken Kern (whose book, *The Owner-Built Home*, was the bible for a generation). The energy crisis of the mid-'70s focused public attention on our use of natural resources and the energy efficiency of our buildings. Around that time, a great deal of research and writing was done on passive solar building, alternative energy systems, and sustainable resource use. But much of that knowledge was swept under the carpet by government policy and public apathy during the '80s.

Although no longer receiving much popular press, the experimental work of conservation-minded builders continued. In the late 1980s, a flurry of activity surrounded the rediscovery in the Southwestern United States of straw bale building, a technique that had gained brief popularity in Nebraska in the early part of the century. In Tucson, Matts Myrhman and Judy Knox started Out On Bale, (Un)Ltd., an organization devoted to popularizing this elegant and inexpensive construction system. Around the same time, Ianto Evans and Linda Smiley, inspired by the centuries-old earthen homes in Britain, built their first cob cottage in Western Oregon. The interest generated by this wood-free wall building technique, which had proven itself well-suited to cool, rainy climates, led them to found the Cob Cottage Company. Meanwhile, Iowa-based Robert Laporte was teaching natural house building workshops that combined traditional timber framing techniques from Japan and Europe, light-clay — a German infill of clay-coated straw, and earthen floors and plasters. In Upstate New York, Rob and Jaki Roy taught cordwood masonry and earth-sheltered housing at their Earthwood Building School. Persian architect Nader Khalili established Cal-Earth, a center in Southern California devoted to developing, educating about, and gaining

The Save the Children office building in Ciudad Obregon, in Sonora, Mexico was constructed primarily of local straw, clay, and reeds – including the built-in shelving.

CATHERINE WANEK

code acceptance for earthbag construction systems. Also in California, David Easton was breaking into the contract building market, first with monolithic rammed earth walls, and then with a sprayed-on soil cement technique he dubbed P.I.S.E..

By the early 1990s, there were dozens of individuals and small organizations in the United States researching, adapting, and promoting traditional building systems. These visionaries proceeded with their work independently, largely unaware of the existence of the others. Then the straw bale boom in the Southwest began to attract the interest of the mainstream national media. When movie star Dennis Weaver moved into a passive solar earth-bermed house made of recycled tires and soda cans, he brought instant fame to New Mexico-architect Michael Reynolds, developer of the 'earthship' concept. As increasing numbers of hands-on workshops were offered around the country, the isolated teachers and innovators began to hear about one another.

In 1994, the Cob Cottage Company organized the first Alternative Building Colloquium, inviting natural builders and teachers from around the country to spend a week together in Oregon. The idea was for these leaders to meet each other, to share the building techniques they knew best, and to begin to join their various philosophies and experiences into a more cohesive system of knowledge. During that gathering, and the annual Natural Building Colloquia that have followed at sites around North America, hundreds of people from diverse backgrounds attended workshops on wall building systems ranging from adobe to wattle and daub; roofing techniques including sod and thatch; and foundation systems including the rubble trench, dry stone, and rammed earthbags. Through lectures, slides, and demonstrations, innovators presented their work with structural testing and building codes; composting toilets and graywater systems; designing with natural forces; co-housing; creating sacred space; and a hundred other topics. The energy and enthusiasm of the group were expressed physically in the construction of ornate timber frames, experimental straw bale vaults, and multi-colored clay murals. Ideas and techniques collided and merged, coalescing into hybrid structures including a straw bale/cob dome and a straw bale/cob/light-clay/wattle and daub cottage on a stone and earthbag foundation.

From the seed of these colloquia, a new movement has been born. The many disparate efforts to relearn ways of building with local materials and adapt them to modern needs have been brought together into a single conceptual basket with an easily understood name: 'natural building.'

Representing every major natural building technique, and written by some of the most prominent innovators and advocates in the field, this collection attempts to document the current state of the art of the natural building movement. But this book is far more than just a survey of techniques. It provides a philosophical framework for the entire natural building movement, as well as a set of design principles broadly applicable to ecological design projects everywhere. Our goal is a whole systems approach to natural building. By integrating the work of the dozens of visionaries presented here into a single coherent text, we hope to provide newcomers with a comprehensive introduction to the field, while filling in gaps in the knowledge of readers already familiar with some pieces of the puzzle.

DONI KIFFMEYER

A stone arch in southern Utah. These natural forms undoubtedly inspired the earliest builders, and still do today.

But our aspirations go beyond just informing our readers of what other people are doing. Our greatest desire is that this book will be a doorway through which many of you will step in order to join the natural building movement. We hope that the case studies at the end of the book and the photographs throughout will help make the concepts and techniques discussed elsewhere more real and get you excited about handcrafting your own personalized structure. The chapters describing construction techniques should give you a good basis for determining which ones appeal to you and make the most sense under specific circumstances, but they will not give you all the details you need to go out and start building. Therefore, at the end of each chapter, we have listed a few of the best books, periodicals, and websites where you can find more information about that technique, as well as providers of workshops and other hands-on learning opportunities. We strongly encourage you to take advantage of the latter; a few days spent practicing a natural building technique with a skilled instructor will give you more confidence and ability than all the volumes ever written.

So come on in; the door is open. We're very pleased to take you on a tour of the rambling, varied, and often surprising edifice we call natural building and to introduce you to some of our friends, colleagues, and teachers along the way.

THE CONTEXT
FOR NATURAL BUILDING

There is some of the fitness in man's building his own house that there is in a bird's building its own nest. Who knows but if men constructed their dwellings with their own hands, and provided food for themselves and their families simply and honestly enough, the poetic faculty would be universally developed, as birds universally sing when so engaged.

Henry David Thoreau, *Walden,* 1854

The Case for Natural Building

Michael G. Smith

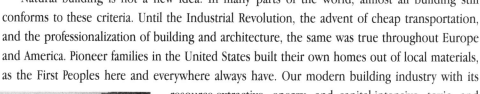

Natural building is any building system that places the highest value on social and environmental sustainability. It assumes the need to minimize the environmental impact of our housing and other building needs while providing healthy, beautiful, comfortable, and spiritually uplifting homes for everyone. Natural builders emphasize simple, easy-to-learn techniques based on locally available, renewable resources. These systems rely heavily on human labor and creativity instead of on capital, high technology, and specialized skills.

Natural building is necessarily regional and idiosyncratic. There are no right answers, no universally appropriate materials, no standard designs. Everything depends on local ecology, geology, and climate; on the character of the particular building site; and on the needs and personalities of the builders and users. The process works best if the designers, the builders, the owners, and the inhabitants are the same people. Natural building is personally empowering because it teaches that everyone has, or can easily acquire, the skills they need to build their own home.

Natural building is not a new idea. In many parts of the world, almost all building still conforms to these criteria. Until the Industrial Revolution, the advent of cheap transportation, and the professionalization of building and architecture, the same was true throughout Europe and America. Pioneer families in the United States built their own homes out of local materials, as the First Peoples here and everywhere always have. Our modern building industry with its resource-extractive, energy- and capital-intensive, toxic, and inaccessible practices must be seen as a temporary deviation from this norm. Let's look at some of natural building's many advantages over conventional modern building practices.

Environmental Impact

It's no secret that the global ecosystem is ill. The housing industry is a major contributor to the problem. We in the Pacific Northwest see the evidence all around us; the trail from clearcut to sawmill to building site is easy to follow. Other major modern building components depend on destructive mining: gypsum for plasterboard; iron for hardware, rebar, and roofing; lime and other minerals for cement. Every material used in a typical modern building is the product of energy-

A Mexican woman near Ciudad Obregon rediscovers ancestral building techniques.

intensive processing. The mills that saw our lumber, the factories that make plywood and chipboard, the foundries that make steel, the plants that turn natural minerals into cement by subjecting them to enormous heat — all consume vast quantities of power, supplied either by the combustion of coal and oil, the damming of rivers, or the splitting of atoms.

Manufacturing processes also release toxic effluent into the water and hazardous chemicals into the air. The manufacture of Portland cement, for example, is responsible for as much as eight percent of greenhouse gas emissions. And even after our building materials are made, modern construction depends on an endless stream of polluting trucks to deliver them to us, usually from hundreds of miles away.

This chart illustrates the relative 'embodied energy' of a variety of industrial and natural materials.

In contrast, straw and other materials favored by natural builders are biological by-products that would otherwise create a disposal problem. Until recently, nearly all the straw produced in California was burned in the fields — enough to build tens of thousands of family homes. But clean-air legislation has outlawed that practice. Faced with the problem of what to do with all the straw that they can no longer burn, California rice growers have thrown their political clout behind legitimizing straw bale building, with the result that the state of California has adopted straw bale building guidelines.

It's impossible to build a house with no environmental impact, but it's our responsibility to minimize and localize the damage. Many of us religiously protect the trees on our property, then go to the lumberyard to purchase the products of wholesale clearcutting. If we choose to build with wood, it seems a lot less hypocritical to take down a few select trees near

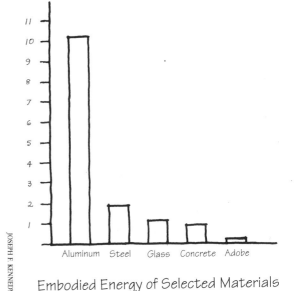

Embodied Energy of Selected Materials

JOSEPH F. KENNEDY

our home sites and run them through a small portable mill, or to thin overcrowded woodlands of small-diameter poles and build with those. Digging a hole in your yard for clay to make a cob house may look ugly at first, but it's a lot less ugly than strip mines, giant factories, and superhighways. Nature has an enormous capacity for healing small wounds — and that hole in your yard would make an excellent frog pond. Building with natural, local materials also reduces our dependence on the polluting and energy-intensive manufacturing and transport industries. When our environmental footprint is under our very noses, it helps ensure that we will minimize its impact. Since we see and walk through our local ecosystems every day, we are more likely to protect their health.

HUMAN HEALTH

Many of the most fervent supporters of natural building are people with acquired chemical sensitivities and other environmental illnesses. These people are particularly aware of how modern buildings make us sick, but we all know it. Even the mainstream press carries frequent stories of cancers and respiratory problems linked to formaldehyde-based glues, plastics, paints, asbestos, and fiberglass, to name a few favorite culprits. The toxicity of these materials has an impact on everyone associated with them: the workers in the factories and warehouses, the builders on the construction site, and the inhabitants of the poisonous end products. Natural materials like stone, wood, straw, and earth, on the other hand, are not only non-toxic, they are life-enhancing.

Vernacular traditions, in this case of South Africa, have much to teach us.

JOSEPH F. KENNEDY

Clay, one of the most useful natural building materials, is also prized for its ability to absorb toxins and restore health.

There is increasing evidence that modern buildings compromise our psychological and emotional health. Right angles, flat surfaces that are all one color, and constant uniformity don't exist in the natural world where our ancestors evolved. Most modern homes certainly don't stimulate our senses with the variety of patterns, shapes, textures, smells, and sounds that our pre-industrial ancestors experienced. The uniformity of our environments may contribute to our addiction to sensory stimulation through drugs and electronic media.

In contrast, we get a good feeling from natural buildings that is difficult to describe. Even though conditioned to prefer the new, the shiny, and the precise, we respond at a deep level to unprocessed materials, to idiosyncrasy, and to the personal thought and care expressed in craftsmanship. Nearly all the natural buildings I have seen, regardless of the level of expertise of the builders, are remarkably beautiful. Living in a handcrafted cob house, I grew to expect the looks of mesmerized awe I saw on the faces of first-time visitors and the difficulty they had prying themselves from the warm earthen benches when it was time for them to leave.

EMPOWERMENT

We grow up being told you can't build a house unless you're a professional builder. If we want a house, we have to work full-time at a job we often dislike to make enough money to pay a builder who may not like his or her job, either. But it doesn't have to be that way. By using local, unprocessed materials like earth and straw, building smaller than the conventional house, and providing much of the labor yourself, you can create a home that is almost unbelievably affordable. As the price tag drops from the hundreds of thousands to the tens of thousands or even a few thousands of dollars, it becomes easier to shrug off the yoke of loans and mortgages. Save yourself money with a more efficient house that uses simple passive solar technology for heating and cooling. You may find your cash needs dropping. You can cut down the hours you work and spend more time with the kids or grow a big vegetable garden that will save you even more money.

Techniques that rely on human labor and creativity produce a different social dynamic than those that depend on heavily processed materials, expensive machines, and specialized skills. When you build with straw bales, cob, adobe, or rammed earth, the whole family can get involved. A building site free of power tools is a safe and supportive environment for children to learn valuable skills. Or invite your friends and neighbors for an old-fashioned barn raising. Offer them food and an education in exchange for their time and energy. It's a good deal for everyone and a lot of fun. While building your home you're also building a different kind of social structure where people depend on themselves and each other — instead of on governments, corporations, and professionals — to get their basic needs met.

MICHAEL G. SMITH

Natural buildings can be constructed by their owners at very little expense. This cob cottage in Oregon was built by Michael G. Smith and the Cob Cottage Company for only about US $700 in materials.

Out of the many gatherings and collaborations of people interested in natural building, a few things have become clear. One is that we are all working together. Even though we may have chosen to focus on different techniques or aspects of natural building, we are all motivated by the same concerns, and our personal experience makes up part of a consistent larger body of knowledge. Two, we are not alone. As word gets out to the greater public, we find enormous interest and support from a growing community of owner-builders, professional builders and designers, activists, educators, writers, and conservationists. And three, together we hold a great deal of power. The power in our ideas and collective action is capable of influencing the way our society thinks, talks, and acts regarding building and resource use. We are helping to create a society where, someday, natural building will again be the norm in the United States, as it still is in much of the world, and where a new cob house with a thatched roof in any American town will draw only an appreciative nod.

Michael G. Smith teaches workshops on natural building and permaculture. He is also a founder and several-time organizer of the Natural Building Colloquium.

RESOURCES
Books

Chappell, Steve, ed. *The Alternative Building Sourcebook: Traditional, Natural and Sustainable Building Products and Services.* Fox Maple Press, 1998. This directory of natural-building-related people, products, and services provides a good starting place for those looking for information or training on building a natural house.

Chiras, Daniel. *The Natural House: A Complete Guide to Healthy, Energy-Efficient, Environmental Homes.* Chelsea Green, 2000. A homeowner's guide to a wide range of natural building systems, comparing the advantages and disadvantages of each. Contains excellent chapters on energy independence, sustainable water systems, and site considerations.

Elizabeth, Lynne, and Cassandra Adams, eds. *Alternative Construction: Contemporary Natural Building Methods.* John Wiley and Sons, 2000. A thorough and scholarly treatment of the contemporary natural building revival, with good introductory material, as well as in-depth descriptions of specific techniques. Excellent bibliography and resource list.

Videos

A Sampler of Alternative Homes: Approaching Sustainable Architecture. Produced by Kelly Hart. Hartworks, Inc., 1998. 120 min. Available from Hartworks, Inc., P.O. Box 632, Crestone, CO 81131, U.S.A.; 719-256-4278; email: kelly@hartworks.com; website: www.hartworks.com. This two-hour video features a number of different natural building alternatives, including adobe, earthbags, earthships, papercrete, rammed earth, straw bale, and more.

The Importance of Housing Ourselves

Ianto Evans

I ONCE HEARD A CHILEAN named Ana Stern give a speech on "The Difference Between Peasants and Farmers in Mexico." Peasants, she said, satisfy their own basic needs: they grow their food, build the houses they live in, and often make their own clothes. Most peasants collect medicinal herbs, treat medical emergencies, and supply their family entertainment. They experience fully what they do every day; they have time; they feel joy. Their culture is integrated; it makes sense.

Farmers, by contrast, grow things to sell. With what they earn from their products, they buy their groceries, building materials, clothes, entertainment, and medical care. They must also buy into a system that demands they drive to market, pay taxes, perhaps send their kids to agricultural college. Increasingly they must buy machinery, seeds, and farm chemicals. Farmers have no time to directly enjoy satisfying their own needs, so they purchase their satisfactions; they buy ready-made clothing and convenience foods.

I've thought a lot about Ana's presentation. Her definition shook my worldview. In her terms we are all farmers — there are few peasants in the U.S.A. I've always felt comfortable in the traditional villages of Africa and Latin America, and now I understand why. The parts of my own life that I truly enjoy are the peasant parts, the parts I don't pay for, the parts that I myself create. A life of working for someone else and paying for basic needs is essentially unsatisfying. Why? Because our links to nature are severed when we live this way.

Why do we grow garden vegetables? It's not the easiest way to obtain food. The simplest cost-benefit analysis will show that it's hard to make the same money from growing lettuces as from going to the office. Otherwise wouldn't most of us be lettuce farmers?

We grow food (or flowers) for completeness, for the grounded understanding that comes from putting seeds in the ground feeding, watering, picking, and eating the plants that grow. To be complete we need to have a constant awareness of our cosmic bearings, of where and how we fit into nature's

This South African woman is learning natural building techniques to help solve her nation's desperate housing crisis.

JOSEPH F. KENNEDY

patterns. If you compost your excrement as the Chinese do, use your own urine for fertilizer, and grow your own vegetable seeds from the plants you raise, the cycle is complete: you have inserted yourself into a completely visible ring of cause and effect. You experience the whole natural process, and the better you observe how that process works, the easier you slide into it.

The peasant/farmer analogy works equally well for house building. For most of history, humans have created their own homes. The whole family helped when the work would otherwise be too heavy or too slow. Sometimes the entire community assisted, as with an Amish barn raising. Only recently have we traded outside the circle of friends and family in order to have homes. At first we traded only for parts or techniques beyond the reach of the homemade. For example, the village blacksmith made the hinges and we gave him eggs. Later we paid money to skilled local artisans for more durable, better-made work. Then, not long ago, we started to pay complete strangers and distant corporations our hard-earned cash to supply us with skilled trades and manufactured components. To earn that money, we had to grow a surplus. The self-sufficient plot was no longer big enough.

Peasants became farmers. Yet small landholders often can't survive in a cash economy, and when they fail, their land is sold to a bigger operator. Not having land, they don't have access to the earth, rock, trees, or straw that were previously at hand for building materials. In order to pay for housing, they turn to producing artifacts or services to sell.

The Taos Pueblo people have continually inhabited this ever-evolving earthen structure for at least the past 1,000 years.

CATHERINE WANEK

That's the stage set. We go to jobs doing possibly meaningless work for 30, 40, or 50 years to pay for a house with which we no longer have any direct connection. How many of us have been in a steel mill or a plasterboard factory? If we have, do we enjoy what we smell and hear and feel there? When schoolchildren take a field trip to the slaughterhouse, they often stop eating meat. When we see how building components are made, perhaps we will seek better ways to house ourselves.

The natural building movement has helped us reconnect with our tradition of self-reliant shelter, surely one of our natural rights. We take the free building materials from the ground beneath our feet — stones, soil, trees, and grasses — and shape them into foundations, floors, walls, roofs, plasters: in short, homes.

A shift in attitude comes of making what you need for yourself. You change your outlook from "I want, so I have to buy ..." to "What's here? What can I best do with it?" The first attitude is how a consumer society approaches life. The second is how people in traditional societies have always looked at their world. It's called 'creativity,' and it's enormously satisfying. Now you see the role of roundwood thinnings in framing a roof and realize how easy it is to build door frames from poles, to shovel sod onto your roof, to set frameless glass shards for windows into a cob wall. Once you learn to create your basic building materials from the ground beneath your feet, your vision opens up.

Central to building your own natural house is the lifestyle change that frees you from tedium and debt. If you follow the thought processes and building principles explored in this book, your housing costs may almost disappear, creating an opportunity for you to take the time to build a house that really inspires you. Most importantly, remember that natural building is not something you do quickly to get a finished structure. Building and living in your house can be spiritual processes; and joy, reflection, and connection with nature, daily experiences.

Ianto Evans is an applied ecologist, landscape architect, inventor, writer, and teacher, with building experience on six continents. With his partner Linda Smiley, he is responsible for reintroducing cob to North America. He is a founder and director of the Cob Cottage Company, cofounder of the Natural Building Colloquium, and coauthor of Hand-Sculpted House: A Practical and Philosophical Guide to Building a Cob Cottage *(Chelsea Green, 2002).*

RESOURCES
Books

Evans, Ianto, Linda Smiley, and Michael G. Smith. *Hand-Sculpted House: A Practical and Philosophical Guide to Building a Cob Cottage*. Chelsea Green, 2002.

Kahn, Lloyd. *Shelter*. Shelter Publications, 1973. An intoxicating celebration of owner-building in all of its forms, from vernacular architecture around the world to the unique artistic products of the American back-to-the-land movement. Many drawings and photos.

Kern, Ken. *The Owner-Built Home*. Charles Scribner's Sons, 1972. The bible for a generation of owner-builders, this book provides practical instructions for first-time builders in site evaluation, design, and planning; and specific techniques such as poured concrete, stone masonry, and roof framing.

Nearing, Scott, and Helen Nearing. *The Good Life: Helen and Scott Nearing's Sixty Years of Self-Sufficient Living*. Schocken Books, 1990. This book describes the Nearings' pioneering work in homesteading based on a philosophy of social justice and peace. Includes detailed descriptions of the process of building their slip-form stone and concrete house.

Thoreau, Henry David. *Walden*. Dover, 1995. Originally published in 1854. A classic on the philosophy of simple living close to nature, this poetic journal particularly extols the virtues of building one's own simple shelter with available materials. Filled with timeless wisdom.

Natural Building and Social Justice

Robert Bolman

Elsewhere in this book there are various arguments for natural building from environmental, health, and esthetic points of view. Here I wish to make the case for natural building from the standpoint of social justice. We all know that there is poverty in the world. The scale of that poverty and the root causes behind it must be understood and accounted for if we, as a society, are ever going to complement our concern for environmental responsibility with an equally passionate concern for social responsibility.

The extremely poor distribution of the world's wealth is not a coincidence. It is not an unfortunate inevitability. It is not a mechanical result of preexisting conditions that we are conveniently powerless to change. The poor distribution of the world's wealth is a direct and deliberate result of foreign policies first pioneered by colonizing European countries and then honed to a fine art by the United States. To a certain extent, wealth and prosperity in the U.S. is directly related to poverty and suffering, often imposed at gunpoint, elsewhere in the world. (An examination of the history of the CIA will bear this claim out in shocking detail.)

For many decades, the Cold War served as a convenient pretext to impose U.S. political will around the world. Now that the Cold War is over, the push toward globalization serves as yet another pretext for the continued imposition of U.S. economic order on the rest of the world's population — many of whom would choose something else if they had any say in the matter. The stated objective in promoting free-market capitalism the world over has been that only through economic growth and development can the world's poor be lifted up out of poverty. But this has only happened to a very limited extent. The far more pervasive reality is that the poor of the world are sinking into greater poverty while the wealthy are becoming much wealthier.

We must consider social realities when we contemplate building our houses. Since the 1940s, although our families have gotten smaller, our houses have doubled in size. And there's no end to the consumer goods that big business is happy to help us fill these houses with — much of it entirely unnecessary and destined simply to end up in a landfill in a relatively short time. While there is some question as to whether or not there's any such thing as an environmentally

We must find better housing solutions, for our children's sake, if no other.

JOSEPH F. KENNEDY

responsible 5,000-square-foot, $600,000 single family house, there certainly is no such thing as a socially responsible house of that size and scale. We are doing our souls a disservice if we concern ourselves only with environmental issues while ignoring the immense, heartbreaking social issues that exist right in front of us.

The spirit behind natural building speaks to the all-consuming sickness of consumerism. Instead of using undue wealth to purchase toxic, energy-intensive building products made in a factory in Mexico, we could humbly assume our place in the world community by using our hands to build our houses out of naturally available, inherently safer materials — much as human beings have done since the dawn of civilization. Instead of buying pesticide-laden strawberries from Chile or lettuce from Mexico, we could grow natural, healthy food in our own gardens. We would do this using the time that we have as a result of not working at a job we hate, to pay the mortgage on our over-sized, over-priced, environmentally clueless house.

The natural building movement exists hand in glove with the 'voluntary simplicity' movement. Growing numbers of people in the U.S. and other affluent countries are recognizing that not only will material abundance not make us happy but that the time spent working to accumulate it can make us miserable. Certainly, many recognize that material abundance doesn't just appear out of nowhere, that the fabulous wealth 'here' and grinding poverty 'there' must somehow be related. As more people turn in the direction of simplicity, of finding happiness in activities other than material consumption, then hopefully, more of the world's wealth can find its way into the lives of all the world's people — not just the wealthiest 20 percent. Natural building can play a major role in helping the human species evolve into a happier and more harmonious global family.

Robert Bolman is a builder, activist, and artist living in Eugene, Oregon.

Hundreds of millions of humans call structures like this tar-paper shack in northern Mexico 'home.'

Building As If the Future Matters

Ted Butchart

L OCAL, NATURAL MATERIALS have almost dropped out of American and Canadian building practices over the last half-century, abandoned not because they are inferior in any way but due to historical forces that worked to reduce manual labor. Reducing hard labor is not a horrible goal by any means, but we have tended that one tree too long and have begun to reap the bitter fruit. Our current construction materials and the buildings we design are, to a significant degree, the children of war and of good intentions gone awry. Let me give you a bit of history, and then I will talk about an alternative path.

Go back in your mind to 1918. Much of Europe was devastated. Whole societies were in rubble, homelessness was rampant, and people were desperate for housing and reconstruction. A few architects, moved by this plight, argued that a return to the earlier esthetic of embellishment and highly decorated buildings was inappropriate — immoral, in fact. What they pushed for was a stripped-down design where form only followed function; this is what came to be known as Modernism in architecture. No higher artistic drive or spiritual resonance was allowed to get in the way of rapid rebuilding — not an unreasonable stance in postwar Europe.

Fast-forward to 1945. As soldiers returned from World War II, the U.S. launched a concerted effort to build huge quantities of single family houses. Below-cost logging was initiated, national transport of manufactured items was subsidized, and, as a result, it was no longer cheaper to use labor-intensive materials. Combined with the effects of Modernism, the subsidies accelerated the simplification and standardization of the building process. The evolution since has been to reduce the need for trained labor on-site, leading to the mechanization and industrialization of the building process. Again, the original impetus for change was laudable enough: to provide quality housing while offering a route to recovery from a devastating war. But we are no longer living in the ruins of war. The immediate pressing need those

The doorway of the past can lead us to the future.

CATHERINE WANEK

people faced no longer faces us, yet we continue the wartime mentality. And now the war is waged against nature and against our own inner nature. It is high time to stop and reevaluate what we are doing and what the real costs might be.

I won't belabor the issue of what our building practices are doing to nature. Let us look instead at what they are doing to us humans. The rush to uniformity and subsidized materials has led to boxy houses that have no soul; that do not support us as feeling, thinking beings; that belittle the workers who produce them; that often make us physically sick; and that require many times as much energy to run as is necessary. All that and they despoil the resources of the Earth in the bargain!

The human need for growth has been eliminated from much of the building process. What room exists tends to be only in the analytical area, cut off from the physical, cut off from the artistic and the emotional. We have to go elsewhere to develop that part of ourselves, but when we cut the emotional, spiritual, and artistic out of our work lives it is darn hard to reinsert it elsewhere. We really do need materials that allow us to be fully human as we assemble them and processes that allow us to grow and deepen as we go about our work.

Any vision of an ecologically fit future must include a vision of a radically reordered building process. In America today 30 to 35 percent of all energy use can be traced back to the decisions of architects; presumably a similar order of materials use originates there, also. The path to finding building systems that can truly fit within broad ecological networks has been confusing and, in the end, ironic: confusing due to numerous and conflicting definitions of what 'ecological' might mean and ironic because the long journey has led back to the ground the builders were standing on when they started the pilgrimage. We have not yet figured out all the details, and we have not yet communicated our methods widely enough, but many courageous builders are already pioneering for that ecologically sane day ahead.

We need to build smaller. Period. From the mid-1960s to the early 1990s the size of the average American house doubled, while the size of the average family dropped. Meanwhile the rest of the world wants that same lifestyle. Oops.... The gross quantity of material used today is unsupportable even in the very near future, much less in 1, 2, or 500 years.

Building smaller immediately lessens the demand on resources, but it has some other interesting features that makes it ecologically sane. Smaller means less risky. The potential for problems, even collapse, rises dramatically as a building increases in size. Beams and posts get bigger as spans increase. The criticality of connections is slight in a small structure, very important in big ones. With smaller buildings there is less need for narrowly focused experts and less need for governmental oversight, which puts modest structures well within the grasp of the owner-builder. Homeowners need not engage in a lifetime of hectic work to pay off the strangers who built the house. The economy as a whole can slow way, way down without 30-year mortgages forcing people to play the bill-paying game.

Building smaller leaves people the time, energy, and enthusiasm for embellishing and personalizing their living space. Building small allows time, perhaps, for the kind of growth and interaction that increases the likelihood of longer home tenancy. Right now, the main impediment to achieving smaller homes is, frankly, the lack of spiritual maturity in the owners. People who know who they are and are comfortable within themselves do not require ego monuments or excess space to escape to.

As building practices change, so will the materials we use. What Americans have done in the last 60 years is to trade knowledge of local materials for easily replicated, dumbed-down knowledge of standardized manufactured goods. Straw bale construction, for example, was a perfectly good system for the treeless portions of the Midwest. But studs and plywood shipped from Oregon all but killed the tradition, even though the local solution was considerably more responsive and adapted to the local climate. As we shift to systems that actually make sense, we will go back and reclaim the use of on-site and regional materials. In so doing we will reclaim healthier, more easily tempered homes and a healthy dose of personal empowerment.

Modern building techniques use enormous quantities of concrete, steel, and other materials with high embodied energy to construct alienating urban environments.

CATHERINE WANEK

Energy systems will also change. Energy use will be a much more conscious, deliberate act, not something that drones on in the background. And that means energy harvesting and use have to be designed into the building from the start, not added on as an afterthought. The systems powering these new buildings will use less energy, and that energy will come from gleaning the forces passing through our systems rather than from harvesting pooled energy and transporting it around the globe.

Design in this era will be characterized by closed loops, including a way of thinking that marries the linear with the circular, the logical with the intuitive. This means using natural contours for siting, instead of plowing roads in straight lines; orienting buildings according to the path of the sun, instead of facing them toward the road; utilizing passive water harvesting and thoughtful land forming, rather than pumping water around. In general, designers will be taught to sense the existing patterns and respond to them instead of beating them down to fit preconceived, two-dimensional plans. They will be taught to think in terms of mass insulation and shading, rather than how to look up a central heating system in a catalog.

Buildings of the future will be made to last for centuries, not just for years or decades. This means that they must be built carefully, with much attention to the details of weathering. Parts must be replaceable as they fail, and reusable directly. Too many alternative houses from the '60s and '70s are already abandoned and rotting, simply because they were built cheaply and with little thought to longevity. This waste is as gross as any tract development.

Buildings that last require materials that last. An aging building is, in some ways, like an aging person. There comes a time when the easy beauty of youth fades. At that point either the soul glows forth, or no amount of powder will disguise the lack. The plastic laminates and synthetic wood trim in current use look good when new, but only when new. One chip and they look terrible. There is no depth, no resilience to the material. Contrast that to a hardwood newel post that grows more beautiful with generations of touch, or to a stone step that records in its shallow, worn curves the footsteps of all those who have used it.

Would the use of wood disappear in an ecologically sane future? Not likely. There are few, if any, materials that combine the lightness, strength, and workability of wood. Could we continue to use and harvest wood as we do today? Not a chance. But it is possible to harvest in a responsible way. Merv Wilkinson has been harvesting wood on his 600 acres on the east side of Vancouver Island since 1938. And he is harvesting more wood every year, not less. He makes more money, employs more people, and derives more lumber per acre from his land than any forestry giant. How does he do it? Attention. He pays exquisite attention to the trees in his care. He knows when they are declining and thins them out. He watches the squirrels: when they are working a tree less it means the tree is producing less seed and is in decline. He knows those trees. Could Boise Cascade do that? Yes, but they would have to hire a huge army of foresters, who would have to get out of their trucks and take the time to really learn their 600 acres. And what is wrong with that?

Having looked far and wide for workable systems, we find the most appropriate materials lying at our feet: mud, rocks, straw, and some wood where we can see and feel it. I think of them as a spectrum of materials with the heat-holding mass of rock at one end and the heat-blocking insulation of straw at the other. Add a bit of straw to earth and we get cob and adobe. Cob is hand-worked into monolithic walls and resists earthquakes and the passage of time well; some cob structures have been in use for many centuries. Adobe is made into blocks and mortared with mud; unlike cob, adobe would be catastrophic in a big quake. Add a bit more straw and we get light-clay, a fireproof infill used for centuries in the heavy timber frame structures of northern Europe. Go all the way to the straw end of the spectrum and we get straw bales, the youngest of these natural building techniques. Combine the high insulation value of straw with a thick heat-absorbing layer of adobe plaster on the inside and you have the genesis of a well-tempered house.

As you consider the use of natural materials, be aware that in general they take time. Sometimes lots of time. On any project there are three interrelated qualities: speed, quality, and price. You can't have them all. If you have little money, then you either have to spend more time or accept lower quality. If you want to save time, then you have to expect the project to cost more or accept lower quality. If you are willing to spend time, then you can have high quality and a lower price. Remember, human labor is one of the only truly renewable resources. If we are going back to a value system that uses cheap and available material, we must be willing to spend the time and money for the human labor to shape them.

The rewards from investing extra time on your project can be invaluable and unexpected. Cob builders sometimes physically heal just from getting down in the dirt and making a building with their own hands. I have watched hope rekindle in people who have been introduced to straw bale building. Your ability to truly invest yourself in a building and have it truly reflect you is greatly enhanced when you take time: time for the structure to evolve, time to feel the poetic potentials of the space, and time for your evolving craftsmanship to be expressed.

A whole house made of clean, non-polluting waste material makes a huge contribution to a better environment and inspires others to see that one person can truly make a difference and still live beautifully. It is time to demand more from our structures by re-involving ourselves in the building process and spending the care and time required to reinvest our creations with reflections of our higher nature.

Ted Butchart is director of the GreenFire Institute, a research and education organization centered on issues of sustainable culture, especially in health, housing, and food production. He is also chief designer for GreenFire Designs, greenfire@igc.org, an architectural design firm specializing in natural materials, with a focus on medical and healing environments.

Resources
Books

Loos, Adolf. *Ornament and Crime: Selected Essays.* Ariadne Press, 1997. A collection of essays that describes the historical movement away from ornament/detail and toward a stripped-down esthetic that would theoretically yield a more affordable product.

McDonough, William. *Cradle to Cradle: A Blueprint for the Next Industrial Revolution.* North Point Press, 2001. The latest book on the big picture from one of the clearest voices out there.

Vernacular Architecture of the Desert

Jean-Louis Bourgeois

B Y TURNS DELICATE and awesome, fastidious and free, traditional desert architecture displays an extraordinary variety of moods. The desert's dryness transforms properly treated, sun-dried mud into a building material of surprising versatility — it can be twisted into playful corkscrew columns, sculpted into fine relief, and formed into lofty walls and towers.

In temperate zones, the sandcastle is the symbol of fragility and fantasy, powder masquerading as permanence, softness as solidity. But in the desert, mud is made dependable, the stuff of sanctuary as well as play. If, as the philosopher Gaston Bachelard says, "the house protects the dreamer," then desert building, offering itself as both the subject and the shelter of dreams, reaches the primordial poles of our imagination, for it forms images of both security and energy, both peace and expression.[1]

A great belt of desert stretches nearly halfway around the world. Starting in North India, it passes west through Pakistan and Afghanistan, continues through the Near East, crosses Africa as the Sahara, and leaping the Atlantic, ends in Mexico and the Southwest United States. In and near this and similar zones, perhaps one quarter of the world's population lives in buildings constructed of sun-dried mud.

The desert is at once harsh and generous. The intense heat, cold, and scarcity of water in this environment are well known; but the desert also provides abundant means with which people can shelter themselves against these extremes. For thousands of years, earth has been used as building material in the desert and dry savannah. Mud architecture is highly resistant to temperature change and insulates against the day's heat and the night's cold.

Desert architecture is the product of a relatively simple yet highly effective technology. Clay and sand are dug from the ground and mixed with water and a binder of dung and/or straw. In some areas, the mixture is tamped in place in a large wooden form or coffer. The block is allowed to dry, the coffer removed and lifted on top of it, and the process is repeated.

Replastering the Great Mosque of Djenne, Mali.

CAROLLEE PELOS

21

This is called 'pisé' or 'rammed earth' construction.

Another method of construction, used in northern Sudan, is called 'coursing' or 'puddling.' A thin layer of mud is shaped by hand, and after it dries, another is added and the wall gradually rises. Indians in the Southwest United States used the coursing technique until the 17th century, when the Spanish introduced the cast, sun-dried brick.

Today brick construction is the most widely used method of building, a technique dating from before recorded history. Hand-molded bricks sometimes dry in place in a wall, but more frequently, cast bricks are left on the ground to bake in the sun. After they are laid in place, the bricks are usually secured by mud mortar and covered with mud plaster. This technique is called 'adobe,' a word borrowed from Spanish. Still earlier, 'adobe' was borrowed by the Spanish from the Arabic *al-tob*, which referred to the earth from which sun-dried bricks are made.

CAROLLEE PELOS

In Burkina Faso, walls are built of hand-molded mud courses.

Houses in the desert tend to be clustered, and isolated dwellings are rare. The fields where farmers grow such grains as millet or wheat and the grazing ranges for herders' camels, goats, or cattle lie outside the settlement. In villages, households are often arranged in extended-family compounds, with structures facing a common open area. In towns and cities, houses tend to have common, windowless walls and usually enclose a central courtyard. In general, the dwellings face inward, away from the heat and dust of the landscape, lane, or street.

Traditional desert structures are designed, built, decorated, and maintained by ordinary people rather than by specialists, although master masons plan and supervise the erection of major buildings such as mosques. But even when trained builders work to construct a house, the entire family works too, often with the help of relations and neighbors. Generally, men are responsible for raising the walls and roof, and the women finish interior surfaces with modeling, paint, or plaster. Maintenance consists largely of exterior replastering, a task performed by men or women, depending on the culture. Upkeep is a dry season activity during which swirling hands, applying new mud like balm on weathered skin, heal the erosion of annual rains.

A single rainy season, even if mild, will soften a mud structure's finer detail. Untended after several such seasons, a mud building may begin to 'melt.' Still, with minimal but continual maintenance, mud architecture may survive an extremely long time. Some mud architecture is now more than 400 years old.

Until recently, the deserts of West Africa and Southwest Asia were thought to be architecturally barren. Architectural standards were such that 'high style' monuments and buildings constructed from 'permanent' materials were considered the only viable and praiseworthy structures. But more contemporary taste has recognized the value and importance of architecture in sun-dried mud.

'Vernacular' is local, folk, or popular architecture. Interest in the broad spectrum of vernacular styles springs in part from the current skepticism about the concepts of progress and technology. A growing interest in climate-responsive building suited to dwellers' needs has led to a reconsideration of building. Vernacular is now seen as an ideal of purity: architecture in practical, spiritual harmony with its site and society. At last vernacular is graduating from 'shelter' to 'architecture.'

Among vernacular architecture, that of the desert is a special case. Despite many obvious differences, desert architecture resembles the architecture of our own temperate climate in an important way — buildings must protect from seasonal and daily heat and cold. In the humid tropics such protection would be inappropriate. There, ventilation provides comfort, not distress. Shelter from nature is needed from above, from sun and rain — but not from the side. Buildings are basically umbrellas, not envelopes, as in the desert and cooler climates.

Western and desert architecture share similar attitudes toward the wall. In both, the wall, having a physical as well as social function, is substantial, not merely a screen. Consequently we Westerners read the desert dwelling as providing a psychological security absent in a vernacular building in the humid tropics, whose open form and woven walls connote 'temporary camp' not 'home.' Desert vernacular is, in this regard, more familiar and more vicariously accessible as a place of permanent comfort, not just for 'them,' but for 'us.'

Permanence is, of course, relative. In the desert, stone tends to be rare and wood often too scarce to fuel brick kilns. As a result, structures are built mainly of sun-dried mud. By temperate climate standards, mud is a material disconcertingly — even alarmingly — soft, a substance so fragile that when hearing of its use as a building material, many people from temperate climates scoff. How, after all, can one build serious structures presumably no more rugged than that symbol of the ephemeral, a child's sandcastle on the beach?

One reason Westerners are surprised by the sophistication of traditional desert architecture is that we find it difficult to believe such architecture exists at all. A region so dry, we assume, cannot allow human life to prosper, let alone flourish with the formal exuberance of the murals of Oualata, Mauritania; the mud embossing of Gujarat, India; or the abacus-like colonnades of

JOSEPH F. KENNEDY

The earth houses of the Ndebele of South Africa demonstrate their exuberant artistic traditions.

eastern Senegal. In a climatic inferno where we expect to find esthetic poverty and people reduced to the struggle for existence, we find instead esthetic abundance and are amazed.

In the industrialized West, our built environment consists of solids once molten, now cool and rigid: plastic, asphalt, glass, concrete, and steel have been heated to hundreds, even thousands of degrees. In the production of building materials, the hotter the process, the visually and psychologically colder the product. But since the heat of the sun is relatively mild, sun-baked mud looks and 'feels' warm and soft. Not cooked out of the natural cycle, mud buildings are less a product of man's ingenuity and power than of the Earth molded by hand.

To a Westerner, desert vernacular can prompt languor or energy. In the first case, resigned to industrialization's advance, we focus on vernacular's poignancy. We imagine one more humane tradition crushed by development, the melancholy passing of yet one more impractical anachronism.

But in the second case, vernacular is seen as vital, not doomed. It inspires hope — resistance to the false, enervating myth that high technology shall triumph everywhere. Cement's appeal is that it proclaims participation today in the progressive worldwide culture of 'tomorrow.' But in fact cement is regressive. Since in most of the Third World there is an excess rather than a shortage of labor, the annual maintenance required by village construction in mud is not a problem. The shortage of capital is. Cement's finance, energy, water, and transportation costs are high. Its use in Third World deserts, because it is a poor insulator, turns houses into expensive ovens.

Mud is not a backward material that progress will replace. In the desert, vernacular, because profoundly local, is increasingly seen as more efficient than centralized industrialization — more adaptive to local climate, local society, and local ecology. Mud's benefits are psychological, too.

As a striking example of appropriate technology surpassing industrial technology, mud reduces neocolonial dependence by promoting cultural self-respect.

Western interest in desert vernacular architecture is very new. We are learning respect and gratitude for beauty that yesterday we ignored. But desert vernacular is more than lovely. It is also practical and ethical. With minimum means, it shelters against nature without abusing her. Spiritually starved by the impersonal purities of modern architecture, many people are grateful to find in traditional desert buildings the grace and splendor of the human touch.

Architectural historian Jean-Louis Bourgeois is author of Spectacular Vernacular: The Adobe Tradition. *He splits his time between his traditional earthen homes in Taos, New Mexico and Djenne, Mali, West Africa.*

NOTES
1. See Gaston Bachelard, *The Poetics of Space* (Beacon, 1969), p. 6.

RESOURCES
Books
Bourgeois, Jean-Louis, and Carollee Pelos. *Spectacular Vernacular: The Adobe Tradition.* Aperture Foundation, 1989. Combining outstanding color photographs and poetic text, this book celebrates both the sensual beauty and the elegant functionality of adobe architecture in desert Africa and Afghanistan, arguing for the respect and protection which vernacular architecture deserves.

Dethier, Jean. *Down to Earth — Adobe Architecture: An Old Idea, a New Future.* Facts on File, 1981. Growing out of a photographic exhibition of traditional adobe building, this book combines superb photographs, mostly from Africa, with a brief, clearly written overview of the history of earthen architecture and the threats facing it today from international development.

Komatsu, Yoshio. *Living on Earth.* Fukuinkan-Shoten Publishers, 1999. Unparalleled in the quality, clarity, and variety of its full-color photographs, this book documents traditional building around the world. Captions are in Japanese, but it doesn't matter; maps help identify the location of each photo.

Oliver, Paul. *Dwellings: The House Across the World.* Phaidon, 1987. This well-illustrated book explores vernacular architecture as an expression of culture, climate, and available resources in many different parts of the world.

Rudofsky, Bernard. *Architecture without Architects: A Short Introduction to Non-pedigreed Architecture.* Doubleday, 1964. This classic book combines photos from Europe, Asia, and Africa with very brief explanatory text.

———. *The Prodigious Builders.* Harcourt Brace Jovanovich, 1977. Rudofsky's magnum opus explores architecture and building from a naturalist's point of view, as a tangible expression of a way of life. Entertainingly written and beautifully illustrated.

Sustainability and the Building Codes

David Eisenberg

Bᴜɪʟᴅɪɴɢ ᴄᴏᴅᴇs are based on a societal decision that it is important to protect the health and safety of people from the built environment. If, inadvertently, these codes actually jeopardize everyone's health and safety by ignoring their impacts on the environment, resulting in the destruction of the ecosystems that sustain us all, then we are obligated to reinvent the codes from that larger perspective. Certainly, it cannot be more important to protect individuals in specific buildings than to protect all of us and all future generations on this specific planet.

This larger view of the consequences of codes provides a crucial, previously missing context. We could think of building codes and standards as describing a sphere of concern — those things we've come to agree must be dealt with to protect people in and around buildings. On further thought, we realize that there is also a sphere of consequence — those things that happen as the direct and indirect results of satisfying the requirements of the sphere of concern. The sphere of consequence is actually much larger than the sphere of concern, because it not only includes the consequences that we intended but also all the unintended impacts, including the environmental ones. There is also a sphere of responsibility, which must be the size of the sphere of consequence, since we are, in fact, responsible for what happens as a result of what we require people to do. Ignorance is no excuse in the eyes of the law, nor does it release us from responsibility. The challenge we face is to expand our awareness and concern to encompass as much as possible of the spheres of consequence and responsibility.

Another piece of the larger context that is often overlooked is the actual current state of the global built environment. Few people in

Current building codes fail to acknowledge the wisdom and continued viability of ancient building traditions such as those of the historic Anasazi of the Southwest U.S.

the developed world realize that fewer than one-third of the more than six billion people on Earth today live and work in buildings like those described in our building codes — modern, industrially based buildings. More than one-third of Earth's people live in earthen structures — adobe, rammed earth, puddled earth, cob, wattle and daub, and so forth — built almost entirely without building codes or standards. The remaining roughly two billion people live in other types of non-industrial, indigenous buildings or shelters assembled out of scavenged materials. Or they live in no buildings at all. And yet, we seem to think that we can go out and house that two-thirds of the world's population in the resource-, pollution-, and waste-intensive ways of building that are mandated by our building codes. We need to take a big step back and reexamine our assumptions about buildings, resources, technology, impacts, and equity.

The evolution of building codes has closely followed the shift in the building industry toward the use of ever higher levels of technology and, almost exclusively, industrially processed materials. This trend greatly amplifies the unintended consequences of building, as the whole system moves continually away from low-impact, local materials and methods and toward higher-impact, less sustainable materials and systems. Not all technologies yield negative outcomes, but there has been almost no attention paid to these issues until the last decade or so and almost none directed toward the role codes and standards play in these impacts.

Building codes ignore such enormously significant factors as where resources come from, how efficiently they're used, and whether or not they can be reused at the end of the structure's useful life. They ignore the environmental impacts of resource acquisition or depletion, transportation, manufacturing processes, disposal after use, embodied energy of materials, and contribution to global warming. Though resource issues are often identified as being at the heart of sustainable patterns for building and development, they are totally absent from building codes.

Why is this important? Buildings account for one-quarter of the world's wood harvest, two-fifths of its material and energy usage, and one-sixth of its fresh water usage. In the past 100 years the level of carbon dioxide in the atmosphere has risen 27 percent, one-quarter of which has come from burning fossil fuels just to provide energy for buildings. During the same period, the world lost more than 20 percent of its forests.

These are the impacts at a time when only two billion of the six billion people on the planet live and work in modern resource-intensive buildings. Projections from the World Watch Institute estimate that in 50 years, it could be four times that many.[1] If we were to apply the level of resource intensity that is essentially required by our modern building codes in the U.S. to the world population, it would be apparent that it's not even remotely possible to house that

At the Center for Maximum Building Potential in Austin, Texas, architect and innovator Pliny Fisk pushes the envelope, combining traditional materials, such as adobe, with modern ones, such as glass block.

number of people in this manner with the available resources. What do we do about that? Deny decent housing to the majority of people on Earth? Or invest resources in finding ways to improve lower-impact and indigenous ways of building and then include these materials and building systems in our codes?

If we can redefine progress to mean 'increasing benefit to the well-being of individuals, communities, and the Earth' rather than 'increasing levels of technology,' then we can begin to see the potential of simpler, more sustainable ways of doing things. Many of the worst examples of architecture and building are the short-lived, high-impact structures that today are being built all over the world out of code-approved materials and systems. Some of the oldest building materials and methods of construction can be seen in some of the most beautiful and enduring

CATHERINE WANEK

buildings in the world. Yet we have relegated indigenous, natural, low-tech materials and building systems to the status of 'alternative' materials and methods, even though in many climates, indigenous buildings are far more comfortable and less expensive than the modern buildings that have replaced them.

Sustainable building requires more than just sustainable resource management. The toxicity and impacts of the processes by which materials are extracted, manufactured, and used must also be considered. The development of tools for life cycle assessment is a necessary step toward beginning to account for and reduce these impacts. We will feel the impacts of these issues whether we choose to face them now or to ignore them into the coming decades.

The necessary changes can happen in a variety of ways. Awareness of the need for change is certainly a fundamental precursor. But there is also a need for research, testing, and development for many low-tech materials and systems, even those which have been in use for centuries. And there is a rapidly emerging need for technical support, educational resources, and training for building officials who are ready to embrace these changes. These issues, which a few short years ago were virtually unheard of, are becoming much more widely recognized, even if appropriate responses are slower to emerge.

The drivers for change may themselves be changing. Modern building codes were initially developed by insurance interests and have been influenced heavily by the industries that produce the materials and building systems that are code regulated. But today, major insurance underwriters and reinsurers around the world are recognizing the enormity of the threats posed by global warming and are becoming interested in climate-change mitigation strategies related to buildings. This should bode well for low-impact building technologies and for the needed research and development, education, and dissemination of information about them.

The development and increased adoption of model energy codes are also encouraging. Model energy codes are not strictly limited to the health and safety of individual occupants of buildings but preserve health and welfare on a community, or even larger level. As we learn to factor in the larger web of interrelationships to what we do — especially where the impacts are so great — we will see large-scale returns from even incremental improvements.

The Development Center for Appropriate Technology (DCAT), through its program, "Building Sustainability into the Codes," is leading a collaborative effort by many organizations and individuals to focus attention on the issue of sustainability and building codes. DCAT also seeks to foster support for a national partnership for the research, development, and testing of low-impact building materials and systems in order to bring them into more common and practical usage within building codes. Since these materials and systems are often in the public domain and lack a developed industry or large profit base for their development and promotion, they are unable to attract the type of investment — readily available for proprietary materials and systems — to pay for extensive research and testing. There is a legitimate role for government to play here. DCAT has been promoting the creation of a national laboratory for sustainable materials (not limited to building materials and similar to the Forest Products Laboratory) or, at the very least, a program within the national labs.

The seriousness of the sustainability crisis has started to affect the way the design and construction industries conduct their business. Organizations such as the U.S. Green Building Council (USGBC) are bringing the building industry together in an effort to address sustainability issues. The Leadership in Energy and Environmental Design (LEED) green building rating system that USGBC has developed is a good starting point for developing sustainable practices in the design, construction, and development industries. The proliferation of green building programs around the U.S., Canada, Europe, and elsewhere indicates an emerging awareness of the need to address these issues. It is only a matter of time before this need is addressed in the building regulatory sector.

Building codes are not static but living documents, representing the best efforts of people seeking to create safe and healthy structures. In the U.S., anyone can propose changes and additions to the building codes — the process is open to the public. Needed changes will come about most effectively when those with the knowledge of more sustainable building practices become directly involved with the code-change and code-development process. (All other sectors related to buildings engage in this way to change and influence the codes.) If there are deficiencies that only we see or know about, it is our obligation to become involved in the process of bringing that awareness to those who work with these regulations professionally.

Changing the way buildings are designed and built starts with developing an awareness of the complexity of the impact of what we do. Although the challenges are monumental, we are not starting from zero in our endeavors. We must not be paralyzed by the difficulty of the task at hand, nor can we be lulled into thinking that it will happen without our committed, focused, long-term efforts.

David Eisenberg is director of the Development Center for Appropriate Technology in Tucson, Arizona. His more than 20 years of construction experience include troubleshooting construction of the steel and glass cover of Biosphere 2 in Oracle, Arizona, building a $2 million structural concrete house, a hypo-allergenic structural steel house, and building with masonry, wood, adobe, rammed earth, and straw bale. He is coauthor of The Straw Bale House *and helped write the first load-bearing straw bale construction building code for the City of Tucson and Pima County, Arizona.*

NOTES

1. See David Malin Roodman and Nicholas Lenssen, "A Building Revolution: How Ecology and Health Concerns Are Transforming Construction," Worldwatch Paper #124, March 1995.

RESOURCES
Periodicals

Building Standards: The Magazine of the International Conference of Building Officials. 5360 Workman Mill Road, Whittier, CA 90601, U.S.A.; phone: 562-699-0541; fax: 562-699-8031; website: www.icbo.org. Through a collaboration with David Eisenberg, this trade magazine for building officials has several times featured natural building techniques such as straw bale, rammed earth, bamboo, and earthships.

Organizations

Development Center for Appropriate Technology (DCAT) P.O. Box 27513, Tucson, AZ 85726-7513, U.S.A.; phone: 520-624-6628; fax: 520-798-3701; email: info@dcat.net; website: www.dcat.net

Life Cycle Cost and Value of Four Homes

David A. Bainbridge

THE GOAL OF THE SUSTAINABLE BUILDING MOVEMENT is to improve the comfort and health of the built environment, while maximizing the use of renewable resources, minimizing life cycle costs, and maximizing life cycle benefits. Life cycle costs and value provide an accounting over the lifetime of a building or project (often 50 years or more in the U.S. but up to 200 years or more in Europe, a difference also reflected in loan repayment periods, which are 30 or so years in the U.S. but 100 years in Switzerland and Japan).

The costs of maintaining and operating a building or project are the life cycle costs. Benefits include the economic return and also the productivity, health, and well-being of the users who live in or work in a building. We rarely consider life cycle value because there is a wide gap between economics as accountants and developers currently know it and a wiser, sustainable economics that considers the future. Some traditional societies have more carefully considered the future, reflecting on possible outcomes and impacts for generations to come (up to seven generations, perhaps a 150-year planning horizon).

Life cycle considerations are particularly important for institutions that cannot count on an increased income to offset foreseeable large increases in costs for energy, water, or other resources. Comfort and health, energy and water use, waste, and recyclability are key issues.

If we compare four houses, we can see the impacts that design and building choices have on life cycle costs.

Life cycle costs of four homes (1,400 sq.ft. [430 m2]) Fresno, CA				
	Conventional	Straw bale	SB solar	Owner-built SBS
FIRST COST				
Construction cost	$112,000	$112,000	$112,000	$42,000
Cost to utility*	$8,000	$6,000	$4,000	$4,000
(*new generating capacity needed at peak)				
ANNUAL OWNERSHIP & OPERATION				
Finance cost annual (4%)	$3,500	$3,500	$3,500	$1,344
Heating and cooling BTU sq.ft.	$37,868	$24,892	$5,893	$5,893
Utility costs annual (10¢kwh)	$1,555	$1,021	$241	$241
ANNUAL OPPORTUNITY COST[+] (at 5%)				
Finance (80% of cost)	$4,480	$4,480	$4,480	$1,680
Utility	$400	$300	$200	$200
Utility bill	$78	$51	$12	$12

SB = STRAW BALE   SBS = STRAW BALE SOLAR   [+]opportunity cost is the often neglected cost of what the money could do if it was invested instead of spent.

This isn't the full cost, which also includes health and environmental costs from carbon dioxide, nitrous oxides, sulfur dioxide and global warming.

	Conventional	Straw bale	SB solar	Owner built SBS
ANNUAL ENVIRONMENTAL COST				
CO_2 emissions tons (from coal 1 lb kwh, 80% effic.)	9.3	6	1.4	1.4

This neglects the energy costs of building the power plant, mining the coal, shipping the coal, air conditioner construction and repair, and maintenance of the power system. These can be significant. Other environmental costs include nitrogen pollution from nitrous oxides, and asthma, pulmonary disease, and other health problems in the vicinity and downwind of the power plant, and significant and far reaching effects on ecosystems over hundreds of square miles. These are often estimated to double or triple the current cost of energy but are not well studied.

Lifetime cost comparison (100 years)	Conventional	Straw bale	SB solar	Owner built SBS
Dollars	$947,900	$935,200	$843,300	$347,700
CO_2 emissions tons	930	600	140	140

The straw bale solar house would be the healthiest and most economical option because the direct solar heating and climatically adapted cooling is basically free. The owner-built solar straw bale would clearly be the best choice for long-term savings — if the owner could build it. If we had more flexible building codes and gave home photovoltaic installations the same subsidies we give utilities, it would probably be cost effective to build a solar stand-alone straw bale house with super-efficient appliances. This would dramatically reduce the environmental and health impacts from the house.

David Bainbridge is associate professor and coordinator of Environmental Studies at Alliant International University, San Diego. His career has included research and development work in passive solar heating and colling, passive solar hot water, sustainable agriculture, agroforestry, straw bale building, and ecocomposite materials. He has written 8 books and more than 250 articles and was selected as one of the top 40 socially conscious designers in the world by International Design Magazine.

Energy estimates adapted from: Elizabeth, L. and C. Adams. *Alternative Construction*. John Wiley and Sons, 2000. Energy modeling by Jennifer Rennick, energy analyst, San Luis Obispo.

A Case for Caring Craftsmanship

Duncan MacMaster

SOMETIMES I LOOK at a piece of wood that I have just made satiny smooth with my hand planes, and I wonder what it really is. What is this stuff called wood? This fibrous substance created by a life force called a tree, produced out of minerals, water, atmosphere, and sunlight? Nature certainly knows how to do many things that humans don't, but how many of us today think of giving credit to the intelligence of nature for supplying our food, houses, clothing, medicine, or anything else? We readily acknowledge science, industry and other people, but do we acknowledge nature or the Earth or the plant world? In this modern world we have been blinded by technology, but throughout the ages, native peoples and cultures have understood and appreciated that they were part of a greater intelligence and that they needed to respond to the laws of nature in order to thrive.

Fine detail is important where the hand and eye are led.

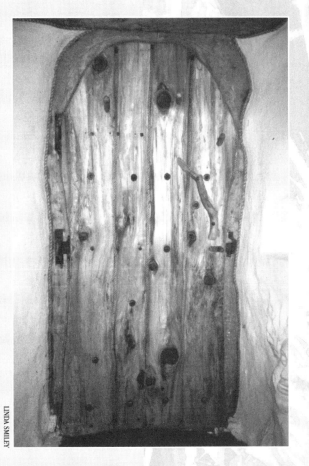

A walk in the woods, in the mountains, by a stream, or on the shore can certainly fill me with peace and wonder. However, it is when I work natural materials (those with minimal processing) with my hands that I begin to respect the creative intelligence of nature the most. I deeply feel the crafts are a way of grounding our spirituality; they are a necessary component of life, not to be relegated to spare time. Whether we are gardening, cooking a meal with love, woodworking, or making pottery or basketry, what is important is that we take the time to be consciously involved on all levels — physical, emotional, mental and spiritual.

We need to find ways to put life and nourishment back into our environments. And it is my observation that this can only be achieved by the willing attention of people. Machines can't do it; in fact, they leave a tangible accumulation of irritating vibrations in their tracks. And industry is replacing people with machines. It is only when a craftsperson — child or adult, accomplished or beginner — works lovingly and perhaps wonderingly with the natural inclinations of the materials which nature has given us, that alchemy really begins.

When our living environments are made and furnished from a level of caring artistry, they feel more balanced, wholesome, and grounded — and so do we. Wood that one can feel, wood that can

LINDA SMILEY

breathe, feels different from wood encased in plastic. It may also cost less. A handwoven rug or a handmade tool feels different from a machine-made one. It has the feeling of the maker in it. Handmade baskets feel wholesome because they are made by people's hands. I am not suggesting that we never use any machines, but prudence and understanding would lead me to the conclusion that if we minimize our machine work and finish with hand tools, both the work and we will feel better.

I think that is why antiques and contemporary items from cottage industries around the world are popular today — they were/are made by people, and we want that richness of feeling in our homes. By surrounding ourselves with and using handcrafted wares, furniture, and houses, the loving comfort of our living spaces become even fuller, and our appreciation and respect for nature and the Earth increases proportionately.

What is it like to live in this way? Can you begin to imagine it with me? Have you ever been in a colonial house that has been lived in and cared for for 200 hundred years? Have you ever been in an old cabin in the woods that has handmade furniture, baskets, and sweaters? These are, by and large, buildings that have been created mostly with hand tools and natural materials. They have a different feel from most new houses or office buildings. They feel rich, solid, grounded, alive. People made these places, and in a caring way. A few new buildings feel this way, too, when timber framers, earth builders, or others put enough of themselves into the work that their love and respect are transferred to the product. Such attention creates a tangible feeling that is very recognizable. We have all noticed it in one place or another. We appreciate the silence. Our senses open and we want to touch and look at things. We are like children wanting to be involved with our environment again, as if we were playing along a stream or walking in the woods.

Duncan MacMaster is a designer, teacher, and master artisan. He designs and creates small houses and furniture to incorporate craftsmanship, natural materials, and simplicity of form and process found in Japanese and Shaker style. Duncan works with the spiritual dimensions of the crafts and presents workshops on the use of Japanese planes and other ways by which to cooperate with nature.

DESIGN AND PLANNING

Have you ever watched the millions of stars in the sky on a moonless night, or seen the wind waver over a field of grass, or noticed the dust at play in a shaft of light, or felt the warmth of another's hand ... someone you cared for? This is where architecture must come from. Architecture must take measure of all that it is to be human in a world that is whole.

James Hubbell, 1974

Designing for Vitality

Carol Venolia

THERE IS MUCH MORE to natural building than simply building with natural materials. To really embrace the potential of natural building, we must view a building as an ongoing process, not a static object. A building is a system within systems of human culture, resource flows, daily and seasonal cycles, and numerous other natural rhythms.

The look and feel of earth, straw, and bamboo stir our senses and remind us of our ancestral roots. The desire to build with material that is close to its own roots often comes from a desire to feel more alive and to behave more responsibly in relation to the larger environment. Natural building provides an opportunity for us to look at how our lives interact with our buildings and how our buildings can help us live in harmony with the greater biosphere.

In order to vitalize the process of creating and inhabiting buildings, we need to overcome some culturally ingrained habits. The buildings to which we have become accustomed in Western civilization reinforce the myth that humans are separate from the rest of nature. For the last several decades, our homes, schools, and offices have increasingly cut us off from the world outside. Inside, we have created artificial systems for providing warmth, coolness, lighting, humidity, sound, and scent — and often inadvertently we have created atmospheres of energy-sapping monotony, noise, odor, and toxicity.

As we now know, the costs of such a narrow approach are many, including an excessive use of energy and other resources, the production of land-choking volumes of waste, and damage to the health of inhabitants. But perhaps the greatest unexamined cost is in the attitudes we have learned — the myth of human separation. Conceivably, if we carry these attitudes into our new building creations, we can make buildings out of natural materials that are still toxic, soul-killing, and grossly consumptive of our Earth's resources.

Building for human vitality can be the core of an approach that brings us back to life in all its dimensions. As we are beginning to remember, human vitality is inseparable from biospheric vitality.

This teepee, handmade by Blue Evening Star, is a portable home with a minimal separation from the natural world.

CAROL VENOLIA

THE PALEOLITHIC TOUCHSTONE

Looking to our biological origins provides us with a useful touchstone and suggests guidelines for living harmoniously with our environment. Our bodies are essentially the same as those of Paleolithic hunter-gatherers — anatomically, physiologically, and psychologically. The human organism has evolved through millennia of constant interaction with sun, wind, rain, soil, fire, plants, and animals in daily and seasonal cycles. Our Paleolithic ancestors lived tribally in the open air, stalked game, gathered plants, and were acutely alert to sounds, smells, sights, and changes in temperature, sunlight, and air movement.

Contrast the sensory richness of Paleolithic times to life today, most of which we spend indoors breathing tainted, recycled air; being warmed by circulated, heated air; seeing by monotonous, artificial light; hearing the droning of equipment; surrounded by motionless walls and furnishings; and having our senses both understimulated and overstimulated in meaningless ways. It becomes clear that few contemporary buildings are places where human beings can thrive.

By examining the sorts of 'environmental nutrients' our body/beings crave, we can create buildings that keep our books dry and our activities private, while resynchronizing ourselves to natural cycles and restoring the rich sensory textures with which our nervous systems function best.

NATURAL CYCLES

Daily and seasonal cycles of light and dark, warm and cool, are basic to our existence. Within our bodies, we experience daily biological rhythms that are synchronized to the sun — in sleep and wakefulness, body temperature, blood pressure, hormone secretion, cell division, and virtually all bodily functions. There are also monthly physiological cycles in both women and men that may be synchronized to the changing light and the gravitational pull of the moon. And we have seasonal rhythms in mood, nutrient absorption, sex drive, growth, and physical ability, also synchronized with seasonal fluctuations in sunlight.

Many researchers believe that we rely on environmental cues to reset our body clocks daily. The morning sunlight triggers and synchronizes certain internal rhythms, while the approach of darkness cues other rhythms to rise and fall. Changes in air temperature, the Earth's magnetic field, and other environmental clues also stimulate biological cycles.

But our built environment typically estranges us from these natural time clues. When our body rhythms get out of sync with each other or with the Earth, our health declines, often resulting in tiredness, depression, anxiety, sleep disturbances, and general vulnerability. Electric lighting lengthens the days and blurs the distinction between the seasons. Street lighting entering bedrooms alters the essential darkness of night and obliterates the subtler periodicity of moonlight. Mechanical heating and cooling systems damp out natural temperature variations. And artificial electromagnetic fields overwhelm the Earth's electromagnetic field and its cyclic variations.

LIGHT

Sunlight tells us a great deal about the type of lighting we need. Natural light is constantly changing in intensity, color, and angle throughout the day and the year. We are biologically accustomed to morning light that is warm in color, low in intensity, and coming from a low angle, gently grading into noon light that is cool in color, high in intensity, and coming from above. We are also accustomed to shorter periods of light in winter and longer periods in summer. Any departure from these conditions challenges both our biological functioning and our sense of esthetics and 'rightness.'

The obvious implication is to design for daylighting wherever feasible and to orient interior spaces for appropriate natural light. For example, an east-facing bedroom allows you to be awakened by the sun and to begin the day by synchronizing your biological rhythms.

Though sheltered by the surrounding straw bale walls, windows allow the outdoors into this cozy nook that functions as both seating and sleeping space. Designed by Dan Smith and Associates.

CATHERINE WANEK

When artificial light is used, it should allow for variety: brighter, cooler-colored light for visual tasks and lower, warmer colored light for relaxing. Research shows that monotony and overstimulation can actually lead to loss of visual acuity. We need variety in our visual field, and we need different kinds of light for different tasks. Keep in mind that light is a stimulant: in this productivity-oriented culture, we use artificial lights to keep banks of chickens laying eggs all night long and fluorescent ceilings to keep office workers producing after dark.

Consider what it might do for your vitality if you let yourself wind down as the sun goes down. Lower lighting levels in the evenings — even going to bed when it gets dark — allow your body to repair itself and your mind to roam freely. Sleeping longer in the winter is a time-honored practice, too; perhaps there would be less Seasonal Affective Disorder if we got more exposure to daylight and allowed ourselves to hibernate in winter.

HEAT

The sun was also our first source of heat, providing a combination of direct and indirect radiant warmth. Direct heat is felt when sunlight falls on us, and indirect heat is felt when nearby materials absorb the sun's heat and later reradiate it. Not surprisingly, studies have shown that radiant heat is the most healthful form of heat for humans.

The sun remains our best source of radiant heat. Designing to admit an appropriate amount of sunlight, and incorporating thermal mass materials that can absorb and reradiate the sun's warmth should be basic to most buildings; this is called 'direct-gain passive solar heating.'

When passive solar heating is inadequate, artificial radiant heating systems can fill the gap. Hydronic systems use heated water flowing through radiators or through tubes in the floor or walls to provide radiant heating. Electric-resistance radiant heating systems are also available but are not recommended due to their excessive fuel consumption and production of high electromagnetic fields.

Our thermal sense can also be a source of richness or tedium. Lisa Heschong, author of Thermal Delight in Architecture, feels that we have cut ourselves off from enjoying the potential sensuality, cultural meaning, and symbolism of our thermal environment. Some people believe that by experiencing natural changes in temperature throughout the day and the year, we keep our internal thermoregulatory mechanism tuned up and improve our immune systems. Heschong states a general principle well: "Uniformity is extremely unnatural and therefore requires a great deal of effort and energy to maintain."[1]

SOUND

Our hearing evolved in a relatively quiet setting in which every sound had meaning; the ability to detect and understand subtle sounds was important to survival. The snapping of a twig, the call of an animal, and the tone of the wind all provided a constant sonic picture of the state of things. The rare loud noises carried important messages (rain is coming; a boulder is headed for you) and evoked an appropriate adrenaline rush. Today, most people are surrounded by inescapable background noise that dulls the senses, and the personal meaning of the sounds is minimal.

When building, you can restore a meaningful sound environment in several ways. First, when possible, site your building away from noise pollution. Second, insulate and weather-strip to block sound that you can't control — earth and straw used as building materials provide excellent sound insulation. Third, minimize the use of noise-producing appliances and mechanical equipment. And fourth, encourage a rich tapestry of pleasant sounds: plant trees with leaves that rustle in the wind; plant fruit-bearing shrubs that attract songbirds; hang wind chimes; install a fountain.

AIR QUALITY

Our bodies process and eliminate toxic substances on a regular basis, but nothing in our evolution equipped us to handle the volume of pollutants that modern life delivers via our air, water, and food. Although we can't immediately control many of these pollutants, we can make our homes and workplaces into oases of low toxicity where our bodies can rest and repair.

There is a threefold approach to keeping the level of indoor toxins low: eliminate, separate, and ventilate. 'Eliminate' means to just say No to highly toxic carpets, paints, adhesives, sealers, and other materials. You don't need them, and there are affordable less toxic options available. How far you go with this approach is a function of your health and your level of commitment, but it is your first and best defense.

'Separate' means that you minimize the impact of interior pollutant sources that it is impractical to eliminate. For example, apply a sealer to cabinets that are made of materials that off-gas formaldehyde; locate office equipment or combustion appliances that create fumes in a separate room.

On a cold February morning in the Sierras, a floor with radiant heat offers comfort to bare feet.

CAROL VENOLIA

'Ventilate' is a good idea in any case. Fresh air is not only important to our health in itself, but it can dilute any pollutants that happen to be in our indoor air, rendering them less harmful. Ventilation can be as simple as an open window or as high-tech as a heat-recovery ventilator. If you have a mechanical ventilation system, adding filtration can also remove some gases and particles from the air.

IMPLICATIONS FOR DESIGN

The beauty of designing with natural cycles and for sensory richness is that it is also energy efficient. We are best adapted to the cyclically changing colors and intensity of light from the sun; therefore, design for daylighting — this saves electricity. We are best adapted to the radiant warmth of the sun and the natural cooling of shade and breezes; therefore design for passive solar gain and natural cooling as appropriate — again, this saves on the energy cost of heating and cooling. We thrive on the visual and auditory textures of rich landscapes and small animals; therefore plant abundantly around buildings as appropriate — this attracts songbirds, provides food, enriches vistas, and helps with natural heating and cooling.

We can also get our environmental nutrients and conserve fuel by creating more indoor/outdoor living areas. Modern building has focused so thoroughly on enclosure and protection that we have lost much of the art of semi-enclosed spaces. But the blessings of screened porches, outdoor kitchens, solariums, and sleeping porches should not be forgotten. If the outdoor environment is at all appealing (and even the tiniest yard can be made more vital with plants, a fountain, and wind chimes), tempering only the unwanted climatic influences can allow us to migrate to indoor/outdoor spaces as the time of day and season allow. Sometimes shade, a windbreak, or protection from the rain are all we need to allow us to work, socialize, or sleep outdoors. And the fresh air, gentle breezes, and sunlight can create deep feelings of satisfaction and vitality that are hard to find indoors.

CAROL VENOLIA

This light-filled conservatory protects from the weather, yet the indoor green space brightens up guests on rainy days at the Empress Hotel in Victoria, British Columbia.

THE HEART OF THE MATTER

You might have noticed something: all of the suggestions I'm making feel good. This is the most important part to keep in mind. Even if you forget all the theory and facts, you will always have this most important touchstone right at hand: what feels good to your body, mind, senses, emotions, and spirit? Don't get so stressed out about saving the planet that you forget to have fun or to take good care of yourself. After all, if your energy is depleted you can't help the planet much. So play, have a good time, let your friends help you, and surround yourself with the things and feelings you love.

> *Carol Venolia is an architect, author, and teacher who has pursued her passion for understanding the relationship between life and buildings for 30 years. She conveys her unique perspective in her book* Healing Environments: Your Guide to Indoor Well-Being *(now in print for 12 years and in three languages); through her newsletter,* Building with Nature; *in her designs for responsive homes of wood, earth, and straw; and in her lectures and workshops internationally.*

NOTES

1. See Lisa Heschong, *Thermal Delight in Architecture* (MIT Press, 1979), p. 19.

RESOURCES

Books

Ackerman, Diane. *A Natural History of the Senses*. Random House, 1990. A delicious exploration of the human senses, weaving science and culture in Ackerman's poetic style.

Eaton, S. Boyd, et al. *The Paleolithic Prescription*. Harper and Row, 1988. An eye-opening look at how we evolved and how current lifestyles do violence to our basic nature.

Heschong, Lisa. *Thermal Delight in Architecture*. MIT Press, 1979. The classic work on the many effects and levels of meaning that our thermal environment has; a lush, sensual read that opens our awareness to how subtle and powerful other aspects of our surroundings may be, as well.

Lewis, Charles A. Green Nature, *Human Nature: The Meaning of Plants in Our Lives*. University of Illinois Press, 1996. Another angle on how much humans need other life forms in order to thrive, and how to include plants in our living, working, healthcare, and institutional environments.

Liberman, Jacob. *Light: Medicine of the Future*. Bear and Company, 1991. An overview of how light affects humans, and how we can use it to improve our well-being.

Mazer, Susan, and Dallas Smith. *Sound Choices: Using Music to Design the Environments in Which You Live, Work, and Heal*. Hay House, 1999. The authors are both musicians and consultants on the design of sound environments for healthcare; they expand and inform our awareness of the power of sound in all our environments.

Perry, Susan, and Jim Dawson. *The Secrets Our Body Clocks Reveal*. Rawson Associates, 1988. A good summary of what was known in 1988 about chronobiology (circadian rhythms, etc.), written in terms non-scientists can grasp.

Venolia, Carol. *Healing Environments: Your Guide to Indoor Well-Being*. Celestial Arts, 1988. A soulful overview of how our organism relates to the world organism — symbolism, light, color, sound, indoor air quality, other life forms — and how that relationship can be healing to both.

Intuitive Design

Linda Smiley

Model of a house designed by several students at a natural building course in South Africa.

Designing a natural home can be a personal and sacred intuitive process. It can have a profound effect on one's life, relationship to the environment, and to the world. As we use our intuitive tools to create magical spaces, learning without interpretation from others, it can be a healing way for us to find a special place in the world. Through this playful art form, similar to art therapy, we explore our boundaries in relationship to friends, family, and ourselves; solve problems, heal emotional wounds, and experience joy.

Every human being was born from a natural home. As fertilized seeds we took our first place in our mother's womb — a connected, loving, protected, and nourishing space for us to grow and thrive. Our psyche knows this womb-like place very well and often seeks its qualities and comfort in relationships and in the world.

As children, we were all intuitive designers and natural builders. Recall the indoor forts you built in the living room using anything you could find. Remember the spaces you created by transforming closets, basements, rooftops, garages, backyard tree houses, old outbuildings, or chicken coops into your own special spot. Recollect the natural structures you found — beaver dams, bird nests, tunnels, caves, rock quarries. And the ones you created from found natural materials — driftwood beach huts, igloos, snow caves, and lean-tos in the forest. What about the places you explored in and under the water, in oceans, lakes, rivers, bathtubs, and swimming pools?

When children design their magic spots, they unconsciously emphasize the qualities that make them feel good. They follow their intuition to find what feels right. In her book, *Anatomy of the Spirit*, Caroline Myss states, "Intuition is the ability to use energy data to make decisions in the immediate moment. Energy data are the emotional, psychological, and spiritual components of a given situation. They are the here and now of life." [1]

We each have woven a lifetime 'memory blanket' of places we have been to and seen. Every thread, rich in color and texture, symbolizes a place that has had a powerful impact on our lives. We can unfold this memory blanket any time we wish to integrate the sacred qualities it contains into our designs as natural builders. Owner-builders can integrate messages from the unconscious into their design through a process of dream work, meditation, and authentic movement.

Start by closely observing your body reactions to different places. What is your reaction to oceans, streams, rivers, lakes, mountaintops, and rock bluffs? How do you feel in sand dunes, meadows, forests, crowded city streets, winding country lanes, open fields, churches, temples, or ancient ruins? Do you feel differently in fast food restaurants, prisons, courtrooms, hospitals, schools or libraries? What is the energy embodied in these places? What qualities of these places do you wish to integrate into your home?

INTUITIVE TOOLS FOR DESIGNING NATURAL BUILDINGS

I carry four tools in my 'tool kit' for designing natural buildings: intuition, dream work, meditation, and sculpting. I use these tools to sculpt sacred space and awareness through cob art.

The following design exercise grew out of my work with Dr. Arnold Mindell, the founder of process-oriented psychology, and with Gary Reiss, author of *Changing Ourselves, Changing the World.* It involves: 1) guided meditation; 2) journal writing; 3) model-making; and 4) storytelling. In a workshop or group setting, each part may take an hour or longer, so allow plenty of time to complete the whole process. If you are doing the exercise on your own and cannot find someone to read Part 1 to you, tape record it and play it back later.

Part 1: Guided Meditation

Sit in a comfortable position. If you need extra support for your back, find a backrest or lie down. You may wish to bend your knees and place the soles of your bare feet in direct contact with the floor or ground. Feel your feet rooted into the Earth. Feel your body contact the surface upon which you sit.

Allow your gaze to soften. When you're ready, close your eyes. Relax deeply with each breath into a new space within you. When you find yourself in this new place of your imagination, tune in to your sensory channels.

Body Feeling

Notice how you feel in your body. Does this place make you feel well or sick, happy or sad? Feel all your sensations, starting with your feet and working your way up your body. Do you notice any places of tension, constriction, or pain? Is the space embracing and protecting you, or are you exposed to the sun and wind? Allow your attention to come to your heart. Be still and feel.

Visualization

Allow yourself to see the shapes that surround you. Notice the colors. Notice the ground or floor of the space, its walls, roofs, windows, and doors. Are you facing the light or avoiding it? What spectacular qualities do you see? Notice it all more clearly and exactly.

Hearing

Listen carefully to the sounds within and around you. Turn up the volume. Notice the subtle and faint sounds, distant and close sounds. Are they loud, clear, and beautiful or horrible? Melodious, staccato, and rhythmic or non-rhythmic? What are you not hearing?

Movement

Within your imagined still space, allow yourself to move in an immediate, authentic expression of how you feel in the moment. Wait for an impulse, a felt sensation. What part of you wants to move? Let your dance unfold. Notice your urge to move or not to move.

Relationship

Notice your relationship to other people within the space, if any. Notice any conflict. What is your relationship to the place itself? What is your connection to the world while you are in this space? How is this space physically and psychologically just right for you? See being in your sacred space as a vision quest; experience the Earth as a wise teacher sending you messages.

Part 2: Journal Writing

Journal writing is an optional step and is used to record symbolic seed concepts for your design. Write down the special qualities of your imagined sacred space and what you have just experienced in the meditation. List the feelings you associate with each quality. Pick out qualities as though you are selecting seeds that you wish to plant and have grow into your home.

Part 3: Model-Making

Model-making integrates your symbolic seed concepts into a model of your dream home. Choose those concepts that are most important to you. Collect and prepare the following materials:

Cob Sculpting Mixture

Mix clay soil (screened in advance), sand, water, and chopped straw or manure, as if you are making a stiff earthen plaster. (Modeling clay will work as well.) Form a ball the size of a small melon and keep it moist until needed.

Building Materials

Collect miniature natural building materials, including small pebbles, stones, sand, mica, driftwood, sticks, bark, sod, bamboo, straw, leaves, and flowers.

Work Surface

Prepare a platform for your model for ease of transportation. Use a piece of plywood, a board, a piece of bark, a flat rock, or other durable material. Ideally, it should be at least 2 feet by 2 feet (0.6 by 0.6 meters).

To make your model, take your ball of sculpting mix or modeling clay, sit still, and without thinking or planning, begin to play with and shape the ball. Do what your hands want to do. Trust your hands to sculpt your seed concepts into your model.

Use the other natural materials that you have collected. If you wish, you can build miniature foundations, floors, walls, windows, doors, and roofs. Or you can choose to symbolically represent a single quality of your sacred space instead of modeling your entire dream home. Place an object or cob figurine in the model to represent yourself and to give scale.

The intuitively designed 'Heart House' is Linda Smiley's and Ianto Evans's home, and headquarters of the Cob Cottage Company.

MARK LAMBERTH

Part 4: Storytelling

Share your model with someone. If this exercise is done in a workshop setting, share as a group, telling stories about your sacred space. Take a tour of each person's model. Notice what symbolic seed concepts are expressed through each person's sculpture. The exercise can be extended by celebrating your creative work and expressing your spirit through singing or dancing.

THE HEART HOUSE

Frank Lloyd Wright evoked the spirit of intuitive design with his statement, "Architecture is born in the heart." When my husband Ianto Evans and I designed our heart-shaped cob cottage, we weren't fully aware at the time of its embracing hug and womb-like shape and qualities, nor could we predict the powerful effect this space would have on our daily lives and relationships.

With the Heart House, we ignored classical notions of design, in which every last detail is figured out and drawn in advance. Nature doesn't design with paper, rulers, and scale models; she begins with a template, which is a fairly rigid idea of what's possible, then creates endless diversity by responding to every nuance of the surroundings. In a similar way, once the foundation was built, we made nearly every design decision by intuition — how it felt at the time and how we imagined it would feel when finished.

The floor plan was not intentionally shaped like a heart. We designed by verb and adjective, the activity and the qualities of the place. Need space to cook in? Well, standing at an imaginary wraparound counter, I spread my arms. You really can't stretch easily beyond that span, so for a solitary cook, the kitchen ended there. Within my reach, and without my needing to walk, are fridge, stove, sink, dishes, pots, food, storage, and counters. 'Desking' space, directly above, turned out to have the same plan, only with a lower ceiling. The spaces fitted the activity as the shell fits the snail. What emerged was a quirky sort of heart shape, with a step, a buttress, and a loft edge separating the tiny space into two tinier places.

Serendipity even had a hand in our design. While the house was under construction, we happened to be on the site at the right time and noticed the light shining through the trees. Intuitive design (and a little careful pruning of tree branches) invited this sacred light into the cottage. At sunrise on August 1 (Lammas), sunlight

CATHERINE WANEK

A cob interior space, sculpted around the human activities that take place here.

floods through a window and hits a spot above the wood stove for precisely seven minutes. After August 4, that spot is not lit again until the following Beltane, when the sun traverses the same path in the sky.

Nature prescribes exactly what we need to heal ourselves. By listening to our body signals and our spirit signals, we can integrate our symbolic seed concepts into the designs of our homes. By consciously responding to place and space, we can create places that will lift our spirits, soothe our souls, and create positive relationships with self, spirit, and others. We can free ourselves from self-destruction, heal our illnesses, and transform conflict into awareness.

Linda Smiley is a founding co-director of the Cob Cottage Company in Cottage Grove, Oregon. After working for many years as a recreational therapist and environmental educator, she has taught cob and natural building since 1993 in the U.S., Canada, New Zealand, Australia, Sweden, and Denmark. She helped found the first Alternative Building Colloquium in Oregon in 1994.

NOTES

1. See Caroline M. Myss, *Anatomy of the Spirit* (Harmony Books, 1996), p. 179.

RESOURCES
Books

Day, Christopher. *Places of the Soul: Architecture and Environmental Design As a Healing Art*. Harper Collins, 1990. Describes how architecture can grow organically out of the needs and intentions of its users and the qualities of the environment.

Evans, Ianto, Linda Smiley, and Michael G. Smith. *Hand-Sculpted House: A Practical and Philosophical Guide to Building a Cob Cottage*. Chelsea Green, 2002. Contains an expanded description of Linda's work with cob art therapy and sculpting sacred space.

Lawlor, Anthony. *The Temple in the House: Finding the Sacred in Everyday Architecture*. Putnam, 1994. Explores the connection between sacred geometry and architecture, following its development through temples of many cultures and many ages and into our modern houses and workplaces. Filled with exercises and meditations to help develop your powers of intuition and observation.

Mindell, Arnold. *Working on Yourself Alone: Inner Dreambody Work*. Arkana, 1990. A guide to process-oriented meditation that can be used by the individual as a means of resolving conflict and increasing awareness from within.

Pearson, David. *Earth to Spirit: In Search of Natural Architecture*. Chronicle Books, 1994. With beautiful color photographs, this book documents the author's quest for an architecture that integrates ecology, health, and spirituality. Focus on ancestral archetypes, vernacular wisdom, permaculture, and climate responsiveness.

The Healthy House

Paula Baker-Laporte

Paula Baker-Laporte
used natural light and
non-toxic materials to
create this beautiful
space in Santa Fe,
New Mexico.

BUILDING-RELATED ILLNESS, 20th-century (21st-century) disease, multiple chemical sensitivities, sick building syndrome, environmental illness: these terms are recent additions to our vocabulary. Until about 25 years ago, indoor air pollution was a very limited phenomenon, but three basic things have changed in the evolution of building technology, resulting in the current widespread concern about environmental quality inside our homes.

First: The very fabric of our homes has changed. Postwar industrialization has introduced mass-produced building components and transportation networks to distribute these products nationwide. Building materials and methods, once regionally derived, have been replaced by manufactured components that promise to provide better performance for less cost. Have these products fulfilled this promise? Certainly not, when environmental and life cycle costs are considered in the cost equation.

Furthermore many of these new products have had a negative and costly impact on our health. Until very recent history, our built environments have always been free of man-made chemicals. There are now more than 4 million registered man-made chemicals; between 70,000 and 80,000 of them are in common use. We know very little about the health effects of most of these chemicals and even less about what happens when they interact with one another in an enclosed environment. We do know that many chemicals found in building products — and once thought to be safe — are making people ill.

Second: As the cost of home heating and cooling skyrocketed, we recognized the need for more energy-efficient buildings. In solving this problem, however, we inadvertently created another, further contributing to the demise of our indoor environmental quality. For several decades now, new building technologies have been invented in order to seal homes more tightly, thus making them more energy efficient. However, in order to maintain health, a well-sealed home requires a ventilation system to replace stale and humid air. Given the number of synthetic and fuel-derived toxins that we have introduced into our homes, the need for fresh air exchange is especially significant in standard home construction. And yet no fresh air exchange is required by law, and most tight homes are insufficiently ventilated for optimal health.

Third: We have become accustomed to a new level of comfort and convenience undreamed-of just 100 years ago. These amenities have placed unanticipated performance demands on our buildings. We have introduced huge amounts of moisture into our homes through daily indoor bathing and the use of laundry and dishwashing appliances. In addition, with the advent of modern heating, ventilation, and air-conditioning (HVAC) equipment, modern architecture has abandoned climatically responsive vernacular design in favor of the mechanically dependent 'machine for living in.' We have succeeded in equipping our homes so as to provide uniform temperature continuously, regardless of climate and independent of architectural form. We have also created extreme moisture and temperature differentials between the inside of our homes and the outside environment. The stresses placed on our building envelopes have contributed to health-threatening conditions, such as mold.

In response to the problem of building-related illness, two very different models for the healthy home have emerged. The first, more mainstream, approach involves eliminating as many pollutants as possible from within the building envelope and sealing it very tightly on the inside so that there is less need to worry about the chemical composition of the structure or insulation. Clean, fresh air is then mechanically pumped in, keeping the house under a slightly positive pressure so that air infiltration is controlled and pollution caused from human activity is purged from the home. This is a technologically-based solution to a technologically-created problem. Impermeable or 'sealed' wall construction is a relatively new concept that relies on manufactured synthetic products to create diffusion-retardant walls. Mainstream building practices and codes are now based on sealed-construction theory.

The second approach involves designing and landscaping the building to be responsive to the local climatic conditions and building the structure out of natural or non-toxic materials that are permeable to air and moisture. The building is seen as a third skin (clothes being the second) — a permeable organism interacting with the natural world and facilitating a balanced exchange of air and humidity. This approach is based on the precepts of 'Bau-biologie.' Bau-biologie is a health-based approach to building, popular throughout northern Europe, that recognizes humans to be part of, and not apart from, a greater natural system. Although technological innovation has been somewhat successful in both dominating and replicating the natural environment, many of the subtle benefits provided by nature have been overlooked (for several decades, as mentioned before, the need for fresh air was one such subtlety). (See "Designing for Vitality.")

The Bau-biologie vision of a healthy indoor environment encompasses several criteria that are not often considered in the more mainstream technology-based approach to the healthy home. These include the study of earth energies and geopathic disturbances; the elimination of man-made electromagnetic fields; the benefits of color, light, and harmonic proportions in building design; and the role that breathable natural materials play in balancing humidity and electro-climate.

Ironically, natural building materials, once the norm for us and still the norm for the majority of humankind, are viewed with great suspicion and skepticism in current mainstream building culture. Even though people have surrounded themselves with natural, permeable materials throughout human history, and even though enduring models of these buildings are found throughout the world, mainstream building practices and codes promote manufactured building commodities that are laboratory tested, standardized, stamped, packaged, and shipped. In this current building climate, applying for a permit to build a natural home can be a discouraging process.

Cob and lime plaster create a healthy place in which to give and receive a massage.

However, the natural building movement, championed by the theories of Bau-biologie and a small but growing sector of environmentally concerned builders, designers, and homeowners is gaining momentum. This is partially due to a burgeoning mainstream green building movement. In the past, issues of health, energy, and the environment were considered in isolation from one another by different sectors of the building industry, resulting in solutions that worked for one but were at cross-purposes to another. For example, an energy-efficient home often resulted in insufficient air exchange for health, while unsophisticated attempts to allow more fresh air into the house were not energy efficient. Recycled materials containing toxic glues may have been an efficient resource use but did not promote health. Natural building by its very nature exemplifies a balance between energy efficiency, health, and a wise use of natural

MARLEY PORTER

Plants can be used to help absorb toxins in the environment.

resources. Currently, the American Institute of Architects and the National Association of Home Builders are embracing an approach in sustainability that is inclusive of all three of these aspects. As green building rating programs are being developed throughout the country, natural building is gaining more recognition in mainstream American building culture.

Paula Baker-Laporte, A.I.A., has headed a prolific and wide-ranging residential architectural practice in Santa Fe since 1986. Together with husband and builder Robert Laporte, she cofounded the Econest Building Company. She has lectured widely on the precepts of environmentally sound and non-toxic architecture and is the primary author of Prescriptions for a Healthy House *(New Society Publishers, 2001).*

RESOURCES
Books

Baggs, Sydney, and Joan Baggs. *The Healthy House: Creating a Safe, Healthy, and Environmentally Friendly Home.* Harper Collins, 1996. Informed by Bau-biologie and *feng shui*, this book leads you on a journey through designing a healthy house, from sacred geometry to sewage treatment.

Baker-Laporte, Paula, Erica Elliott, and John Banta. *Prescriptions for a Healthy House: A Practical Guide for Architects, Builders, and Homeowners.* New Society Publishers, 2001. A thorough introduction to the problem of toxic building materials, including medical research. Clear suggestions on what you can do differently, and where to get products and information.

Bower, John. *The Healthy House: How to Buy One, How to Cure a Sick One, How to Build One.* 4th ed. Healthy House Institute, 2000. This encyclopedic book for builders, buyers, and remodelers identifies threats to indoor health and suggests strategies for improvement in a system-by-system fashion.

Organizations

Building for Health Materials Center, P.O. Box 113, Carbondale, CO 81623, U.S.A.; phone: 800-292-4838; website: www.buildingforhealth.com. Extremely knowledgeable and helpful about healthy building options. They ship hundreds of non-toxic building materials direct from the manufacturer all over the U.S.

Earth Sweet Home Institute, 98 Falk Road, East Dummerston, VT 05346, U.S.A.; phone: 802-254-7674; email: earthswt@sover.net; website: www.envirolink.org/orgs/earthsweet. Educational materials on low-tech building materials and methods, focusing on non-toxicity and low embodied energy.

International Institute for Bau-Biologie and Ecology, P.O. Box 387, Clearwater, FL 33757, U.S.A.; phone: 727-461-4371; fax: 727-461-4373; email: baubiologie@earthlink.net; website: www.bau-biologieusa.com. Offers books, videos, equipment, seminars, and a correspondence course on building health, the environment, and electro-magnetic issues.

The Healthy House Institute, 430 N. Sewall Road, Bloomington, IN 47408, U.S.A.; phone: 812-332-5073; email: healthy@bloomington.in.us; website: www.hhinst.com. Independent resource center for designers, contractors, and homeowners interested in healthy houses.

Responsive Design: Integrating the Spirit of Place with the Vision of Home

Susie Harrington

THE SUBURBAN HOUSE sitting in the middle of its perfect lawn, framed on each side by a driveway, its landscape lobotomized by a strip sidewalk leading to the front door has done much to deaden our sense of what is possible. Not surprisingly, the desire for a more natural home is often accompanied by the desire to live in a rural setting far from other houses, driveways, and lawns. What we are seeking, though, is not just plenty of space but a more intimate relationship with our surroundings. Responsive design enables us to consciously create that relationship on any site.

When we explore how to build sustainably, we discover new possibilities at every level from community organization to our choice of paints. Through careful consideration of the site and our own needs, we are able to build a place that is not only more environmentally sustainable but also more satisfying and healthy to live in.

Responsive design can be likened to a tree, in which roots, trunk, and crown are seamlessly integrated. The roots of responsive design are twofold. The physical, ecological, and historical information inherent in the site itself composes one root. Individual social, cultural, and programmatic desires compose the second root. The two roots reinforce one another and fully support the character of the site and the people using it. The trunk of the tree corresponds to the actual constructed environment. When the roots are healthy and the trunk well established, the crown — delightful branches, flowers, and fruit corresponding to ongoing integration and growth — can flourish.

This sculptural cob courtyard wall, built by Linda Smiley and Ianto Evans outside their Oregon home, helps to define a cozy outdoor living space.

LINDA SMILEY

THE ROOTS
Site Inventory: Physical, Ecological, and Historical Considerations

Although we often neglect to fully assess human needs for a site, we more frequently fail to look carefully at the site itself. A full understanding of the site should include the substrate (rock, soil, groundwater), drainage patterns, vegetation (existing, historical, and potential), climate (wind, rain, temperatures), sun and shade patterns, views, and special opportunities and challenges (a

CATHERINE WANEK

Natural light improves our mood, enhances performance, and saves energy.

noisy road, a north-facing aspect, a tall neighboring building, etc.). It is also important to respond to the site as a whole. Getting the feel of the site might involve just sitting and noticing. What are the attractive spots? Where are you drawn? What areas do not seem so great? (See also "Siting a Natural Building.")

Programming: Individual, Social, and Cultural Considerations

Having looked at the site itself, we need to consider the proposed human needs for its use, including the amount of time we would like to spend outside or in semi-enclosed spaces. What specific activities will take place, and what are their spatial needs? What is the desired feel for each of those activities? What are the shapes, sizes, and relationships of spaces that will facilitate the proposed uses?

It is easy to say that we need, for example, a three-bedroom, two-bath house with a home office, a big kitchen, and an open living space. But such a description tells us almost nothing that would facilitate a responsive design. If, on the other hand, we create a detailed description of the ambiance we want for our sleeping, eating, or working spaces, then a picture starts to appear. Books, photographs, and visits to existing structures are wonderful resources for this process, as is taking time to look at the details of one's own experiences, routines, and internal vision. (See also "Intuitive Design.")

Flexibility is an important aspect of the programming stage of responsive design. Since it is difficult to balance immediate needs with needs that change over time, it helps to simply play out a few scenarios in your imagination. What minor adjustment might allow an office to become a bedroom, for instance, or two bedrooms to become an apartment for an elderly parent?

THE TRUNK
Finding Form
Site Repair

The place to which you are most attracted may not need to be altered; in fact, building there would likely destroy whatever it is that makes it so attractive. The less desirable or more damaged part of a site, however, may benefit from being altered, screened, planted, and built on. It is the damaged, uninviting spot that allows us the most freedom and opportunity to create something beautiful without sacrificing beauty in the process.

Orientation

The sun is the single strongest organizer of a responsive design. It is a common mistake to orient a building exclusively to the view and ignore the variety of experiences provided by sun and shade. Feeling the sun streaming in the windows on an early winter morning, wandering into the garden on a spring afternoon to read the mail, dining under a cool trellis late in the summer — these experiences depend on a careful orientation of the building with surrounding spaces. When you organize in response to the sun, you might orient a bedroom toward the east, build closets and utilities on the north side of the house, and create a cool-weather outside sitting area within a southwest-facing courtyard. (See also "Designing with the Sun.")

Well designed external spaces are just as important as those inside a house.

Indoor and Outdoor Space

It is important to consider each space on its own, with an eye to having all the spaces of a site form a coherent whole; this helps to tie together a building with its site. When we create outdoor spaces that interlock with interior spaces, it encourages our sense of connection to both kinds of spaces and offers us the opportunity to relate to the living world around us in diverse ways. Such outdoor spaces need not be large. There are intimate gardens of 50 square feet (5 square meters) that create daily magic in owners' lives.

Designing from the Outside In

Synergy of Site and Building

In order to relate well to its larger context, a house should complement the landscape. A desert environment, with flat mesas and few tall trees, is the quintessential horizontal landscape. Complementary building forms for this environment are long, low shapes with flat roofs and sharp short verticals. Conversely, a tall, narrow building with steeply pitched roofs complements an alpine village that is surrounded by evergreens. Within the higher density area of a town or city, the natural landscape is often not predominant, and the fabric of pre-existing buildings is the larger context to consider.

Attention to detail gives a design completeness and repose, as in this Southwestern straw bale home.

Balance

It is important to create balance in one's experience of space. Each site has its own particular feel that can affect the building design. A site may feel expansive, or it might feel intimate and enclosed. It might have a special place, tree, or built feature that suggests a relationship to the building. For example, a building on an expansive site with long views would ideally be expansive, but would also have within it places of intimacy and enclosure. When large views predominate, close views may need to be created.

Scale

The character and scale of a house establishes its relationship to its site. A modest cottage on a small town lot can successfully relate to its site through its size and by dividing its walls, roof, windows, etc. into smaller pieces and carefully detailing them. Intimate gardens and narrow paths will further integrate a building with its site. Although a larger site with a grand landscape suggests a larger scale of building, fine details will complement it, even as the grandest landscape is broken into smaller elements. No matter how large, a building requires a variety of scales.

Designing from the Inside Out

Organizing Rooms

Using the external site as a guide, the location, orientation, and relationship of internal spaces can be organized into a layout. Each space or room will have its preferred view, time of day for sun, access to the outdoors, privacy requirements, etc. When the natural character of each interior space is aligned through appropriate placement with its location on the site, the experience of the site and the rooms can flow together more easily. Once the approximate locations and relationships are determined, the next challenge is to unite the spaces. Circulation is the key element that ties everything together.

Circulation

Circulation in a building should be both efficient and interesting. Efficiency can be best accomplished by having a central core of circulation. Storage, closets, bookshelves, and windows can combine nicely with circulation spaces to make them more interesting and multifunctional.

Defining Spaces

After the basic layout is determined, attention should be brought to the design of each space. Just as with exterior spaces, internal spaces need edges and definition. On the other hand, especially in smaller houses, creating a visual connection between spaces allows for an overall feeling of spaciousness.

Connection

Each room can have its own feel and particular connection to the surroundings. Views can be either of faraway hillsides or of plants just outside the window. When it is easy and inviting to sit outside, flow is initiated. Once begun, this flow becomes a fundamental aspect of the way in which a house and its outdoor spaces work together. Drinking a cup of tea on the patio below a trellis, for instance, may lead you to curiosity about a newly blooming flower. On closer examination, you may notice a bee and a beetle and an unfamiliar sprout nearby. The warmth of the sun on the back of your neck and a bird chirping from a nearby branch complete the moment.

Arcades create shade and conviviality, especially in urban contexts.

Detailing

A clear intention to retain the connection to place will assist us in keeping details simple. Large quantities of mass-produced parts and pieces will perhaps contribute little, while a single coat rack, handmade from a branch of a nearby tree, will weave us closer. Locally produced and crafted finish details also have the soft, unprocessed, natural feel of the world outside our door. Although the financial cost is usually higher for this sort of finishing, the additional

CATHERINE WANEK

environmental cost is minimal. Beautiful, handmade, and locally acquired details allow us to rejoice in our own artistic and creative spirit.

THE CROWN
Only the Beginning

A design process that integrates our own lives with the life of the site provides the opportunity for ongoing growth and change. By gently and sensitively creating human habitation, we have the chance to share and even enhance the wildlife habitat, plant diversity, and inherent character of a place. Our daily experience engages us in the great cycle of growth, decay, and the rebirth of life. The roots of site and human need join and nourish the trunk that is a responsive and integrated built environment. The trunk, in its turn, upholds a crown of new growth, so that flowers may bloom and the whole tree flourish.

> *Susie Harrington is immersed in the grassroots effort to find ways that people can inhabit a place without destroying it. This has led to straw bale house design, co-housing community and development, site design, landscape planning, and teaching.*

RESOURCES
Books

Alexander, Christopher, et al. *A Pattern Language.* Oxford University Press, 1977. This book breaks the constructed environment down into individual desirable elements. These 'patterns' are explained both in how they are formed and in how they are used by people.

Connell, John. *Homing Instinct: Using Your Lifestyle to Design and Build Your Home.* Warner Books, 1993. A thorough and readable walk through designing a home; directed specifically for the first-time owner-builder. Includes detailed construction information.

Lyle, John Tillman. *Regenerative Design for Sustainable Development.* John Wiley and Sons, 1994. This book is an inspiring and detailed exploration of the theory and application of integrating human and natural systems.

Thompson, J. William, and Kim Sorvig. *Sustainable Landscape Construction: A Guide to Green Building Outdoors.* Island Press, 2000. A comprehensive look at designing and altering landscapes in ways that favor long-term sustainability and the integration of human construction into existing patterns.

Wells, Malcolm. *Gentle Architecture.* McGraw-Hill, 1981. An excellent book for thinking about building impact and appropriate design with respect to landscape and construction.

Eighteen Design Principles to Make Square Feet Work Harder

Robert Gay

BEFORE YOU BEGIN designing, do this four-part exercise in self-knowledge.

1. Study your lifestyle very carefully.

2. Think as freely as possible about the qualities of the spaces and places you have most loved and hated.

3. Fight to minimize your clutter and accumulations.

4. Free yourself up from advertising, media imagery, and pressures to consume, since if you don't, the urge to buy will terrorize you.

Then, when you begin designing or working with a designer, use as many of the following principles as possible.

1. Minimize circulation space by reducing or eliminating hallways and paths to and from the doors. Excessive circulation space is one of the biggest drawbacks of many floor plans.

2. If you do have to have a hallway, enrich the pass-through experience with bookcases, niches, photos, mirrors, art objects, skylights, or textures.

3. Avoid circulation paths that cut diagonally through a space. This almost always chops something up that would otherwise be a whole with its own integrity. (An exception is that sometimes a large space can successfully be cut into two groupings of furniture.)

4. Don't close rooms off from each other unless you have to. It's easy to see how this helps minimize interior walls.

5. Consider partial separations between rooms to create an ambiguity of connectedness: arches, interior windows, half-walls, curtained spaces, freestanding headboards (for beds), interior columns, and similar features. Often there are reasons for partially separating one space from another, without needing to devote a separate room to each.

6. Let interior walls be as thin as possible. (This contrasts to the many compelling reasons for having thick exterior walls.) Something thinner than an inch (2.5 centimeters) can often serve as a wall, as with Japanese *shoji* doors.

7. Organize the floor plan around activities, such as eating dinner, doing a craft or hobby, or greeting visitors, rather than around preconceived rooms. Look for the centers of action, movement, and attention; then shape spaces around them.

1. Minimize circulation space.

2. Enrich hallways with bookcases, niches etc.

3. Avoid circulation paths that cut diagonally.

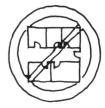

4. Don't close rooms off from each other.

5. Consider partial separations between rooms to create connectedness.

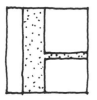

6. Let interior walls be as thin as possible.

9. Consider a sliding 'pocket' door.

10. Relate carefully to different views in different directions.

11. Have easy connections between inside and outside spaces.

12. Consider creating other planetary connections.

8.   Minimize the number of doors, after considering your real need for privacy.

9.   If a door swing seems to take up too much space or unavoidably conflicts with something else, consider a sliding 'pocket' door.

10.   Relate carefully to the different views in different directions; include connections with the heavens above, via roof windows, skylights, or porch roofs high enough to let you see some sky from inside the house. Look also for ways to appreciate or enhance the smaller views, since intimate, small-scale views can be just as enjoyable as sweeping, dramatic ones. The perceptual effect of a view is to expand the space from which you see it.

11.   Have easy connections between inside and outside spaces, such as patios, decks, and out door showers, designing them as outdoor rooms with their own definition and sense of partial enclosure. Because of seasonal variations in your climate, you may need different out door spaces for winter and summer use.

12.   Consider creating other planetary connections: a compass in the floor, a Stonehenge-like shaft of light at the equinoxes or solstices, a sundial or shadow-casting play place, or prisms in a window that send rainbows flying around. These connections help make a house feel part of a much larger whole.

13.   Avoid right angles as much as is permitted by your budget, your building system, and your skill in building. Where you do have them, consider softening them by sculpting your wall material by using trim, ornament, or a built-in feature like a fireplace or display cabinet.

14.   Vary ceiling height by generally giving smaller spaces lower ceilings. This will dramatize the perceived size of the larger spaces by increasing the contrast between spaces. Floor levels can also be varied — even a few inches of difference adds to the diversity and apparent size of a space. (This, of course, is at odds with the desire for maximum accessibility for potential wheelchair-bound or otherwise infirm users of a house.)

15.   Avoid flat ceilings; instead, use open trusses, curved vaults, or cornices. A shape that rises will pull your feelings up with it.

16.   Have a diversity of windows. A single glass block or 1-square-foot (.09-square-meter) window can energize a large blank wall, and 'zen views' can make much of a smaller window.

17.   Plan lighting to create pools of light, rather than uniform illumination everywhere.

18.   To extend rooms and create diversity, use 'non-room' spaces, such as window seats, sleeping alcoves, niches, built-in benches, and recessed shelves. Thick-walled building systems like straw bale and rammed earth naturally allow these kinds of spaces, but thin-wall methods can also incorporate them. One result on the outside might be 'bumpouts.'

Of course these guidelines aren't absolute, and sometimes the exceptions are as intriguing as the rules! Nevertheless, I believe that in well-crafted houses that embody most of these principles, small spaces can be intensified to become richer and more enjoyable. A vibrant level of complexity will automatically unfold. And it might just be that houses made in this way will be understood to be a contribution to the well-being of the planet.

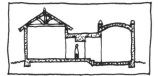

14-15. Vary ceiling height by giving smaller spaces lower ceiling.

> *Robert Gay, an architect in private practice in Tucson, centers his largely residential practice on human needs and sustainable building practices, with a specialty in straw bale design. He's also done university teaching, a college master plan, general contracting, furniture making, stonework, and small playful art projects. He lives near the Catalina Mountains with his wife, two small boys, and many other creatures, some domesticated.*

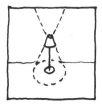

17. Plan lighting to create pools of light.

RESOURCES
Books

Cline, Ann. *A Hut of One's Own: Life Outside the Circle of Architecture.* MIT Press, 1997. This intriguing book weaves together many threads: the failure of modern architects to meet the needs of their clients, historical accounts of downwardly mobile hut dwellers throughout the ages, and the author's own experience of building and inhabiting a tiny teahouse.

Susanka, Sarah. *The Not So Big House.* Taunton Press, 1998. A thought-provoking book on techniques for designing houses that use less space while increasing quality of life for their inhabitants.

Walker, Lester. *The Tiny Book of Tiny Houses.* Overlook Press, 1993. A series of case studies of tiny (less than 300-square-foot [27-square-meter]) houses, with excellent illustrations.

18. Use non-room spaces to extend rooms like window seats.

Combining Natural Materials for Energy Efficiency

Catherine Wanek

The Save the Children office in Cuidad Obregon, Mexico, by Bill and Athena Steen, is a masterful example of combining several materials – in this case, straw, clay, and reeds – to create a beautiful and energy-efficient building.

IT'S NATURAL to use available, on-site materials to build our homes. Doing so conserves energy and resources — our own and the planet's. And understanding the specific qualities of our on-site resources and how they can be combined allows us to create efficient and elegant homes that require the least energy input and return the greatest comfort.

Beginning always with choice of building site, two effective strategies for energy efficiency are solar orientation and earth-coupling. If we simply design window placement to capture the winter sun, a major part of our heating needs in many climates can be accommodated with minimal effort. If your site happens to be on a hillside and you couple your home with the constant year-round temperature of the earth below the frost line — about 55 to 65 degrees Fahrenheit (13 to 18 degrees Celsius) — it will keep indoor temperatures within a relatively few degrees of the human comfort zone. Combining earth-coupling and passive solar design enhances the effectiveness of both but requires fine-tuning to climate, and works less well in cold climates and where sunlight is scarce in the winter.

THERMAL MASS, INSULATION, AND STRUCTURE

Earth is common to nearly every building site — in fact to build a sturdy foundation, it's generally necessary to excavate. After the topsoil is set aside for gardening or landscaping, the subsoil must be dealt with. Very often it can be combined with other natural materials to form wall systems. Stones and timber are other materials often found on-site — both of which can be utilized in construction. But to utilize them appropriately and most effectively, it's essential to understand what each material does best.

Although timber in our dry-land bioregion is a precious resource, it can still be harvested sustainably and used in construction. Wood has great structural strength, rigidity and beauty, and a medium insulation value. But it shrinks as it dries, so wooden wall systems are prone to small gaps that

CATHERINE WANEK

can let in a lot of cold air. Thus, on most sites, it probably makes the best use of timber to use wood structurally for your roof system. Smaller trees not normally considered for building can be quite useful. The locally ubiquitous juniper tree grows slowly and in organic shapes; hence it is not well suited for milling. On the other hand, this scorned tree is a member of the cedar family and so is extremely rot resistant and strong. It makes good structural posts, sills and trim, and, when left in its organic shapes, can be amazingly beautiful. Willow, maple, and other saplings that often need to be thinned can be used in wattle and daub walls or for pinning straw bale wall systems (instead of rebar).

Stone and earth can also be utilized as structural materials. Their density makes them good 'thermal mass,' which means that they absorb heat or cold from the air around them; then, as the

Structural wooden posts, harvested from trees killed in a forest fire, also serve as part of the forms for a straw-clay interior wall. Straw bale exterior walls insulate this passive solar residence at the Lama Foundation, New Mexico.

air temperature changes, they slowly equalize to match it, releasing the stored heat or cold. Thermal mass material absorbs heat most effectively when it is dark colored and the sun hits it directly. Used well, thermal mass can help to warm or cool our homes, but misunderstood, it can be an energy drain or cause discomfort. The 'heat island' effect in some urban areas is due to excess thermal mass (and lack of shading). Masonry buildings, asphalt streets, and concrete sidewalks soak up the hot summer sun during the day and radiate it out during the night, keeping the city continually hot. This cycle can continue day after day, and it requires massive energy inputs to create human comfort zones.

Straw is not often found on-site but is cheap and available in nearly every region. Since humans first began to build shelters, straw (or grass) has been used as a building material in combination with earth — in bricks, walls, and floors. When the baling machine was invented, it became possible to turn straw

CATHERINE WANEK

into big, highly insulating building blocks. In bale form, straw can be used structurally, and it provides something few other natural materials can — excellent insulation. It is the dead-air space contained within the hollow stalk of straw and around the individual stalks that make straw bales such a good insulator, provided that any walls made with them are well sealed with plaster to prevent air infiltration.

Wall systems that combine thermal mass with insulation will, not surprisingly, perform somewhere in between those systems that use only one or the other. Although definitive R-values

R-Value Comparison Chart

Source: U.S. Department of Energy

Wall Type	R-value (hr-sqft-F/Btu)	U-value (Btu/hr-sqft-F)	Weight (lb/sqft)	Heat Capacity (Btu/sqft-F)
Wood Frame				
2x4 studs w/R11 batts	10.2	0.098	9.2	2.2
2x6 studs w/R19 batts	15.4	0.065	10.5	2.6
Compressed Straw panel				
uninsulated 4.8" panel	10.1	0.099	13.4	4.9
insulated 4.8" panel	18.4	0.054	13.7	4.9
Fibrous Concrete Panel				
insulated 3" panel	16.7	0.060	16.9	4.7
insulated 4" panel	19.1	0.052	20.1	5.7
Straw Bale				
23" bale @ R-1.8/inch (-25%)	42.7	0.023		
23" bale @ R-2.4/inch	56.5	0.018	21.4	6.4
23" bale @ R-3.0/inch (+25%)	70.3	0.014		
Foam Blocks				
6" form w/concrete/adobe fill	26.3	0.038	40.8	7.5
8" form w/concrete/adobe fill	28.0	0.036	54.2	9.8
Adobe				
uninsulated 10"	3.5	0.284	95.0	17.9
insulated 10"	11.9	0.084	95.3	18.0
uninsulated 24"	6.8	0.147	183.4	34.2
exterior insulated 24"	15.1	0.066	183.6	34.3

Notes:

• All walls have stucco exterior and drywall interior, except adobe and straw walls have plaster.

• Wood frame walls have 25 percent (R-11) and 20 percent (R-19) stud areas. The R-19 batt compresses to R-18.

• Compressed straw panel, insulated case, has 2 inches polystyrene on exterior.

• Fibrous Concrete panels have 1-inch polystyrene inside and out.

• Straw bale wall R-value is calculated for 3 unit R-values for straw to cover potential variability.

• Average material thickness across foam block wall sections is as follows:

•6-inch foam has 2.9 inches polystyrene each side and 3.4 inches of fill.

•8-inch foam has 3.1 inches polystyrene each side and 4.8 inches of fill.

• Wall properties are based on 75 percent adobe and 23 percent concrete fill.

• Adobe walls, insulated case, have 2 inches of polystyrene on exterior.

• 24-inch wall is two 10-inch layers with 4-inch air gap.

are not established for straw-clay, woodchip-clay, cordwood masonry, papercrete, fidobe, and the like, these materials retain thermal mass characteristics with moderate insulation properties. When sealed against air infiltration and combined with passive solar design and a well-insulated roof, these materials can create a comfortable and energy-efficient home in moderate climates.

Good insulation in walls and ceilings protects indoor environments from daily and seasonal temperature swings and provides the greatest comfort for the least energy input — which is why I favor straw bales for exterior wall systems. But bales take up a lot of space and are less suitable as interior partitions, where insulation isn't needed. So, for inside walls, a thermal mass material is most useful, where it will serve to moderate temperature. Earth and straw combinations, such as adobe, cob, straw-clay, etc. also offer infinite possibilities for sculpting interior spaces and built-in furniture. And clay has a preservative effect on straw and wood, reducing their vulnerability to moisture and rot.

Another reason to use earthen materials inside the home is its ability to absorb sound, odors, and moisture. Water vapor from bathing and cooking can build up inside and provide an environment for mold and fungal growth, but earthen walls and plasters, with their enormous capacity to moderate humidity, resist this buildup. Used to create floors, earth provides thermal mass for direct solar gain and a surface to stand on that is easy on the body. And an earthen plaster covering interior walls adds up to a lot of thermal mass, augmenting passive solar design.

Although the cost of using on-site natural materials is often 'dirt cheap,' techniques vary in how much work they take. Even when you are using machinery, walls made from cob, straw-clay, adobe, rammed earth, etc. are quite labor intensive to build. But building with bales can go very quickly, so the use of bales for exterior walls and thermal mass techniques for interior walls is also consistent with conserving fossil fuel and human energy in constructing our buildings.

We can create a comfortable environment with primarily natural materials by simply orienting our homes to the sun and combining exterior insulation with interior thermal mass. Understanding the properties of natural materials and how they can complement each other will lead to healthy and energy-efficient built environments that nurture human life.

Catherine Wanek lives in a historic stone and brick lodge that faces north, with leaky old windows. The quest for energy-efficient comfort has led her to the preceding conclusions. She and her husband Pete Fust hosted the first Natural Building Colloquium in 1995.

RESOURCES

Books

Anderson, Bruce, and Malcolm Wells. *Passive Solar Energy: The Homeowner's Guide to Natural Heating and Cooling.* 2nd ed. Brick House Publishing, 1994. An easy-to-read overview of strategies for passive systems, with sufficient detail to help you design a new building or retrofit an old one.

Elizabeth, Lynne, and Cassandra Adams, eds. *Alternative Construction: Contemporary Natural Building Methods.* John Wiley and Sons, 2000. See especially Chapter Three: Natural Conditioning of Buildings, by Ken Haggard, Polly Cooper, and Jennifer Rennick for a detailed description of the relationship between natural materials and passive solar heating and cooling.

Kachadorian, James. *The Passive Solar House — Using Solar Design to Heat and Cool Your Home.* Chelsea Green, 1997. This tome describes the timeless principles of solar design, including charts and tools to make solar calculations for a variety of latitudes. Suggested building materials are of a conventional nature.

Workshops

Build Here Now — a Natural Building and Permaculture Convergence; annually at The Lama Foundation, P.O. Box 240, San Cristobal, NM 87564, U.S.A.; phone: 505-586-1269; email: registrar@lamafoundation.org; website: for photos and descriptions, visit www.strawhomes.com. A great introduction to many natural building systems, permaculture, earth-based spirituality, and cooperative ethics.

Natural Building Colloquium; annually, at various locations. Contact: The Black Range Lodge, 119 Main Street, Kingston, NM 88042, U.S.A.; phone: 505-895-5652; email: blackrange@zianet.com. The gathering that brought the natural building movement into focus and that has inspired the construction of many hybrid natural structures.

Designing with the Sun

Susie Harrington

THE SHAPE AND ORIENTATION of a house, as well as its window locations, determine not only its direct experience of sun and shade but also how its internal climate responds to seasonal climatic conditions. Rather than controlling temperature using mechanical devices and fossil fuels, we can rely on the three key components of solar design — insulation, insolation, and thermal mass — to create a comfortable environment.

INSULATION

The more extreme the environment, the more insulation is appropriate. It is simpler and less expensive to install high quality windows and insulation materials than to heat a 'leaking sieve.' The use of passive heating or cooling strategies presupposes that the building is well enough insulated that the low-intensity heat of the sun or the coolness of nighttime breezes will make a difference. Some insulation materials, such as straw bales, have low environmental cost and toxicity, are inexpensive, and do not require high-tech installation methods.

INSOLATION

Insolation — bringing the sun's heat into a building — occurs through the windows. The sun's rays pass through the glass, hit a surface, become heat, and are then trapped within the space. As often occurs in a greenhouse, insolation can easily lead to high temperatures. In solar design a moderating influence is provided by thermal mass.

THERMAL MASS

Any material that has the capacity to absorb large amounts of heat can be called a thermal mass. Rock, earth, masonry, concrete, and water are common thermal mass materials. These materials change temperature slowly, coming to equilibrium with the surroundings over a period of time.

The capacities of thermal mass can be put to good use. In a solar-heated space, a thermal mass will slowly increase in temperature as the sun heats up the ambient air. If sunlight falls directly on the mass, then heating will occur even more rapidly. The more surfaces in the room with heat-storing capacities or the more depth to the mass, the more total mass there is to come into equilibrium with the air temperature. As a result, the room will be slower to heat (regardless of

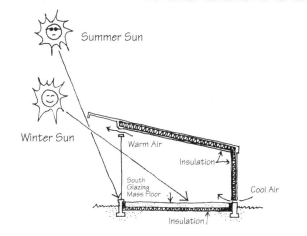

Diagram of an overhang design for summer shading and winter sun penetration.

Summer Sun

Winter Sun

Warm Air

Insulation

South Glazing Mass Floor

Cool Air

Insulation

JOSEPH F. KENNEDY

whether or not the mass is in the sun). If there is sufficient thermal mass, enough heat will be absorbed to prevent the air temperature from becoming uncomfortably high. After the sun has set, the warm mass will cool down over the course of the night, radiating heat to the surfaces and people within the room. Thus, thermal mass acts as an equalizer, harnessing a few hours of intense sun in the middle of the day to provide heat all day and night, without overheating at the peak insolation period.

The same principles apply to summer cooling. It is a common experience to walk into a masonry building in the middle of the summer and find it refreshingly cool. That is because when nighttime temperatures are low enough, the mass of the building gives up its heat at night and then slowly heats up over the course of the day.

The primary challenge in designing a passive solar house is to balance the amount of sun coming in the windows throughout the year with the thermal mass.

The Magic of Sun Angles

Fortunately it is easy to design a building to receive sunlight through south-facing windows in the winter but not in the summer. The sun is high in the sky during the summer months, and its rays can be blocked by roof overhangs, trellises, awnings, and other shading devices. Because the sun is low in the sky during the winter months, the winter sun will shine in below these shading devices, providing heat to the interior. Overhang dimensions can be optimized for summer protection and winter penetration on south-facing windows. It is this wonderful ability to control solar heat gain that gives south-facing windows their magical quality in building design.

Shading on east and west faces is more challenging since the sun is lower in the sky in the morning and evening, diminishing the usefulness of overhangs. So, in general, most of the glass in a passive solar building should face south, with limited windows on the east and west sides. To maximize the advantage of passive solar design, a building can be elongated in an east-west direction (with a long south face). North-facing windows are kept to a minimum in cool climates because they allow heat to escape, without providing any opportunity for insolation.

Susie Harrington received a Masters in Architecture and a degree in Landscape Architecture from the University of Oregon and is currently a landscape architect and building designer. In her free time, she wanders the red-walled canyons near her home in Moab, Utah.

Siting a Natural Building

Michael G. Smith

S ELECTING A BUILDING SITE is one of the most critical design decisions you will ever make. The wrong choice can have long-lasting negative effects that are difficult (or impossible) to mitigate. Many of the characteristics that most strongly determine what it will be like to live in a place are not immediately obvious during a quick visit. To find the best building site, you need to spend a lot of time on the land through different seasons and in extreme weather conditions. If possible, spend a full year camping on the site, or visit it frequently before pinning down the precise building location. Also speak to neighbors and look through county records. The care you take will pay off.

The following suggestions are intended specifically for siting dwellings on rural land, but most are applicable to other situations and building types (in the Southern Hemisphere, reverse north and south notations).

PHYSICAL SITE CHARACTERISTICS
Slope

Don't assume you need a level building site. Often it's best to build on a slope and leave the flattest places for gardening. Slopes can provide the best views and offer advantages in water

This house by Christopher Day blends into the landscape to such an extent that it becomes nearly invisible.

and air drainage, since gravity will help move water and wastes. Excavating a flat pad on a sloped site can provide earth for building, gardening, or landscaping. On the other hand, very steep slopes may complicate access, require excessive digging, and be difficult to get around on during building.

Aspect

The direction a sloped site faces makes a big difference in ground temperature. South-facing slopes, with their surface more nearly perpendicular to the rays of the winter sun, collect more heat in the winter, which could translate into substantial energy savings.

Drainage

If possible, pick a naturally well-drained site. It will save you work, expense, materials, and repairs. Avoid marshy areas, flood plains, and depressions. Stay away from seasonal creeks and gullies where surface water may flow only during part of the year (or maybe only once every several years). If you can't be on site during the heaviest rainfall of the year, imagine a storm of Biblical proportions and figure out where the water would flow. If you're stuck with a poorly drained clay soil and a rainy climate, put the building on a slope so that you can create artificial drainage.

Subsurface Geology

One of the first things I do when exploring a potential building site is to dig a lot of holes. I want to know how far down it is to bedrock (which will inform my excavation plans and foundation design), how much topsoil there is, and what kinds of amendments the soil needs for building with. If the site has deep, rich topsoil, then it might be better used for a garden or orchard. I also look for evidence of landslides and try to determine whether the site is seismically stable.

MICROCLIMATE

Solar Access

In any climate, you can save a lot of money and energy in heating and/or cooling your home by using simple passive solar design strategies. Where winter heating is needed, windows on the south side (or an attached greenhouse) make a big difference but only if you have winter sun on the building! The best sites for passive solar heating (and for photovoltaic electricity) have an unobstructed view to the horizon from the southeast to the southwest. If trees to the south shade your site, consider respectfully harvesting or substantially pruning them. The number of trees you will save by decreased heating needs over the lifetime of the building can easily make up for the ones you take now.

Shade

In hot summer climates, afternoon shading can make the difference between a cool, comfortable retreat and an oven. Look for tall trees to the southwest and west of the site. Deciduous trees are especially useful since they block the summer sun but drop their leaves and let the winter sun through. In general, trees and vegetation around a site will keep it cooler and moister. Deciduous trees and vines can also be planted after the structure is complete.

The Wimberley House of Healing by architect Marley Porter is a manifest match of building and site.

MARLEY PORTER

Prevailing Wind Direction

Because of local topography, wind direction on a specific site can vary enormously from the regional norm. Find out from which direction the biggest storms approach your site. (If you live in the woods, look for big fallen trees. Which direction did they fall?) Will there be wind-driven rain, sleet, or snow? Are you in a valley that channels cold winds past your site, increasing your future heating costs? Are you on a ridge with a spectacular view of the ocean but no protection from whipping gales?

Air Drainage

On clear winter nights, air cools off and condenses wherever it is exposed to the sky, flowing downhill like a viscous fluid. Wherever its passage is blocked by a rise in the ground, a line of trees, or even a building, it comes to rest, creating 'frost pockets' of much colder air. These are the places that freeze first — not a good location for your tomatoes or a cozy home. Valley floors are often the worst. If your site is on a slope, then make sure that cold air can drain away downhill. Also position your buildings where early morning winter sun will warm them up sooner.

Fire

Wildfire runs uphill and in the direction of the wind. Ridges and hilltops are the most susceptible to burning. Waterways, roads, and irrigated gardens all make effective firebreaks.

Floods

If you're near a river or stream, find out where the 100-year flood plain is and site any buildings beyond its reach. Get to know old-timers in your area and ask them about the most extreme weather conditions they can remember.

SITE PLANNING

Master Plan

It's incredibly useful to have a good understanding of overall land usage before you site any building. Look as far into the future as possible. What buildings, gardens, orchards, pastures, ponds, woodlots, and wild areas might you eventually want on the land, and where does it make the most sense to put them? How can you position them relative to each other in a sensible way so that each part of the system meets the needs of the others and of the whole system? For example, can you dig a pond to provide earth for your cob house, fire control, and a home for the ducks and geese, which will also help with erosion and drought control, be part of your graywater system, and irrigate your fruit orchard? This sort of design takes thought and careful planning.

Access

Although it's not always necessary to have a permanent road to a building site, it's important to think about these questions: How will you transport materials to the site during construction? How will the inhabitants get themselves, their babies, groceries, and the like to the building in rainy or snowy weather? What about emergencies — getting sick people out or fire engines in? It's very romantic to build on a remote site with no vehicle access. But a few experiences of hauling heavy materials like sand, cement, and foundation stones uphill via wheelbarrow makes me recommend that you seriously consider at least a temporary road, which can be decommissioned or shortened after construction is complete. If you do create a new permanent road, then plan it very carefully.

Water and Utilities

Drinking water, wash water, electricity, phone lines — if you need them, where will they come from? Avoid having to pump sewage uphill to a septic system or leach field. Plan for your graywater to be useful downhill from the building site in an orchard, garden, woodlot, or pond. Wastewater considerations suggest that it may be best to avoid locating your home at the lowest point of the property.

The Earth Sweet Home Institute is sited so as to take advantage of the sun's energy.

DAVID SHAW

Building Materials

If you plan to use materials from the land (such as earth, sand, stones, trees, straw, or water) in construction, where are they located and how will you transport them? It's much easier to roll stones downhill than up.

SOCIAL AND POLITICAL CONSIDERATIONS

Zoning and Regulations

Different counties have different land use policies and varying abilities to enforce them. Within a county, areas are zoned for different purposes, such as residential, forestry, or light industry. If your plans include agriculture, manufacturing, multiple residences, or building with alternative materials and you pick the wrong location, then you may find yourself fighting your neighbors and the county government. Neighbor relations are of primary importance, so nurture them. Try to a find an area where other people are doing the sorts of things you would like to do. Zoning and regulatory considerations should affect your choice of a building site on a much larger scale — at neighborhood, county, and state levels.

Do not build on good agricultural soils. Plant a garden there instead.

CATHERINE WANEK

Privacy

Think about not only visual privacy but also protection from noise, smells, and light pollution. A nearby highway may be loud on one side of the property and impossible to hear just around the side of the hill. Some kinds of noise and smells (hunting, field burning, etc.) are seasonal. If you want to keep a low profile, then figure out where your building site is visible from. Can it be seen from a neighbor's property, a driveway, or a major highway? Remember that visibility can be much greater in winter when some trees drop their leaves.

Community

Would you like your home to be clustered near friends and neighbors for mutual support, safety, and companionship?

Easements

Owning the title to a piece of land doesn't mean that you own all the rights to it. A neighbor might already have permission to put a road through your property. The phone or utility company may own a corridor where they plan to put a cable or pipeline. A mining company may own the mineral rights to your land, allowing them to drill or tunnel beneath the surface. These rights are called 'easements,' and should be recorded on the property title.

Future Development

Find out who owns surrounding land and what they plan to do with it. Clearcut the forest? Build a housing development? Get to know your neighbors and ask them what rumors they've heard. Also check with your county planning department to find out about their plans to widen roads or change the zoning.

Other Important Considerations

Views

Although you can establish beautiful short views by landscaping your site, you can't do much about the long views. Either you have them or you don't. Views of the sky and the distant horizon do a lot to combat feelings of claustrophobia and cabin fever, especially for people who live in the forest or in places with cold or gray winters, or for those who spend a lot of time at home. Sometimes you can open up long views by judiciously pruning or clearing trees around your site.

History

It's always useful to know what human beings before you have done on the land. Who were the original human inhabitants of this place? Are there sites of archeological or religious significance that it would be better not to disturb? In recent times, have people used chemicals that might still be present in the soil and water? If there's a history of manufacturing, agriculture, or even previous building, it might be a good idea to get the soil tested for toxins.

Ecological Impact

It hardly seems necessary to suggest that you think seriously before cutting down a lot of trees or draining a wetland for your building site. But all outdoors places are habitat. Get to know the plants and animals that you will displace or kill during construction. Find out where deer trails pass through, where owls roost to hunt, and who is living underground. Try to locate your building where it will cause the least disruption to natural cycles. Many people advocate building on the most damaged sites: clearcuts, logging depots, or abandoned pastures. That way, through erosion control, revegetation, and so on, you can actually improve the ecological health of the site.

Feng Shui

The Chinese art of building placement is based on the interrelationships of factors like geometry and subterranean waterways, but you don't have to be a trained specialist to use your intuition. Different places have different kinds of energy. Spend time on a proposed building site, meditating or just living, and see how it feels. Is the energy happy or sad, welcoming or resistant? Would you be comfortable with it in your home? Usually the most magical spots, like that special

Our houses and landscaping can reflect our sensitivities to a site, as amply demonstrated by this garden in Japan.

natural meadow in the back woods, are exactly the places where you should not put a building. Any intervention changes the feeling of a place, and building a house has an extreme impact. If the place is already as good as it can be, leave it alone.

Michael G. Smith provides consultation to owner-builders on the placement and design of natural buildings.

RESOURCES
Books

Chiras, Daniel. *The Natural House: A Complete Guide to Healthy, Energy-Efficient, Environmental Homes.* Chelsea Green, 2000. Contains an excellent chapter on site considerations.

Evans, Ianto, Linda Smiley, and Michael G. Smith. *The Cob Cottage: A Philosophical and Practical Guide to Building an Ecstatic House.* Chelsea Green, 2002. Contains detailed instructions on how to approach a building site with sensitivity, as well as more information on site selection and many useful anecdotes.

Mollison, Bill. *Permaculture: A Designer's Manual.* Island Press, 1990. The bible of permaculture; lays out an entire system for master planning.

Scher, Les, and Carol Scher. *Finding and Buying Your Place in the Country.* Dearborn, 1992. An excellent guide to selecting rural property and navigating the complexities of real estate transactions.

The Permaculture House

Peter Bane

PERMACULTURE IS A SYSTEM of design for managing energy that arose from the 1970s revolution in thinking about humankind's relation to the natural world. Permaculture works as a set of principles within a matrix of ethics. It encourages individual initiative toward care of the Earth, care of people, a fair sharing of surplus resources, and the limiting of our own consumption and population.

Informed by ecology and a growing awareness of global limits, permaculture is also a response to the failure of institutionalized development policies. Hunger in the world today is a problem not of production but of distribution of land and resources. In the same way, renewable energy solutions are limited not by technology or economics but by politics and ignorance.

An example of 'stacking functions': a garden is planted next to this traditional South African building, with fruit-bearing vines forming a shade trellis.

JOSEPH F. KENNEDY

Homelessness and inadequate shelter will not be remedied by agencies or contractors but only by people empowered to build their own houses. In every case, says veteran permaculture teacher Lea Harrison, "The problems are large and complex, but the solutions are embarrassingly simple." Permaculture emphasizes ethics because to change behavior, attitudes and thinking must change first.

Originating from conversations between Australians David Holmgren, a student in ecological design, and Bill Mollison, a professor of environmental psychology, permaculture has spread through more than 60 countries and dozens of languages in rural villages, isolated farms, and giant cities. Its basis of grassroots education — 'each one, teach one' — aims to empower individuals and local communities to restore degraded environments, create local employment and housing, generate energy, and improve food security. Though specific strategies vary with climate, culture, and the resources available, the principles of sound design are universal and form the core of permaculture education.

Permaculture design gives us a new way to see energy flows and material cycles in the world around us — a way that aligns us with the workings of the natural world. If we are to reduce the negative impacts of human activity on the biosphere or even repair the damage done, it's important that we apply this new understanding to what we create. Permaculture design has tremendous relevance for the way we cultivate the Earth — agriculture and forestry — and for how we build our homes and towns. Permaculture can improve the comfort, durability, healthfulness,

Permaculture Design Principles

To create human settlements that restore fertility, generate more energy than they consume, and heal disrupted societies, it's necessary that all our planning, building, agriculture, forestry, and commerce be based on the principles that underlie successful natural communities. These communities provide the only evidence we have of sustainable, permanent systems of land use. Let's look at these principles and see how they can help redirect our thinking toward more harmony with the natural world.

Location and Connection

To properly manage our supply of energy and materials, we must place every element of a productive system (a town, farm, household, or woodland) in beneficial functional relation to everything near it. To keep a house warm in winter, for example, locate it halfway up a south-facing slope so that frost and cold air drain away, winter winds and storms are blocked, and free energy can fill the dwelling. To avoid pumping water, hook roof gutters up to a storage tank. Put the garden below the tank and irrigate by gravity.

Multiple Functions

If everything in the system serves multiple functions, we can do more with less. Permaculture means that you see your roof not only as shelter,

➤ CONTINUED ON PAGE 77

and economy of any building by helping us make intelligent choices about placement and orientation; the design and layout of the space within and around the building; and the way it harnesses and disposes of energy, water, and waste.

ASSESSING YOUR NEEDS

Our first consideration in the creation of any structure should be our need for it. Built space is expensive — the most energy- and materials-intensive area of any property. Getting clear about our need for a building helps us meet those needs without building more than we can afford.

Though the standard American house is still being built for a married couple with two or three children, most families these days don't match that picture. It's possible to live comfortably in a very small space; I know because my partner and I live in a 300-square-foot (27-square-meter) house. We built small to save money and avoid debt. Our house doesn't include some things the typical American house is expected to have. Instead of an attic, we built a loft for our sleeping space, eliminating the need for a separate bedroom. We have no closets, though there are plenty of built-in or movable cupboards, shelves, and hooks to keep the things we really use. Surplus belongings are stored in a nearby shed, which is about the same size as the house; it, however, doesn't have to be heated or finished to the same degree as the dwelling, and cost only one-third the price of our already inexpensive home. A small kitchenette meets most of our needs for cooking. For major food processing, baking, or entertaining, we have access to two larger, community kitchens nearby.

Instead of building a bath and toilet inside the house, we share these facilities with some ten other households in our immediate neighborhood. We have access to a shower, a composting toilet, and soon, a sauna; we rarely have to wait to use any of them, always have enough hot water, and do less maintenance on average than if we kept our own.

Our house, though small inside, has a large roof. The large overhang not only provides good protection for our exterior plaster and straw-clay walls but ample sheltered space for tool and fuel storage, cool food storage (on the north side), a small graywater treatment cell, and a sheltered walkway to access the cistern, which stores water collected from the roof.

Building small to meet our most essential needs allowed us to finish and move into our own home much sooner than if we had built a larger space. By moving into our own off-the-grid, debt-free home, we started saving money by not paying rent and by lowering our utility costs. We got on to the land we're cultivating: gardens are just outside the door, and other crops are within easy walking distance. This proximity gives us the chance to enrich our landscape by continuous care and to harvest and sell crops. The benefits of building small and debt-free are well worth the small inconveniences of limited space.

BUILDING SITING AND DESIGN

The choice of land for a building is next in importance after assessing your real needs. The ideal situation is a small lot in a clean environment, with friendly and cooperative neighbors and reasonable local government regulation. Most of us can't make good use of more than a quarter-acre, which is enough land to grow all the vegetables for a dozen families. And if the land around ours is clean and well managed in a compatible use, we needn't pay taxes on it. The purpose of good placement for a building is to conserve and capture energy throughout the life of the structure. Poor placement is a 'Type One' error, a mistake for which you will pay forever after — an energy sinkhole. (See also "Siting a Natural Building.")

The shape of a building strongly affects its energy performance. The most compact shape in nature is a sphere; the most compact rectilinear space is a cube, which is somewhat easier to build. The longer a building is in relation to its depth and

but as both a part of the water supply and as a producer of energy (solar collectors). Houses that stack functions to meet their own needs approach the elegance of living systems.

Redundancy

Let every essential function be met by multiple elements. Have more than one source of water, heat, and income. Parts always fail; larger systems are more stable because their energy pathways are flexible.

Energy Cycling

Capture, use, and recycle energy many times before it leaves the system. Turn sunlight into plants; plants into animals; and animals into manure, meat, compost, heat, and other animals. Catch water high and move it slowly through the landscape, building fertility with every turn.

Zones, Sectors, and Elevations

Plan for energy efficiency by analyzing the influences from outside a system (sectors), the intensity of activity within a system (zones), and the differences of elevation on the landscape itself. Place elements requiring high levels of interaction (such as children, a plant nursery, and small livestock) at the center of the system and autonomous elements toward the outer fringe.

➤ CONTINUED ON PAGE 79

height, the less efficient it is at conserving heat. However, a longer south side allows a building to capture more solar gain relative to its volume, so building shape and proportion is a tradeoff between these factors. In far northern or cloudy winter climates, where solar gain is less effective, buildings should take a more compact shape. In locations with more winter sun, buildings should stretch out on the east-west axis to a length that is from 1.4 to 1.7 times their north-south depth.

Buildings in hot climates should avoid large exposures on the west and south sides to limit daily heat gain. Ventilation is more important in hot climates, so the sector from which summer breezes blow should be planted in deciduous trees to cool and direct air toward the dwelling. In hot, humid climates, successful traditional buildings are usually elevated on posts to allow cooling

Local materials creatively combined achieve shade and beauty at this permaculture center in South Africa.

JOSEPH F. KENNEDY

breezes beneath the structure and have deep overhangs to shade the windows and doors. Heavy, heat-retaining materials, such as masonry, should be limited in favor of lightweight materials like wood, straw, and thatch. Hot, dry climates (which often have wide daily temperature variations) are well suited to massive masonry or earthen walls, which can act as a thermal flywheel to hold cool evening temperatures throughout the day. In cold climates highly insulating materials, such as straw bales, serve admirably.

Borrowing from successful traditional knowledge is important to permaculture. By starting with the best of what has worked for vernacular builders and then refining those ideas from our own experience and the learning of other innovators, we can define an appropriate building design for our climate and circumstances.

Permaculture design means applying environmental considerations to the shaping of buildings and their surroundings. For example, the interior layout of rooms should reflect their function. Rooms benefiting from morning light (bedrooms, kitchen) ought to be placed on the east side of the house, rooms for living (kitchen, sitting room) to the south or sunny side, and rooms and spaces with infrequent or nighttime use (bath, utility room, closets) to the north.

In choosing materials for a building, keep in mind their embodied energy costs. Aluminum, steel, concrete, brick, and glass have relatively high environmental impacts because of their energy-intensive manufacturing processes. Wood is a wonderfully strong, light material that is easy to work with, but most commercial lumber is harvested unsustainably. If you can't acquire wood from sustainably harvested sources, limit its use to essential structural elements. Wood siding, for instance, doesn't make a lot of ecological sense even though it can be beautiful.

To build houses that are durable, comfortable, energy-efficient, non-toxic, friendly to the Earth, and easy to reuse or recycle at the end of their useful life, we should build with materials that themselves meet these criteria. In general, our buildings should be mostly constructed of local, abundant, cheap natural materials that do not damage the environment where they are produced, used, or disposed of. Not surprisingly these are the same materials people have built with for millennia: earth, clay, lime, straw, wood, and local stone. The use of natural materials is not dogma but a practical means for making buildings inexpensive and recyclable, while minimizing environmental costs and toxicity. Low cost is not just about initial investment; it also means low energy, operating, and maintenance costs. Overall, an energy-efficient, durable design can be far more easily achieved with the judicious use of a few high-tech modern materials: steel and rubber for roofs, glass for windows, closed-cell foam for subgrade insulation. The energy embedded in these materials can be justified by their limited use and by the amount of energy they allow us to capture and conserve over the life of a building. For the functions they perform, they represent appropriate technology.

Scatter hostile energies (noise, pollution, storms, cold winds) and focus beneficial ones (winter sunlight, good views, cooling summer breezes, customers, bird manure). Plan to move water, waste, fuels, and construction materials downhill.

Use Biological Resources

Biological resources are cheaper and safer. Automobiles pollute the air, kill innocents, and break down to junk, but horses run on grass, create food for mushrooms, and replace themselves. Air conditioners cost kilowatts and destroy the ozone layer; deciduous trees can cool just as effectively while making rain, building soil, feeding animals, and growing money.

Appropriate Technology

If you can't afford it, repair it, fuel it, and recycle it locally, look for something else. Make sure it meets the energy test: will it produce more energy and resources over its lifetime than were required to make it? Don't forget the cost of disposal. Atomic science hasn't learned to put its toys away yet.

Succession and Stacking

Use time in your favor. Anticipate natural succession and plan for your house, garden, or neighborhood to change. As things naturally grow up, plan to use

➤ CONTINUED ON PAGE 81

Much of the energy impact of a house lies in its interactions with its surroundings, for a building is not static. Even if our skillful design of the structure has limited the need for combustion heating by allowing for solar gain, the building's inhabitants will require food and water and will generate waste that must be managed. The energy benefits of good initial placement of the building can be augmented by planting trees for windbreaks and shade. The judicious location of roads supports fire control and allows us to take advantage of gravity in moving heavy building materials, farm produce, and so on, downhill.

With the modern food system wasting ten calories of energy in transport and processing for every calorie of food value delivered, it's imperative that we shift food growing closer to home. The best place for a garden starts at the kitchen door of the house. If that garden emphasizes herbs and salads, includes some small fruits, and incorporates a few poultry and fish in a pond to add eggs and meat into the diet, much of the toxicity, nutrient and soil loss, and wasted energy of industrial food can be eliminated. If the water for the garden is harvested from the roof of the house (easily done with gutters and a tank or cistern), and the nutrients in the human waste stream are returned to the soil through composted or biologically treated 'humanure,' then most of the major energy cycles of the domestic economy can be closed.

Making beneficial and functional connections between a house and its surroundings is the essence of permaculture design. When the yields of a landscape can supply the needs of its inhabitants and all the other elements of the cultivated system, we approach the standard that nature has demanded of us. If this good design can be implemented mainly with local materials, local labor, and community financing, then we'll be well on our way to a whole different world.

A small shed nestled into a garden space illustrates an integration of landscape and structure.

CATHERINE WANEK

CATHERINE WANEK

An enormous amount of diversity can thrive at the edge of a wetland ecosystem.

Peter Bane publishes The Permaculture Activist, *North America's oldest journal of permanent culture. A published author and photographer, he also teaches and consults about permaculture design and is a founder and resident at Earthaven Ecovillage in the Blue Ridge Mountains of North Carolina.*

all the layers and spaces in three dimensions. Harvest from the canopy as well as from the ground. The forest does; why shouldn't we?

Observe and Replicate Natural Patterns

Organic life has demonstrated what works cheaply and cleanly. If we pay more attention, we'll get along much better.

Incorporate Diversity and Edge

Diverse ecosystems are more stable than simple ones. Variety is the name of life itself. Edges are where the variety is greatest; that's where the action is.

Attitude Matters

Think positively. Turn problems into solutions. Work for the good of life itself and remember to share your surpluses. The natural world is abundant and life begets life. Our individual efforts can and do make a difference.

Start Small

Build out from a controlled front. Bite off no more than you can chew, and meet your own needs first; then you'll be in a better position to help others. ✑

RESOURCES

Books

Mollison, Bill. *Permaculture: A Practical Guide for a Sustainable Future.* Island Press, 1990. The bible of permaculture, this large, dense volume covers the same material as *Introduction to Permaculture,* only in greater detail, with specific strategies for different climate zones all over the world.

Mollison, Bill, and Reny Mia Slay. *Introduction to Permaculture.* Tagari Publications, 1991. The best single introduction to the subject, this slim, readable volume describes the basic principles and strategies for creating a sustainable world.

Todd, Nancy Jack, and John Todd. *Biosbelters, Ocean Arks, City Farming: Ecology as the Basis of Design.* Sierra Club Books, 1984. A wide-ranging and inspirational book on the application of nature's design principles to everything from urban agriculture to building remodels.

Periodicals

The Permaculture Activist, P.O. Box 1209, Black Mountain, NC 28711, U.S.A.; phone: 828-669-6336; email: Peter@PermacultureActivist.net; website: www.permacultureactivist.net. Available by subscription for US$19 per year. The North American permaculture movement's best resource for networking and keeping up on new developments.

Regenerative Building: An Ecological Approach

Michael G. Smith

In the last 20 years, restoration ecologists have developed techniques for healing damaged ecosystems, detoxifying hazardous chemicals, restoring interrupted flows of water and nutrients, and reintroducing vanished species. This work is essential not only from an ethical standpoint, but because natural ecosystems ultimately provide human beings with everything that sustains us: soil, clean air and water, climate regulation, pest control for our crops, and the genetic source of all our foods and most of our medicines. The developing concepts of 'restoration forestry' and 'regenerative agriculture' have spread this awareness among producers and consumers of food, fiber, and forest products. Those of us concerned with shelter need to take a similar step. If we wish to heal the scars caused by the non-sustainable resource exploitation of the past, and to ensure the continuing health of our ecosystems into the distant future, we must do more than merely reduce our environmental impact by substituting natural materials for processed ones.

How can regenerative builders improve ecological health? First, we can study ecology — the science of living systems. Before we can know what building materials are most appropriate to a particular place, we need to determine how their production, extraction, transportation, assembly, and presence in a building will affect the environment on all levels.

Second, we can emphasize the use of local resources. A full ecological analysis will mandate that we eliminate long-distance transportation of bulk materials. This requires that we get to know the places where we live — not only our houses but our back yards, watersheds, and bioregions.

Finally, we can incorporate site influences, energy flows, and landscape interactions into our designs for homes, neighborhoods, and towns. Our buildings consume, breathe, and excrete just as animals do but often on a far larger scale. We must understand their material and energy cycles to minimize the need for industrial energy and the production of hazardous wastes.

As we come to understand how our local ecosystems work, we can see how our own behaviors and choices affect them. When we recognize our dependence on the landscape in which we live, we are compelled to take responsibility for our actions. When we value the long-term stability of the ecosystem, we can develop integrated practices of building and resource management that will enhance the health of the nonhuman communities surrounding and protecting us. Let's look at an example of how this might work in practice.

A cross-section of the hermitage wall system.

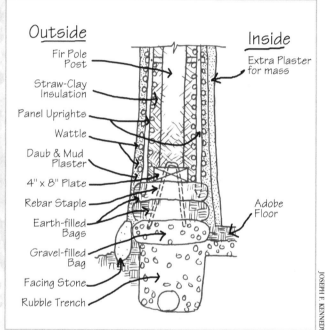

Outside

Inside

Fir Pole Post

Straw-Clay Insulation

Panel Uprights

Wattle

Daub & Mud Plaster

4" x 8" Plate

Rebar Staple

Earth-filled Bags

Gravel-filled Bag

Facing Stone

Rubble Trench

Extra Plaster for mass

Adobe Floor

JOSEPH F. KENNEDY

THE HERMITAGE

Near my home in Northern California, I worked with the staff of an environmental education center to design and build a small structure that demonstrates the principles of natural and regenerative building. Located in a small meadow surrounded by mixed forest, the hermitage offers temporary retreat for people wishing to slow down, relax, meditate, write or paint, observe, and commune with the natural surroundings. It contains a bed, desk, tiny wood stove, an altar, comfortable sitting areas, and a minimal kitchenette.

Soil from the site, a mix of clay and rock fragments ranging from sand to small cobbles, made an excellent base material for rammed earth, cob, earthen floors, and plasters. We also built a section of straw bale wall, pinned with bamboo stakes and covered with earth and lime plasters. We made the roof trusses from bamboo poles harvested 150 miles (240 kilometers) away. All of these techniques would be called 'natural building': they are very low-cost, low-embodied energy, non toxic, easy-to-construct systems that use few manufactured products and mostly local materials. But they don't necessarily cross the bridge into regenerative building by improving the health of the surrounding ecosystem.

We wanted to demonstrate true regenerative building in the hermitage. Before beginning construction, we took a close look at the ecology of the site: what resources did it offer and in what ways had it suffered from past mismanagement?

Perennial native bunch grasses, herbs, and shrubs once grew thick in the meadow where the building now stands. This ecological community underwent a major transformation due to the introduction of cattle and the suppression of wildfire. Quick-growing wild oats and other introduced annual grasses now predominate, out-competing the natives for light and nutrients.

We decided to push the ecological balance in favor of the native grasses. After collecting their ripe seeds in late summer, we mowed the meadow, setting aside the hay for building material. Broadcasting some of the seed over the mown area, we grew the rest out in the nursery to be transplanted later into areas affected by the construction.

The forest surrounding the meadow still shows the effects of heavy logging. Fire suppression in the vicinity has allowed Douglas fir to grow back in thickets, crowding and shading out the hardwoods: live oak, madrone, and bay laurel. Under Native American management, frequent low-temperature forest fires used to thin these groves, killing many of the fir seedlings. This also reduced the fuel load near the ground, making severe canopy fires less likely. As a result of recent management, the forest is much more vulnerable to fire damage, and the population balance is shifting from native hardwoods and the wildlife they support, toward the reduced complexity of Douglas fir stands.

We went into the forest with saws and pruners, 'thinking like fire.' We thinned overcrowded stands of fir by selectively harvesting young trees and pruned lower branches to increase light penetration and reduce fire danger. We wound up with fir poles of up to 9 inches (23 centimeters) in diameter and branches of all sizes.

CHRIS BLUM

The harvesting of undergrowth and non-native species can improve the health of a forest, while providing useful building material.

Logging and grazing had compacted the soil and increased erosion from the area. To remedy this, we dug swales (on-contour ditches) to catch the winter rain runoff, increase infiltration, and slow down the loss of topsoil and nutrients. By digging the swales deep, we harvested extra earth for construction.

Our aim was to reverse ecological deterioration caused by former land management practices, and our efforts created an abundance of local, natural building material, including clay soil, hay, fir poles, and branches. Putting these into the building was the link we needed to make our project truly regenerative.

From the larger poles we constructed a post and beam frame to support the roof. On either side of these posts, we wove wattle wall panels using straight branches and small fir saplings. At the same time we prepared our wall insulation by coating the hay with a thin clay slip to protect it from fire and insects. This hay-clay was sun-dried, then packed into the 8-inch (20-centimeter) cavity between the inner and outer wattles. Then the wattle was covered with a daub made of clay soil, horse manure, and chopped hay. Finally, the wall was plastered with a fine mix of screened clay, sand, and horse manure or cattail fluff.

This experimental system combines traditional techniques: wattle and daub, light-clay straw, and earthen plasters. The specific building method was chosen to make use of the materials yielded by ecological restoration, with a desire to improve the building's thermal efficiency by combining insulation and thermal mass in the most efficient way.

BIOREGIONAL BUILDING

Over time, if encouraged to observe and experiment, local builders will develop construction methods and land management strategies ideally suited to their regions. Over several generations, we can imagine a distinct architectural style evolving in each bioregion, along with a unique system of food production, and so on, all of which will reflect what local people know about their climate, resources, and ecosystems. This process — now in its incipient stages — has been called 'reinhabiting the landscape,' or 're-indigenization.'

Building can be considered the art and practice of creating homes. But in the industrialized world especially, building our homes too often destroys the homes of other creatures. Some of us are moving toward a way of building that respects those other homes and the rights of their animal and plant dwellers to inhabit the Earth indefinitely. The next step involves creating homes for ourselves in ways that repair the damage we have already done to the homes of our co-inhabitants.

Ultimately, to live in harmony with our neighbors on this planet, we must expand our concept of home. It must encompass not only the structure of the house but also the yard and garden, the surrounding site, the watershed, and the entire bioregion. That way, in taking care of our home, in maintaining it and beautifying it, we will make life better not only for ourselves but also for the greater world of which we are an inseparable part.

RESOURCES

Books

Drengson, Alan, and Duncan Taylor. *Ecoforestry: The Art and Science of Sustainable Forest Use.* New Society Publishers, 1997. A superb introduction to the philosophy, science, and sociology behind the current efforts to develop sustainable forest management practices.

Pilarski, Michael, ed. *Restoration Forestry: An International Guide to Sustainable Forestry Practices.* Kivaki Press, 1994. A resource guide and anthology of articles about international efforts to heal the world's forests.

Ecovillages and Sustainable Communities

Joseph F. Kennedy

THE PROCESS OF CONSTRUCTING and inhabiting human landscapes is destroying our capacity to live on this planet, and we have approached, if not exceeded, the limit of human activities the Earth can sustain. If we are to have a 'tolerable planet' to live on, we need to choose a new way to dwell. Ross Jackson, Albert Bates, and Philip Snyder of the Global Ecovillage Network (GEN), describe our choice:

> *We can have a world of industrial smog, diminishing diversity, vanishing rainforests, the threat of nuclear annihilation, and the lurking hazards of genetic engineering, or we can have a world in which there are no 'environmental' diseases, no malnourished children, no warfare between social classes, no poor. A world in which rainforests expand, oceans and lakes teem with fish and marine mammals, new coral reefs are born, the variety of species of life expand and the human prospect grows ever more secure.* [1]

Ecovillages are a way we can manifest the latter, more positive choice. They are human communities that strive to combine the best of the old with the innovations of today.

Why ecovillages? Why now? Many people seek to satisfy their basic needs in sustainable, pleasant, and healing ways. They desire security, community, a sense of identity, and self-esteem. Many wish to reduce the stress in their lives through living creatively in a beautiful natural setting. They want more meaningful social interaction and to spend more time with family and friends. Ecovillages are designed to satisfy these needs. In addition, they support the notion of 'right livelihood' where shared, local, satisfying work can minimize commuting and environmental impact. Ecovillages are diverse places, where people of different ages, races, incomes and spiritual paths are accepted within a common vision.

Although the term 'ecovillage' is relatively new, perhaps dating from the mid-1980s, communities described by that term have been around for much longer. Steinerian communities, like Solheimer in Iceland and Jarna in Sweden that emerged in the late 1920s and early 1930s, continue to this day. The concept continued to evolve through the Danish co-housing movement. The first Ecovillages and Sustainable Communities conference was held in Scotland in 1994 and gave rise to the Global Ecovillage Network, a non-governmental umbrella organization. Ecovillages have now been formed on five continents, and interest in the concept is growing exponentially.

Certain features characterize ecovillages. Their populations are usually less than 500 people, in order to maximize trust and cooperation. The full range of human activity is supported through facilities for residence, work, leisure, social activity, and commerce. In addition, ecovillages actively support the health of their residents on a physical, emotional, and spiritual level.

CREATING AN ECOVILLAGE

There are a number of challenges in the creation of a successful ecovillage. Ecovillage planners realize that a sustainable process is as important as a sustainable village and place a strong emphasis on all phases of the project, from initial research and development, through creation and implementation, to the ongoing maintenance of the final ecovillage itself.

When people decide to build an ecovillage, they must first determine how decisions will be made and how things will get done. To live peacefully at the high densities typical of ecovillages

Ecovillages are as much about human community as physical infrastructure, demonstrated by this ceremony at Earthaven Ecovillage.

ARJUNA DA SILVA

requires highly developed social skills and careful community design. The consensus decision-making process is one of several techniques that have evolved to achieve this.

Many ecovillages are in rural locations, which provide the natural resources and way of life sought by many residents. However, others in the ecovillage movement feel that taking land away from nature for human habitation is a serious breach of principle. As a result, some very exciting work is being done with urban restoration of 'brownfield' sites into ecovillages. Whether rural or urban, numerous factors must be considered when deciding upon a site for an ecovillage. The more ideal the site, the better the chance for success. Some of the variables to consider when selecting a site include: the size and price of the land; climate; availability and quality of water and other natural resources; existing buildings and other improvements; governmental regulations and restrictions; commercial development potential; access to roads, public transportation, electricity, and other utilities; proximity to surrounding communities; and physical site factors such as slope, aspect, and geology.

Once a site is determined, the planning process is initiated. The process must be flexible and sensitive, engaging the future residents in a participatory process. Ecovillage designers draw on lessons from many disciplines, including architecture, planning, wilderness conservation, ecology, and landscape design to create as rich and diverse a physical and social landscape as possible.

Before beginning any physical changes, the group undertakes a holistic land-planning process. This determines the carrying capacity of the site and the placement of elements, through a 'zone and sector' analysis (*see* "Permaculture and Design"). Access and energy flows, social zones, and special places are all discussed and mapped through numerous iterations until a mutually agreed upon plan has been developed. Such a plan will consider the following.

Ecosystem

In creating an ecovillage, natural habitats for wildlife must be preserved. Soil, air, water, and biodiversity are carefully preserved or improved. Waste products are recycled or managed on site. Ecovillagers also endeavor to obtain food, wood, and other biological resources from the region, or, ideally, from the site itself.

The Built Environment

Houses and other structures are designed to use ecologically friendly materials and renewable energy sources. Planning minimizes the need for automobiles in favor of walking and biking. Proper siting of buildings reduces the impact of construction on local plants and animals. For social harmony, a balance between public and private space is crucial. 'Cluster' development encourages community interaction and minimizes the physical footprint of structures. The full range of human activity is designed for, from work to play and from quiet time to community gatherings.

Economics

Ecovillages attempt to reduce exploitation of other people, distant places, and future generations through fair and sustainable practices and policies. Ecovillage residents must also discover sustainable economic activities for themselves. Some of the challenging questions include: Will ownership of land and buildings be handled privately or cooperatively? Are there alternatives to the money economy, including barter, local currency, and the like? How can ecovillages be ecologically and economically efficient at the same time?

Government

Ecovillage residents must create a structure for community decision making. How will conflicts between people be resolved? How will group decisions be enforced? What will be expected of leaders, if any? How will the ecovillage deal with local and national governments?

Pedestrian walk ways, bike paths, and social gathering spaces are designed in between multi-family dwellings at Le Domaine de la Terre, France.

Group Vision

A strong shared vision is one of the most important factors that holds an ecovillage together. Is the ecovillage composed of individuals with divergent views, or are there common values regarding community life? What should be the balance between unity of purpose and diversity of views? Are the ecovillage members close interpersonally, or do they lead separate private lives? How does the community relate to those outside the ecovillage? How will the ecovillage evolve over time?

CATHERINE WANEK

There are no easy or right answers to these questions. Success depends on many factors, including the location and qualities of the site and the willingness of its residents to work through the many questions and conflicts that may arise. Many believe that the process of creating ecovillages is crucial for human survival. Happily, increasing numbers of people are willing to take on the challenge. They not only see the manifestation of this new vision as necessary but filled with immeasurable rewards — those of a life of hope.

Joseph F. Kennedy has lived and worked in ecovillage projects in the U.S., Argentina, Ireland, and South Africa.

NOTES

1. See Ross Jackson, Albert Bates, and Philip Snyder, "The Ecovillage Vision: White Paper 2000" (GEN International Secretariat, 2000), p.2.

RESOURCES

Books

Communities Directory: A Guide to Intentional Communities and Cooperative Living. Fellowship for Intentional Community, 2000. This incredible book lists and describes over 700 intentional communities around the world, along with relevant books and organizations.

Corbett, Judy, and Michael Corbett. *Designing Sustainable Communities: Learning from Village Homes.* Island Press, 2000. A book with information and examples of how, through proper planning and development, it is possible to create successful communities.

Directory of Ecovillages in Europe. GEN-Europe, 1998. Available for DM 30, Euro 15 from GEN-Europe, Ginsterweg 5, 31595 Steyerberg, Germany. An excellent compendium of ecovillage projects in Europe, with useful descriptions of each one.

Ecovillages and Communities Directory: Australia and New Zealand. GEN-Oceania, 2000. Available for AU $14.95 from GEN-Oceania, 59 Crystal Waters, MS16, Maleny, Queensland, 4552, Australia. A directory similar to the European directory. Includes useful articles on ecovillage design, natural building, etc.

Organizations

Ecovillage Network of the Americas, c/o EarthArt Village, 64001 County Road DD, Moffat, CO 81143, U.S.A.; phone/fax: 719-256-4221; email: ena@ecovillage.org; websites: www.gaia.org/secretariats/ena/, www.earthart.org.

Ecovillage Training Center, The Farm, P.O. 90, Summertown, TN 38483-0090, U.S.A.; phone: 931-964-4324; fax: 931-964-2200; websites: www.gaia.org, www.i4at.org/, www.thefarm.org/etc, www.ena.ecovillage.org. A whole systems immersion experience of ecovillage living, together with classes of instruction; access to information, tools, and resources; and on-site and off-site consulting and outreach experiences.

The Fellowship for Intentional Community, 138 Twin Oaks Rd. Louisa, VA 23093; phone 800-462-8240; email: PubsList@ic.org; web: www.ic.org/. FIC promotes community living and cooperative lifestyles. Publisher of *Communities* magazine, the *Communities Directory* and an upcoming video.

Global Eco-Village Network (GEN) Oceania/Asia, 59 Crystal Waters, MS 16, Maleny, Qld. 4552, Australia; phone: +61 7 5494 4741; fax: +61 7 5494 4578; email: lindegger@gen-oceania.org.

Ecovillage residents may share communal cooking space, as in this large, well thought out kitchen at the Lama Foundation near Taos, NM.

CATHERINE WANEK

Videos

Crystal Waters Video. GEN Oceania, 1998. 14 minutes. Available in PAL format for AU$14.95 plus shipping/handling (total of $AU19.50 within Australia); NTSC AU$20 plus shipping/handling from GEN Oceania. A video on the Crystal Waters Permaculture Village. Includes footage of this World Habitat Award-winning, ecologically sustainable development (homes, lands, gardens) and a 12-page booklet with more detailed design information.

The Habitat Revolution. The Global Ecovillage Network, 1998. Available for US$20 plus $5 shipping/handling from the Ecovillage Training Center. Visit ecovillages around the world!

Websites

Ecovillage Audit Document: www.gaia.org/internationalprojects/evaudit/evaudit/pdf. An excellent means to see how 'ecological' your community is.

Global Ecovillage Network: www.Gaia.org. A detailed and well-linked site that is the best first place to go for learning the most up-to-date information on the ecovillage movement.

Natural Building Materials and Techniques

Don't be afraid of being called 'unmodern.' Changes in the old methods of construction are only allowed if they can claim to bring improvement; otherwise stick with the old ways. Because the truth, even if hundreds of years old, has more inner connection than the falsehood that walks beside us.

Adolf Loos, 1913

Natural Building Materials: An Overview

Joseph F. Kennedy

NATURAL BUILDING has emerged as a response to an increasing concern for our built environment. Natural materials are an alternative to the toxic substances that have led to widespread environmental illness. Those seeking to simplify their lives can build their own homes using such techniques, with community help and local, inexpensive materials. Those who recognize the environmental, social, and economic costs of our current ways of construction believe that natural building provides part of the solution to the complex worldwide problem of sustainable living.

Sticks and mud make wattle and daub.

JOSEPH F. KENNEDY

While interest in natural building has surged in the industrialized West, many ancient roots have been lost in traditional areas in favor of capital-and energy-intensive industrial building methods. In the name of progress, crucial cultural and technological riches continue to be abandoned. Ironically, some builders in industrialized countries are now turning to these very cultures for solutions to their building problems. It is to be hoped that a resurgence of interest and research into vernacular building systems will increase respect for these timeless ideas in their native lands.

Though often appropriate in their original contexts, many ancient techniques are benefiting from scientific study and engineered applications for a variety of new situations. Modern structural and other performance tests, which also point out directions for further research and improvement, are validating these techniques.

Most natural builders would agree that a natural material is one that is closest to the state in which it is found in nature. Although natural builders and designers generally prefer these materials when creating structures, other non-natural materials are also used, such as metal roofing, glass, and/or waterproof membranes. Deciding whether to use one material or another depends on such factors as ecological impact, availability, and workability. Some materials, even though they are natural, are difficult to obtain or work with.

Local availability is the most important factor in deciding which materials to build with. It is also important to know how these materials are harvested, to determine whether their use has a disturbing effect on the local ecosystem.

Here are some of the materials most commonly used by natural builders. Most are natural materials, but some of the commonly used manufactured materials are listed as well.

EARTH

Earth construction has been practiced for thousands of years and still shelters more than a third of the world's population. Earth is composed of stones, gravel, sand, silt, and clay, in decreasing order of particle size. The best earth for building contains 20 to 30 percent clay and 70 to 80 percent sand. Although widely available, versatile, and highly workable, earth is not as strong as other materials, especially in tension, and must be protected from water and earthquakes.

STONE

Stone is the mineral bedrock of the planet and comes in endless varieties. Igneous stone is formed by the cooling of liquid magma. Some igneous stone (pumice and scoria) contains air bubbles, which make it a good insulator. Sedimentary stone is formed by the cementing together of sediments resulting from erosion by wind or water. Sedimentary stone is layered, which allows it to be split into flat pieces that are easy to stack into walls. Metamorphic stone is igneous or sedimentary stone that has been altered by heat or pressure. The best stone for building is angular, with parallel flat sides. Round stones are not recommended, but they can be used if that is all you have. Stone can be used as is or shaped with tools. Stone makes an excellent foundation for wall systems. Flat, thin stones like slate can be used as a roofing material or to make durable floors.

MICHAEL G. SMITH

Test samples of various building materials, made by combining clay with straw, sawdust, wood, chips, hemp hurds, and pumice.

GRAVEL

Gravel is composed of small stones. It is useful for filling drainage trenches and rubble trench foundations, as it is strong in compression, yet lets water flow through. It can also be used to fill bags, which are then stacked into walls. This type of gravel bag foundation keeps water from reaching materials like adobe or straw bales that can easily be damaged by moisture.

Builders in South Yemen use earth as the primary material in their homes and cities, which can reach a dozen stories high.

SAND

Sand is small gravel. It is an essential ingredient (mixed with clay and/or fibers in various proportions) in cob, adobe, plasters, rammed earth, and compressed earth blocks. Angular sand is best for most purposes but is often created by destructive mining practices. Well-graded (many different-sized grains) sand is best. While not as strong, rounded sand found in streams or riverbeds can be used, and in some cases, as for finish plaster, it is even preferred.

DANNY GORDON

CLAY

Clay results from the chemical weathering of the mineral feldspar. It is composed of small flat plates that stick well to themselves and to other materials. Clay is the essential binding ingredient in any earthen building system. To find soil with a high clay content, notice if the soil cracks after it is wet, or if it is difficult to dig and clumps together. Some clays shrink considerably as they dry, requiring the addition of a great deal of sand or fiber to prevent cracking.

BRICK

Bricks are made from clay that is formed into (usually rectilinear) shapes then fired (baked) in a kiln. The hotter they are fired, the harder they become. Bricks come in many shapes and sizes. They are commonly used in walls, floors, and vaulted roofs. Other brick-shaped building elements are adobes, which are sun-dried mud bricks, and compressed earth blocks, which are unfired.

TILE

Similar to bricks, tiles are flat, thin elements made from fired clay. They are often glazed with a compound which, when fired, makes them waterproof. Glazed tiles are available in many different colors and are commonly used for decoration. Tiles are usually attached to a base material which is structurally strong (for example: stone, brick or concrete). They are often used for floors and for waterproof walls and counters.

SOD

Sod is the interwoven roots of grasses and the soil they trap. It can be cut into bricks and stacked to form a wall. Sod can also be used to create a 'living roof.'

WOOD

Wood is very strong in compression and tension. It can be used for many purposes, including posts, beams, floors, roofs, windows, doors, and furniture. It is an essential material for natural builders but must be used wisely to help decrease deforestation. Wood in log form can be used like bricks in cordwood construction. Longer logs are used for walls, posts, or roof beams. Notching logs helps them to interlock to form the walls of log cabins. However, all-wood construction is now unsustainable in many parts of the world because of the overharvesting of forests.

Palm leaves are traditionally used for thatched roofs in tropical climates.

BAMBOO

Bamboo is the largest of the grasses and is most common in the tropics. The culms (stalks) of the plant are used in construction. Bamboo is very strong in tension and compression. It grows very quickly and can be used as a substitute for wood in many cases. Strong bamboo construction requires special joinery techniques.

STRAW

Straw is the hollow-stemmed stalk of cereal grains and grasses such as rice, wheat, oats, and barley. It can be baled into large blocks and stacked to make walls. Straw improves tensile strength, resistance to cracking, insulation value, and increases workability of earthen materials. It is used full-length or chopped fine as an ingredient in cob, straw-clay, and plasters. If the straw is particularly long and strong, it can also be used as a thatching material.

REEDS

Reeds are hollow-stemmed water plants, similar in appearance to grasses. Because they are straight, long, and shed water well, they are often used for thatching roofs.

LEAVES

Leaves of plants have been used throughout history as a building material, mostly to shed rain or create shade. An example is to use palm leaves for roof thatching.

HEMP AND OTHER FIBERS

Hemp and other fiber-producing plants such as kenaf, flax, and sawgrass are currently being investigated as potential building products. Hemp particularly has several advantages, as it provides four times the usable fiber per acre as wood, grows in degraded soils, and needs little chemical processing. Commonly used for numerous purposes before drug laws made its cultivation illegal, non-psychoactive hemp is being rediscovered as a source of fiber, oil, and hurd (the pithy inner stalk left over after the fibers are removed). These can replace wood and petrochemical products in a variety of building applications, including pressed-board products, and a concrete-like hemp-hurd/lime material.

You can determine the relative proportions of sand, silt, and clay in a soil sample by using a 'shake test.'

CHRIS BLUM

PAPER

Paper is made of compressed plant fibers, usually from wood. Paper can be used as a wall material (as in Japanese *shoji* screens) or to cover other materials (wallpaper). A recent experimental use is to soak recycled paper in water to release the fibers, which are then mixed with cement and sand, or with clay, to make lightweight blocks. This is called 'papercrete,' 'fibrous cement,' or 'fidobe.'

CLOTH

Cloth is made by weaving natural or artificial fibers together to make a continuous sheet. Cloth can be used to make bags (used in earthbag construction), as roof coverings, ceiling treatments, or to provide shade.

MANURE

Manure from cows and horses is a common additive in earthen plasters, replacing chopped straw. Very fine plasters can be created using cow manure, because the cows' several stomachs break up the plant fibers into very small pieces. The stomach enzymes also act as a preservative and hardener in earth plasters. In Africa, fresh manure is spread to create a floor, which is often sealed with ox blood.

ORGANIC ADDITIVES

A number of products derived from animals and plants have been used as additives to earthen and lime plasters. Properly used, they can improve hardness, workability, and water resistance. Such additives include: eggs, milk, blood, urine, linseed and other oils, cactus juice, starch, tallow, tree sap, wheat flour paste, and molasses.

SHELLS

In some coastal areas, shells have been used to build houses. They are mixed with lime and put in forms, which set up to create solid walls. Shells can also be burned to create lime. In Northern Europe, waste shells from food production are being used below floors for insulation and drainage.

LIME

Lime is a traditional binding agent made from limestone or seashells that are burnt in a kiln, then crushed. The resulting powder is combined with water, causing a chemical reaction (slaking) and forming lime putty. Kept wet, lime putty can be stored indefinitely, and it improves with age. It was commonly used in mortars and plasters before cement was available. True lime putty is difficult to find in the U.S., and the inferior dried (mason's hydrated) lime is used instead. Lime putty is also a by-product of acetylene gas production, and some natural builders are obtaining high-quality putty in this way. Lime is mixed with sand to create 'breathing' plasters and mortar. It can also be used to make paint. Because it is less brittle and less environmentally damaging to produce than Portland cement, many natural builders are rediscovering lime.

CONCRETE

Concrete is made of sand, gravel, water, lime (sometimes), and Portland cement. These ingredients are mixed together to form a thick liquid, then poured or sprayed into forms. The mixture solidifies and cures over time. Concrete has high compressive strength and can be used in foundations, walls, roofs, etc. However, the making of the cement in concrete is a highly energy-intensive and polluting process and a major contributor of greenhouse gases. It can also be difficult to recycle, though some natural builders are finding uses for old concrete, such as for building foundations.

STEEL

Steel is iron that contains carbon, making it harder and more flexible. It is used to make metal roofs, structural elements, and hardware. Because it has very high embodied energy, natural builders use it sparingly. However, it can be easily recycled, making it more appropriate than some other manufactured materials.

GLASS

Glass is quartz sand, limestone, and additional minerals heated until molten. It is then cast, blown, rolled, or spun into a variety of building products including blocks, window glass, and fiberglass insulation. While its manufacture is high in embodied energy, it is easily recyclable, and its physical properties of light transmission are impossible to duplicate with non-industrial materials. Some natural builders use recycled glass windows and bottles in creative ways.

RECYCLED MATERIALS

In an effort to lessen waste, some builders and manufacturers are reusing materials that would otherwise end up as trash. Bottles and cans can be used like bricks. Large cans may be flattened to make roofing shingles. Old plastic bottles are ground up and mixed with sawdust to make artificial 'lumber.' Many natural builders prefer to recycle materials such as bricks and lumber from old structures or other sources than to use new materials. Windows, doors, and other fixtures can be refurbished and reused, saving valuable architectural heritage and cutting down on waste.

CONCLUSION

The use of natural building materials in construction has a bright future. Increasingly, innovative systems such as cob and earthbag construction are becoming code approved and are joining more established systems such as rammed earth, adobe, and straw bale construction. As techniques evolve and more builders, architects, and developers employ them, structures that meet human needs while assisting in the regeneration of the planet will become more common. While many challenges still lie ahead, this is a hopeful and exciting time to be part of the quest to create a sustainable human culture.

Joseph F. Kennedy is an architect, writer, and peripatetic scholar of natural building and ecological design.

RESOURCES
Books

Stulz, Roland, and Kiran Mukerji. *Appropriate Building Materials: A Catalogue of Potential Solutions.* SKAT Publications, 1993. This book is an excellent catalog of many of the materials mentioned here, with many illustrations. It is conveniently keyed (wall materials, roofs, etc.) for easy reference.

van Lengen, Johan. *Manual del Arquitecto Descalzo (Manual of the Barefoot Architect).* Editorial Concepto, 1980. Although this Spanish-language book is difficult to track down, it is worth the search for its simple, comprehensive, and well-illustrated discussion of a wide range of natural building techniques.

Woolley, Tom, Sam Kimmens, et al. *Green Building Handbook: A Guide to Building Products and Their Impact on the Environment*, Vols. 1 and 2. E&FN Spon, 1997, 2000. Has an excellent chapter on insulation (Vol. 1).

Periodicals

Environmental Building News. 122 Birge Street, Suite 30, Brattleboro, VT 05301, U.S.A.; phone: 802-257-7300; fax: 802-257-7304; email: ebn@buildinggreen.com; website: www.buildinggreen.com. This excellent monthly newsletter, targeted toward professional designer-builders, contains frequent updates on environmental building products and systems.

CATHERINE WANEK

Transporting stone to the building site in a wheelbarrow.

Natural Insulation

Joseph F. Kennedy and Michael G. Smith

INSULATION MATERIALS are used to prevent heat or cold from entering or exiting a building through the walls, roof, and floor. They work by trapping small pockets of air that do not transmit heat well. Natural insulation materials must be kept dry, as moisture greatly decreases their effectiveness (though some materials, such as wool, pumice, and vermiculite can be used in moist situations). In addition, air leaks greatly decrease the effectiveness of any insulation, an effect that is magnified in cold climates. Fibrous or loose insulation must be protected from animals, such as rodents, who like to use it for nesting material. Some organic insulation materials, such as loose straw and cellulose, are very flammable and therefore should be carefully enclosed and treated with a fire retardant.

Different insulation materials are most suitable for different applications, and the choice of insulation can affect choice of building system, and vice-versa. Effectiveness of insulation is measured by its thermal resistance (R-value), which measures how well it resists the passage of heat. The inverse (U-value) that measures conductivity, is used in Europe. The natural insulation materials with the greatest thermal effectiveness are wool, cellulose fibers, cork, and vermiculite. The first three compare favorably with conventional fiberglass insulation, although no natural material compares with modern foamboards on an R-value-per-inch basis.

Natural builders use the following materials as insulation:

A waste product of the seafood industry, seashells of all kinds are being used in Europe to insulate foundations.

CATHERINE WANEK

WOOL

Wool makes an excellent insulation and is one of the only materials that still insulates when wet. In some places, such as New Zealand, wool batts are commercially available. But in North America, natural builders usually make their own woolen insulation. This can be done either by washing and carding the wool and treating it with borax or Quassia chips to protect it from moths, or by stuffing raw wool into plastic garbage bags to keep the smell in and the moths out. A worldwide surplus has made it difficult for U.S. sheep farmers to sell their wool, so it is often available cheap directly from the source. One danger to avoid is the organophosphate used in some sheep dips.

STRAW

Straw is an excellent insulator if installed correctly. Bale walls are highly insulating, and baled or loose straw (coated with clay or borax to reduce the fire hazard) can also be used as roof insulation. If bales are used, they should be installed tight together, with cracks carefully stuffed to avoid heat leakage. Straw bales are heavy compared to other insulation options, and a ceiling structure must be designed accordingly. Loose straw is often combined with clay to make it more resistant to fire, mold, and rodents. This straw clay mixture can be made into insulating tiles, compacted into the ceiling cavity, or placed loose in the roof. Straw boards, such as Stramit, provide modest insulating qualities. Other fibers such as hemp, coir, flax, cotton, or textile wastes could be used for insulation in ways similar to straw.

CELLULOSE

Cellulose insulation is a popular product; it is inexpensive, non-toxic, and made from recycled newspapers. It is usually blown dry into the wall or roof cavity with a special machine. Borax and other additives make it resistant to fire and insects, but it is not good in moist situations. The disadvantage of dry cellulose is that is settles over time, but new techniques of blowing moist cellulose result in a much more stable material.

CORK

Cork is the bark of a particular oak tree that grows only in Spain and Portugal. Cork granules can be used for loose fill insulation, and cork board products are dimensionally stable and useful for roofs, walls, and floors. Although cork is produced from sustainably harvested forests by small firms, the high energy costs of shipping should be carefully considered when using it outside of Europe.

COTTON

Recycled cotton in batt form has insulation values comparable to that of fiberglass insulation. Made from 100% post-industrial denim and cotton fibers by the Bonded Logic Corporation, this insulation is treated with boron to discourage pests and retard fire. It passes all ASTM test, produces no chemical outgassing or airborne particulates, and is produced with minimal energy inputs. One

ARJUNA DA SILVA

Straw, ideally treated with a fire retardant such as clay, can be stuffed into roof cavities as insulation. This example is at Earthaven Ecovillage in North Carolina.

Pumice, a lightweight volcanic stone, can be used as insulation below a slab or as an aggregate in a stemwall. It must be sealed to prevent air infiltration.

drawback to cotton, however, is that most conventional cotton growers use high levels of pesticides and herbicides to produce the crop.

FIBERGLASS

Fiberglass is currently the most commonly used insulation in conventional building. It is essentially glass heated to high temperatures and spun into fibers. It is not recommended by natural builders because of its high embodied energy and the toxicity of the formaldehyde resins and other chemicals used to form it into batts. Small glass fibers may be carcinogenic if inhaled, and fiberglass creates a disposal problem when it reaches the end of its useful life.

PLASTIC FOAMS AND BOARDS

Because of a lack of alternatives, foam boards are also often used, especially for below-grade applications like foundation perimeter insulation. These products are highly efficient insulators but are also toxic and contain high embodied energy. In addition, ozone-depleting blowing agents are often used in their manufacture.

EXPANDED MINERALS

Perlite and vermiculite are heat-expanded minerals that have very good insulating qualities. They can be more expensive than other options but are particularly good in areas that might be exposed to water or fire. These minerals are usually obtained from open-pit mines and can contain asbestos-like fibers. Pumice and scoria are naturally occurring, porous igneous stones available in some parts of the U.S. They are sometimes used to create insulated concrete products called 'pumicecrete.' They can also be used in earthbags to build walls and domes and as floor insulation". (See "An Earthbag-Papercrete House.")

Foundations for Natural Buildings

Michael G. Smith

IT IS OFTEN SAID that natural buildings appear to grow right out of the ground. It's true that the materials from which they are built may be harvested from the site, and their form and appearance may mimic the natural landscape. Yet the relationship between any building and the earth beneath it is always more complicated than meets the eye. Even a tree, which does in fact grow out of the ground, needs a specialized root system to support the trunk; in some species, the root system is bigger than the tree we see. In a similar way, the below-ground parts of a building are often among its most complicated and expensive systems.

FOUNDATION FUNCTIONS

'Foundation' is the general term used to describe the lower structure of a building that comes in contact with the ground. A foundation may serve any or all of the following important functions.

Support

One of the fundamental purposes of a foundation is to spread the load of the structure above it. In the same way that your foot is wider than your ankle, the bottom of a foundation (called, logically enough, the 'footing') is often wider than the wall above. This stabilizes the wall and reduces the likelihood that the ground beneath the structure will settle unevenly. Strong, wide footings are especially important in post-and-beam buildings like traditional timber frames, where all of the weight of the roof and wall structure bears on a few small and widely spaced points.

JOSEPH F. KENNEDY

One purpose of a foundation is to provide continuous reinforcement at the base of the walls to resist earthquakes or other ground movement.

Reinforcement

When the ground moves, either as a result of a sudden, catastrophic earthquake or landslide, or of slow slippage or settling over years or centuries, the part of the building that meets the ground is most vulnerable. Especially in seismically active regions, it's important to tie the base of a building together with a continuous structure capable of resisting bending and twisting forces.

Protection from Water

Most kinds of walls can be damaged by excessive moisture. This is especially true if they are built of natural materials like wood, earth, and straw. Foundations serve to protect the walls and the interior of the building from moisture in the soil. Some foundations, often called 'stemwalls' or 'plinths,' extend well above ground level to protect the walls from wind-driven rain and from splashing roof runoff. In rainy climates, foundations for earth and straw structures should generally extend from 12 to 18 inches (30 to 40 centimeters) above ground level.

An elegant example of keeping a water-sensitive material (wood) away from the ground by using a water-impervious material (stone).

Drainage

Good site drainage is very important in natural building. Especially in rainy climates and on sites with poorly drained (high clay content) soils, great care must be taken to prevent the moisture in the soil from migrating into the building. In conventional modern building, this is achieved by using highly processed waterproofing materials including concrete, plastics, tar, and other sealants. If we wish to reduce the use of industrial materials for environmental, health, and/or economic reasons, the only reliable replacement is good drainage.

Site drainage can be enhanced in a number of ways. The ground immediately around the building should be re-graded as necessary so that surface runoff flows away from, rather than

TOM LANDER

toward, the foundation. Uphill from the building, ditches can be dug to catch surface and subsurface runoff and carry it around or away from the building. A deep drainage ditch close to the building, backfilled with gravel and often with a perforated drain tile at the bottom, is called a 'curtain drain' or 'French drain.' Curtain drains are a good idea on poorly drained sites in rainy climates, especially if any part of the inside floor will be lower than the exterior ground level ('below grade') or made of earth.

Drainage can be combined with the load-bearing function of the foundation. (See "Rubble Trench Foundations.") Rubble trenches are very popular among natural builders because they provide excellent protection from ground moisture and frost heave while minimizing the use of concrete. They may also reduce earthquake damage by allowing the building to slide around a bit when the ground moves, dissipating the violent forces before they are transferred to the structure.

Even when a rubble trench is used, there is generally some kind of above-grade foundation to hold the building together and elevate the bottoms of the walls. There are many materials and construction systems to choose from. Your choice will depend on what you can gather or acquire locally; what you know how to build; and how strongly you value natural materials, proven performance, and engineering rigor.

ROBERT BOLMAN

Robert Bolman built the foundation for his straw bale house in Eugene, Oregon from 'urbanite' (recycled concrete), cutting down the amount of new concrete by 75 percent.

FOUNDATION MATERIALS

Concrete

Concrete is a combination of sand, gravel, water, and Portland cement — an artificial compound made by baking lime, clay, and other chemicals together at a very high temperature. Nearly all foundations for conventional modern buildings are made of concrete in one of its several forms, whether as a monolithic pour, concrete block masonry, or various kinds of recycled foam and concrete units. Poured concrete reinforced with steel rebar is most common, due to its great strength, flexibility of form, and ability to withstand earthquakes well. Many natural builders prefer to minimize the amount of concrete in their buildings because of its high embodied energy, the environmental costs of its manufacture, and disposal issues.

One way to reduce the use of new concrete is to build a foundation out of recycled concrete chunks. The easiest chunks to use are broken-up slabs and sidewalks, sometimes called 'urbanite' because they are such an available resource in cities. In Eugene, Oregon, Rob Bolman received a building permit for a straw bale house with a foundation made of stacked urbanite with a cement-sand mortar and a poured concrete bond beam on top.

There are various products available commercially that combine concrete with recycled plastic foam for insulation. One such product is Rastra, a foam block system into which steel is inserted and concrete poured. This reduces the amount of concrete used, eliminates the step of building forms, and improves the energy performance of the foundation.

When used in combination with natural materials, concrete can cause problems by wicking or trapping moisture. Straw bales particularly should never be placed directly on concrete because of the danger of moisture build-up on top of the foundation. Usually a pair of wooden 'sleepers' is set atop the concrete foundations to create a 'toe-up' that keeps the bales away from water.

An example of a dry-stacked stone foundation for a straw bale house. This one is at Earth Sweet Home Institute in Vermont.

DAVID SHAW

Stone

All around the world, for thousands of years, stone has been the material of choice for foundations. Its advantages are obvious. Stones are heavy, strong, extremely resistant to weathering, and readily available in many areas. Traditional stone foundations are built either with or without mortar. The mortar is made of sand bound together with clay, lime, and/or Portland cement.

An unreinforced stone masonry foundation is held together primarily by gravity. In severe earthquakes, these foundations can crack and crumble. To prevent this, steel reinforcing can be embedded in liberal amounts of cement mortar between courses of stone. Another strategy is to cast a concrete bond beam above and/or below the masonry part of the foundation to tie it all together.

One of the disadvantages for owner-builders is the amount of skill and time required for stone masonry. These vary widely, depending on the type of stone you have to work with. Sedimentary stones like sandstone, which break naturally along flat planes, are much easier to build with than harder, irregularly shaped stones. Round river stones, although beautiful, are very difficult to stack solidly and require lots of mortar. One technique promoted by early owner-builder movement leaders, including Helen and Scott Nearing and Ken Kern, is the 'slip-form method,' in which concrete is poured between stones that have been placed in a temporary wooden form.

Wood

Foundations can be made of wood in either of two ways. The more common option is to raise the entire building on wooden posts, as is often done in the hot, humid tropics. This has the advantage of getting the main structure away from the wet, heat-retaining earth and into the cooling breezes higher up, and of making the invasion of pests like termites easier to see and to control. Modern buildings are sometimes set on 'post and pier' foundations, in which the wooden posts are either placed on concrete footings to spread the load or are replaced entirely with concrete or steel. Post foundations are most suitable for lightweight, wooden buildings. The weight of most of the wall systems featured in this book makes a post and pier system impractical. Great care must be used in seismically active regions to engineer a post foundation that will resist earthquakes.

The other way to use wood in foundations is to build with heavy beams on grade. This brings the building in direct contact with the earth, which is more appropriate for passive solar designs. Wood has the advantage over stone masonry of being easier to shape and to fasten together. The major issues are the capacity of the wooden members to withstand the loads placed on them and to resist rot. One inexpensive solution used in several straw bale structures is to place used railroad ties, which are impregnated with creosote as a preservative, onto a bed of gravel for drainage. I have also used salvaged redwood beams, which are naturally rot resistant, on top of a rubble trench.

Earthbags

"Building with Earthbags" describes a system for building using burlap or woven polypropylene bags filled with rammed earth. Although this technique has been used primarily to construct self-supporting domes and vaults, it has also been adapted as a very easy-to-build, inexpensive foundation system. In rainy climates, the bags should be placed atop a rubble trench; the earth inside can be replaced with gravel, in effect creating an above-ground rubble trench. Often, strands of barbed wire are used between courses of bags as a type of 'Velcro mortar.'

Cob can be built directly onto earthbag foundations. To improve the connection and keep the cob from sliding off during an earthquake, stout wooden stakes are pounded into the top course of the bags. Straw bales can also be placed directly on the bags. After the first course or two of bales are in place, sharpened rebar pins can be driven down through them and all the way through the bag foundation, helping to hold the layers of bags together.

In rainy climates, I prefer to install an additional drainage layer between straw bales and polypropylene bags, to prevent the possibility of condensation buildup on the water-resistant bag surface. One way to achieve this is to build a wooden frame the width of the bales and fill it with pea gravel or pumice. In post and beam wall systems, the posts can either sit on a wooden beam that is pinned into the earthbags, or they can rest on separate footers placed to one side of the bag foundation.

KATE LUNDQUIST

Barbed wire 'mortar' provides tensile strength to an earthbag foundation.

The biggest concern about earthbag foundations is their durability. Polypropylene degrades rapidly when exposed to sunlight. It is not known how much thickness of plaster is necessary to preserve it. This is particularly important when the bags are filled not with rammed earth but with gravel, making the bags permanently structural.

Rammed Tires

The concept of reusing car tires filled with rammed earth as a foundation is similar to the use of earthbags. Again, whole buildings can be made this way. (See "Earthships, An Ecocentric Model.") Stacked rammed tires can create a stable, earthquake-resistant base for various wall systems. Like earthbags, they lend themselves to curved, organic wall shapes. The large diameter of the tires can present an interesting design challenge when the wall above is much narrower. One solution is to sculpt indoor or outdoor benches at the base of the wall.

Michael G. Smith likes to experiment with low-tech, natural building systems. He currently lives in a small cement-free house with earthbag and redwood foundations on a rubble trench, a timber frame of round redwood poles, straw bale and clay wattle walls, clay and lime plasters, and a living roof.

RESOURCES

Periodicals

The Last Straw: The International Journal of Straw Bale and Natural Building, HC66 Box 119, Hillsboro, NM 88042, U.S.A.; phone:505-895-5400; email: thelaststraw@strawhomes.com; website: www.strawhomes.com. Issue #16, Fall 1996 is devoted to discussing the many different foundation systems possible for straw bale (and natural building in general), ranging from the cheap and simple to the elaborate and expensive.

Rubble Trench Foundations

Rob Tom

WHEN WATER FREEZES, it expands volumetrically by 9 percent and in so doing, exerts a force of 150 tons per square inch (2100 megaPascals). When that water is found in poorly draining soils, nature, as usual, chooses the path of least resistance and dissipates much of that force by popping things up and out of the earth; much like what happens when one squeezes on a bar of soap. If a mere house, whose footings may only be carrying a few tons per linear foot, happens to be buried in that earth above the frost line, then it too gets heaved upward. As houses aren't usually dynamically balanced assemblages, there's no assurance that the bathroom will get heaved the same distance as the kid's bedroom. Speculation as to where the randomly displaced elements will fall when the earth thaws again presents odds that would delight any bookie.

A good solution to the freeze/thaw problem is the rubble trench foundation which, as the name suggests, consists of a trench dug down to a depth below the frost line. The trench is then filled with clean stone ballast in which drainage tile has been embedded to ensure positive drainage. The compacted stones bear solidly against each other and effectively transmit building loads to the supporting earth below. Furthermore, the voids between adjacent stones provide space for any water that may collect to freely expand, without detrimental consequences to the structure. Rubble trench foundations work in most soils whose bearing capacity exceeds 2,000 pounds per square foot (95 kiloPascals).

Rubble trench foundation for a cold climate region.

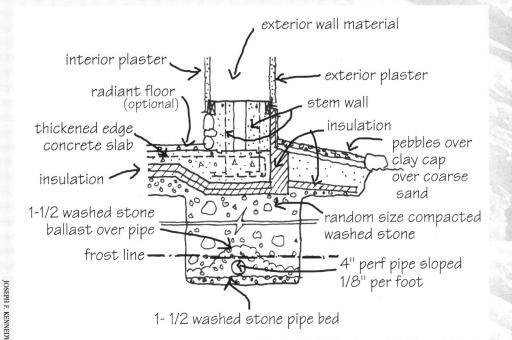

interior plaster

radiant floor (optional)

thickened edge concrete slab

insulation

1-1/2 washed stone ballast over pipe

frost line

exterior wall material

exterior plaster

stem wall

insulation

pebbles over clay cap over coarse sand

random size compacted washed stone

4" perf pipe sloped 1/8" per foot

1- 1/2 washed stone pipe bed

JOSEPH F. KENNEDY

Before digging the trench, topsoil should be peeled away (and saved for grading and landscaping) in the area of the building footprint to create a level building site. After laying out the foundation in the usual fashion, a line denoting the center of the wall is marked onto the earth (using garden lime, brightly colored stones, etc.). As the trench is dug, that line is kept in the center. The general rule is that footings are at least twice the width of the wall thickness. However, since straw bale walls include a lot of structurally redundant width, the footing width can be reduced in this case if the soil-bearing capacity is adequate.

The shallowest part of the trench (high point) will be dug to below the frost line and then sloped from there to one or more outlet trenches at the lowest parts of the building footprint. The outlet trenches leading away from the building are run out to daylight or to a dry well and, like DWV plumbing, sloped at least 1/8 inch per foot (1 centimeter per meter) horizontal run. Take care to ensure that the bottoms of the trenches are flat, free of loose debris, and properly sloped to the outlets.

The bottoms of the trenches are filled with a few inches of washed stone to provide a firm bed for a 4-inch (10-centimeter) perforated drainage tile. Then the trench is filled with washed stone (1.5 inches [38 millimeters] is a nice size for shoveling, but larger random sizes are okay, too), compacting at every vertical foot or so it as it is filled. In sloppy, oversized excavations, in an attempt to minimize the amount of stone rubble required, larger stones can be laid up in the manner of dry-stacked walls where the sides of the excavation should have been (it's easier than it sounds). Then use smaller, irregularly shaped stone (the turtles and footballs) to fill in between, backfilling and compacting the rubble in 12-inch (30 centimeter) lifts.

The drain tile only requires a foot or so of stone around it. To prevent fine soil particles from washing down and plugging the drainage media, a filter of landscape fabric, asphalt-impregnated felt, reclaimed woven polypropylene lumber tarps, or burlap should be laid over the stone before backfilling. The sidewalls of the trench would benefit from the use of a filler membrane, as well, to prevent clogging of the voids by loose dirt washed into the trench by the movement of subsurface groundwater. The outlet end of the drain tile should be capped with stout, corrosion-resistant mesh to keep critters out.

Rob Tom is a builder who now spends most of his days as an architect.

Earthen Floors

Athena and Bill Steen

EARTHEN FLOORS are one of the oldest flooring methods and have been used throughout the world in many climates and conditions. They have ranged from basic dirt, hardened and sealed from years of use, to elaborate clay mixtures poured in place, leveled, and highly polished. Because of their natural warmth, softness, and 'breathability,' earthen floors make very comfortable living surfaces.

Since local clay soils can often be used and specialized labor is not required, earthen floors can be inexpensive. They are easier to install and to repair than brick, tile, or concrete. Well-built earthen floors can be quite durable even under high traffic. Once sealed, they can be swept, mopped, or waxed the same as other floors.

Earthen floors can be finished to look as one likes: smooth and shiny or more earthy — slightly matted and textured with flecks of straw. Wood can be placed into the floor to create a grid pattern, or the surface can be scored to look like tile. Different colored clays can be added to vary the color. Earthen floors can also be used as sub-flooring for coverings such as tile or carpet and can be installed directly over existing concrete slabs.

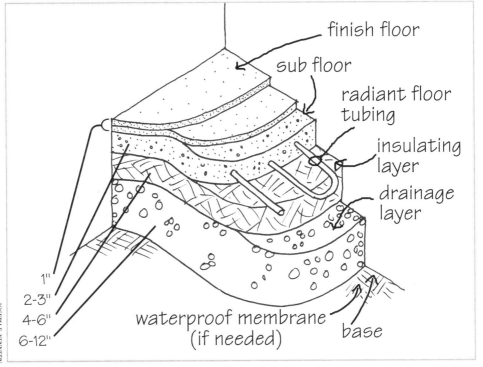

Earth Floor

One of the most beautiful things about earthen floors is that there is no single right way to construct them. Formulas and techniques vary according to available materials, cultural traditions, climatic conditions, and individual preferences. Here we describe one particular system that we have worked with successfully. With some experimentation and testing and a basic

113

understanding of the general principles, it will be possible to create your own long-lasting, beautiful earthen floor.

PREPARING THE BASE, DRAINAGE, INSULATION, AND SUB-FLOOR

To help prevent the floor from cracking or settling, the ground should be well compacted, with all organic and plant matter removed. The ground should also be dry before beginning construction of the floor.

In rainy climates and on poorly drained sites, steps need to be taken to improve drainage and stop the upward movement of moisture into the floor. In most situations, a layer of 6 to 12 inches (15 to 25 centimeters) of gravel or coarse sand may be adequate. Certain volcanic stones like pumice could also provide the additional benefit of insulation. If more drastic measures are required, a plastic membrane can be laid down (cushioned with a layer of sand to prevent punctures) but at the cost of losing breathability.

If insulation is desired, it should be laid on top of the gravel drainage layer. Some of the natural options include 4 to 6 inches (10 to 15 centimeters) of straw light-clay (See "Light-Clay: An Introduction to German Clay Building Techniques"), perlite-clay, pumice fines, or expanded clay (clay which has been heated, expanded, and filled with small air spaces.) A solid and compact layer of straw light-clay requires practice and can be labor intensive. One can also resort to rigid foam insulation.

The finished earthen floor needs to rest on a solid, level surface. If the drainage and insulation layers have been omitted, then the sub-floor can be nothing more than the well-compacted ground. Otherwise, use 2 to 3 inches (5 to 7.5 centimeters) of moistened — and then compacted — silty or sandy soil, with enough clay to hold together when dry. This sub-floor can serve as a good working surface during construction of the building, as foot traffic will help to compact it. But wait until all heavy construction (including interior plastering) is complete before installing the finished floor.

TESTING THE MIX

The most critical step of the finished floor layer is determining a suitable mixture, usually a combination of clay, sand, and chopped straw. The mixture needs to have enough clay to bind all the ingredients together with good strength, yet not so much that it cracks. Cracks, even when filled or grouted, remain the weakest part of the floor and the most vulnerable to damage. It is critical to create test samples to see how they dry.

Combine different ratios of clay soil and sand, starting with pure soil, then ½ part sand to 1 part soil, and so on up to 3 parts sand. Both soil and sand should be sifted through ³/₈-inch

(1-centimeter) hardware cloth to remove stones and debris. Add just enough water to thoroughly blend all the ingredients. Mix enough material to create test samples that are 1 inch (2.5 centimeters) thick and at least 12 inches (30 centimeters) square. When they dry, choose the sample that has no cracking and has sufficient strength. If no such sample exists, you have several options: add chopped straw to reduce cracking; add clay to improve strength; choose a different soil to work with; or stabilize the mix with 6 to 10 percent Portland cement.

Chopped straw or sifted cow or horse manure can always be added for visual effect, even if the test sample produced good results without it. Once a mix has been selected, make a larger test sample (10 square feet [a square meter]) for final confirmation.

INSTALLING THE FINISHED FLOOR

If the sub-floor has been properly prepared, the finished floor can be quite thin, anywhere from 1 to 2 inches (2.5 to 5 centimeters). Typically, we have had good results with a 1-inch (2.5-centimeter) finished floor, applied in two separate $1/2$-inch-thick (1-centimeter-thick) layers. It is conceivable that it could be done in one layer, although there would be more problems with shrinkage and cracking.

When preparing your mix, measure the ingredients carefully so that each batch is consistent. Mix the dry ingredients thoroughly before adding water, and set some of this dry mix aside for future repairs. Add just enough water to make the mix workable; the drier the mix, the less the floor will shrink and crack. The sub-floor should be swept or vacuumed clean and then dampened before applying the mix.

Applying the floor mixture is most easily done with a trowel. Swimming pool trowels, which have rounded corners, are easier to use with earthen materials than standard square-cornered trowels. A 3- to 4-inch (7- to 10-centimeter) putty knife, Japanese finishing trowel, or small mason's trowel can be useful in the corners.

It is usually easier to apply the mix in 2-foot-wide (0.6-meter-wide) strips across the room. The edge of each strip should be beveled and then scored or scratched, so that the following section will overlap and bond to it. Failure to bevel and scratch these edges will typically result in long cracks between sections. It is best to do an entire room at one time. The sub-floor needs to be kept damp where the mix is being applied to keep the mix from drying out too quickly and cracking.

There are several ways to keep the floor level as you go. Level lines traced onto the walls at the height of the top of each floor layer will help you keep on track as you move across the room. Use a level, taped to a straight board 3 to 4 feet (90 to 120 centimeters) long, to check the level and remove any excess material. Pieces of rebar or strips of wood the same thickness as the depth

CATHERINE WANEK

Carole Crew's trowels smooth the finish layer of an adobe floor.

of the floor application can be laid at intervals across the sub-floor as guides. As each section of floor is completed, remove the guides and reposition them for the next section, making sure to carefully fill the gaps left behind.

The first layer of earthen mix can be left slightly rough so that the second layer will adhere better. Optimally, the second layer should be applied while the first layer is still damp, yet leather hard. If the first layer dries out completely, dampen it well before starting the second layer, and keep it damp as you work your way across it. If the first layer shows any cracking, adjust your mix for the second layer.

The second layer is applied in the same manner as the first. Once it has hardened, but while still damp, it can be troweled with a little water to achieve a smooth, fine polish. Wiping it lightly with a wet sponge before troweling brings out the flecks of straw.

Depending on the weather, the entire floor could dry in anywhere from a few days to several weeks. A fan could help speed up the drying process. All traffic should be kept off the floor during this time.

Sealing the Surface

Once it is completely dry, the earthen floor needs to be sealed to make it harder and to prevent dusting and water damage. Traditionally, the most successful sealants have included oils, animal urine, and blood. Boiled linseed oil is probably the most cost effective and widely available option today.

To be effective, the sealant needs to penetrate deeply into the earthen floor rather than form a skin or shell on the surface, as do acrylic sealants. The problem with a thin, hard shell on top of a relatively soft material is that it is fragile and susceptible to damage. When broken, the result is potholes in the floor.

To improve penetration, a solvent will be necessary for thinning the oil. The options include everything from common mineral spirits and turpentine to more expensive but environmentally friendly citrus oils and odorless turpentine. Oils penetrate deeper when they are warmed (carefully) and when the surface of the floor is also warm.

Generally, it is better to apply the oil in a stronger concentration in the initial coats, gradually reducing the ratio of oil to solvent in each successive coat as the floor becomes less porous. We

A completed, sealed, and polished earth floor.

BILL STEEN

usually use four coats, starting with full strength oil, then 25 percent solvent, then 50 percent, then 75 percent. Each coat should be applied as soon as the previous one is no longer tacky to the touch. Periodic applications of 25 percent oil, 75 percent solvent can be used to maintain the sheen. Hard wax can also be used.

Through the Canelo Project, Athena and Bill Steen teach workshops on straw bale and natural building in the United States and Mexico. They are coauthors of the bestselling The Straw Bale House *and authors of* The Beauty of Straw Bale Homes.

RESOURCES
Books

Smith, Michael G. *The Cobber's Companion: How to Build Your Own Earthen Home.* 3rd ed. Cob Cottage Company, 2001. Contains detailed instructions for the author's system of poured adobe floors.

Steen, Athena, and Bill Steen. *Earthen Floors.* Canelo Project, 1997. This booklet contains construction details for several types of earthen floors, including poured adobe and tamped earth.

Steen, Athena Swentzell, Bill Steen, David Bainbridge, and David Eisenberg. *The Straw Bale House.* Chelsea Green, 1994. Along with lots of information about straw bale building, this book describes a number of flooring options for natural houses, including earthen floors.

Organizations

The Canelo Project, HC1 Box 324, Elgin, AZ 85611, U.S.A.; phone: 520-455-5548; fax: 520-455-9360; email: absteen@dakotacom.net; website: www.caneloproject.com. Athena and Bill Steen's non-profit educational organization offers workshops on earthen floors and plasters, straw bale construction, and more.

CATHERINE WANEK

A sample of an earth floor, showing the different layers.

A Tamped Road Base Floor

Frank Meyer

Afew years ago, when asked to make an earthen floor, I started by collecting samples of all the soil types available in our area. Austin, Texas is situated in a geologically diverse area, so I got samples from several places, including the building site; my backyard; and commercial suppliers of dirt, loam, and road base. After weeks of playing in the dirt, mixing in stabilizers and trying to strengthen and harden the earth to make it suitable for a floor, I came to an interesting conclusion. One particular road base would make the hardest, prettiest, and quickest floor without any stabilizers at all. Its rich red color and excellent blend of silt, clay, sand, and gravel made test bricks that were more impressive than anything else I came up with.

Not all road bases are created equal. The one I chose is what is known here as 'city base.' Engineers for building roads and streets in Austin have approved it. It originates in a quarry where the material is taken from the earth and the silt, clay, sand, and gravel are separated, then reblended to specified proportions. It has a plasticity index of 12, which relates to the way it shrinks and swells. It costs US$2.48 per ton, plus hauling. A 500-square-foot (45-square-meter) floor will require two 12-ton truckloads, costing between US$200 and US$300 delivered. When estimating the amount of material to use, figure it will lose about one-third of its original volume when compacted.

By using this material and applying basic road building techniques, we have a big advantage over traditional poured earth floors. The process uses relatively little water, thereby requiring a much shorter drying time. It can typically be walked on a day or two after installing.

Before proceeding with the installation process, it is necessary to consider vapor barriers. I have done earth floors with and without vapor barriers. Unfortunately, the recent drought has made it difficult to compare the performance of the earthen floors with and without vapor barriers. My feeling is, if in doubt, use a vapor barrier. If your location is high and dry and you want your floor to 'breathe,' consider not using one.

To begin the process of building a tamped road base floor, make sure the ground is fairly level, smooth, and compacted to at least 6 inches (15 centimeters) below the planned finished height. If a vapor barrier is used, spread a layer of sand 1 or 2 inches (2.5 to 5 centimeters) thick both below and above the barrier to prevent gravel from puncturing it. Apply the first layer of road base to a thickness of about 2 inches (5 centimeters) and wet it with a hose or watering can. There is no need for soaking; just get it wet enough so that the silt and clay stick to the aggregate.

Compact the first layer. A plate compactor, available at tool rental outlets, works well (be sure to vent the building with fans if using a gas-powered compactor). Hand tamping — another option — is slower but much quieter and doesn't produce fumes. Hand tampers are easily made from wood or by welding a steel plate to a piece of pipe. Hand tamping the edges works best even if a powered compactor is used.

Repeat layers as necessary until they reach about 1 inch (2.5 centimeters) from the finish height.

At this point we need to level the floor. Sift the road base through a piece of $3/8$-inch (1-centimeter) hardware cloth to produce a mixture of silt, clay, sand, and small gravel. Layer it on and level, using screed boards (much like concrete workers use).

After leveling, wet and tamp the mix again, making sure that it bonds with the layer below. For the top coat, we screen the material again, this time using $1/8$-inch (3-millimeter) hardware cloth. This fine mixture can be applied dry and wetted like all the preceding layers or mixed wet and troweled on. The most important thing is to make sure it bonds with the layer below. I have had better success applying the top coat dry. The top coat is not compacted but hand troweled and burnished, using enough water to make it bond and be workable. Trial and error will give you a feel for it.

We seal our floor only after it is thoroughly dry. In the summer in Texas, thorough drying may take only a few weeks. In cooler, moister climates it may take several months. The floor can be used during this drying period. Cracks from drying, and any chipping or gouging that may occur during drying, can be patched by again screening the road base, this time using window screen. What is left is a fine powder of silt, clay, and fine sand, which makes an excellent patching and burnishing material. It can be sprinkled on, wetted, and blended in. The more time and patience you have at this point, the better your results will be, as burnishing with a pool trowel brings out the beauty and character of the earth.

The best sealer I have found is boiled linseed oil, thinned with turpentine and brushed on in several coats (the odor dissipates in a week or two). This is an all-natural, non-toxic floor that has relatively low embodied energy. With time, patience and an affinity for getting dirty, anyone can do it. Enjoy!

Frank Meyer of Thangmaker Construction has over 25 years of construction experience. His focus is sustainable and green building. He specializes in straw bale construction and earth floors and is available for consultation and workshop facilitation.

Adobe Building

Paul G. McHenry

This adobero from Sonora, Mexico makes three adobes at a time – 250 to 300 per day – and polishes them so that they can be fired in a simple kiln to make 'burned' adobes. He is mining an arroyo, where the soil is good for adobe making. His main complaint was that in order to do the firing, he had used all the available firewood for 15 miles (25 kilometers) around.

EARTH BUILDINGS in many forms are found in most parts of the world, in various degrees of sophistication. They range from mud-covered brush shelters to magnificent palaces in the Middle East to luxury homes in Santa Fe, New Mexico. The choice of earth building method is dictated by climate, as well as by tradition developed by trial and error through the centuries. Frequently, through cultural influence, various styles are found side by side. Earth building techniques from ancient peoples on every continent are well documented in the reports of explorers and archeologists. What may come as a surprise is that at least a third of the world's people still live in earth homes today.

The basic principle in building with earth is to keep it simple. Good shelter can be built with a minimum of skilled labor and tools or even with no tools at all. Modern efforts to mechanize, standardize, and improve earthen building may lead to unnecessary complexity and other problems.

Adobe bricks are blocks made of earth and water that are dried in the sun. Sizes vary widely, mostly determined by historic tradition. After the bricks have been cast, it may take a week or more for them to be dry enough to handle. A larger and thicker brick will tend to crack more and will take longer to dry. Heavy rains can damage the bricks as they are drying, so brick making must be done in a period where the possibility of rain is low.

Bricks can be made in a number of ways, depending on site, climate, and tools available. The simplest way is with a single mold. Mud is mixed and placed in the molds by hand on a smooth surface. The mold is removed and the bricks allowed to dry sufficiently to stand on edge, after which they are trimmed and allowed to dry completely before stacking or use. The whole process takes about one week in most favorable dry climates.

The brick making process can be expanded with the use of shovels, wheelbarrows, multiple forms, front-end loaders, and concrete or plaster mixers. The use of a hydraulic pressing machine that can create a large number of bricks (compressed earth blocks) — up to 4,000 per day — is another option. This type of production has many advantages but requires a large capital investment. (See "Compressed Earth Blocks.")

PAUL McHENRY

Once they are dry, adobe bricks are stacked to make walls. The bricks are cemented together with a mud mortar made up of water and screened soil taken from the same sources as the soil used to make the bricks. Although early buildings in the Southwestern U.S. were sometimes placed directly on the ground, adobe walls should be built on a foundation of concrete or stone to protect them from moisture damage. Frames for windows and doors are set in place as the wall goes up.

Soils

Contrary to popular belief, most soils will make suitable building bricks. Adobe soils contain a mixture of clay, silt, and sand or aggregate, with the individual percentages being relatively unimportant. Clay provides the waterproofing and is the glue that holds the aggregate together. Bricks have been made that have no clay, but they are prone to rapid erosion. Expansive clays can cause cracks as the bricks dry. Many natural soils have too high a clay content and must be modified with a tempering agent of sand or straw. (In the book of Exodus in the Bible, the need for straw to make bricks is mentioned; this perhaps verifies the tradition in many places that straw is necessary when the clay percentage is too high.) Most good adobes will have a mix of approximately 50 percent clay and silt, and 50 percent sand and aggregate. The resulting brick should be dry, hard, and free of major cracks.

The rate of erosion of mud surfaces from rain is much slower than might be expected. Historic examples in the Southwest indicate an erosion rate for vertical wall surfaces of perhaps 1 inch (2.5 centimeters) in 20 years, in an area with average rainfall of 25 inches (64 centimeters) per year. Unprotected horizontal surfaces, such as tops of walls, will erode much faster.

CATHERINE WANEK

Wooden boxes laid in place of adobe, called 'gringo blocks,' provide an attachment place for window and door frames.

Energy, Ecology, and Insulation

Energy and ecology go hand in hand. We are spending the world's non-renewable resources at a frightening rate. An often-overlooked feature of energy consumption is the cost of producing our primary building materials — its embodied energy. An adobe brick made by hand on the building site uses no fuel except the builder's sweat. Earth building holds answers to many of our energy and ecology concerns.

Tests indicate that adobe has the capacity to absorb, store, and release heat, making use of solar energy and damping ambient temperature swings. These tests found that the interior wall temperature of a 10-inch-thick (25-centimeter-thick) adobe wall on the south side of a building was the average outdoor temperature through the previous week. Interior wall temperature varied only by 2 or 3 degrees in any 24-hour period, while outside air temperatures varied from 60

Taos Pueblo is multi-storied and has been continuously occupied since before the Spanish Conquest. The historic pueblo has no electricity or plumbing, and the mud plaster is redone every few years by the women of the village.

to 90 degrees Fahrenheit (15 to 32 degrees Celsius). At midday, with outdoor temperatures in the 90s (30s), the interior temperatures, at 75 degrees Fahrenheit (24 degrees Celsius), felt cool. At night, when the exterior temperature was 60 degrees Fahrenheit (15 degrees Celsius), the interior temperature at 75 degrees (24 degrees) felt warm. Other tests on 24-inch (60-centimeter) walls had the same results, but the interior temperatures only varied by 1 or 2 degrees. This is called the 'thermal flywheel effect.'

The insulation value, however, is quite low, and if the building needs to be heated continually, the wall loses heat unless additional insulation is supplied. The flywheel effect is most effective in areas with highly variable ambient temperatures.

PAUL McHENRY

HISTORIC USE

Prehistoric peoples every-where used earth and other natural materials for building. When traders and invaders came, they adapted the same local materials to the archi-tectural styles of their countries of origin. Adobe was the most widely used form in most of the Southwestern United States and Northern Mexico. It did not always follow the local architectural style of Pueblo or American Territorial; adobe bricks were also used in place of fired brick in Victorian-style buildings.

When the railroads arrived, offering economical transportation of manufactured goods, those who could afford them began using more modern materials. But in difficult economic times, people always returned to earthen buildings to meet their needs. If funds were scarce, then churches, schools, public buildings, and homes were built with adobe. The government found this useful as well. When the New Mexico State Fairground in Albuquerque needed buildings, money was scarce and there was massive unemployment. As material was available on-site, what better way to meet both needs than to build with adobe?

During the Great Depression, The Farm Home Administration and other government agencies sponsored another program to assist farmers who had been broken by the drought. They obtained land in the Rio Grande River valley, portioned it off into various size plots, and sent tools and supervisors to build simple adobe homes. This allowed the motivated farmers to build new lives for themselves. Of the 40 or more homes built during this program, all but 2 are still occupied by satisfied owners.

CHALLENGES TO CURRENT AND FUTURE USE

Adobe construction in New Mexico has a split image. On the one hand, a person with few resources can build a snug shelter with the materials under his feet, using only his hands. On the other, a wealthy person can build an adobe palace, paying top dollar (mainly for labor). Adobe is now thought of in New Mexico as a luxury material that only the wealthy can afford.

Today, the primary enemies of building with earth are ignorance and building regulations. Prior to World War II, most people in the Southwest were familiar with adobe construction. After World War II, when professionals went back to school and work, earth building got lost among the new materials. As a result, we now have an entire generation of professional engineers, architects, and building officials who are unfamiliar with this type of construction. The only people familiar with the material are those in developing nations and a small number of professionals who specialize in natural building. Even the people of the developing nations are rapidly losing their earth building skills.

Building regulations were frequently written by people who had no knowledge of adobe. Some current building regulations place such limitations on its use that the cost becomes prohibitive. The answer to this is education.

Three things need to be done.

1. Change building codes to recognize the centuries of earth building experience and tradition.

2. Establish community and higher-education programs that provide real, hands-on experience. Use these people to train more trainers.

3. Build full-scale demonstration projects that people can walk into and experience.

Paul G. ("Buzz") McHenry is an architect and builder specializing in adobe construction. He teaches in the architecture department at the University of New Mexico, and founded the Earth Architecture Center International, Ltd. in 1994 and the Earth Building Foundation in 1998. The author of Adobe and Rammed Earth Buildings: Design and Construction *and* Adobe: Build it Yourself, *McHenry researches innovations in earth building and ecological design.*

RESOURCES

Books

Gray, Virginia, and Alan Macrae, authors; and Wayne McCall, photographer. *Mud, Space, and Spirit: Handmade Adobes.* Capra Press, Santa Barbara, 1976. Takes you inside beautifully sculpted, owner-built adobe homes.

Khalili, Nader. *Ceramic Houses and Earth Architecture: How to Build Your Own.* Cal-Earth, 1986. Although focused on the technique of 'geltaftan' or fired earth, this book contains valuable information for adobe builders, including structural principles and weather protection of arches, domes, and vaults.

McHenry, Jr., Paul. *Adobe and Rammed Earth Buildings: Design and Construction.* University of Arizona Press, 1984. Includes history, engineering, and overview of construction techniques, including soil testing, windows and doors, and plastering options.

———. *Adobe: Build it Yourself.* University of Arizona Press, 1985. A thorough and readable introduction to many aspects of adobe construction.

Norton, John. *Building with Earth.* Intermediate Technology Publications, 1997. A good, brief introduction to the general principles of earth building, including testing. Contains instructions on building adobe vaults and domes.

Tibbets, Joseph. *The Earthbuilder's Encyclopedia.* Southwest Solaradobe School, 1989. Useful pictorial reference to materials, tools, techniques, and details of adobe and other earth building systems. Out of print but available as CD-Rom.

Periodicals

The Adobe Builder. Southwest Solaradobe School. P.O. Box 153, Bosque, NM 87006, U.S.A.; phone: 505-861-1255; fax: 505-861-1304; website: www.adobebuilder.com. Oversized, glossy trade journal, mostly targeted toward professional earth builders in the Southwestern U.S., but with good articles about history, restoration, and new techniques.

Organizations

The Earth Building Foundation (www.earthbuilding.com) is a non-profit foundation dedicated to the collection and dissemination of information on earth building and can supply accurate, technical information on earthen building. Bibliography searchable on-line.

Bamboo Construction

Darrel DeBoer

Many Americans see bamboo as invasive and at odds with our chosen landscapes, but in the southeastern U.S., it was once an integral part of the landscape, covering millions of acres. Native to every continent except Europe — with its use as a building material traced to 3500 B.C. — bamboo tools, utensils, food, and buildings still strongly influence the lives of half the world's population. In Asia, thousands of potential uses make bamboo not just desirable but a required element in every house.

A comprehensive system of growing, processing, and (especially) understanding bamboo does not yet exist in this country. And although there are already thousands of timber bamboos growing in the western and southern U.S., many Americans have never seen one. Yet, given the joinery system developed in Colombia over the last several decades, now is the ideal time for us to draw upon the proven methods of bamboo construction from Southeast Asia and South America.

In the United States, for the first time in our history, an unlimited, highly subsidized supply of structural-quality timber does not exist. Bamboo can be a key element in creating large structures with minimal environmental impact. It allows afford-able construction without highly industrialized, proprietary systems — wood, concrete, and steel production are not needed — while taking some of the pressure off of the forests. Bamboo structures can make a significant contribution to local self-reliance, and because of the speed and density of bamboo growth, a builder with access to a relatively small amount of land can be in full control of his or her source of construction materials.

We need to develop a bamboo culture — one that recognizes the value in the use of this plant. We will have many challenges along the way, including: gaining access to inexpensive land that is not valued for other purposes; choosing appropriate species; allowing time for the bamboo to mature; understanding the esthetic of working with cylindrical materials in a predominantly rectilinear society; learning to distinguish exceptional working stock; and developing a design approach that takes full advantage of both the strength and the beauty of timber bamboo.

This elegant tropical home, designed by Colombian architect Simón Vélez, uses bamboo for most of its structural elements.

BAMBOO AND SUSTAINABILITY

Bamboo meets the basic criteria for a sustainable building material by being

- renewable: The *Phyllostachys* species — those most suitable for growing and building in the U.S., surviving temperatures as low as 0 degrees Fahrenheit (-18 degrees Celsius) — will grow 10 to12 inches (25 to 30 centimeters) a day once a grove is established. The record is 49 inches (124 centimeters) in a single day. Culms (the living stalks) achieve all of their growth in an initial six-week spurt, then spend the next three years replacing sugars and water with silica and cellulose, after which they are useful structurally. Once established, one-third of a mature grove can be sustainably harvested annually.

- plentiful: Our current meager U.S. supply of timber-quality bamboo could increase greatly within a decade with species selection appropriate to various microclimates and levels of water and nutrient availability. For now, strong tropical varieties are imported from Asia and South America, along with temperate varieties such as *Moso*. For microclimate information, look at the American Bamboo Society's Species Source List at www.Bamboo.orgs/abs.

- local: Bamboo concentrates a large amount of fiber in a small land area, creating a rare situation in which a single person can be both the producer and consumer of a building material.

- waste-reducing: As is nature's general practice, nothing goes to waste. At some times of the year, the leaves are a more nutritious animal feed than alfalfa, and bamboo compost serves to fertilize the next generation of plants.

Bamboo production systems in Japan, Southeast Asia, and Central and South America allow a small number of people to carry out the process from planting through utilization, with only minimal infrastructure and equipment. Every part of the plant has a use, and harvesting for that use at the appropriate time not only doesn't hurt the plant but encourages future vigor. Groves can be located to take advantage of the plant's unusual ability to quickly process water and nutrients left over from livestock farms, sewage treatment plants, and industrial processes. In contrast to most plants, the addition of fertilizer does not diminish the quality of bamboo poles, since energy is stored in the rhizomes for later release in the formation of the next year's culms. Meanwhile, those rhizomes are useful for securing topsoil and for erosion control. The plants use transpiration to create their own microclimate, cooling a grove (or a house located in a grove) as much as 10 to 15 degrees Fahrenheit (6 to 8 degrees Celsius).

STRUCTURAL PROPERTIES

Bamboo is an extremely strong fiber, having twice the compressive strength of concrete and roughly the same strength-to-weight ratio of steel in tension. Its hollow shape approximates the ideal shape of a beam, and testing has shown that the hollow cylinder has a strength factor of 1.9 over a solid pole of equivalent mass. The useful life of a pole ranges from two years, if buried underground, to several hundred years, as seen in the rafters of traditional Japanese farmhouses.

The strongest bamboo fibers have a greater shear resistance than structural woods, and they take much longer to come to ultimate failure. However, the ability of bamboo to bend without breaking may make it unsuitable for building floor structures in this country

SIMÓN VÉLEZ

because of its natural flexibility. (It works very well as a replacement for hardwood in finish flooring.)

Through most of the world, there is no provision in the codes for bamboo construction. Successful experiments by Colombian architect Simón Vélez to achieve 66-foot (20-meter) spans and 30-foot (9-meter) cantilevers were conducted in areas not requiring inspection of structures. Now that these buildings exist, they stand as proof of what works and as models for future designs. Even one-quarter of Vélez's spans would be adequate for most of our needs. Because of the increasing scarcity of timber bamboo in the U.S., one of the best uses for this giant grass is as a roof truss.

Although bamboo is a bending and forgiving material, structural redundancy is a must in truss design. It is imperative that we overbuild; a structural failure at such an early stage of the introduction of bamboo architecture would be catastrophic. It is crucial to understand which members

Simón Vélez has taken bamboo architecture in new directions, showing that it is not (as is often perceived) a poor person's material.

are in tension or compression and which points in a structure experience maximum shear and moment forces. Ambitious designers should do some small-scale work with the material to get an idea of what feels right, then find a structural engineer who can do the calculations for them.

There are two strategies for overcoming lateral forces in a bamboo structure. The first, represented by recently engineered Latin American structures, relies on the shear resistance provided by mortar on both the bamboo-lathed walls and the roof. The success of this approach was demonstrated in April 1991, when 20 houses constructed in Costa Rica for the National Bamboo Foundation survived a 7.5 Richter scale earthquake. The second approach takes advantage of the forgiveness of the traditional lashed, pinned, or bolted joints found in both Asia and the Americas.

A bamboo tower in Colombia demonstrates the strength of bamboo.

In the Colombian earthquake in January 1999, which destoyed 75 percent of the buildings in the region, nearly all of the 500 people killed were hit by falling concrete. Bamboo structures survived uniformly unscathed, including a tower with a bamboo roof structure located within a few thousand meters of the epicenter.

DARREL DEBOER

Even structures created with intuitive engineering and non-optimized joinery take great advantage of the broad elastic range of bamboo; a structure can deform and return to its original configuration once the load has been removed. It is difficult to cause failure of bamboo in pure compression or tension. Truss designs remove the bending forces and put all the weight along the axis of the pole in complete tension or compression. What has been lacking until now is a joint capable of making that smooth transition.

JOINERY DESIGN

Simple joinery systems based on pegging and tying have evolved to take advantage of the strong exterior fibers of the hollow bamboo tube. Lashed joinery has been used successfully for millennia.

It allows for movement, and if natural fibers such as jute, hemp, rattan, or split bamboo are used for lashing while still green, they will tend to tighten around the joint. Unfortunately, the seasonal moisture changes in most of the U.S. will cause bamboo to expand and contract by as much as 6 percent across its diameter, causing a slackening, and not all joints remain accessible for tightening.

More recent systems have been engineered to make joinery stronger and less labor-intensive. The joint of preference has become the one developed by Simón Vélez in Colombia. He relies on a bolted connection but with an understanding that the bolt alone concentrates too much force on the wall of the bamboo. Therefore, the void between the solid internal nodes is filled with a solidifying mortar. Where members of a truss come together at angles and tension forces are anticipated, a steel strap is placed to bridge the pieces. It is important to design with redundant systems, capable of both tension and compression. Nevertheless, as Vélez told me, "I have never seen the bamboo fail; only the steel straps have failed under load testing." The bamboo can split and pull away from the mortar, but small stainless steel straps are easily available to prevent that in critical situations.

THE CHALLENGE

From our orientation toward wood as the most common building material, bamboo is an awkward shape and doesn't have the forgiveness of wood when mistakes are made. Our tendency is to try to make bamboo into wood. Flooring milled from thin strips of bamboo and woven matting are two very simple substitutions for commonly used materials. These changes require no training or shift in mindset. The problems will have more to do with the inherent difficulties of industrialization: demand outstripping sustainable supply, local producer economies

Checklist for Obtaining Construction-Quality Poles

- **Age** — *three- to five-year-old culms best, depending upon species.*
- **Starch content** — *harvest at right time of year to minimize beetle/fungus attack.*
- **Appropriate species** *for the intended use.*
- **Sufficiently adapted to local humidity** — *especially for interior use.*
- **Stored** *out of direct sun, preferably vertically.*
- **In the running bamboo species**, *use the bottom five feet or so for other purposes, as it is usually crooked, with nodes too close together and with density characteristics different than the rest of the pole.*

Checklist for a Well-Designed Bamboo Structure

- *Thorough static analysis to ensure that loads are distributed evenly among the joints and axially along the pole.*
- *Slenderness ratio of less than 50.*
- *Bolted joints with solid-filled internodes.*
- *Dry poles that are still easily workable — about six weeks after harvest is ideal.*
- *Find a way to obtain lateral strength. Either create a shear panel consisting of a mortar bed over lath, or avoid mortar altogether and allow the structure to deflect and return.*
- *Refer to the engineering formulas and testing criteria developed by Jules Janssen.*

CATHERINE WANEK

This tropical timber, known as Guadua, can grow to over 6 inches (15 centimeters) in diameter and 100 feet (30 meters) high.

destroyed by outside owners and cash economy demands, short-sighted use of cheap materials, etc.

A model non-prescriptive code written by Jules Janssen for the International Network on Bamboo and Rattan (INBAR) is intended for inclusion in the year 2000 International Building Code and could have a lasting impact on widespread acceptance. Jeffree Trudeau and David Sands of Bamboo Technologies in Hawaii have been working to achieve code acceptance by first building a ferrocement house with stay-in-place formwork panels and joists of bamboo. They are currently working with ICBO Evaluation Service, Inc., to prepare both the acceptance criteria and an evaluation report to provide future guidelines and reference. So, with the aid of a patient building official, the language is now in place to use bamboo in code-approved structures in the U.S.

> *Darrel DeBoer is an architect and furniture builder who became possessed by the idea of building with bamboo several years ago after seeing the structures of Colombian architect Simón Vélez. He has co-written two books on alternative building material,* Building Less Waste *and the* Architectural Resource Guide *to more sustainable building materials, written by members of Architects/Designers/Planners for Social Responsibility (www.adpsrnorcal.org). His traveling exhibit of resource-efficient building materials can be seen at www.stopwaste.org/gmat.html.*

RESOURCES

Books

Bell, Michael. *The Gardeners' Guide to Growing Temperate Bamboos.* Timber Press, 2000. Good introduction to the running species.

Cusack, Victor. *Bamboo World.* Kangaroo Press, 1999. Growing and the many uses of tropical clumpers. The definitive work for regions where temperatures don't get below 15 degrees Fahrenheit (-.9 degrees Celsius).

Farelly, David. *The Book of Bamboo.* Sierra Club Books, 1984. Great stories and inspiration around the many uses for bamboo, but low in technical detail.

Hidalgo, Oscar. *Manual de Construcción con Bambíe (Bamboo Construction Manual).* National University of Colombia's Research Center for Bamboo and Wood (CIBAM), 1981. In Spanish, but so well illustrated that the intent is clear. Focus is on short-span, low-cost structures.

Institute for Lightweight Structures; Dunkelberg, Maus, et al. IL31: *Bamboo as a Building Material.* Karl Kramer Verlag, 1985. In-depth analysis of the possibilities of bamboo design and joinery. Doesn't predict the optimized joinery techniques now practiced in Colombia.

Janssen, Jules. *Bamboo: A Grower & Builder's Reference Manual.* American Bamboo Society, Hawaii Chapter, 1997. 73-4533 Kohanaiki Road, 8b; Kailua-Kona, HI 96740, U.S.A. Out of print, but this extraordinary researcher will soon publish an extended version. See also his *Building with Bamboo* (Intermediate Technology Publications, 1995).

Vélez, Simón, et al. *Grow Your Own House.* Vitra Design Museum, 2000. Slightly quirky imperative leading to the construction of the amazing 20,000-square-foot (1,860-square-meter) ZERI pavilion for Expo 2000 in Hanover, Germany. If you can only get one book, make it this one.

Periodicals

American Bamboo Society Newsletter. 750 Krumkill Road, Albany, NY 12203, U.S.A.; website: www.halcyon.com/abs.

Newsletter of the Pacific Northwest Chapter of the ABS. Phil Davidson, Newsletter Editor, 10416-107 Street CT SW, Tacoma, WA 98498-1599, U.S.A.; phone: 253-588-0662 or 253-512-0754; email: phildavidson@worldnet.att.net. An exemplary newsletter; consistently much more information than requisite.

The Temperate Bamboo Quarterly. 30 Meyers Road, Summertown, TN 38483, U.S.A. Detailed information for bamboo growers. Has much on bamboo crafting.

WEBSITES

See www.bamboodirect.com for the latest list of available bamboo books and periodicals.

DARREL DeBOER

An interior view of some of the amazing bamboo architecture of Simón Vélez.

Cob Building, Ancient and Modern

Michael G. Smith

Cob lends itself to many different architectural styles. This Victorian mansion in Nelson, New Zealand, was built in 1856 and survives in perfect condition today.

ᴮᴇᴄᴀᴜsᴇ ᴏꜰ ɪᴛs ᴠᴇʀsᴀᴛɪʟɪᴛʏ and widespread availability, earth has been used as a construction material on every continent and in every age. It is one of the oldest building materials on the planet; the first freestanding human dwellings may have been built of mud or wattle and daub. About 10,000 years ago, the residents of Jericho were using oval, hand-formed, sun-dried bricks (adobes), which were probably a refinement of earlier cob. Even today, it is estimated that between one-third and one-half of the world's population lives in earthen dwellings.

'Cob,' the English term for mud building, uses no forms, no bricks, and no wooden framework. Similar forms of mud building are endemic throughout Northern Europe, the Ukraine, the Middle East and the Arabian Peninsula, India, China, the Sahel and equatorial Africa, and the American Southwest.

Exactly when and how cob building first arose in England remains uncertain, but it is known that cob houses were being built there by the 13th century. Cob houses became the norm in many parts of Britain by the 15th century and stayed that way until industrialization and cheap transportation made brick popular in the late 1800s. Cob was particularly common in southwestern England and Wales, where the subsoil was a sandy clay and other building materials, like stone and wood, were scarce. English cob was made of clay-based subsoil mixed with straw, water, and sometimes sand or crushed shale or flint. The percentage of clay in the mix ranged from 3 percent to 20 percent. It was mixed either by people shoveling and stomping, or by heavy animals such as oxen trampling it.

The stiff mud mixture was usually shoveled with a cob fork onto a stone foundation and trodden into place by workmen on the walls. In a single day, a course or 'lift' of cob — anywhere from 6 inches to 3 feet (15 centimeters to 1 meter) in height but usually averaging 18 inches (45 centimeters) — would be placed on the wall. It would be left to dry for as long as two weeks before the next lift was added. Sometimes additional straw was trodden into the top of each layer. As they dried, the walls were trimmed back substantially with a paring iron — commonly to between 20 and 36 inches (50 and 90 centimeters) thick — leaving them straight and plumb. In this way, cob walls were built as high as 23 feet (7 meters), though they were usually much less. Frames for doors and windows were built in as the wall grew.

Many cob cottages were built by poor tenant farmers and laborers who often worked cooperatively. A team of a few men, working together one day a week, could complete a house in one season. A cottage begun in the spring would receive its thatch roof and interior whitewash in the fall, and its inhabitants would move inside before winter. Often they waited until the following year to plaster the outside with lime-sand stucco so that the walls would have ample time to dry. Cob barns and other outbuildings were sometimes left unplastered.

But cob buildings were not reserved solely for humble peasants. Many townhouses and large manors, built of cob before fired brick became readily available, survive in excellent condition today. An estimated 20,000 cob homes and as many outbuildings remain in use in the county of Devon alone. It was common for well-built cob homes to go for a hundred years without needing repair.

British settlers to other parts of the world took the technique of cob with them. Early colonists of New Zealand found the clay soil and tussock grass common on the South Island to make excellent cob, and constructed at least 8,000 houses there, of which several hundred survive today. Cob was less popular in Australia, where mud bricks and rammed earth were the preferred earth building techniques, but a few cob buildings survive in New South Wales, Queensland, and the vicinity of Melbourne. Cob buildings in North America dating from the same era are few and far between but include a house built in 1836 in Penfield, New York and a church in Toronto.

By the late 1800s, cob building in England, considered primitive and backward, was declining in popularity. In recent decades, however, public attitudes have slowly evolved and traditional cob cottages with their thatched roofs are now valued as historical and picturesque. As there was virtually no new cob construction in England between World War I and the 1980s, traditional builders took much of their specialized knowledge with them to the grave. But enough information survived to allow a cob building revival in the 1990s that was fueled largely by historical interest and the real estate value of historic cob homes.

Many cob homes are sculptural works of art. This thatched cob house built by Mike Carter and Carol Cannon evokes the architecture of southern Africa, but it is actually located in Austin, Texas.

THE ENGLISH COB REVIVAL

The English place great value on tradition and take good care of their historical buildings. In recent decades many long-neglected cob homes have needed repair, causing a resurgence of interest in traditional building techniques. People involved in the restoration of ancient cob buildings have become the greatest advocates for the reintroduction of cob as a contemporary building technique. The first new construction project of the English cob revival was a bus shelter built by restorationist Alfred Howard in 1978. Since then there has been a slow increase of new cob built in England, particularly in Devon. Kevin McCabe received a lot of press in 1994 for his two-story, four-bedroom cob house, the first new cob residence to be built in England in perhaps 70 years.

The building technique of these revivalists closely resembles that of their ancestors. They mix Devon's sandy clay subsoil with water and straw and fork the mixture onto the wall, treading it in place. Walls are generally 24 inches (60 centimeters) thick and straight, applied in lifts up to 18 (45 centimeters) inches high. The machine age has altered the traditional process in only minor ways: McCabe and others use a tractor rather than oxen for mixing cob and often amend the subsoil with sand or 'shillet' — a fine gravel of crushed shale — to reduce shrinkage and cracking.

THE DEVELOPMENT OF 'OREGON COB'

Concurrent with the renewed interest in cob in England, there has been a parallel revival in the United States, led by the Cob Cottage Company in Western Oregon. With less access to traditional knowledge, the building system that has arisen here is sufficiently distinct from British cob that it merits a separate name: 'Oregon cob.'

By 1989, Cob Cottage Company founders Ianto Evans and Linda Smiley recognized the need for inexpensive, healthy, bioregional housing. Ianto grew up surrounded by cob in Wales and later took part in earthen construction in Africa and Latin America. Experimenting with earthen building in rainy Western Oregon, Ianto and Linda chose British cob as a model because of its demonstrated durability in a cold, wet climate.

When starting their first cob structure, Ianto and Linda were unable to locate anybody with first-hand experience. They relied entirely on their explorations of existing cob structures in Britain and a very sparse literature on the subject, much of it inaccurate and contradictory. The system they developed involved making loaves of stiff mud, called 'cobs' ('cob' itself is an Old English word for 'loaf'). The system has advantages: the mix can be made at some distance from the wall and easily transported by tossing the cobs from person to person as with a bucket brigade. As construction progresses, cobs can be thrown to a builder much higher on the wall than a pitchfork can be raised.

More recently, Oregon cob builders have shifted to a building technique we call 'Gaab cob,' which combines the control of hand-worked loaves with the speed of traditional trodden cob. Larger chunks of cob mix, stiff but still sticky and workable, are lifted onto the wall. By using either one's fingers or a wooden tool called a 'cobber's thumb,' the new material is married firmly to the wall beneath. The result is a strongly bonded, monolithic wall that should be considerably more resistant to earthquakes and other shear forces than traditional cob.

Another way in which Oregon cob differs from traditional cob is in the attention given to the quality of ingredients and to the proportions of the mix. Whereas cob builders in previous centuries had to use whatever soil was on hand with little or no amendment, we can now cheaply import as much sand or clay as is necessary to make the hardest, most stable mixture. Furthermore, whereas grain straw was formerly a valuable resource for animal bedding, thatching, and the like, it is now an under-utilized waste product available in huge quantities for little cost. Oregon cob is characterized by both a high proportion of coarse sand and lots of long, strong straw, which helps strengthen the earthen mass. Since soils vary so much from site to site, mix proportions should always be carefully tested before a wall is built.

This cob cottage in Dawlish, England, was built in 1523 and is still inhabited. Note the buttresses and traditional reed thatch roof.

Most Oregon cob is mixed by foot on a tarp. Wet or dry clay soil and sand are mixed by rolling the tarp back and forth; then water is added. Builders dance on the mix to forcibly combine the clay and sand particles. Straw is added slowly as the dancing continues and the tarp is rolled back and forth. Although the tarp method works well for many owner-builders, there is often a desire for increased mixing speed on large or contract-built projects. Many people have had good results with commercial mortar mixers. A tractor or backhoe can be used to mix very large batches, but then quality control is a challenge.

Better ingredients, more precise proportions, and thorough mixing allow the construction of stronger, narrower, and more sculptural walls. Exterior walls of Oregon cob are typically between 12 and 20 inches (30 and 48 centimeters) thick; non-load-bearing partitions taper to as little as 4 inches (10 centimeters) but are more commonly 8 inches (20 centimeters). Most Oregon cob buildings have curved walls, niches and nooks, and arched windows and doorways. By adding extra straw in the needed direction, the Cob Cottage Company developed a system for corbelling arches, vaults, and projecting shelves beyond the capability of traditional cob.

One quality which attracts many artists and owner-builders to cob is its extreme fluidity of form. Hand-formed from pliable mud, a cob cottage literally becomes a living sculpture. Cob combines nicely with other natural materials including stone, roundwood, and straw bales. Because of its capacity to stick to almost anything and to fill awkward gaps left by other materials, cob has been dubbed 'the duct tape of natural building.' Cob is one of the simplest and cheapest building techniques imaginable, making it particularly appealing to first-time builders. Since it requires no machinery, little training, and few tools, cob building is accessible to almost everyone, including children, the infirm, and the very poor. Many new cob buildings are created by community efforts similar to an old-time barn raising.

Since 1993, the Cob Cottage Company has taught scores of week-long training workshops throughout the United States and Canada, as well as in Australia, New Zealand, Mexico, and Denmark. We have trained hundreds of people in cob construction, some of whom have gone on to build homes for themselves or teach workshops of their own. These efforts have produced over 100 cob buildings. Since the cob revival is still in its infancy, the rate of new developments in technique has been astounding. In eight years we have doubled or tripled the speed and efficiency of manual mixing and building. Recent efforts have turned to making cob more thermally efficient for cold climates by combining it with more insulating materials like straw bales.

Careful detailing makes all the difference in any owner-built home. Jan Sturmann, the designer of this cob cottage in Massachusetts, has exquisitely blended cob, plaster, stone, and unmilled wood.

JAN STURMANN

The future of cob is difficult to predict. Due in part to the wide variability of soils from site to site and in part to the amount of labor required for manual mixing and building, cob has yet to make it into the North American mainstream. Nonetheless, in combination with other natural building materials, cob provides a real solution to many of the economic, social, and environmental problems associated with the modern building industry.

Michael G. Smith was a co-director of the Cob Cottage Company from 1993 to 1998. He is the author of The Cobber's Companion: How to Build Your Own Earthen Home *and coauthor of* Hand-Sculpted House: A Practical and Philosophical Guide to Building a Cob Cottage. *He teaches workshops on cob, natural building, and permaculture.*

DANNY GORDON

Buildings of unbaked earth can be astoundingly strong and durable. These cob and adobe towers in the city of Shibam, South Yemen, are up to ten stories high.

RESOURCES
Books

Bee, Becky. *The Cob Builder's Handbook: You Can Hand-Sculpt Your Own Home*. Groundworks, 1997. A clearly written step-by-step guidebook, including everything from design to plasters.

Cob Cottage Company, 1994. *A Cob Reader*. A collection of hard-to-find articles about historical cob and earthen building.

Evans, Ianto, Linda Smiley, and Michael G. Smith. *Hand-Sculpted House: A Practical and Philosophical Guide to Building a Cob Cottage*. Chelsea Green, 2002. The most comprehensive and up-to-date book on cob construction; with extensive new material on natural building philosophy, site considerations, and designing a compact, comfortable cottage; along with updated how-to information.

Norton, John. *Building with Earth*. Intermediate Technology Publications, 1997. A good, brief introduction to general principles of earth building.

Smith, Michael G. *The Cobber's Companion: How to Build Your Own Earthen Home*. 3rd ed. Cob Cottage Company, 2001. A well-illustrated and detailed step-by-step guide to every aspect of cob construction, including site selection, mixing and testing, windows, doors, roofs, floors, and plasters.

Periodicals

The CobWeb. Cob Cottage Company. P.O. Box 123, Cottage Grove, OR 97424, U.S.A.; phone/fax: 541-942-2005; website: www.deatech.com/cobcottage/. Newsletter of the Cob Cottage Company, published twice per year with inspirational stories, recent technical updates, and networking resources.

Videos

Building with Earth: Oregon's Cob Cottage Company. Inner Growth Videos, 1995. A brief, entertaining introduction to the 'whys' and 'hows' of cob. Available from the Cob Cottage Company.

Organizations

Cob Cottage Company. Workshops, consulting, mail-order books and videos, networking, and information on cob and other natural building systems.

Devon Earth Builders Association, 50 Blackboy Road, Exeter EX4 6TB, England. Dedicated to the research, promotion, and revival of traditional cob building in Devon. Publishes excellent informative pamphlets and a newsletter.

Groundworks, P.O. Box 381, Murphy, OR 97533, U.S.A.; website: www.cpros.com/-sequoia/workshop.html. Information, books, and workshops on cob, especially for women.

Compressed Earth Blocks

Wayne Nelson

Compressed Earth Block (CEB) is one term for earthen bricks compressed with hand-operated or motorized hydraulic machines. In many areas of the world, suitable materials are available for making CEB, and thus this type of block may be an excellent building choice. The decision to use CEB is dependent on several factors, including culture, labor force, and, most importantly, the preference of the homeowner.

There are hundreds of types of presses. Hand-operated presses have been used for many decades. Historically and even today, some people have made the blocks by beating soil into a wooden mold with a stick. Other presses are designed with simple levers, and since they are easily manufactured in local machine shops, they have seen widespread use in many countries. Some presses contain a variety of compression mechanisms such as cams, hand-operated hydraulic assists, toggles, and motorized hydraulics. As these presses are more complex and expensive, they have had less frequent use.

Modern equipment, with hydraulics driven by diesel, gas, or electric motors, may be useful in urban areas or for large multi-house sites. However, motor-driven equipment is less appropriate for smaller jobs and in rural areas. People in these situations are often the ones who need the most help with improving their housing, and manual compressed earth block machines offer a solution. Builders who have tried to use motorized presses without understanding the local economy have experienced significant problems with maintenance, the expense of fuel and spare parts, and the availability of the tools and expertise required for maintenance and repair.

ADVANTAGES

Compressed earth block construction offers uniform building components that use locally available materials, which reduces transportation cost. Uniformly sized building components can result in less waste, faster construction, and the possibility of using other pre-made modular building elements, such as sheet metal roofing.

The use of natural, locally available materials makes good housing available to more people and keeps money in the local economy, rather than sending it off in exchange for materials, fuel, and replacement parts. The earth used is generally subsoil, leaving topsoil for agriculture. Building with local materials can employ local people and is more sustainable in times of civil unrest or economic difficulties, as good shelters can be built regardless of the political situation of the country.

The reduction of transportation time, cost, and attendant pollution can also make CEB more environmentally friendly than other materials. Soil for CEB can usually be found on-site or within a short distance. In most of the world's economies, cost-effective transportation is often that provided by people or animals. In Ghana, for instance, small wagons are built with old car wheels and tires. It is less expensive to have a few people move wagonloads of cement and sand a couple of miles than to hire a bus, truck, or tractor, because the latter are dependent on fuel and parts purchased from economies outside the local community.

INNOVATIONS

Over time, CEB manufacture has seen some interesting innovations. One was to change the shape of the block from a solid rectangle to one that incorporates holes or grooves that will allow for the insertion of mortar and steel or bamboo for earthquake resistance. Another was to create interlocking shapes that don't need to be laid in a bed of mortar; yet another was to create U-shapes and tapered bricks for use in reinforced lintels and arches. Some machines even make tiles for floors and roofs. Sometimes a press is used to make bricks, which are then fired in a kiln — although once fired they are no longer referred to as CEBs.

CATHERINE WANEK

A compressed earth block home constructed at the Habitat II conference in Istanbul.

The interlocking shapes of the improved bricks help to reduce the skill level needed by owner-builders and allows for several layers of blocks to be placed in the wall at a time. A supervisor checks that a wall is straight and plumb, and then mortar is poured into the hollow blocks to lock them together and eliminate gaps which would otherwise allow air infiltration.

My favorite hand-operated press is the 'TEK' from the University of Science and Technology in Ghana. The TEK ram is simple and inexpensive. (There is a similar French machine which is great and simple to operate as well, but it costs ten times as much. Both machines create a CEB block using only one operation.) I like the size of the brick from this press, as it is bigger than most. It measures 12 by 9 by 6 inches (30 by 23 by 15 centimeters). Wall thickness can be made to correspond to any of the three dimensions simply by turning the block. Bigger blocks mean fewer elements to move around during construction, which speeds up the process.

Auroville architects adapted this simple hand press to create compressed earth blocks with a variety of interlocking designs. Faster hydraulic machines do exist, but they are far more expensive to buy, run, and maintain.

SATPREM MAÏNI

THE EARTH MIX

There are several simple publications on selecting earth and using a press. Volunteers in Technical Assistance (VITA) has a good one, as do some machine manufacturers. The UN has simple soil-testing information, and many universities can help test soils as well. However, there is nothing like experience to tell how the soil will work, and many indigenous folks know which local soils are good for building. If you are on your own, look at road cuts or riverbanks to see how different soil types resist erosion. If the soil resists erosion well, it could be a good building material.

There are two simple soil tests that I like to use to determine the proper soil mixture. For the first test, fill a clear, straight-sided jar half full of soil, add water until the jar is three-quarters full, and add a pinch of salt. Cap the jar tightly and shake it up until the soil is in suspension; it is good to let it soak for a few minutes and then shake the solution again to get it mixed well. Normally, layers of different particle sizes will form as everything settles, a process that will take a few minutes to a few hours. The large particles on the bottom of the jar will be sand; then silt will settle out, and finally a clay layer will form on top. Mark the height of each layer to make a rough calculation of the percentages of each material. With hand presses 10 percent clay is a minimum amount to make strong blocks.

For the second soil test, fill a form 2 feet long by 1-$\frac{1}{2}$ inches wide by 1-$\frac{1}{2}$ inches high (0.6 meters long by 4 centimeters wide by 4 centimeters high) with moist soil. Wait a week, letting it dry in the shade. Once the soil sample is dry, you will notice a gap between the end of the block and the inside of the box. The less shrinkage, the better the soil. Acceptable shrinkage is less than 2 inches (5 centimeters) and preferably $\frac{1}{4}$ inch (6 millimeters) or less. If you have a lot of shrinkage, indicating a high clay soil, add sand to make a better mix. A very expansive soil should be rejected for building after this test, but soils nearby or deeper in the ground may have suitable, less expansive clays.

The stability of the clay can also be observed by placing the brick in a bucket of water after it is compressed and seeing how quickly the clay will expand. Placing a stabilized, well-cured brick in a bucket of water can be a great way to demonstrate its water resistance to those who doubt that soil can be used to build a good house.

STABILIZERS

Stabilizers such as cement, gypsum, lime, and asphalt emulsion have all been used in the body or on the surface of bricks. Sometimes it is less costly to make a soil block with no cement and then to use cement mortar and a cement plaster. (Cement plaster doesn't stick well to unstabilized earth bricks, so the mortar joint is necessary to hold the plaster.) Natural earth plasters can also be used on unstabilized walls. Wide roof overhangs will help protect earthen plasters from wear; still these plasters may require maintenance on a regular basis, in the same way that you give your house a fresh coat of paint. (See "Earth Plasters and Aliz.")

When using cement stabilizers, it is very important to cure the bricks slowly. This may mean watering twice a day for a couple of weeks and covering the wall with plastic or leaves to keep the sun and wind off and the moisture in. Cement cures with water, so letting it dry too quickly, especially during the first week or two of curing, reduces its strength. Blocks without stabilizers should also be dried in the shade to avoid rapid drying, which may cause cracking.

It is important to make sure that the stabilizer is mixed thoroughly with the earth. I recommend using a garden rake, rather than a shovel, because it breaks up lumps of dirt, spreads the water through the mix more easily, and mixes more thoroughly.

PRODUCTION

Moisture content distinguishes CEB from other earth building techniques. People often have experience with concrete or adobe, which are mixed much wetter. The moisture content of a good CEB mix is so minimal that it never really seems wet. Take a handful of CEB mix and squeeze it into a ball as tight as you can. If the mix stays in a ball when you open your hand, then the moisture content is good. If it falls apart, then you need to wet it more. Once you have a ball that stays together in your hand, drop it from your waist to the ground. If it flattens but sticks together when it hits the ground, then it is too wet. If it shatters into dozens of pieces, then it's too dry. If the mix is just right, then it should retain much of its spherical shape, while breaking into several parts.

When a block machine compresses a block, it reduces the volume by 30 percent. It does this by mechanically aligning the moist clay particles, removing the air pockets, and sticking the clay to the sand. If too much water is in the mix, then there will be more air space between the particles when the brick dries. This reduces strength and thermal mass; the surface is more porous and less resistant to water and scratches. If there is more clay than is needed to fill the spaces between the sand particles, then the block becomes weaker because clay compresses more than sand, especially when wet.

How fast can you make blocks and begin building? Efficient workers using hand presses can make 500 bricks a day, perhaps producing all the bricks for the walls of a modest house in one week. A hydraulic machine can make all the blocks for a large house in a day if you can feed the soil to it fast enough.

After they are pressed, blocks are set aside to cure. If you are using hand-operated presses, then it is best not to stack the blocks on top of each other the first day. You should handle them as little as possible so as not to knock off the fragile corners. The next day the blocks can be stacked several layers high to make room for the next batch. It is also possible to place bricks directly in the wall, either dry-stacked or mortared; with enough people and the right equipment, the walls of a simple house can be completed in a day.

Most people who build with earth find it quite enjoyable. It can be just plain fun to make your house from the earth under your feet.

Wayne Nelson works with Habitat for Humanity's Department of the Environment and is an international provider of construction information and training. Trained as a carpenter and builder, he has experience creating shelters with compressed earth blocks in Africa and other countries.

RESOURCES
Books

Houben, Hugo, and Hubert Guillaud. *Earth Construction: A Comprehensive Guide*. Intermediate Technology Publications, 1994. This detailed, well-illustrated technical guide to many forms of earthen building contains good information on CEB. The authors are from CRATerre, and the book focuses on disaster-resistant earthen building for developing countries.

Norton, John. *Building with Earth*. Intermediate Technology Publications, 1997. A good, brief introduction to general principles of earth building, including production and testing of CEBs.

Organizations

CRATerre, Maison Levrat, Rue de Lac B.P. 53, F-38092 Villefontaine Cedex, France;   phone: 33-474-954391; fax: 33-474-956421; email: craterre@club-internet.fr; website: www.craterre.archi.fr. Professional school of earth architecture, engineering, and construction, especially for developing nations; excellent technical publications.

Auroville Building Centre, Earth Unit Auroshilpam, 605 101 Auroville, Tamil Nadu, India; phone: 91-4136-2168/2277; fax: 91-4136-2057; email: csr@auroville.org.in; website: www.auroville.org. Research, publications, and information on earth building for development, especially with compressed earth blocks.

Cordwood Masonry: An Overview

Rob Roy

ORDWOOD MASONRY is a technique by which buildings are constructed of short logs — sometimes called 'log ends' — laid up transversely in the wall, much as a rank of firewood is stacked. The walls consist of an inner mortar joint, an outer mortar joint, and an insulated space in between. The log ends are structural, tying the two mortar matrixes together.

Despite a continuous history of at least 250 years, cordwood masonry remains the best-kept secret of the natural building movement. And those few people who have heard of the technique often aren't aware of its compelling '5-E' advantages: economy, ease of construction, energy-efficiency, esthetics, and environmental harmony.

ECONOMY

Because cordwood masonry can make use of so-called junk wood unsuitable for milling, the cost of structural wall materials can be extremely low in forested bioregions. When cob mortar is used, the cost can be next to nothing if both wood and suitable earth are available on-site. As the log ends are typically 8 to 24 inches (20 to 60 centimeters) in length, suitable pieces can be derived from fire- or disease-killed wood, logging slash, driftwood, sawmill scrap, even pieces left over from log cabin manufacturers and furniture makers. Insulation cost is also very low, as lime-treated sawdust is the typical insulation of choice. My wife Jaki and I insulated our 2,000-square-foot (183-square-meter) Earthwood house for US$75 worth of sawdust, delivered.

EASE OF CONSTRUCTION

My favorite gag line is that children, grandmothers, and beavers can (and all do) build cordwood masonry buildings. It wouldn't be so funny if it wasn't so true. If you can stack wood, you can build a cordwood home. With many cordwood homes, the heaviest lift in the wall-making process might be a 20-pound (9-kilogram) log end or, perhaps, a window frame.

ENERGY EFFICIENCY

Cordwood masonry combines insulation and thermal mass in a wonderful way. The key is the insulated mortar matrix, and it surprises many people to learn that the superior thermal characteristics of a cordwood wall are found in the mortared portion. Mortar makes up about 40 percent of the total wall area, the log-ends about 60 percent, although these figures can easily go up or down by 10 percent, depending on the skill and style of the mason.

The Earthwood Building School where Rob and Jaki Roy demonstrate cordwood and other natural building techniques.

Insulation values of wood, on end grain, vary from approximately R-0.5 to R-1.0 per inch, with dense hardwoods toward the bottom of the insulation list and light and airy woods, such as Eastern white cedar, at the top. The wooden parts of our 16-inch-thick (40-centimeter-thick) white cedar walls at Earthwood have a theoretical value of about R-16. The calculation for the mortared portion is: 6 inches (15 centimeters) of sawdust at R-3/inch = R-18, plus a nominal R-2 assigned to each mortar joint, totaling about R-22. The theoretical average R-value of such a cordwood wall would be about R-19. In an actual test, done to Canadian national testing standards, a 24-inch (60-centimeter) section of cordwood masonry, composed of mixed woods and having 12 inches (30 centimeters) of sawdust insulation, was found to have an insulative value of R-24.

ROB ROY

However, insulation is only part of the story. Equally important is the great thermal mass of both the log ends and the mortar joints. The entire mass of the inner mortar joint is correctly placed on the warm side of the insulation for winter heat storage and summer cooling. Thus, thanks to this wonderful juxtaposition of insulation and mass, cordwood homes stay a steady comfortable temperature, summer and winter.

ESTHETICS

Jaki and I were first drawn to cordwood masonry by its appearance, which combines the warmth of wood with the texture of fine stone masonry. We soon discovered that all sorts of special design features, including shelves, patterns, and 'bottle-ends,' could be incorporated into a cordwood wall. Some cordwood homes are sculptural works of art. And the work is fun!

ENVIRONMENTAL HARMONY

Cordwood masonry makes good use of indigenous and recycled materials: wood, sand, sawdust, even bottles. Although we have had good success over the past quarter-century with Portland cement mortar mixes, some natural builders may object to the environmental impact of cement. I will not argue the point. There are pros and cons too numerous to list here. But those who can not or will not use Portland will be glad to know that a cordwood wall can also be built with cob instead of cement mortar. When such a home finally gives up the ghost — after hundreds of years if it is built right — it will simply recede gracefully into the landscape whence it came.

THREE BUILDING STYLES

Cordwood masonry houses come in three distinct styles and various hybrids of these styles. They are (1) cordwood infill within a post and beam frame, (2) stackwall (or built-up) corners, with regular cordwood masonry between the corners, and (3) curved wall or round houses, such as Earthwood. With the first style, the timber frame supports the load, but in the other styles, the cordwood masonry itself is load-bearing.

The stackwall corners method, popular in Canada where 24-inch-thick (60-centimeter-thick) walls are common, involves building up the corners first with regular units (called 'quoins'), such as six-by-six timbers or quartered logs. The quoins are crisscrossed on alternate courses, and my guess is that the technique evolved from a similar stacking method used to support the ends of firewood ranks. After stackwall corners are built up, say, 3 feet (1 meter), a mason's line is stretched from corner to corner and the sidewalls are built in the regular way. A typical 8-foot-high (2-meter-high) wall can be built in three lifts by this method.

FREQUENTLY ASKED QUESTIONS

Here are the three most frequently asked questions that we have heard at Earthwood Building School over the past 20 years.

Won't the wood rot?

No. But to understand why, you have to know about the critters that cause rot in the first place — fungi that literally digest the wood. Fungi need air, food, and moist conditions to propagate. With cordwood masonry, which breathes along end grain, the wall may get wet in a driving rainstorm, but it very quickly dries out again, and fungi cannot get a foothold. The Mecikalski Store in Jennings, Wisconsin — now a museum — was built over 100 years ago and the log ends are still in excellent condition. Many cordwood homes and barns built in the middle of the 19th century in Wisconsin, Canada, and Sweden, are also still in good condition.

ROB ROY

A 'stackwall' corner, with regular cordwood masonry built up between the crisscrossed 'quoins.'

To cover my bets, I recommend four simple rules: (1) Use only sound wood with the bark removed. (2) Do not allow two log ends to touch each other, as this could trap moisture. (3) Use a good overhang of at least 16 inches (40 centimeters) all around the building. And (4) keep the cordwood masonry at least 4 inches (10 centimeters) clear of the ground, supported by a rot-proof foundation, such as block or stone masonry, concrete footings, a floating slab, or railroad ties supported on a gravel berm or a rubble trench.

What kind of wood should be used?

Short answer: Use what you've got. If there is a choice, though, it is better to go with the lighter, airier woods, such as white cedar, spruce, loblolly pine, and poplar, than the harder denser woods like oak, hard maple, beech, or southern pine. The lighter woods have better insulation value, but, perhaps more importantly, they are more stable, with less tendency to shrink or expand. With the preferred woods, it is good to air-dry them in single ranks, covered, a full year before using them. With the dense woods, there is a danger of wood expansion if the log ends are seasoned too long, so just cut and bark them, split them if desired, and dry them for only a few weeks before use. They will probably shrink in the wall, but they will do that anyway, even if you dry them for a year.

Wood shrinkage is only a temporary cosmetic problem, not structural, and after a year or two, the shrinkage gaps (if they occur) can be filled cheaply, easily, and beautifully by a method developed by Geoff Huggins of Winchester, Virginia. Geoff fills the shrinkage gaps with any cheap caulk. Then, while the caulk is still gooey, he presses a slurry of mortar into the caulk with a half-inch-wide (1.25-centimeter-wide) brush. The slurry is the same mix as was used on the mortar joints but thinned with extra water. In about 20 minutes, Geoff has a virtually invisible repair.

What is the best mortar mix?

A full discussion of mortar mixes is not possible here, but I will share a mix that has stood the test of time at Earthwood for over 20 years: 9 parts sand, 3 parts sawdust, 3 parts lime, 2 parts Portland cement. The sand should be fine, not coarse, to retain plasticity and to allow good smooth 'pointing' (also called 'grouting').

The sawdust is used to retard the set of the mortar, thus reducing mortar shrinkage and cracking. To accomplish this, the sawdust must be of the light and airy variety, as described previously, and needs to be passed through a ½-inch (1.25-centimeter) screen to remove bark and chunks of wood. The sawdust is then soaked — at least overnight — in an open vessel such as a 55-gallon (250-liter) drum, and introduced wet into the mix. Oak and other hardwood sawdust do not seem to work, and the worst thing you can do is to put unsoaked sawdust into the mix, as this accelerates rather than retards the set of the mix. If the right kind of sawdust cannot be obtained locally, it is safer to go with a commercially available cement retarder such as Daratard-17 (W.R. Grace & Co.) or Plastiment (Sika Corporation). Leave out the sawdust and add an extra shovelful of sand to replace the missing bulk.

Lime is used to make the mix more plastic (workable) and to add strength. Use builder's lime, also called 'slaked lime,' 'Type S,' or 'hydrated lime'. Do not use agricultural lime, intended for lawn and garden use; it will not calcify.

And water? Add just enough to make a good stiff mix. We use a 'snowball test.' Throw a snowball-sized ball three or four feet (about a meter) in the air. It should not splatter when you catch it (too wet) nor should it crumble apart (too dry). Only with the correct consistency can you juggle two or three

MICHAEL G. SMITH

snowballs. In masonry parlance, you want stiff — yet plastic — 'stone' mortar, not the thinner mortar used for brickwork.

COBWOOD

Over the past few years, several people around the world have been experimenting with using cob instead of cement mortar. The early returns on these projects are very encouraging. Tony Wrench in Wales has been living in his lovely cordwood and cob round house for four years. Beautiful work has also been done by Steen Møller in Denmark. In late 2000, Jaki and I collaborated on cobwood building with Ianto Evans and Linda Smiley of Cob Cottage Company, both at Earthwood in August and at the Natural Building Colloquium in Kingston, New Mexico in November. We have learned that we can substitute Oregon cob, as described elsewhere in this book, for the mortar. We found that the cob points quite well with our regular pointing knives. Another option is to apply a finer cob plaster to a recessed mortar joint later on for a pleasing finish.

Cordwood has traditionally been mortared together with a cement or lime mix, but in this wall at Sandy Bar Ranch in Northern California, cobbers experimented with a mud mortar.

From a cordwood masonry perspective, the advantage of cob is that no Portland cement is needed; walls can be built entirely of indigenous materials. From a cob builder's perspective, the log ends save one heckuva lot of cob mixing. The insulated space should still be retained for energy efficiency, particularly in the north, and this further reduces cob mixing.

Is 'cobwood' really a new development? Probably not. My guess is that we are just returning to the cordwood masonry of a thousand years ago, when the use of clay as a binder was much more likely than the use of lime mortars. In this scenario, cordwood masonry may simply be coming full circle.

Rob Roy is director of Earthwood Building School, which he cofounded with his wife Jaki in 1980. He has written and edited several books on cordwood masonry, including The Complete Book of Cordwood Masonry Housebuilding: The Earthwood Method.

Resources

Books

Chiras, Daniel. *The Natural House: A Complete Guide to Healthy, Energy-Efficient, Environmental Homes.* Chelsea Green, 2000. Contains a good introductory chapter on cordwood, along with many other alternative building systems.

Flatau, Richard. *Cordwood Construction: A Log-End View.* Quality Print, 1983. Available from Earthwood Building School.

Henstridge, Jack. *About Building Cordwood.* Self-published. Available from the author at RR 1, Oromocto, New Brunswick, Canada E2V 2G2.

Roy, Rob. *The Complete Book of Cordwood Masonry Housebuilding: The Earthwood Method.* Sterling, 1992. The most complete guide to the technique, along with useful information on many other topics of interest to the owner-builder, including masonry stoves and solar greenhouses. Available from Earthwood Building School.

Videos

Basic Cordwood Masonry Techniques. 1995. In-depth how-to introduction with Rob and Jaki Roy, showing every step of the wall building process. Available from Earthwood Building School.

Cordwood Homes. 2000. A tour of seven cordwood houses, featuring interviews with owner-builders and experts. Available from Earthwood Building School.

Organizations

Earthwood Building School, 366 Murtagh Hill Road, West Chazy, NY 12992, U.S.A.; phone: 518-493-7744; website: www.cordwoodmasonry.com. Offers workshops, mail-order books and videos, and consulting on cordwood masonry, earth-sheltered construction, mortgage freedom, and stone circles.

Today's natural builders look to ancient structures like these for inspiration. Every indigenous culture developed a vernacular building tradition using available materials in response to the local climate.

BETTY WANEK

JOSEPH F. KENNEDY

Top: The Greek village of Santorini was built of local stone, plastered and white-washed with lime. White walls and roofs help deflect the heat of the Mediterranean sun.

Left: At the UN sponsored Habitat II conference in Istanbul in 1996, a builder from Harran, Turkey demonstrates the traditional method of mortaring adobes into a corbelled dome. Some of the adobe bricks he is using are 2000 years old.

Lower left: The St. Francis Church in Ranchos de Taos, New Mexico, was built of adobe bricks in 1815. The massive earthen walls and structural buttresses create a dramatic exterior, and a cool, comfortable interior in this desert climate.

JOSEPH F. KENNEDY

CATHERINE WANEK

Lower right: This Troglodyte or "cave dweller" home is carved into the soft lime-stone strata of the Loire Valley, France. Earth-coupled dwellings are sheltered from seasonal temperature changes.

Stone is among the oldest and most durable of all building materials, and it is still widely used today. Stone buildings from different cultures are visually distinct, whether dry-stacked or mortared, rough or finely worked.

Top left: this shepherd's hut in Sardinia is one of the simplest buildings imaginable. The entire structure is made of stones stacked upon each other, without mortar.

JOSEPH F. KENNEDY

CATHERINE WANEK

Top right: Although recently built, this dry-stacked stone wall at the Centre for Appropriate Technology in Wales uses age-old techniques.

Bottom right: The stones in this farmhouse in Brittany, France, have been individually shaped. Stones are utilized for door and window lintels, and the slate tile roof.

CATHERINE WANEK

Timber framing, which relies on the strength of intricate wood-on-wood connections (no nails, screws, or bolts) evolved in both Europe and Asia. Panels in the frame may be filled with various materials, including wattle and daub, adobe, fired brick, straw-clay or straw bales.

Top: For many centuries in Europe, timber frame homes with fired-brick infill were a sign of wealth, while peasants lived mainly in cob, or earthen, houses. This historic Danish house has been maintained in its original condition, including the thatched roof.

Lower left: Welsh furniture-maker David Hughes is constructing this whimsical workshop for himself, from oak logs rejected by conventional builders.

Center right: Nearly a lost art, thatching is being revived by determined craftsmen like David Hughes, who must harvest their reeds in the dead of winter.

Lower Right: Historic timber frame buildings in Vannes, France, utilize a straw-clay infill. The hydrophillic clay helps preserve both the wood and the straw, and the overhanging upper floors divert rain away from the building, and pedestrians below.

CATHERINE WANEK

Living roofs like these help connect the building to its site, both visually and ecologically. They also protect the building from summer heat, provide habitat for birds and insects, and can even yield an edible crop!

Top: The roof of Thierry Dronet's workshop in France is planted with perennial herbs and ornamentals. The walls are of plastered straw bales and cordwood masonry. (see cover for front view.)

Bottom: The sanctuary at Hollyhock retreat center in British Columbia, Canada, is truly a 'hybrid' natural building. The foundation is of local stone, the structural framework of driftwood logs gathered from the nearby beach, and the walls of cob and cordwood, with earthen plasters and a heated adobe floor.

CATHERINE WANEK

GORDON BROWNE

Contemporary natural building involves the harmonius blending of traditional materials from all over the globe with modern design strategies. The results are beautiful, innovative, and sustainable.

CATHERINE WANEK

CATHERINE WANEK

Top: In Sonora, Mexico the straw-clay courtyard walls of the Save the Children office building are shaded by traditional palm-thatched ramadas.

Center: Andre and Coralie de Bouter enjoy the south-facing patio at Steen Møller's owner-built home. Steen combined rammed earth trombe walls with passive solar design to create a handsome thatched-roof home near Sondre Felding, Denmark.

Below right: All the timber was milled locally, and cob made from local clay mortars together Steen Møller's beautiful log-end wall.

CATHERINE WANEK

Top: Anne-Marie Warburton acted as general contractor for her family's 2,500 square foot, post and beam home in the Hockley Valley, Ontario. The framing was done by professionals and the straw bale walls were raised by volunteers.

Center: The Sanctuary House in Crestone, Colorado shelters visitors inside sturdy straw bale walls, offering a peaceful respite.

Straw bale construction, invented in Nebraska a century ago, has gained international prominence as one of the most successful modern natural building techniques. An agricultural waste product, straw bales provide solid walls and superior insulation.

JOHN MARROW

CATHERINE WANEK

Bottom: In "The Butterfly House," Dutch homeowner Jan Sonneveld created a structure that seems like it could take flight, from earth-bound straw bales and lime plaster.

CATHERINE WANEK

Integrating straw bale insulation with interior thermal mass materials creates a comfortable human environment and inviting aesthetic possibilities.

Top left: Straw bales offered New Mexico builder Tony Perry a sculptable surface, which he personalized with inviting niches and window seats.

Top right: Sun streams in through south-facing windows, warming the adobe bancos and stained concrete floor of the Hughes/Rhoades straw-bale home in Santa Fe, New Mexico.

Lower left: Athena and Bill Steen's guest house in Canelo, Arizona shows how decorations and furniture can be as simple and elegant as polished clay.

Lower right: Clerestory windows bring daylight into this living space, saving energy and brightening the ambiance in the Butterfly House, The Netherlands.

Top right: In an annual ritual, community members prepare a clay plaster to touch up the adobe church in Ranchos de Taos, New Mexico. Built in 1815, this historic structure was almost destroyed by the application of cement stucco in 1967.

T here are an enormous range of finishing options for natural buildings, many of which are cheap, easy, non-toxic, beautiful, durable, and fun.

Top left: The inside of Sun Ray Kelley's cob yoga studio in Washington State sports a colorful aliz (clay-slip finish) over earthen plaster. Stabilized with flour paste and made sparkly by the addition of mica flakes, aliz can be mixed up with safe ingredients in your kitchen, then painted on with a brush.

Lower left: Earthen plasters can be made from most local soils and applied with bare hands. This clay plaster in Nova Scotia protects the straw bale wall beneath from fire, moisture, and pests.

Lower right: Bill Steen demonstrates an essential step in natural plastering — testing samples of various mixes for color, texture, hardness and durability.

CATHERINE WANEK

NYGEL FUSELLA

JOSEPH F. KENNEDY

CATHERINE WANEK

Building with Earthbags

Joseph F. Kennedy

EARTHBAG CONSTRUCTION has recently emerged as an important technique in the natural building movement. Sandbags have, of course, been used for many decades by military forces to create bunkers and other structures and for temporary walls by archeologists. In recent years, however, the earthbag technique has been advanced by Persian architect Nader Khalili. He and his students and associates have built a number of prototype structures at his school and research center, the California Institute of Earth Art and Architecture (Cal-Earth). Building with bags emerged out of Khalili's exploration of how to build structures on the moon and Mars. His vision was to create domed and vaulted buildings of site-woven sacks filled with lunar soil to save the immense costs of rocketing building materials from the Earth. I was working with Khalili at the time and helped to build our initial lunar prototype structures using flood control sacks that we obtained from the local fire station.

The technique is essentially flexible-form rammed earth. It is literally dirt cheap, as it uses locally available site soil and polypropylene or burlap sacks, which often can be obtained free or at low cost. It demands few skills, is easy to learn, and can go extremely quickly, much faster than any other manual earth-building technique. Earthbag construction is adaptable to a wide range of site conditions and available fill materials. When built properly, earthbag structures — especially domes — are extremely strong, as shown by recent ICBO testing. While some structures have proven resistant to earthquakes, fires, and floods, additional testing is necessary to determine the most appropriate detailing. As the bags themselves are lightweight and easily transported, they are useful for remote locations and as emergency shelter.

MATERIALS

The essential material in building with earthbags is, of course, the bags themselves, which are commonly made of polypropylene. Woven polypropylene sacks come in a variety of sizes for grain, feed, and flood control and also come in a tube form, which is much cheaper to buy per foot. Burlap sacks have also been used but are not as durable and are often more expensive. I have used custom-sewn bags for an art piece in Prague, and site-sewn custom bags can easily be made using bent nails or wire.

The other essential material is the fill, which may include sand, clay, pumice, and/or gravel. While an ideal mixture would be a standard adobe mix of sand and clay, pretty much any subsoil can be used. The fill can be used either wet or dry, but moistening it creates a more stable structure.

The California Institute of Earth Art and Architecture, founded by Nader Khalili. The domes in the foreground are made of fired brick; the one in the distance of earthbags.

Steve Kemble and Carol Escott have used decomposed coral in the Bahamas with excellent results.

The most important consideration for bag choice is the kind of fill. The weaker the fill material, the stronger the bag must be. In some cases, once a strong (high-clay) fill material has set, exposed parts of the bags can be removed or allowed to deteriorate without any loss of structural integrity. On the other hand, if a weak material such as sand is used, it is essential that the bags be kept integral and plastered as soon as possible to protect them from deterioration due to ultraviolet solar radiation.

Additional materials include barbed wire, used to keep the bags from slipping, and regular wire, used to tie the bags together. For extremely strong structures, cement can be added to the fill to create soil-cement. Old nails and fencing staples are often used to pin bags closed, create new shapes, and keep barbed wire in place.

PROCESS

The process of building with earthbags is quite simple. The site is first prepared; often a rubble trench foundation is used as a base for bags. Material removed during excavation can be saved to fill the bags, setting aside topsoil and organic materials.

JOSEPH F. KENNEDY

The fill material is then prepared by removing large rocks and sticks from the subsoil. For short non-structural walls, this soil can be used dry, but for structural purposes, the fill material is evenly moistened and left overnight. The material should be made wet enough to compact well. In moist climates the first couple of rows are filled with gravel to preclude vertical wicking of water into the wall.

Necessary tools are easily available or constructed. The basics are a shovel, wheelbarrow, and tamper. A tamper is essential to compact the bags once they are in place. For sufficient compression, the face of the tamper should be no more than 5 inches by 5 inches (12 centimeters by 12 centimeters), and as heavy as the person tamping can handle. They are often made of welded steel or wood. A good homemade tamper can be made from a quart yogurt container filled will concrete attached to a stout staff. A large coffee can is handy for tossing soil up to those working higher on the wall. The longer tube-shaped bags are filled easily using inserted tubes of cardboard or PVC.

The bags can be filled in several ways. They can be partially filled using a homemade stand or by one person holding the bag while another fills it. The bags can then be moved into position and filled completely. Large bags can be filled in place from a wheelbarrow. Bags higher on the wall can be filled using shovels or cans. It is preferable to fill the bags in position in order to avoid having to pick up and move the heavy bag. Tubular bags can be filled from both ends by placing soil in the end, then picking up the ends of the tube and shifting the soil to the middle of the bag. To avoid straining your back, tubes should be no longer than 20 feet (6 meters). Another technique is to gather the tubular bag around a 1- to 2-foot (0.3- to 0.6- meter) length of pipe that holds the bag open and allows the bag to be let out gradually as it is filled. A mechanical pump can make these filling processes extremely fast and easy.

Before the bags are filled, their bottom corners are poked in, squaring the bag ends. This process produces a more uniform wall surface, minimizing the use of plaster. The bags are gently laid into place before being tamped. The first bag in a row is usually pinned securely, and subsequent bags are folded closed and laid down with the folded end butted up to the factory-sewn end of the previous bag — much easier than sewing each bag closed. It is important not to overfill the bag in order to get a secure fold. Once a row of bags is laid, they are checked for plumb or properly placed in the ring of a dome, adjusted if need be, then gently pressed into place by standing on them. The tamper is used for final compaction.

It is important to lay the bags in a 'running bond' as with bricks; the joints of the previous row are covered by the bags of the next row. In earthquake prone areas, a strand or two of barbed wire is laid between courses to keep the bags from

Procedure for laying an earthbag wall.

Put bag in place on wall. Fill with soil or gravel. 'Diddle' bottom corners of bag.

'Diddle'

Fold Bag. Lean gently into position. Adjust if necessary.

Gently tamp bag with feet.

Lay down barbed wire or dimple with sledge hammer as shown.

Compress bag using tamper.

JOSEPH F. KENNEDY

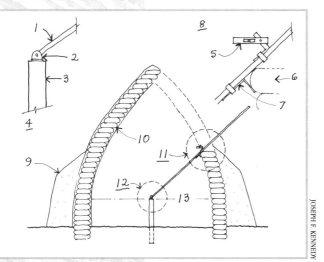

JOSEPH F. KENNEDY

Creating a corbelled earthbag dome with the help of a compass.

1. *Steel/Aluminum Pole*
2. *Caster*
3. *4 x 4 Post*
4. *Detail A*
5. *Level*
6. *Earth Bag*
7. *Extendable Guide*
8. *Detail B*
9. *Buttress*
10. *Corbelled Bags*
11. *Detail B*
12. *Detail A*
13. *Spring Line*

slipping. The wire can be held in place using nails. Another way to keep the bags from slipping is to interlock them by pounding a 'dimple' into each bag, creating a void which will be filled when the bag above is placed.

STRUCTURAL CONSIDERATIONS

Different structural issues arise depending on how the bags are used. In foundations, for instance, bags should be filled with gravel to at least a foot above grade, with the top row relatively level to receive the wall material (straw bales, adobe, wood, etc.). Retaining walls can be built with bags, but it is important to provide drainage behind the wall and to make sure that the bags are properly secured against slipping. Leaning the wall against the bank ('battering') improves stability, as does compacting the tops of the bags such that each slopes back toward the earth bank.

Small openings (1 foot [0.3 meters] or less) can be created by spanning the opening with a lintel of wood or metal. A common way to build windows and door openings is to build an arch over a rigid form. The gothic and catenary arch forms have been found to be much more stable than hemispherical arches. When creating arches it is crucial to fill the bags in place and to tamp them to create wedge shapes, which will not slip when the form is removed. Small vaults for door openings have been built with earthbags, but larger vaults are probably not practical.

A special use for the earthbag technique is to make domed structures. A simple, rotating guide (see illustration) makes this simple. The only really practical dome has a pointed or catenary shape and is built on a round base with supporting buttress. Kelly Hart built an oval dome but encountered structural problems that required additional support. (See "An Earthbag-Papercrete House.") It is important to lay the bags in corbels (each ring is flat) in order to prevent slippage in the upper rings. Hemispherical domes are impossible without additional formwork and are not advised. Over small spans, earthbags can be easily used to create 'free-form' domes and arch shapes. A direction worth pursuing is to make domes using bags filled with a straw-clay mixture (as was done with the roof of the first Cal-Earth dome) or pumice (by Kelly Hart), in order to reduce weight and provide good insulation.

PLASTERING

It is important to plaster a structure built with polypropylene bags as soon as possible, as their worst enemy is sunlight. The bags can be protected with a scratch coat as they are built. Sticks laid between bags can also be useful to key the plaster.

To date, mud plasters have been most commonly used on earthbag structures. When using lime/sand or cement plasters, lath may be desirable. Strings laid between bag courses could be a convenient attachment point for such lath. Domes should be plastered with a cement or lime-based plaster and thoroughly waterproofed except in the driest areas, where mud plaster could be possible. Kelly Hart's intriguing house in Colorado utilized fibrous cement (paper pulp mixed with sand and cement) as a plaster. (See "An Earthbag-Papercrete House.") As all these techniques are experimental, plastering is a subject that needs much additional research.

Joseph F. Kennedy is an architect, writer and peripatetic scholar of natural building and ecological design. A former student of Nader Khalili, he teaches earthbag construction as well as other natural building techniques.

RESOURCES

Books

Elizabeth, Lynne, and Cassandra Adams, eds. *Alternative Construction: Contemporary Natural Building Methods.* John Wiley and Sons, 2000. Includes a thorough introductory article on earthbag construction.

Wojciechowska, Paulina. *Building with Earth — A Guide to Flexible Form Earthbag Construction.* Foreword by Bill and Athena Steen. Chelsea Green, 2001. This book teaches the basics of earthbag construction: how to design and build rounded forms — including arches, vaults, domes, and apses; shows a method for building essentially 'tree-free' structures, from foundation to roof; and explains how to combine earthbags with conventional and ecological building techniques.

Organizations

Cal-Earth, 10376 Shangri La Avenue, Hesperia, CA 92345, U.S.A.; phone: 760-244-0614; fax: 760-244-2201; website: www.calearth.org. Research and teaching center where many of the advances in earthbag construction have been made.

Earth, Hands & Houses, Paulina Wojciechowska, 18 The Willows, Byfleet, Surrey KT14-7QY, England; e-mail: EHaH@excite.co.uk. Ecological design, alternative and conventional building and construction methods, consultation, workshops, with a special interest in supporting, reestablishing and furthering ecological building methods among indigenous people. Provides consulting and workshops on earthbag construction and other natural building techniques.

OK OK OK Productions, 256 East 100 South, Moab, UT 84532, U.S.A.; phone/fax: 435-259-8378; email: okokok@lasal.net; website: www.ok-ok-ok.com. Kaki Hunter and Doni Kiffmeyer offer earthbag workshops and an illustrated manual.

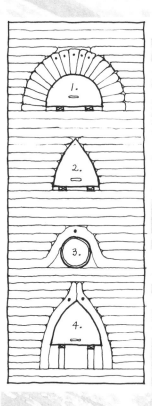

Arched Window Forms
1. Semicircular arch form held up with shims. Bags marked with a '•' must be filled at the same time to create wedge shapes.
2. Corbelled pointed arch.
3. Arch over bucket form. Bag marked with a '•' must be filled with stabilized material.
4. Pointed arch. Bags marked with a '•' must be filled with stabilized material.

Earthships: An Ecocentric Model

Jack Ehrhardt

THE WORLDWATCH INSTITUTE estimates that if the rest of the world used natural resources at the rate we do in America, it would take two additional Earths to meet the global demand. Overall, the 1.1 billion wealthiest people in the world consume 64 percent of the resources, while the 1.1 billion poorest consume only 2 percent. With the Earth's population having doubled since 1950, it would seem that the real shortage of affordable housing has just begun. Sustainable building — using earthen and recycled materials and implementing principals of energy efficiency to take advantage of free, clean, renewable energy — will help to solve many of these problems.

The European-American wood-framed building system, the way we have built our homes for centuries, is being challenged by more 'ecocentric' methods of construction. We have to face the fact that a leading cause of global deforestation is the demand for the wood products used to construct wood-framed houses, apartments, and small commercial buildings. We can't put a tree-hugger in every forest in the world to save the old growth, but we can change the way we think. The Cartesian mechanistic paradigm we have lived by for the past 2,000 years assumes that the world is a human-centered machine. We now know that this is simply not the case.

Designers and builders of sustainable homes work intuitively to combine natural environmental services with building design. A modern home needs an interior temperature control system, a system providing clean water for consumption and common use, and systems to manage both human waste and garbage — all of which have recyclable elements, if imaginatively conceived and intelligently executed.

Perhaps no other building designer has more radically interfaced all of these living systems than Michael Reynolds of Solar Survival Architecture. He started designing homes based on sustainable principles in Taos, New Mexico, more than 25 years ago. Now over 1,000 homes around the world incorporate his 'living building' systems. These homes, called earthships, have built-in systems that take into account every human impact and need. They are designed to make a family feel as independent and free as if they were on a long voyage, only in this case the ship is their home, their voyage is on Earth, and their goal is to live equably with their environment.

My wife Sharon and I have lived in our 2,000-square-foot (185.8-square-meter) earthship for five years. It could be described as a typical earthship, but like all earthships, it has certain unique features. Earthships, whether built on flat ground, dug down into the ground a couple of feet, or built into a south-facing hillside, are buried in the earth on three sides. (Some people, like me, cheat a little and put some windows and a door on the east side, but doing so reduces energy efficiency.)

The building is oriented such that its long front faces south. This is part of the heating system, which uses solar gain through the windows to charge the thermal mass inside in order to heat our home in the winter. (*See* "Designing with the Sun.") The system works so well without any backup heat that even if it gets down to 16 degrees Fahrenheit (-9 degrees Celsius) outside at night, when we get up in the morning it's 62 degrees Fahrenheit (17 degrees Celsius) inside and quickly warms up with additional solar penetration. We have frequently commented to one another after coming home on a cold, windy night that it feels like a heater has been on.

JOSEPH F. KENNEDY

The office of Michael Reynolds, the innovator of the earthship concept. Earthships are not just a system of building with tires but a design concept for totally self-sustained living. Earthships are passively heated and cooled, collect energy and water, and process solid and liquid waste.

The earth is retained by load-bearing walls constructed of 'engineered rubber-encased adobe building block,' also known as used car and truck tires. Tires are used for the following reasons:

- They have an estimated half-life of 30,000 years.

- They are free (except in northern New Mexico, where so many earthships are being built that they have to be trucked in from elsewhere).

- Once they have been filled with on-site dirt and compacted to 90 pounds, tires make the strongest walls I have worked with or studied.

- They do not outgas. Studies based on leachate monitoring of old dumpsites have not shown traces of tire material. However, tires do outgas when piled in sunlight, which is another reason to build with them and cover them up. This solves the problem of how to recycle waste tires in an environmentally sound way.

- Tire walls covered with natural adobe or stucco are fire- and termite-proof. Tire walls have gone through fires, hurricanes, and earthquakes and have remained standing.

When the first row of tires are laid directly on existing compacted ground and then filled with dirt and compacted, they form a spread footing. Subsequent courses are staggered, as in a block wall. The resulting thermal mass provides excellent cooling in the summer and warming in the winter. In addition, operable skylights at the rear of the home draft warm air out in the summer.

An earthship's passive solar design precludes the need for a forced-air-conditioning unit, the most costly and energy consumptive appliance in many homes. Ninety-nine percent of earthships use a solar and/or wind electrical system for independent power. One of the primary reasons that the solar energy market has not taken off like it should is that it is not always economical to attach solar electric energy systems to conventional, inefficient buildings. They work best when integrated into a complete system of energy efficiency that uses all the free energy available.

Our earthship's 650-watt power system cost US$4,500 and has never failed. As Sharon is typing this article on the computer for me (I'm still a pen and paper person), a clothes iron, a sewing machine, the DC refrigerator/freezer, and our outdoor fountain are all operating at once. If energy-efficient building designs were universally adopted, families would be able to maintain their homes without the need for dangerous nuclear power or polluting coal- or oil-fired power plants. People choose to contribute to a clean environment for future generations when they build homes that use clean, renewable energy sources.

Another design element of earthships that promotes independence and responsibility involves water recycling. Roofs are designed to harvest rain water and divert it to cisterns for storage. Pre-made tanks can be used, but cisterns made of tire walls are frequently built into the sides of earthships. Water from the cisterns is brought into the home, filtered, and used for all purposes, thereby reducing the huge infrastructure development usually required for water supply and the non-point pollution problems clean water is facing these days. We recycle the graywater from our showers and sinks to irrigate gardens inside the front of the house. The organic vegetables and flowers are efficiently top watered, and the remaining water flows down to the deep roots of our fig tree and banana plants. Our 'kitchen sink irrigation system,' which has a sediment containment box to catch food particles, grows red peppers, broccoli, and flowers. The size of the planters was calculated from the estimated amount of graywater use and the plants' projected absorption rate. Growing our own vegetables increases our self-sufficiency and reduces our dependence on mass agriculture and its poisonous pesticides and fertilizers.

Our toilets also use graywater. Michael Reynolds' 'black water' (human waste) system is especially efficient because a huge volume of graywater has already been removed from the waste stream, dramatically reducing the amount of black water to be treated. If you can't get yourself to use a modern composting toilet system, then his above-ground sealed system works the best. Just

An interior view of an earthship in New Mexico.

MELISSA MALOUF

as in graywater sealed systems, the black water goes to a sealed containment tank and then flows to second and third containment beds designed to keep the liquid out of the ground. Moisture-absorbing plants are grown in the second and third containers to draw out the liquids. Again, the size of the system is based on projected volume use. As almost everyone knows, water is a precious part of our environment and vital to all living things. Conservation measures keep our water safe to use and allow us to be in close contact with its life-giving processes.

The earthship and similar designs personify a paradigm shift to a whole systems approach to human sustainability. A sustainable society is defined as one that satisfies its needs without diminishing the prospects of future generations. Just as building codes are written to preserve the health and safety of the public, sustainable building is emerging as a responsible way for humanity to preserve the health and safety of the planet.

Jack Ehrhardt is the cofounder of CERBAT — the Center for Environmentally Responsible Building Alternatives. The center, which also serves as an environmental-education youth camp, is based in Kingman, Arizona, as is Ehrhardt's general contracting business. Ehrhardt has been involved in the building industry for 25 years, is currently contracting the construction of a 5,000-square-foot (465-square-meter) straw bale house, and acting as a consultant to the Arizona National Guard on a 6,000-square-foot (560-square-meter) earthship project in Phoenix.

RESOURCES
Books

Chiras, Daniel. *The Natural House: A Complete Guide to Healthy, Energy-Efficient, Environmental Homes.* Chelsea Green, 2000. Contains an excellent chapter on building with tires, as well as good information on energy independence.

Reynolds, Michael. *Earthship,* Vol. I: *How to Build Your Own House;* Vol. II: *Systems and Components;* Vol. III: *Evolution Beyond Economics.* Solar Survival Press, 1993. The original references by the originator of the earthship concept.

Organizations

Earthship Biotecture, P.O. Box 1041, Taos, NM 87571, U.S.A.; phone: 505-751-0462; fax: 505-751-1005; email: biotecture@earthship.org; website: www.earthship.org. A wide range of services from design to construction.

Earthship Global Operations, P.O. Box 2009, El Prado, NM 87529, U.S.A.; phone: 505-751-0462; email: eartshp@taos.newmex.com; website: www.taosnet.com/earthship/. Michael Reynolds's headquarters, offering books, newsletters, supplies, design services, referrals, and more.

Digging In for Comfort

Kelly Hart

T HINK OF ALL THE ANIMALS that dig into the ground to find refuge, comfort, and security. Their ancestors discovered millennia ago that the earth could provide all of that, free for the digging. We humans have done this too, at times, but we tend to forget the benefits, preferring to follow the trend of building on the surface.

What the animals know is that the earth can shelter them from the extremes of temperature, from the wind and sun and snow. If you dig several feet into the ground, you will discover that the temperature does not vary much there, year round. In fact, 5 feet (1.5 meters) under the ground, temperatures stay around 50 degrees Fahrenheit (10 degrees Celsius) constantly. I'm sure you have experienced the delicious coolness of a basement room on a scorching summer day. Perhaps you've gone into that same basement in midwinter and been surprised how warm it felt. This is the moderating effect of the earth at work.

The people of Cappadocia, Turkey have excavated homes in the area's soft volcanic rock for millennia.

BETTY WANEK

Of course, most of us would not be comfortable in a house kept at 50 degrees (10 degrees), so we would need to bring the temperature up maybe 20 degrees (11 degrees) to relax at home. Compare that 20-degree (11-degree) increase with say the 70-degree (39-degree) increase necessary to be comfortable in a conventional home when it's 0 degrees (-18 degrees) outside. It would take over three times as much energy to stay warm if you have not taken advantage of the earth for shelter. And on a hot day it works in the other direction, requiring tremendous air conditioning energy to stay cool enough if you have not dug into the earth.

Many people think that an earth-sheltered house must be dark, dank, dirty, and doubtful as a pleasant abode. They are wrong. There are many ways to introduce light, views, and an airy feeling into a bermed house. An earth-sheltered house is dug into a hillside, especially if that hillside faces more or less south. Then the windows for solar heating are naturally at ground level, and much of the rest of the house can be surrounded with earth. Of course, even on flat land, soil can be pushed up around the sides of the house to provide the berm.

In building an earth-sheltered house, it is important to pay attention to certain details. As with the rest of the house, the walls that are in contact with the earth need to be well insulated;

otherwise the soil will continually suck warmth out of the house. Also, these walls need to be strong enough to withstand the pressure of that earth and waterproof to keep out the moisture. Traditionally, reinforced concrete has been used to build subsurface walls, and this works well, but it is not the most environmentally friendly way to do it.

Mike Oeler, author of *The $50 and Up Underground House Book*, suggests using heavy timbers to frame the structure, with boards to form the walls and plastic sheeting to waterproof it. He has lived in such a structure in Idaho for quite a few years and is still happily advocating this approach.

I have been experimenting with earthbag construction, much of which has been underground. Polypropylene bags are filled with either sand or volcanic scoria. The lower bags that are filled with sand are insulated from the outside with scoria. I cover all of this with a double layer of 6-mil polyethylene before backfilling. Between each course of bags are two strands of four-point barbed wire. The wall itself has a convex curve set against the earth to withstand the pressure of the soil. The beauty of this technique is its simplicity of construction and the fact that it uses very little industrial material.

A traditional Kiva structure, built undergound by the ancient Anasazi in Mesa Verde, Colorado.

CATHERINE WANEK

I have visited several other local houses that take advantage of the earth for shelter. Mark and Christine started building their house 11 years ago and originally lived in a nearly totally bermed room at the lowest level. This room was built with foam form blocks that were filled with rebar and cement, tarred on the outside, and then Q-bonded on the inside. Mark finds it very soothing to be in that room. The earth makes it snug and cozy and quiet. He also points out that digging in allows for a lower profile that is not as much of an intrusion on the landscape.

Alan and Julie are just moving into their passive solar house that has been two years in the making. Alan designed it with some suggestions from a solar design specialist. The house is

basically set into a south-facing sand dune that was notched all the way through, so that the garage/entrance is on the north side. The exterior walls were formed with Rastra blocks, which were filled with rebar and cement. A Bituthane coating was applied to the blocks below grade, and blue-board insulation was set in place before backfilling. This is one of the best passive solar designs I've seen. I'm sure they will be comfortable.

These people have happily dug into the earth for shelter. They know what the wild animals know: Mother Earth provides for our needs.

This restaurant in Sopron, Hungary, is built in an ancient underground vault.

Kelly Hart has experimented with building technologies most of his life, from miniature rock walls (copying what his father was building), to huts and tree-houses, to professional remodeling. His most recent project is his own earthbag/papercrete house.

RESOURCES

Books

Campbell, Stu. *The Underground House Book*. Garden Way, 1980. Although this book is many years out of print, it is worth trying to find it in used bookstores, as the information, backed by the design expertise of Don Metz, is still good.

McClintock, Mike. *Alternative Housebuilding*. Sterling, 1989. Contains a good, brief introduction to earth-sheltered construction, along with cordwood, log, timber frame, pole, stone, rammed earth, and adobe building.

Oehler, Mike. *The $50 and Up Underground House Book*. 6th ed. Mole Publishing, 1997. Available from the author, Rt. 4, Box 618, Bonners Ferry, ID 83805, U.S.A. A quirky but valuable book on how to build a truly 'dirt cheap' house.

Roy, Rob. *The Complete Book of Underground Housing*. Sterling, 1994. Discusses techniques that can be performed by owner-builders, such as surface-bonded block wall construction and plank and beam roofing. Available from Earthwood Building School, 366 Murtagh Hill Road, West Chazy, NY 12992; phone: 518-493-7744.

Wells, Malcolm. *The Earth-Sheltered House: An Architect's Sketchbook*. Chelsea Green, 1998. A witty and profusely illustrated treatise on the subject of underground houses. For a complete list of Malcolm Wells's books, send a card to Box 119, Brewster, MA 02631; phone: 508-896-6850; fax: 508-896-5116.

Building with Hemp

Tom Woolley

THE FOLLOWING NOTES on hemp building are drawn from ongoing research into the potential for hemp as a construction material. There is an extensive body of literature on hemp as a crop and its many uses for foodstuffs, cosmetics, paper, interior body work for automobiles, and so on. Although the growing of hemp is still illegal in many parts of the world because of its association with marijuana, non-psychotropic varieties are widely grown (under police license) in many parts of Europe. Commercial seed is available from France and Hungary.

Hemp is relatively easy to grow, even in the cold wet summers of Northern Ireland, where trial crops have been grown for the last 2 to 3 years. Farmers, seeking diversification possibilities, have been attracted to hemp by European agricultural subsidies and because there is no need to use fertilizers and pesticides with the crop. However it is important to find local uses for the material, as it does not make economic sense to transport the bulky crop long distances. Initially, hemp is being used as a luxury form of horse bedding as it can absorb a great deal of moisture while remaining relatively dry. It has also been considered as a biomass crop for heating. Such low-value uses seem a waste when hemp can be used for much more valuable purposes, especially as the farmer requires considerable investment for special harvesting equipment and subsequent processing of the crop.

We have been investigating the use of the chopped stem of the plant (the hurd, core, or shive) in composite wall-building materials. Having carried out some work with straw bale building, we have found persistent problems with dampness affecting wheat or barley straw.

We were initially attracted to hemp as a replacement for straw, as it appears to be much more resistant to damp, as well as being tougher and longer lasting. An attempt was made to build a hemp bale building in England, and it was found to be too difficult to pin the bales together because of its toughness. Hemp bales might still work, however, with external pinning methods.

In a different technique, chopped hemp can be mixed with lime or earth, then cast using form-work, to make walls. Normally, the hemp is chopped into pieces less than an inch (2.5 centimeters) long, but it is also possible to use longer lengths. We plan to do some experiments in which we add longer fibers to the wall material, as it seems likely that this will give added strength.

It seems possible that chopped hemp mixed with lime could be used to create freestanding walls, but so far, most hemp builders have used a mix of hemp and lime as a composite form of construction with timber frame structures. A relatively lightweight timber-panel frame can be constructed (one or two stories) and the hemp cast around it. Hemp buildings in France and

TOM WOOLLEY

View of Ralph Carpenter's house in Suffolk, England, with hemp walls built using Isochanvre method.

England have generally been built 8 inches (20 centimeters) thick, with the hemp mixture cast in lifts between 30 and 36 inches (75 and 90 centimeters) in height.

We have experimented with mixing the hemp with different forms of lime, but the most sensible seems to be to use hydraulic lime. (*See* "Working with Lime.") One of the remarkable features of hemp is that it binds so well with the lime with a relatively small amount of water that it is possible to remove the formwork immediately. Two or three weeks are needed for the walls to dry out, depending on conditions. There is little need for protection, as the hemp/lime mixture is relatively waterproof. The wall can then be finished with a skim coat of lime plaster inside and out. Thicker plasters can be strengthened with the additions of hemp fibers.

Discovery of this amazing material came from work on the restoration of historic buildings. Restorers found that a hemp/lime mixture could replace infill in medieval timber frame buildings, where previously manure, horsehair, and straw with lime would have been used. The hemp/lime mixture is dimensionally very stable and does not shrink. It can absorb water vapor to a high degree and still remain warm and dry to the touch. Because of this property, hemp has also been used as a flooring material, laid without even a damp-proof course (vapor barrier). Loosely chopped hemp can also be used as an insulation material in lofts or floors. Hemp/lime plaster is also a very attractive material.

We have also experimented with making 8-inch-thick (20-centimeter-thick) blocks, which can be laid using a lime mortar, but this will not have the shear strength of the timber and cast hemp composite. We have now begun work on mixing hemp with earth, and it seems that this can work as well as using lime. Some work on casting hemp and earth walls has been done by Chris Dancey in Ontario, Canada. The quality of earth material should be similar to that used in rammed earth construction, and Dancey stresses the need for careful quality control.

The use of composite timber frame and hemp walls has been well accepted in France, and several social housing schemes, as well as private houses, have now been constructed with hemp. Two principal companies promote hemp construction in France. *Chenevotte Habitat* has developed a material called 'Isochanvre,' produced using a 'mineralizing' process. They claim that without such mineralization, the hemp will be subject to fungal attack. We have been testing blocks using un-mineralized horse-bedding material and have found no evidence of fungal activity of any kind, even when a block is left out in the rain. Although the secret mineralization process is controversial, the Isochanvre product is well produced, and their literature and supporting documentation (in French) is excellent. They supply two forms of hemp, one for loose insulation and the other for mixing with lime.

The other principal French product is 'Canosemose,' produced by *La Chanvriere de l'Aube*; it is not clear whether or not their hemp is mineralized. *La Chanvriere de l'Aube* produces equally professional literature. Some independent reports, based on tests carried out by the University of Rennes, also exist on their product. In addition to these two producers, a number of smaller companies have emerged in northern France.

The hemp used for Isochanvre comes from a global corporation that grows hemp for use in paper. Multinational corporations increasingly control the manufacture of lime, with the cement companies gaining principal control as interest in lime grows. For the short term, we have imported some Isochanvre material from France via England. But to be fully ecological, we need to grow and process the hemp locally, using locally manufactured lime or earth. As hemp can be grown almost anywhere with adequate rainfall, it ought to be possible to 'grow' our buildings locally.

Construction of a hemp/lime wall using movable form work.

Ralph Carpenter of Modece Architects in Suffolk, England has been the main power for hemp housing in England. He has designed and built several beautiful, private hemp houses and will shortly be constructing a social housing scheme in Haverhill in Essex. He convinced the U.K. Building Research Establishment to carry out some testing and is also involved in a European research project. Carpenter uses Isochanvre material and timber frame methods.

At present, we have not been able to fully test all the claims made for hemp construction, but it does seem to have many advantages.

- The material is natural and fully renewable, with no damage to the environment.

- Processing involves some investment but the technology is fairly simple.

- It seems that hemp mixed with lime has a very high degree of stability, longevity, and resistance to moisture (nothing definite yet on hemp mixed with earth).

- Walls constructed with hemp seem to provide an ideal 'breathing' medium, with potential health benefits.

- Hemp/lime finishes have a very attractive, natural, and warm feel with high surface temperatures.

- Good insulation standards can be achieved. Isochanvre make various claims, but we have not been able to test these yet. Insulation values differ for different densities of material.

- The use of hemp for encasing a timber frame is a very attractive solution, as this eliminates the cold-bridging problems of some kinds of timber frame construction.

- Hemp can be used for flooring and roof insulation and in historic building restoration.

ACKNOWLEDGMENTS

I would like to acknowledge Chris Dancey, Ontario; Francis Aujames (Architect), Rene, France; JB Plant Fibres, North Wales; John Hobson, Hemcore; John McGrady, Seeconnell Initiative; Lindsay Easson, Agricultural Research Institute, Northern Ireland; Loik Lamballais, University of Rennes; and Ralph Carpenter (Architect), Modece Architects, Suffolk, for their help and, in particular, Mark Alexander, whose inspiration set us on the hemp path.

Tom Woolley has been Professor of Architecture at Queens University, Belfast since 1991. He is editor and one of the authors of the Green Building Digest *and the* Green Building Handbooks, 1 and 2. *He is a founding member of the Ecological Design Association and the Ecological Building Network; and a member of the Association of Environment Conscious Builders, the European Green Building Forum Advisory Panel, and chairman of the Northern Ireland Building Regulations Advisory Committee.*

RESOURCES

Books

Roulac, John. *Hemp Horizons: A Comeback of the World's Most Promising Plant.* Chelsea Green, 1997. Well-written book on the many industrial uses of hemp, from food to textiles.

Periodicals

HempPages: The International Hemp Journal. Box 550, Forestville, CA 93436, U.S.A.; phone: 707-887-7508; website: www.hemppages.com

Organizations

Building Limes Forum, Michael Wingate, 82 The Street, Hindolveston, Dereham, NR20 5DF U.K. Mail-order service with a wide range of books on lime and earth construction.

Chenevotte-Habitat, 30 rue Sainte Anne, F-21000 Dijon, France; phone: (33) 03 80 49 85 51; fax: (33) 03 80 50 1 61; email: chenovette.habitat@wanadoo.fr; website: www.isochanvre.com. Distributor of a wide range of hempbuilding materials.

Hempline, 11157 Longwoods Road, R.R.1, Delaware, Ontario, Canada N0L 1E0; phone: 519-652-0440; email: info@hempline.com; website: www.hempline.com. Canadian supplier of hemp material.

La Chanvriere de L'Aube (LCDA), Rue du Gal de Gaulle, 10200 Bar Sur Aube, France.

Modece Architects, 88 St. John's Street, Bury St. Edmunds, Suffolk, IP33 1SQ U.K.

Light-Clay:
An Introduction to German Clay Building Techniques

Frank Andresen

CLAY IS AN EXCELLENT BUILDING MATERIAL, found in most places in the world. It's affordable and recyclable. Being an excellent heat absorber, it regulates indoor temperature variations. Mixed with fibers, it provides insulation, while preserving and protecting the fibers from insects, mice, and fire. It absorbs odors and lends itself to architectural creativity.

Building with clay has a long tradition in Germany and other European countries. Half-timbered houses from the 12th century, framed with wood and infilled with a mixture of clay and straw fibers, still exist. This traditional technique — wattle and daub — is still in use in the preservation of historic buildings. Oak stakes are installed vertically or horizontally into the frame, woven with thin willow whips (wattle), and plastered with a heavy mixture of clay and straw (daub). When the daub is dry, it is plastered with a mix of lime, sand, and animal hair. Finally, the surface is painted with limewash.

Several other historical techniques are still practiced in Germany. *Lehmwickelstaken* consists of oak stakes wrapped with a mix of straw fibers and clay paste and is mainly used as a ceiling infill. *Lehmwellerbau*, a technique already established by the Middle Ages, involves straw-clay loosely stacked with a pitchfork and then compressed with a tamper. After a couple of days drying time, the wall is shaved with a triangular spade and the next layer is added.

Here, straw-clay has been formed into blocks and used to create ceiling insulation.

As modern building materials became common in the last 40 years, many of the medieval half-timbered buildings were renovated, and the clay infill was replaced with modern materials. Within a few years, these buildings began to show signs of decay and structural problems brought about by a combination of moisture infiltration and a lack of flexibility in the new materials. Research began to show that the best way to preserve the buildings was to replace the new infill with the traditional materials that had proven themselves over the centuries.

By the early 1960s, traditional building in Germany had all but died out, but much like the revival of timber framing in North America, a small group of builders began to relearn the craft about 20 years ago. The increased environmental consciousness of the '80s led to a revival of traditional building systems throughout Europe. Clay construction techniques once again began to be studied as a viable building alternative, and many technical advances took place, especially in Germany and France. Because clay building requires relatively simple tools and technical know-how, it has found increased popularity among owner-builders. Clay-building companies have also been established, specializing in a variety of building techniques using commonly available equipment and pre-mixed, delivered raw materials.

The term 'light-clay' refers to the mixing of liquid clay with large quantities of light materials such as straw, wood chips, cork, or minerals. One of the recent refinements has been the development of straw light-clay, a mixture of liquid clay slip and large quantities of straw. More straw added to the clay will result in a lighter mixture, with correspondingly higher insulation values, while less straw creates a heavier wall. Mixtures range between 20 pounds per cubic foot and 75 pounds per cubic foot (300 to 1,200 kilograms per cubic meter). To get a very light mixture, the use of soil with a high clay content is necessary. Medium heavy (between 40 and 50 pounds per cubic foot [650 to 800 kilograms per cubic meter]) mixtures are most realistic for practical work on the building site.

Frank Andresen's test samples of wood light-clay and straw light-clay, showing an earthen base coat and finish plaster.

The straw-clay mix is tossed together, then covered with a tarp for a day or two before the mixture is placed into a form and tamped. To preserve insulation qualities, it is important that the tamping not be too hard. After filling and tamping a section, the form boards can be removed immediately and moved up for the next section. This technique can be used for both exterior and interior walls, as well as for ceilings. Although dependent on water content, outside temperature, and wind conditions, final drying time for a 12-inch-thick (30-centimeters-thick) wall is approximately 12 weeks during the warm season (making sure that both sides of the infill are exposed to the air while drying). Hence builders in northern climates must be prepared to start early in the year.

The use of wood chips instead of straw as an aggregate in light-clay mixtures increased in popularity in the 1990s. The drying time, shrinkage behavior, and (most importantly) labor intensity are reduced when using wood chips. The size of the chips ranges from coarse sawdust to chunks up to 2 inches (5 centimeters) in diameter, depending on the chipper. The chips can be dry or green, but they should be bark-free, as bark decomposes rapidly. Wood light-clay is made of about four parts wood to one part clay slip. These ingredients can be mixed easily and quickly using a mortar mixer or even a cement mixer, then poured or shoveled into the formwork. Hardly any tamping is required.

A variety of forming systems can be used with wood light-clay. When reed mat forms are used as an infrastructure, studs should be no wider than 12 to 16 inches (30 to 40 centimeters) on center. By using wooden laths or bamboo as a light framework to cage the infill, these distances can be nearly doubled. Because the infill is anchored to the laths or matting, the whole wall is stiffer and shrinkage is virtually nil. Temporary plywood forms can also be used to build walls that require no mats or lath. In this case, horizontal or vertical reinforcing such as saplings or small-dimension lumber should be placed in the middle of the wall about every 16 inches (40 centimeters) to add lateral strength. Many types of plaster can then be easily applied, making sure exposed framing is covered. The insulation value for a 12-inch (30-centimeter) wall with plaster can be up to R-25, depending on the quality of the wood chips and clay and the density of packing.

Besides being a strong and efficient building material, light-clay reduces the use of wood in construction. The raw materials — clay, straw, and wood chips — are available at very little cost. In most places, clay is available in the ground in unlimited quantities, making transportation unnecessary. The mixing of the materials requires much less energy than the burning of bricks or the production of cement or synthetic foams. While the installation of light-clay is labor intensive, the low cost of the raw materials can make it cost competitive with some modern building systems.

It is also possible to make bricks, blocks, or panels with clay and fiber, which can then be used in a pre-dried state. With these dry materials the range of construction techniques is even greater and the construction season can be extended. Light-clay bricks can even be used as a ceiling infill between beams. As required, these elements can be made either light or heavy and can be cut quite easily with a band or hand saw. Some producers hope to reduce costs by automating production, enabling them to price clay bricks and other natural products competitively with modern building materials.

An industrial prefabricated dry board has been developed in the last few years. *Lehmbauplatte* is a clay panel board that is burlap-coated and reinforced with plant fiber. Clay paste is applied to jute net fabric, then two to five or more layers of reed mats are laid crosswise with alternate layers of clay paste. Finally, it is covered with another layer of burlap and transported to a drying station. Material tests with this board have shown excellent fireproofing, soundproofing, deformation, and diffusion values. The *Lehmbauplatte* can be used as a permanent form, combined with blown-in cellulose, or used as a ceiling and insulation board. It can be screwed, nailed, and sawed.

All clay construction must be properly protected from the weather with appropriate construction details. Large overhangs are helpful. Lime plaster will protect the clay on exterior walls; also paint, clapboards, or shingles can be used.

Get advice when necessary. Involve friends and family. Then, besides building a healthy home, you can save money, too. Working with clay is labor intensive and requires patience, but you will be using materials from your own property — clay, wood, stone, straw, reed, and other fibers — instead of forking your money over to industry or the bank in return for artificial, potentially toxic, products.

> *Frank Andresen has been involved in professional clay building in Germany since the early 1980s. He has been teaching and applying both traditional and modern techniques in Europe and America for both historical and new buildings. He is available for workshops and consulting on light-clay materials, plasters, and dry clay products.*

RESOURCES
Books
Elizabeth, Lynne, and Cassandra Adams, eds. *Alternative Construction: Contemporary Natural Building Methods.* John Wiley and Sons, 2000. Contains a brief chapter on light-clay by Frank Andresen and Robert Laporte.

Laporte, Robert. *Mooseprints: A Holistic Home Building Guide.* Econest Building Company, 1993. This brief booklet includes an outline of straw light-clay construction, along with timber framing and earthen plasters and floors.

Organizations
Econest Building Company, P.O. Box 864, Tesuque, NM 87574, U.S.A.; phone: 505-984-2928 or 505-989-1813; fax: 505-989-1814; email: info@econests.com; website: www.econests.com. Robert Laporte and crew offer workshops on straw light-clay as well as timber framing and professional design/build services.

Fox Maple School of Traditional Building, P.O. Box 249, Corn Hill Road, Brownfield, ME 04010, U.S.A.; phone: 207-935-3720; email: foxmaple@nxi.com; website: www.nxi.com/WWW/joinersquarterly. Workshops in timber framing and traditional enclosure techniques, including Frank Andresen's workshops on earthen wall systems.

Proclay, P.O. Box 249, Brownfield, ME 04010, U.S.A.; phone: 207-935-3720; email: proclay@hotmail.com. Frank Andresen's professional building and restoration service using light-clay and other earth building techniques, both traditional and modern; fine clay finishes; and workshops.

Mechanizing Straw-Clay Production

Alfred von Bachmayr

MY FIRST EXPERIENCE with light-clay was at a workshop in which the straw and clay had to be mixed by hand with pitchforks. I remember thinking that I loved the finished product but discounted the viability of the material due to the high labor component.

Having grown up on a farm where my father was always creating machines out of items form the junk pile, my mind went to work devising a mixing device that could be easily made out of materials obtainable anywhere. I first tried a conventional cement mixer but found it too small and awkward to process significant amounts of material. I then created a tumbler out of a 55-gallon (250-liter) drum, which replicated a cement mixer; even though the volume was greater, the problem of limited batch size remained. I started thinking about a rotating tube with the raw materials being fed in one end and the mixed product coming out the other.

Alfred shovels straw, clay, and water into his mixer as it turns.

After welding two 55-gallon (250-liter) drums together to form a tube, I attached a driving belt to turn the tube with an HP electric motor. The raw material was fed in the upper end of the tube in sequence (straw, water, and clay) and mixed as it tumbled down the tube. By adjusting its pitch, I could control the rate at which the materials went through the tube. A series of tines welded inside the tube helped the material mix more thoroughly by lifting it at each rotation up the side of the drum and dropping it when the tines approached vertical.

The device allows the ratio of clay to straw to be adjusted as desired. For walls where high insulation values are desired, the material can be mixed at a dry weight of approximately 35 pounds per cubic foot (560 kilograms per cubic meter). Where more mass is desired, a higher percentage of clay is used and the mix can be made to weigh 50 to 75 pounds per cubic foot (800 to 1,200 kilograms per cubic meter). To optimize the thermal performance of a building, the lighter mix is used in north and west walls, while the heavier mix is used on the south, east, and in interior walls.

My mixer design continues to evolve. In order to produce even more material, I developed a larger tumbler, 36 inches (90

CATHERINE WANEK

169

centimeters) in diameter and 10 feet (3 meters) long. It is made of a tractor tire rim split in half, with corrugated metal roofing attached to the inside to create the tube. It is turned with a gear motor at about 30 revolutions per minute, and the whole device is mounted on a trailer that can be pulled to construction sites. This large device can produce enough mixed light-clay to keep a large crew busy compacting it in forms. The next evolution will involve a more automated feeding of the raw materials to the rotating drum and better delivery of the mixed material to the walls for compaction.

Architect Alfred von Bachmayr designs low-cost, energy-efficient, and sustainable buildings utilizing straw bale, straw-clay, pumicecrete, adobe, earthen plasters, rainwater catchment, alternative waste disposal systems, and solar electricity. He also invents devices to aid in the production of alternative buildings. He has small and large light-clay mixing drums for rent.

CATHERINE WANEK

CATHERINE WANEK

Top: After straw-clay is mixed, it is left to rest for a while, then tamped into forms.

Bottom: The Gary Zuker house in Texas is made of straw-clay and other natural materials.

Paper Houses: Papercrete and Fidobe

Gordon Solberg

AMERICANS THROW AWAY enough writing and office paper each year to build a wall 12-feet (3.6-meters) high from New York City to Los Angeles. If we included other types of paper (newspapers, magazines, cardboard boxes, packaging materials, junk mail) we could probably build a wall of waste paper around the whole country each year. Wouldn't it be nice to find something useful to do with it all?

Fortunately, in recent years a hardy band of innovators has been experimenting with turning waste paper into a strong (300 psi compressive strength), lightweight, and insulating building material. The concept is simple. You build a huge blender and pulp paper or cardboard with water to form a slurry. If Portland cement is added to this slurry, you end up with 'papercrete.' If you add adobe dirt, you get 'fidobe' (short for fibrous adobe). Either way, you can pour the slurry into forms for blocks or panels, use it as mortar, or pump it directly into slip-forms.

I am especially excited about fidobe, which has the advantage of not requiring cement. This makes it cheaper and more Earth-friendly, since Portland cement requires a lot of energy to manufacture and transport. Fidobe has several advantages over regular adobe: it weighs less, has considerable insulation value, will hold a screw, and can be painted.

Papercrete is not a new concept. It was patented back in 1928, but the patent expired unused, because there was no way to make any money off an idea that was so cheap and simple. Since then, papercrete has been independently rediscovered a number of times. The present papercrete renaissance owes its existence to Eric Patterson of Silver City, New Mexico, who started experimenting with it in 1990, and Mike McCain of Crestone, Colorado, who began a few years later.

At the present time there are about 50 papercrete or fidobe structures completed or under construction. Most of them are in the Southwest, but we know of some in wetter climates, such as British Columbia, Wisconsin, and Upstate New York. Costs vary widely, but are considerably cheaper than conventional construction.

MIXERS AND PUMPS

Since papercrete blocks are not yet available commercially, most people will have to make their own blocks, and this means building a mixer first. This can be intimidating to all but the most mechanically inclined.

A papercrete mixer is nothing more than a huge blender, consisting of a tank, a blade, and a power source. The most popular mixer design so far is the 'tow mixer' invented by Mike McCain.

With this design, a 200-gallon (900-liter) steel stock tank or plastic water tank rides on top of a recycled automotive rear end. Ordinarily, turning the drive shaft makes the wheel spin. The tow mixer works the other way: turn the wheels and the driveshaft spins. The U-joint between the differential and driveshaft is inserted vertically into the bottom of the tank, and a lawnmower blade is bolted onto it. When you tow the mixer behind your vehicle, the blade spins rapidly, with great force. You can mix a batch of slurry by towing the mixer about 1/2 mile (1 kilometer).

Ideally, you would be able to pump your slurry directly from the mixer into the forms. Several types of pumps are suitable for this application — concrete pumps, shotcrete pumps, etc. — but they tend to be expensive. Ordinary water pumps tend to clog. One builder in Arizona is having great success with a used diaphragm pump. There are a lot of people out there experimenting, and the pump situation continues to evolve.

Sean Sands stands in front of his 300-square-foot (28-square-meter) papercrete home. The walls and roof went up in a month of part-time work. Sand estimates his materials cost was US $0.75 per square foot!

KELLY HART

FORMULAS

Since the most common mixer has a 200-gallon (900-liter) tank, most papercrete builders think in terms of 200-gallon (900-liter) batches. The basic formula for a 200-gallon (900-liter) batch is: 160 gallons (727 liters) of water, 60 pounds (27 kilograms) of paper, 1 bag of cement (94 pounds [43 kilograms]), and 65 pounds (29 kilograms) of sand (15 shovelfuls). The sand adds thermal mass, reduces flammability, and makes the slurry pack down better for a denser, stronger block. Half a bag of cement works fine, but the slurry will dry more slowly and the blocks won't be as hard when dry. Some people add two bags per load, particularly for the bottoms of walls, for roof panels, and for floors. There is no one right formula. Experiment and see what works best for you.

The ideal fidobe formula depends on your dirt. The clay content of the dirt should be anywhere from 30 percent to 100 percent. With regular adobe, too high a clay content causes cracking, but this isn't a problem with fidobe, since the paper fibers hold the block together. It's a good idea to make up small batches with a kitchen blender, vary the dirt to paper ratio, and see what proportion seems best. The more clay you add, the heavier and stronger your block will be, but it will have less insulation value. I prefer a 4-to-1 ratio of dirt to paper, by weight, which yields a strong block that is reasonably lightweight.

Unless you add enough nonflammable material to the mix, both papercrete and fidobe will burn, slowly and without flame, like a charcoal briquette. My experiments show that papercrete made with a 4-to-1 ratio of cement to paper, by weight, will not burn, and fidobe made with 3 parts dirt to 1 part paper, by weight, won't burn. For additional protection from fire, use a non-flammable stucco inside and out, and a metal or tile roof.

WALL-BUILDING OPTIONS

The first decision to make is whether to use papercrete or fidobe. Fidobe is a lot cheaper and more Earth-friendly, but it takes significantly longer to dry, because it hardens up strictly through evaporation. With papercrete, a chemical reaction causes the blocks to harden up more quickly. The more cement you add, the faster the slurry hardens. This is a useful characteristic in wet climates, or if you're in a hurry.

KELLY HART

A more conventional looking house in Colorado, made with poured-in-place papercrete walls.

Papercrete and especially fidobe are admirably suited for dry climates. The wetter the climate, the more precautions you'll have to take. It's important to build only during the hottest, driest time of year. Even here in the desert, during the hottest time of the year, fidobe blocks take two weeks to dry completely. If you live in a cool and/or humid climate, consider building a solar-heated drying shed out of 2-by-4s and clear plastic to speed up the drying process. And always keep your work covered from the rain!

The next question is whether to use blocks or slip-forms. Both have their advantages. With blocks, the slurry is dumped into the forms at ground level, and the blocks don't have to be moved until the water has evaporated out. (Slurry is 85 percent water by weight and water is heavy.) With slip-forms, the material is handled only once, since it's poured or pumped directly onto the wall.

If you plan on using slip-forms, then consider bringing the window frames all the way down to the ground and adding some corner posts to make a post and beam structure. That way, you can fasten your forms directly to the corner posts and window/door frames, which is quick and convenient. Any convenient depth for the form is fine; 8 inches (20 centimeters) deep is typical. Always remember: wet papercrete is very heavy and lacks strength. Newly poured walls need to be securely braced until they dry, as with poured concrete.

And there is another alternative: both papercrete and fidobe can be cobbed. Just dump the slurry onto a piece of shade cloth or window screen for a few minutes till the excess water drains out. Then you can pick up the thick slurry with your hands and sculpt it to your heart's content. Cobbed fidobe offers the best of both worlds — the freeform creativity of cob, plus the higher insulation value of fidobe.

The typical wall is 12 inches (30 centimeters) wide, and the typical foundation (where I am in the Southwest) is 12 inches (30 centimeters) wide and 12 inches (30 centimeters) high, made of poured concrete, with two parallel strips of $1/2$-inch rebar in the foundation for extra strength. As with straw bale construction, papercrete builders are inserting short lengths of vertical rebar into the wet concrete about every 2 to 4 feet (0.5 to 1 meters), on which to impale the first course of blocks. It's important to use a stemwall, or to have the foundation stick up a few inches above ground level to prevent water from getting into the wall during heavy rains. It's also a good idea to paint the top of the foundation or stemwall with concrete sealant, to prevent wicking of moisture into the wall.

If you build with blocks, then you need to drill holes through the first course so they will slip over the vertical foundation rebar. Put down a 1-inch (2.5-centimeter) bed of papercrete or fidobe mortar onto the foundation, and slip the blocks into place. Subsequent courses are laid just like adobe or cinderblock walls.

Since papercrete and fidobe are so lightweight, you can form them into 'logs' which can be anywhere from 4 to 8 feet (1 to 2.5 meters) long. (It will take two people to move an 8-foot [2.5-meter] log, but the wall will go up very quickly.) The logs can be reinforced with bamboo or small saplings for extra strength — they tend to break unless they are absolutely dry. Logs give you a stronger wall, because there are fewer mortar joints between blocks. They can be cut with a chainsaw to fit precisely between window frames.

Every few courses, 1/2-inch rebar is driven vertically through the blocks, about 4 feet (1 meter) apart. Also, it's good to lay horizontal rebar every 3 or 4 courses, wiring it to the vertical rebar for extra strength, especially in earthquake-prone areas. Slip-form walls are reinforced just like block walls.

Most builders use a wooden bond beam to attach the roof trusses or rafters to the wall. Like all bond beams, it should be well attached to the foundation by straps or other device. The rest of the roof is constructed in the standard way.

THE FUTURE?

Papercrete and fidobe won't really take off until large factories start cranking out blocks by the millions. To my knowledge only one factory is making fidobe blocks. Building a mixer so that you can make your own blocks is like a straw bale builder having to build a baler and bale the straw before building the house.

There is little doubt that papercrete and fidobe will ultimately be included in the Universal Building Code after the necessary testing is done. Until then, we have three main options: (1) We can build in areas more likely to accept alternative buildings. In many rural counties, particularly in the West, building codes are either nonexistent or loosely applied. A good way to find out would be to choose a likely looking county, drive around till you find an unusual-looking house, and ask the owner what they did about codes. (2) In many code jurisdictions, we can apply for an 'experimental' permit if we have an architect or engineer sign off on the plans. (In Doña Ana County, New Mexico, where I live, a county building inspector is building himself a papercrete house using just this strategy.) (3) We can talk to our local building inspectors. Some are strictly by the book, but others are remarkably open-minded and flexible. Fidobe, in particular, might qualify under your state's existing adobe code, particularly if you call it 'fiber-enhanced adobe.' We know of one paper-crete house being built with a building permit in Arizona.

The papercrete/fidobe movement continues to evolve rapidly. New mixer and pump designs are being developed and will be available within a couple of years. When this happens, paper-crete/fidobe production will increase enormously, and we can finally start to turn that 12-foot-high (3.6-meter-high) wall of paper around our country into inexpensive, high-quality houses.

Gordon Solberg is an author, publisher, beekeeper, and homesteader living in the fertile valley of the Rio Grande.

RESOURCES

Books

Solberg Gordon, ed. *Building with Papercrete and Paper Adobe.* Out of print. But all the information in the book is available as *Earth Quarterly* and *Papercrete News* back issues and may be ordered from the website www.zianet.com/papercrete.

Periodicals

Papercrete News, Box 23-B, Radium Springs, NM 88054, U.S.A.; website: www.zianet.com/papercrete.

Videos

Building with Papercrete and Paper Adobe. *Papercrete News*, 2000. Available from *Papercrete News.*

Websites

A list of papercrete builders is available from www.egroups.com/message/papercretenews/27. Papercrete e-group (listserv): www.egroups.com/group/papercretenews.

Rammed Earth: From Pisé to P.I.S.E.

Scott Grometer

PEOPLE OFTEN OVERLOOK earth building in the search for environmentally, economically, and socially sustainable building technologies. They associate the term 'earth building' with primitive materials and techniques, limited to the most arid of climates. They imagine that earthen structures built elsewhere would necessarily be dirty, damp, cold, and unlikely to survive the ravages of rain, freezing temperatures, or earthquakes.

A handful of patient and dedicated architects, engineers, and earth builders, however, are working to quell a stubborn resistance to earthen walls as they investigate new ways of applying modern technology to an ancient form of construction. The myths are slowly giving way. The statistics show that earth-walled structures can, and frequently do, outperform many conventional wood-framed versions in many aspects of comfort, efficiency, safety, and longevity. Examples are appearing in a variety of regions, climates, and architectural styles.

While much of North American earth building is still executed in adobe, particularly in the more arid Southwestern states, the greatest advances have come in the age-old technique of rammed earth, or *pisé de terre*. Pisé differs from adobe brick in both composition and technique. Adobes, unbaked mud bricks, are typically high in clay and require a lengthy drying time before they can be mortared in courses to form walls. The bricks are usually of a relatively low crush strength, and if left exposed, are subject to erosion. On the other hand, pisé or rammed earth involves a carefully measured amount of pure mineral earth — with its constituent components of clay, sand, and aggregate — mixed with a small amount of water and compacted into wall forms. After completion, the forms can be removed and reused. As the resulting rock-hard monolith cures, it takes on a greater crush strength than adobe. It is also less susceptible to erosion. Eliminating the extra steps of forming, drying, transporting, and laying up bricks gives pisé the edge in labor costs.

Pisé is a proven building material. For more than 6,000 years, and in virtually every region of the world, rammed earth has been employed for structures great and small, a surprising number of which remain in existence today. Portions of China's 2,000-year-old Great Wall were constructed of rammed earth, as were many of the great archeological remains of the Middle East and Africa. Introduced in Europe by the Romans, one finds rammed earth structures from Italy to England. In some regions of France, particularly the Rhône Valley, virtually every structure is pisé.

French and German immigrants of the late 1700s and early 1800s brought the pisé technique to America. Large stately homes done in pisé, many still in use, ranged throughout New York, New

Jersey, Pennsylvania, and Washington, DC. By the mid-1850s, pisé had spread to the South, and then throughout the Midwest during the westward expansion. The U.S. government became interested in rammed earth, funding a Department of Agriculture bulletin titled "Rammed Earth Walls for Buildings" as early as 1926. Earth building seemed destined to flourish. Research and experimentation by the government and universities continued to expand until the beginning of the Second World War. However, the end of the war brought a dramatic increase in housing demand, and with it a shift to the American tract home, built of lightweight, easily transportable, and seemingly inexhaustible materials. Pisé slipped into obscurity.

Then, in the 1970s, with the energy crisis and an awareness that so-called renewable resources were being consumed faster than they could be replenished, the concepts of earth building resurfaced. In Western Australia, where there was a shortage of timber and an abundance of termites, designers and contractors already familiar with conventional masonry techniques were quick to accept the reintroduction of rammed earth. Giles Honen, who spurred the Western Australian movement, established the firm Stabilized Earth Structures. With ten affiliate companies employing his techniques, production increased to nearly 200 buildings per year.

David Easton's and Cynthia Wright's P.I.S.E. home in Napa, California.

CYNTHIA WRIGHT

In France, graduate students from the architectural school at Grenoble established CRATerre (Center for the Research and Application of Earth). Inspired by a rich history of French earth building, this group set out to study and adapt earth building techniques to modern application. CRATerre gained international recognition by sponsoring an architectural competition for the entirely new earth village of *Le Domaine de la Terre*, near Lyon (early 1980s). The success of this project has prompted plans for the International Raw Earth Institute, a resource and educational center for the applications of earth architecture.

Meanwhile, in North America, rammed earth was being used primarily as an alternative to adobe in the American Southwest. The advent of stabilized rammed earth, with the addition of a small amount of Portland cement to the earth mixture, yielded higher strength walls with a lower rate of moisture transfer. More advanced forming systems were developed, and power equipment helped in speeding up the placement process.

At about the same time in Northern California, an industrial engineer named David Easton formed the design/build and consulting firm Rammed Earth Works. For nearly two decades, Easton has tirelessly pushed the frontier of rammed earth into wider application and greater public acceptance. Situated in a seismically active and climatically diverse region, Rammed Earth Works has pioneered a variety of new techniques and amendments to the materials. Their reinforced structures have been approved by building departments with even the most stringent seismic engineering requirements, and many have been exposed to repeated earthquake loading. To date, more than 100 projects have been completed, ranging in location from the Sierra Nevada mountains to the rain forest of the Northern California Coast. Most of Easton's employees, enthusiastic young architects, split their time between design and field work.

After years of labor-intensive work in stabilized rammed earth, Easton recognized that if the material was to enjoy truly widespread application, a system would have to evolve to speed the process and make it more palatable to the existing construction industry. Inspired by the gunnite shooting technology of swimming pool builders, Easton developed a new technique coined P.I.S.E. (for Pneumatically Impacted Stabilized Earth). In this method, compaction is attained by spraying the earth mixture horizontally against a rigid, one-walled form. This differs from conventional rammed earth, in which the soil is manually tamped or rammed downwards between two form surfaces.

Construct a P.I.S.E. wall as follows. Pour a concrete footing and slab and allow it to cure. Then, using plywood (or other suitable rigid material), erect a form wall to form the inside perimeter of the walls. Attach displacement boxes to the forms to leave openings for doors and windows. Install a wall-high steel reinforcing grid, and set electrical conduit and hardware in place. Then blow the mix against the form to the desired thickness, and finish the outside surface with a hand float.

The resulting exterior surface is not unlike stucco, and apart from a clear sealant, no other treatment is necessary. Paint or other finishing of smooth interior walls is also optional. As with rammed earth, the roof system is the choice of the designer. Because the technique yields considerable labor and time savings over conventional rammed earth, and because it utilizes the services of conventional building trades, Easton is optimistic about widespread acceptance.

Earth construction would seem to offer obvious and immediate environmental advantages. The industry cites the following statistics for a typical earth-walled structure over conventional stick frame: per unit timber consumption reduced by up to 50 percent; reduced energy consumption for heating and cooling through effective use of thermal mass (wall thickness typically ranges from 18 to 24 inches [45 to 60 centimeters]); virtual elimination of toxic substances found in wall coatings, construction adhesives, and wood preservatives.

The less obvious but perhaps most significant benefit of pisé is its longevity. As centuries-old structures throughout the world attest, a properly designed and built earth home is likely to be standing long after most wood framed structures are in landfills.

The process of ramming earth can be done by hand or with machines.

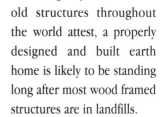

Earth building requires a number of special design considerations. Finding suitable earth for building is important for a quality finished product. If not available on-site, soil needs to be imported. Rock quarries are often a good source since tailings are available inexpensively and are often of ideal composition. The color of the material is also important. Because the addition of a cement stabilizer can alter the appearance, potential soil mixtures should be tested by ramming or shooting a small test wall. The choice of method, either rammed earth or P.I.S.E., will most likely be influenced by site conditions. Small lots with tight setbacks or sites on steep hillsides may not be appropriate for conventional rammed earth, as room for mixing and tractor loading of the material into the forms is necessary. The P.I.S.E method, on the other hand, has been successfully applied in dense urban settings and on steep terrain.

Rammed earth and P.I.S.E. structures require 'a good hat and a good pair of boots.' Sufficient roof overhangs and adequate footings will ensure a dry, comfortable structure. The concern is not that the walls will wash away, but rather that they might become saturated due to excessive exposure. Porosity tests show stabilized rammed earth to be comparable to concrete block, so this point need not be a cause for alarm. For ease of construction and seismic concerns, low-aspect-ratio structures are preferred, though many successful multistory structures have been built. Because forming is an integral part of rammed earth construction, designs that are modular are most efficient to build. By reusing different sized forms throughout the project, labor, costs, and waste can be reduced.

Style considerations are more guidelines than restrictions. Earth building is not limited to prototypical antiquities nor to traditional or period designs. Contemporary examples are being constructed in diverse parts of the world. More recent experiments in color mixing or banding of different color layers have led to some interesting art forms.

The construction costs of rammed earth and P.I.S.E. vary. At present, the square foot cost of the P.I.S.E. technique is roughly comparable to that of wood frame construction. Labor is the major expense, so as more builders enter the field and the process is streamlined, increasing economies of scale will likely result in a net reduction of cost. Those in the industry point out that actual construction costs do not reflect the more significant long-term savings of reduced energy consumption, low maintenance, and long life.

Scott Grometer has a degree in fine arts with an emphasis in architecture, and hands-on experience in French pisé. He currently resides in Northern California.

RESOURCES
Books

Easton, David. *The Rammed Earth House.* Chelsea Green, 1996. A thorough guide to rammed earth, including traditional, mechanized, and P.I.S.E. Good chapters on design and landscape issues.

Houben, Hugo, and Hubert Guillaud. *Earth Construction: A Comprehensive Guide.* Intermediate Technology Publications, 1994. This detailed, well-illustrated technical guide to many forms of earthen building contains good information on low-cost, low-tech rammed earth, with or without stabilization.

King, Bruce. *Buildings of Earth and Straw: Structural Design for Rammed Earth and Straw-Bale Architecture.* Ecological Design Press, 1996. An engineering approach to rammed earth.

Norton, John. *Building with Earth.* Intermediate Technology Publications, 1997. A good, brief introduction to general principles of earth building, including testing soils.

Organizations

Rammed Earth Works, 101 S. Coombs, Suite N, Napa, CA 94559, U.S.A.; phone: 707-224-2532; email: easton@rammedearthworks.com. David Easton's design/build firm; offering also consultation, referrals, and workshops.

Stone Masonry

Michael G. Smith

IF I ASK YOU to think of an ancient building, chances are the structure that appears in your mind's eye is constructed of stone. Stone masonry is, indeed, one of the oldest and most ubiquitous building systems on Earth, but its dominance of ancient sites is more the result of its unequaled durability than of anything else. The intricately fitted defensive walls of Machu Pichu, the soaring cathedrals of Western Europe, and the engineering feats of Roman aqueducts, Egyptian pyramids, and British stone circles all inspire us with awe. The signature characteristics of strength, solidity, heaviness, and durability give stone structures a reassuring timelessness.

In modern industrial society, stone masonry is no longer common; it has been largely superceded by concrete and other manufactured materials. In that process, some ancient techniques for transporting and shaping stones have been forgotten. Yet for the contemporary natural builder, stone can still be both viable and practical. Stone is a particularly good option for those interested in reducing or eliminating the use of Portland cement from their buildings, for environmental or health reasons. Stone makes excellent foundations for other wall systems; durable, waterproof floors for indoor or outdoor spaces; massive, heat-retaining fireplaces and chimneys; cool, moisture-resistant basements and root cellars; and even whole houses, for the especially dedicated. As with many other natural building techniques, stone construction can be very inexpensive if the materials are locally available and if the builder is amply supplied with time and/or volunteer help.

Stone masonry also presents the owner-builder with plenty of challenges. Foremost among these is the sheer weight of the material, which can be a strain on your back, your vehicle, and other tools. The quantity of stone required for most projects is far more than most novices would predict. Shaping and working stone is an art, involving both skill and luck; some types of stone are more cooperative than others. From an engineering perspective, unreinforced stone masonry is vulnerable to damage

Carefully shaped and fitted stones result in durable, massive walls like this one in Japan.

TOM LANDER

from earthquakes. Stone is also a very poor insulator. But with care, practice, and good planning, all of these limitations can be overcome. The best advice for a would-be stone mason is to start small.

Safety is of paramount importance when one is building with stone. Stones are both heavy and hard, providing ample opportunities for injury. Be very careful when lifting; use proper body mechanics and get help if the stone is beyond your safe limit for lifting. Always wear safety equipment: leather gloves and boots when moving stones; gloves when handling cement or lime mortar; eye protection when cutting or shaping stone.

SELECTING STONE

The first consideration for every stone builder is where to acquire the material. There are many options, ranging from having the stone delivered by truck from a quarry to scouting around your own backyard with a digging bar and a wheelbarrow. Before you go out hunting, you need some idea of what you are looking for. The kind and quality of stone you need depends on what you intend to do with it. There are many different techniques for building with stone, some of which are described below. A 'solid wall,' built either with or without mortar, is suitable for a foundation or a load-bearing wall and requires the most precise fit among the stones. Since it is built up of horizontal courses, each stone should have two relatively flat 'faces' — the top and the bottom. It's nice if there is a third attractive face at approximately right angles to the other two, to expose on the wall's surface. Construction will be much easier if there are many stones of about the same thickness top to bottom.

A 'boulder wall' is made of more irregular or rounded stones. It's harder to create a stable wall using this technique. For the beginning mason, a more reasonable option might be a slip-form wall, in which stones are placed in a removable form with plenty of concrete mortar packed or poured between them. Round river rocks, which are very difficult to stack into a solid wall, can be successfully used this way.

A flagstone floor can be made from any stones that are relatively flat and thin. In fact, only one flat face is really necessary, since a rounded or irregular bottom can be dug into the ground or buried in mortar. To build a stone 'veneer' over a wall of brick, concrete block, poured concrete, or even wood, you will need stones that are all about the same thickness.

Stones for any building project should be hard and sound, as opposed to crumbly and fractured. A range of different sizes is good, although none should be so heavy that it is impossible to maneuver into place. Small, flat, wedge-shaped 'chinkers' are very useful for stabilzing larger stones.

WHERE TO GET STONES

Since stones are so heavy and their transport can be expensive, the logical place to build with stone is where stones are abundant. Start by looking around the building site. If surface stones are not plentiful or are eroded and fractured, try looking just below the surface. A heavy digging bar is an excellent tool for probing beneath the soil and for levering stones up to the surface. A large contractor's wheelbarrow can comfortably transport stones of up to several hundred pounds. Lay the wheelbarrow on its side, roll a large stone into it, and then push the wheelbarrow upright. For carrying stones uphill or over uneven ground, a good alternative is to make a simple carrying cradle out of wire fencing. By sliding strong poles through the wire, you can make a litter that can be carried by four people or even more.

If you need to transport rock from outside the immediate neighborhood, a pickup truck is practically indispensable. If you are lucky enough to live in an area with a long history of agriculture or stone building, then you may be able to recycle previously used stones. In the old days, fieldstones were often stacked into fencerows or thrown into piles to get them out of the way of the plow; these may be considered a nuisance by the present landowner. Similarly, abandoned cellars, demolition sites, and excavations for new construction sometimes yield prime building materials.

Another good place to look for building stones is in road cuts. Where a road has been blasted through a hillside, stones often slide down to litter the shoulder. Be careful not to further destabilize the bank or roadbed in your zeal for material. Seashores, creekbeds, and riverbanks can also be sensitively harvested.

If you need to purchase your stone, try to find the most local source, as transportation will likely cost more than the stone itself. Always go to see the stone before you order, to make sure that it will be usable for your purposes — it could be too big or too small, too crumbly or too irregualar in shape.

It's easy to underestimate the amount of stone you will need. Even a modest-sized stone wall or foundation will swallow

A slate roof protects this centuries-old stone farmhouse in Wales.

CATHERINE WANEK

up astounding quantities of material. Estimate the volume of the wall, and then add 25 to 50 percent to that figure when you are assembling your rock pile. Some of the stones will be unusable because they are cracked, irregular, or simply the wrong size or shape to fit. If you are shaping your stones, some will get broken in the process. Others will lose a percentage of their volume under your hammer and chisel.

Shaping Stones

Most stones can be 'cut' or shaped with some degree of success. Soft, sedimentary rocks, such as sandstone and slate, are fairly easy to split into flat planes along the 'grain.' Hard, igneous rocks, such as granite and basalt, are the most difficult to shape. Other types fall somewhere in between.

The most important tool for shaping stone is a stone hammer. A long-handled 8-pound (3.6-kilogram) sledgehammer is useful for breaking large stones into smaller pieces. Smaller hammers come in various weights, between 1-1/2 and 4 pounds (0.7 to 1.8 kilograms). These can be used alone for cutting by repeatedly striking the stone with the square edge of the hammer's face. For more precision, use a heavy cold chisel or brick chisel. A mason's hammer combines hammer and chisel into a single implement.

In theory, if enough force from enough blows is directed along a single plane through a stone, then the stone will eventually break along that plane. The practice is somewhat less predictable, especially for the beginner. The stone is likely to break along any preexisting cracks or faults. Any chips or pebbles caught underneath the stone when it is struck can redirect the force. It's easiest to cut a stone along a visible crack, or to remove a corner or weak protrusion. Several of the books listed in the Resources contain detailed instructions on shaping stone.

Building Techniques

Just as there are multiple ways to build an earthen wall, so there are many ways to build with stone. Here I will focus on two of these options: the solid wall, which can be constructed with or without mortar, and the slip-formed wall.

The Solid Wall

In a solid stone wall, all of the weight is transferred directly from stone to stone, from the top of the wall down to the bottom. A solid wall may be built with or without mortar; the construction sequence is practically identical either way. The purpose of the mortar, if used, is not to cement the stones together but merely to keep them from shifting and to prevent the passage of air, water, and small creatures.

There are many options for mortar mixes. The simplest is a mixture of sand and clay. This works fine in dry locations but is susceptible to erosion if exposed to weather. Another traditional mortar mix is made of lime putty and sand (See "Working with Lime"). Modern masons often use a mortar of Portland cement and sand. Lime is a good addition to this mixture, as it slows down setting, making the mix workable over a longer time period; it also reduces the mortar's brittleness.

A solid wall is built in an orderly sequence. Start with the most visible face. Line up a few stones to form a pleasant-looking row, with a fairly smooth face and an even, level top. It will be very helpful to have a lot of the stones of the same height. If you are using mortar, then remove each stone one by one after the row is in place, put a bed of mortar below it, and then tap the stone down into the mortar. Then move to the other side of the wall and repeat the process, building a second row of stones the same height as the first. Don't worry if there is a space between the two rows; this can be filled in with mortar and small stones.

Continue on along the wall until you have completed the first course. If the wall is longer than a few feet, it may not be possible to make this first course all the same height. You can have steps in it periodically where the level changes, but the fewer of these the better. Fill in all the cracks between stones with mortar, pushing it into place with a mason's trowel.

Shaped cornerstones, called 'quoins,' produce a typical regional window detail on a grain mill in Brittany. Note the visible courses and 'running bond.'

CATHERINE WANEK

When the first course is complete, begin the second. Fit a row of stones in place, then remove them one at a time to place the mortar. Tap each stone down into the mortar until it touches the stone below it. Actually, it should touch at least two stones. The principal rule of the solid wall is the 'running bond.' The joint between every two neighboring stones should be bridged by the stone above it. This is why it is so important for the top of each course to be fairly even. Wherever a step occurs in the top of one course, start the next course with a stone that brings the lower level up even with the upper level. In the next course up, a stone will bridge that gap to reestablish the running bond. When you stand back for a look, the vertical joints should be discontinuous, zigzagging up the face of the wall.

There is an equally important overlap that won't be visible. You've bound each face of the wall together by bridging all the joints. But you must also bridge the two faces with long stones that run through the entire width of the wall. These are called 'tie stones' or 'bonding units.' The more bonding units that are used, the stronger the wall will be.

A solid wall built in this fashion will be very strong in compression but not so strong in tension. Because it is made out of discrete units that are held together mostly by gravity and friction, a big earthquake can bring the whole thing down. There are several ways to reinforce a solid wall to make this less likely. You can pour 'bond beams' of concrete reinforced with steel both beneath the base and on top of the wall. In high walls, you might even want one or more bond beams part way up. These can be poured between rows of narrow stones to make them invisible.

The Slip-Formed Wall

The slip-formed wall requires less care and skill than does a solid wall and depends less on the shape and strength of the stones. It is basically a concrete wall, with a substantial amount of the concrete displaced by stones that are visible on both faces of the wall. Although this technique demands less of the stone, both in quality and quantity, a slip-form wall requires large amounts of concrete and wood for forms, which can raise the cost of materials considerably. Slip-form walls are more difficult to make beautiful; the concrete tends to show in large, uneven joints and to stain the stones, unless great care is used to clean them off almost immediately. However, slip-forms can be a good option for unskilled masons working with poor quality stone. It's easy to add steel reinforcing to make the wall stronger and more earthquake-resistant. Furthermore, insulation can be added either in the middle of the wall or attached to the

Although rounded river stone is difficult to work with, it can make a beautiful wall if handled with skill, care, and plenty of mortar.

CATHERINE WANEK

interior face, helping to solve one of the most significant problems with stone as a primary wall material.

Since their invention in the 1840s, many different forming systems have been developed, ranging from simple, bulky constructions of lumber and plywood to more complex but light-weight forms of pipe and welded steel. Some forms are built in short sections, which must be moved laterally along the wall; others extend the full length of the wall. Most forms allow only a foot or two (30 to 60 centimeters) of height to be built at a time. After that, the concrete is allowed to set, anywhere from an hour (if quick-setting additives are used) to two days, before the forms are removed and raised into place for the next section of wall. Cement mortar can either be set between the stones as they are placed into the form or poured in afterward. In the latter case, the joints must be 'pointed' with more mortar after the forms are removed.

Among the best-known proponents of slip-form masonry are Helen and Scott Nearing, who left the world of urban academia in the 1930s to live a life dedicated to simplicity and social justice. Their classic book, *Living the Good Life* (Shocken Books, 1970), is an eloquent testament to the role stone building can play in the creation of a more sane and harmonious society.

Michael G. Smith lives in an intentional community and learning center in Northern California. He is surrounded by a bounty of natural building materials, including clay, trees, sand, and gravel — but unfortunately hardly any rocks suitable for building.

RESOURCES
Books

Kern, Ken, Steve Magers, and Lou Penfield. *The Owner Builder's Guide to Stone Masonry.* Owner Builder Publications, 1976. Look for this very readable and well-illustrated classic in used bookstores. Introduces three different building techniques: traditional laid masonry, stone 'facing' over other wall systems, and formed masonry.

Long, Charles. *The Backyard Stonebuilder.* Warwick Publishing, 1996. An entertaining, accessible, and non-intimidating introduction to stone masonry for the hobbyist, including detailed instructions for many small outdoor projects.

McRaven, Charles. *Building with Stone.* Garden Way, 1989. An excellent beginner's guide to stone building, both dry and mortared. Contains instructions for many projects, including a fireplace, root cellar, bridge, dam, flagstone floor, and even a stone house.

Nearing, Helen, and Scott Nearing. *Living the Good Life.* Shocken Books, 1970. Reissued by Chelsea Green. Among countless other pearls of homesteading wisdom, these back-to-the-land pioneers describe in detail their system for building a slip-form stone house.

Straw Bale Building: Lessons Learned

Catherine Wanek

A WONDERFUL IRONY about straw bale builders is that they often started out as complete skeptics. "Doesn't it rot? Doesn't it burn? What about the Big Bad Wolf?" We converts who've heard this before have learned to smile patiently. After all, it was just a decade ago that modern-day pioneers seeking affordable, ecological, beautiful housing built the first code-approved straw bale homes. Since then, straw bale houses have been built in every state in the U.S. and all over the world. It's likely that any 'Doubting Thomas' will soon be converted to a grinning, wide-eyed natural builder by the amazing potential of the humble bale.

Individually, a stalk of straw seems fragile, but hundreds together, compressed and baled, make a sturdy building block. Stack a bunch of these blocks together and walls can go up in a hurry — especially if you enlist your family and friends to help. Roof and plaster it, and you have a super-insulated house; the concept is simple and intuitive. And straw bales, soft and easy to sculpt, can be shaped into cozy spaces, forming a home that feels like an embrace.

A straw bale home not only feels good, but you can feel good about it — straw is commonly underutilized, composted, or burned as an agricultural waste product. The 'staff' of the 'staff of life,' straw is available at a cheap price wherever grain is grown. And stacked like giant bricks to form a thick wall, bales offer super insulation from the heat or cold or noise outside, providing a quiet, comfortable living space with modest lifetime energy requirements. Replacing 'stick frame' walls with bales can cut by half the amount of timber needed in a modern home, reducing demand on forest resources.

Unlike manufactured insulation materials, straw is natural and non-toxic, and very low in embodied energy — the energy required to process and deliver a material to a building site. Should a fire get started, lab tests and experience have shown that foam insulation ignites at low temperatures and releases poisonous fumes, and wood studs and trim will burn readily. But bales, compressed and sealed with plaster, are starved of oxygen and resist combustion. If they do catch on fire, they merely smolder, allowing precious time for occupants to exit and for help to arrive.

Building with bales also has the potential to impact global warming by significantly reducing fossil fuel consumption. Preliminary studies in China and Mongolia indicate that each straw bale home built there, over a projected 30-year life (and they should last much longer), will reduce the amount of carbon entering the atmosphere by 150 tons (136 metric tons). Combined with

China's locally available supplies of straw, bale-building technology holds out the promise of affordable, ecological housing to literally a billion people.

GOOD DESIGN AND DETAILING

To live up to its promise, straw bale building systems must be understood and optimized. The number-one nemesis of straw is water, the universal solvent. Exposed to a moisture content above 20 percent (about 80 percent relative humidity), bales will support fungal growth and begin to decompose. Wet bales have also been linked to insect infestations, which disappear as the bales dry out. Conversely, kept perfectly dry, straw can remain inert for centuries, even millennia. It's not surprising that appropriate bale-building design is consistent with good design practice for homes in general.

A well-designed roof and foundation ('hat and shoes') will prevent most problems with moisture in bale structures. Raising straw bales 6 to 10 inches (15 to 25 centimeters) above grade and installing a moisture barrier (or 'damp-proof course') between the stemwall and first course of bales should eliminate moisture wicking up from the ground. It's also wise to create a 'toe-up' for straw bales above the final floor level, in case of interior flooding from a plumbing problem.

A roof design that incorporates wide eaves (2 to 3 feet [0.5 to 1 meter] if possible) is also highly recommended. Not only will it shed rain and snow far from bale walls, but it will protect earthen plasters from erosion and cement stucco from becoming water saturated. Additionally, wide overhangs, portals, and porches offer the cheapest living/storage space possible and are useful in any climate. Flat roofs and parapet walls, common in the Southwest, are not recommended. Unless their detailing and maintenance is impeccable, they will eventually leak, causing problems no matter what your wall system.

Good window detailing is also critical to avoid moisture infiltration. Commonly, windows are set all the way to the outside of an opening, leaving a bale-wide shelf or window seat on the inside and the minimum surface needing protection from the weather outside. Where window ledges are exposed, proper flashing is essential, and a 'drip edge' recommended.

EARTHEN PLASTERS AND STUCCO

Finish plasters serve multiple functions. Protecting straw bale walls from wind and rain, plasters also seal bales from birds and rodents that find them to be an attractive home, too. Plasters add structural strength to the wall — especially cement-based stuccos. In laboratory tests, compression strength, wind resistance, and racking sheer strength were significantly enhanced after stucco was applied, irrespective of whether wire mesh was used. However, in seismically active areas, a bale/stucco/wire-mesh structural combination is recommended — where it has shown great promise as a safe building system.

It's also important to plaster both sides of a straw bale wall to seal out oxygen for fire resistance. For example, if an interior wall were 'furred out' with studs to attach drywall without plastering it first, the resulting air space would act as a chimney in case of a fire. A well-sealed bale wall is also critical for energy efficiency, as even minor gaps will allow air infiltration through the porous bale, reducing its effective R-value.

Conventional builders often want to add an air barrier (Tyvek and the like) to the outside of a bale wall, under the exterior plaster, to eliminate air infiltration. This is not only unnecessary — as a well-detailed plaster is sufficient for this purpose — but can be a critical mistake. Such an air barrier will prevent the exterior plaster from 'keying in' or bonding to the straw bales, reducing the wall's structural strength. Worse yet, as interior water vapor migrates to the colder exterior through the straw bale wall, it will tend to condense on the inside of the air barrier. This moisture will dry out very slowly, and when the temperature warms, it can produce conditions ripe for fungal growth.

Without ceiling insulation, a straw bale house is like a thermos bottle without a lid. Most heat loss and gain is through the roof. Whatever insulation you choose, air infiltration will significantly compromise its performance, so take care to seal any cracks, especially the joint where the walls meet the ceiling. If bales are used as roof insulation, space the trusses or rafters so the bales fit tightly together. It is also wise to plaster any exposed surface, as a fire-retarding measure.

In cold climates, floors and foundations should also be insulated from the ground and outside air. If you incorporate passive solar design, then free heat from the sun can be stored in interior mass floors, walls, and objects. Thermal mass materials equalize to their surrounding air temperatures gradually, tending to moderate the climate around them. A thick plaster on straw bale interior walls adds up to provide a significant part of the thermal mass required for effective solar design. Earthen plasters will also moderate humidity inside homes, providing the perfect range for human health, according to Bau-biologists. Praised for absorbing odors and softening sounds, plasters of earth are also renowned for their beauty.

Earthen plasters have an added advantage of being hydrophilic, which means that they will always wick moisture from straw, acting to protect it from rot. Many historic English and Welsh cob houses and German houses with straw-clay infill walls are still lived in today after centuries of use. It appears that clay combined with straw has a preservative effect and is much less vulnerable to moisture. Earthen plasters on straw bale walls may also have this kind of long-term beneficial effect.

JOSEPH F. KENNEDY

Following the encouraging example of historic Nebraska straw bale buildings, modern bale builders choose load-bearing wall systems typically for modest-sized, single-story structures. This wall raising is part of a self-help housing project in Guadalupe, Arizona.

LOAD-BEARING VERSUS POST AND BEAM

A modest single-story rectangular building lends itself to load-bearing design. It will generally be cheaper to build than a post and beam and bale structure, primarily due to reduced lumber costs. Load-bearing bale walls can generally be erected faster, too, as they avoid the complex interface between bales and the structural system. Both modern testing and the continuing viability of historic straw bale homes in Nebraska indicate that bales are sturdy building blocks that can bear the roof load and stand the test of time in a well-built house.

Larger, more complicated floor plans must generally incorporate a post-and-beam structural system, with bale infill. One big advantage of this method is the possibility of raising the roof before the bales arrive on site. This provides a ready place to store bales out of the weather and virtually guarantees no wet bales — something that has proven to be a nightmare to many a careless builder. Be sure to think through how your structure and bales will meet, as designing to minimize notching and custom bales will pay off in ease of construction. One common approach is to wrap the bale walls around the outside, leaving the posts exposed inside. This results in a tight, insulating envelope and an interior structure that is easy to tie into. If your posts are trees left naturally round, it is all the more beautiful.

CODES

Straw bale construction has been adopted in a number of building codes, including the state of New Mexico and many counties in Arizona and California. This has been both a blessing and a curse for architects and builders. The codes they fought to have accepted are now, just a few years later, inflexible and restrictive, hindering new, improved bale building methodologies.

Still, code approval has helped straw bale building gain acceptance with lenders and insurance companies, paving the way for mainstream applications. And energy efficiency is increasingly being mandated by new codes, which reflect our society's growing awareness of the need for conservation. In this context, straw bale construction offers a 'green' alternative to conventional housing, and, for many, a stepping stone toward natural building and sustainability.

TRENDS

Despite code restrictions, experimentation continues towards simplifying bale wall construction, reducing costs and improving performance. In a poor but vibrant neighborhood in Sonora, Mexico, Athena and Bill Steen have worked with local builders to create affordable straw bale homes from locally available materials. Together they discovered simple solutions to working with poor-quality bales. Many professionals north of the border are adopting one technique known as 'exterior pinning,' 'exterior ribs,' or the 'corset system.' Conventionally, bale builders pin the courses of bales together by pounding rebar, bamboo, or wooden stakes down through them. The Steens discovered that it is far stronger to place a 'pin' vertically on each side of the bale wall and then attach the pins with twine or wire pushed horizontally through the bale. This cinches the bale wall tightly together and can firm up an otherwise shaky wall. The Steens use a local reed called 'Carrizo,' but in other regions, any plentiful sapling would probably serve the purpose.

In Australia, John Glassford of Huff and Puff Constructions has successfully built several large commercial buildings with load-bearing jumbo bales, measuring 3 by 3 by 8 feet (1 by 1 by 2.4 meters). Workers used forklifts to place the bales, which were then sprayed with stucco. Glassford and company constructed a factory and two wineries with this technique. These thick bales, combined with good ceiling insulation, created a large, super energy-efficient structure that can easily provide the proper environment for aging fine wine.

Retrofitting existing buildings with straw bale insulation shows great promise in urban areas. Although a quality job requires much planning and attention to detail, wrapping a sound but inefficient building can make a huge difference in

Although building codes are slow to catch up, most bale builders are now 'pinning' their walls with exterior stakes of bamboo, rebar, willow, etc. Tied tightly in pairs on either side of the wall, exterior pins work better to stabilize tall bale walls. They may be buried in plaster or exposed for decorative effect.

CATHERINE WANEK

One advantage of a post and beam structure is that the roof can be built first and bales safely stored and installed out of the weather. To avoid excessive notching of bales, consider leaving the posts exposed inside the structure.

energy bills, comfort, and esthetics. A recent retrofit by straw bale pioneers Matts Myhrman and Judy Knox in Tucson transformed a homely block home into a work of art. In many situations, the choice to retrofit can save valuable existing resources and reduce the energy drain of poor design.

Pushing the boundaries of straw bale, a number of builders have been experimenting with vaults, notably Berkeley, California architects Dan Smith, Bob Theis, and Kelly Lerner. Using bamboo 'exoskeletons,' bales are carefully stacked and supported with falsework, until the vault is completed; then the supports are removed and the bales plastered. The primary advantage of a vault is its resource efficiency — the inexpensive bale is used for both wall and ceiling insulation and provides its own structure. Disadvantages include difficulties in roofing and/or making the bales watertight. Since creating a waterproof skin will also prevent water vapor from transpiring through the wall/roof area, moisture could condense in the bales. This complex issue needs more study. Still, Smith and Associates have secured the first permit to build a straw bale vault, in a seismic zone of California. With continued pioneering, the straw bale vault may yet emerge as the most cost-effective and energy-efficient bale structure possible.

CATHERINE WANEK

A STRAW BALE FUTURE

Given our rapidly expanding world population and the mounting evidence of global warming, straw bale construction is being embraced by visionaries as a housing solution that minimizes the use of fossil fuels. Currently the United States has more straw bale buildings than any other country. Rather than leading the rest of the world toward resource exhaustion, the U.S. has begun to set an example of resource conservation, as more and more Americans choose to build their homes with bales — and boast about it.

Meanwhile, low-tech straw bale methodologies are already creating affordable homes for people in far-flung communities around the globe. The *Casas Que Cantan* (Houses that Sing) initiative of Athena and Bill Steen in Mexico assists low-income families to construct good, decent homes for around US$500 in materials. In Belarus, a government initiative has built nearly 100 straw bale homes for families displaced by the Chernobyl nuclear accident, at one-quarter the cost of a typical brick home. And in Mongolia and China, the Adventist Development Relief Agency (ADRA) introduced energy-efficient straw bale technology into areas with extremely long, cold winters, saving 75 percent or more of the coal required to heat conventional buildings. A few hundred Chinese straw bale homes may soon inspire tens of thousands more, if costs can be partially subsidized by 'carbon credits,' for coal not burned (and pollution thus avoided) in a snug, warm straw bale house.

The good feelings that seem to emerge when people work together to help each other is probably the strongest magnet attracting people to straw bale and natural building. As we work and sweat and laugh together, we remember our interdependence and connect with those around us in an essential way. That is when building with bales becomes more than a methodology for a resource-efficient future; it becomes a doorway into a community that holds a hand out to those coming up behind.

Catherine Wanek has traveled from Orange County to Red Square, learning about and documenting straw bale projects. Since 1992, she has produced five straw bale videos, and has spent four years managing and editing The Last Straw: The International Journal of Straw Bale and Natural Building.

RESOURCES
Books

Lacinski, Paul, and Michel Bergeron. *Serious Straw Bale: A Construction Guide for All Climates.* Chelsea Green, 2000. This excellent how-to guide focuses particularly on good detailing for cold and wet climates.

Magwood, Chris, and Peter Mack. *Straw Bale Building: How to Plan, Design, and Build with Straw.* New Society Publishers, 2000. This clear, step-by-step guide is especially useful during the planning process, whether you intend to build your own or hire a contractor. Good information on permitting, budgeting, designing and drawing up plans.

Myhrman, Matts, and S.O. MacDonald. *Build it With Bales: A Step-by-Step Guide to Straw-Bale Construction.* Out On Bale, 1997. The indispensable guide to all phases of construction, from planning through plastering.

Steen, Athena, and Bill Steen. *The Beauty of Straw Bale Homes.* Chelsea Green, 2000. A color-photo-filled book that shows the range and esthetic possibilities of building with straw.

Steen, Athena Swentzell, Bill Steen, David Bainbridge, and David Eisenberg. *The Straw Bale House.* Chelsea Green, 1994. This is the bestselling book that helped push straw bale building into mainstream American consciousness. Describes the history and philosophy of straw bale building, design options, and construction details.

In the summer, a concrete block home in urban Tucson is either a sweltering nightmare or an expensive energy hog.

By adding wide shady porches and a straw bale 'wrap,' Matts Myhrman and Judy Knox transformed this building into a home of comfort and beauty.

Periodicals

The Last Straw: The International Journal of Straw Bale and Natural Building. HC66 Box 119, Hillsboro, NM 88042, U.S.A.; phone: 505-895-5400; email: thelaststraw@strawhomes.com; website: www.strawhomes.com. This large quarterly journal is packed with up-to-date information on the international movement, resources, and the latest technical developments.

Video

Building with Straw, Vol. 1: A Straw-Bale Workshop. Black Range Films, 1994. Covers the basics of straw bale construction and the many different reasons that people are attracted to it. Available from Black Range Films, Star Rt. 2 Box 119, Kingston, NM 88042, U.S.A.; email: blackrange@zianet.com; website: ww.StrawBaleCentral.com.

Building with Straw, Vol. 2: A Straw-Bale Home Tour. Black Range Films, 1994. Introduces ten houses with a wide range of building styles, from elaborate mansions to simple bungalows; with narration by the owners. Available from Black Range Films.

How to Build Your Elegant Home with Straw Bales. Sustainable Systems Support, 1996. How-to guide to load-bearing straw bale construction; comes with a manual. Available from Sustainable Systems Support (See "Organizations").

The Straw Bale Solution. NetWorks Productions, Inc., 1997. Superb introduction to bale building; narrated by Bill and Athena Steen and featuring their work in Mexico. Available from NetWorks Productions, Inc., HC 66, Box 119, Hillsboro NM 88042, U.S.A.; website: www.NetworkEarth.org.

Organizations

California Straw Builders Association (CASBA), P.O. Box 1293, Angels Camp, CA 95222, U.S.A.; email: casba@strawbuilding.org; website: www.strawbuilding.org. Good reference for local designers and builders. Holds an annual conference and produces a newsletter.

Mid-America Straw Bale Association (MASBA), 2110 S. 33rd Street, Lincoln, NE 68506-6001, U.S.A.; phone: 402-483-5135; website: www.strawhomes.com/sban. Information, networking, and straw bale publications from Nebraska, the original straw bale heartland.

Sustainable Systems Support, P.O. Box 318, Bisbee, AZ 85603, U.S.A.; phone: 520-432-4292; email: sssalive@primenet.com; website: www.bisbeenet.com/buildnatural/. Steve Kemble and Carol Escott provide straw bale workshops, consulting, engineered building plans, building services, and mail-order resources.

The Canelo Project, HC1 Box 324, Elgin, AZ 85611, U.S.A.; phone: 520-455-5548; fax: 520-455-9360; email: absteen@dakotacom.net; website: www.caneloproject.com. Athena and Bill Steen's non-profit educational organization offers workshops on straw bale and other natural building techniques; work-study tours to Mexico.

Out on Bale (un)Ltd, 2509 N. Campbell Ave. #292, Tucson, AZ 85719, U.S.A.; phone: 520-622-6896; email: biwb@juno.com. The godparents of the straw bale revival, Judy Knox and Matts Myhrman offer public presentations, design consulting, customized workshops, and straw bale wall-raisings.

Websites

CREST Straw-bale Listserve. An email discussion group with lively and often useful discussion on mostly technical aspects of bale building. To subscribe, type "subscribe strawbale" in the first line of an email message to: majordomo@crest.org.

Surfin' Strawbale. A collection of links to other straw bale web pages, on-line at www.strawhomes.com and http://moxvox.com/surfsolo.html.

Timber Framing: A Natural Building Form

Steve Chappell

ARCHITECTURE IS THE ART of building, engineering is the science, but these two elements remain only an illusory concept until the builder picks up the shovel and begins to lay the foundation and turn the illusion into a manifest reality. Both the art and the science of building have evolved throughout the ages based on empirical evidence gathered step-by-step in the field by the builders who actually put the structures together.

The purpose of architecture is to define space; to assure that the space will sufficiently fulfill the requirements of its intended use. The purpose of engineering is to assure safety — to prevent injury or death by designing structures that will not collapse upon their inhabitants. The challenge to the builder is to marry these two, to find practical and efficient approaches to carry out the building process in the field, under real-world conditions. The architect and the engineer each operate more or less on a theoretical level. The builder, however, works on the direct physical level. The theories and concepts of the architect and engineer remain mute until the builder puts them into action.

Until the Industrial Revolution, the indigenous and vernacular building styles of nearly all regions of the world were based on and derived directly from empirical evidence. The laboratory was in the field. Systems that proved to work over time were replicated. The successful builders attracted more apprentices who were then trained to follow the successful formulas of building. For the most part, especially in residential dwellings, the builder served also as the engineer and architect. The variations in design in most medieval dwellings were subtle, dictated more by the materials most readily available at that time. The medieval village homes and country farmhouses from England to Japan all shared a striking similarity. The styles and designs seemed to be developed from a universal intuitive level. The type of structure and the materials used to enclose it were developed directly from the materials at hand. The northern-forested areas all developed a timber framing tradition.

This well-maintained timber frame house in Europe shows that an oak timber frame can last for centuries.

CATHERINE WANEK

197

Enclosures were made up from a mixture of straw and clay in the walls and thatch or stone on the roof — most often directly from the farmer's waste products. The minka farmhouses of medieval Japan share such a close similarity to the farmhouses built in Germany during the same period that one might easily believe the same builder may have built them. Even the materials were the same: timber frames, a mixture of straw and clay in the walls (variations of wattle and daub) and thatch roofs. In the Mediterranean region, stone and clay were the prominent materials. From the dawn of civilization until very late into the 19th century buildings were primarily built with the materials that came directly from the building site. Regional styles and patterns developed in direct relationship to the material resources at hand.

A well-directed work party raises the timber frame for Michael Smith's house in northern California. Note round pole construction.

CRAFTSMANSHIP

If we were to bundle all of the traditional building styles and systems into a bag, one thing above all stands out: craftsmanship. The minka builders of medieval Japan would typically search for the most crooked logs for the principal members of their frames because the challenges they presented would stand as a testament to their abilities as artists and craftsmen.

Throughout a student's long apprenticeship, as great an emphasis was put on developing their skills as a fine craftsman as was the understanding of structure and design. But these both went hand-in-hand. If a structure was to stand for many generations, then no corners could be cut. The 800-year-old timber framed stave churches of Scandinavia stand to this day for two simple reasons: 1) the timber frames were built based on a solid technical understanding of structural design; and 2) the carpenters who built them placed craftsmanship as the top priority. Pure structural forms can often be stark and uninspiring, but take a pure structural form, add an artistic element, execute it impeccably, such that you and your children will be inspired and proud, then respect toward it will be passed down to each succeeding generation. Buildings we respect are buildings we maintain. Without maintenance, no structure can survive more than a generation or two at the most.

TIMBER FRAMING AS STRUCTURE AND ART

The development of timber framing began as a simple solution to create a structural framework. Every forested region of the world developed a form of timber framing. The early examples relied on crude joinery, often lashed together with rope. As the system evolved, sophisticated forms of joinery were developed and the ability to create more complex designs came with it. By the end of the middle ages the system of timber framing had risen to such a high level that it combined structure with art, as evidenced by the great cathedrals of Europe.

By creating a structural framework, the opportunity to use more diverse enclosure systems for both roof and walls became possible. Mixtures of clay and straw became the most common wall enclosure and thatch or stone the common roof enclosure. By the 9th century, the essential system of timber framing — joined timbers with clay walls and thatch roofs — was nearly fully developed. This system remained, with relatively few modifications, throughout Europe and Asia through the 19th century. It became the common mode of house construction for nearly all northern cultures for more than a thousand years. The remarkable thing is that great numbers of these dwellings are still in use to this day.

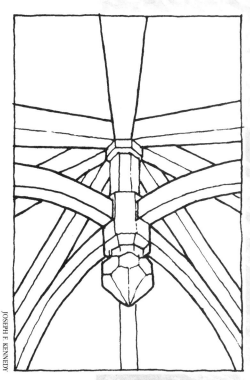

JOSEPH F. KENNEDY

Views from below of an elegant and complex timber frame roof assembly.

EVOLUTION OF TIMBER FRAME DESIGN

The basic system of timber framing is quite simple and straightforward. A common frame in the middle ages would have consisted of frameworks constructed by simply inclining two timbers, or blades (often from one timber split in half lengthwise), to make an A frame. These frameworks were called 'crucks.' The base of the early crucks commonly spanned 12 to 16 feet (3.6 to 5 meters), but spans up to 20 feet (6 meters) were possible. A typical house may consist of two or more crucks, spaced from 10 feet to 16 feet (3 to 5 meters) apart, connected to each other by smaller logs or hewn timbers known as purlins. These were either lashed or set into notches on the cruck blades. The earliest forms of cruck framing were known as 'hovels' because they were often buried, or bermed with earth four or five feet from the sill plate. Impoverished peasants of the lowest class commonly built these dwellings; hence the connotation of the term, "living in a hovel," implies a sub-standard, impoverished existence. Above this level, reed thatch or stone was attached to the purlins. As this form developed into the 13th century, cruck framing became extremely sophisticated, and a common method to construct community halls, chapels and even structural elements in the great cathedral roof frames. The essential design became the pattern for much more sophisticated roof framing systems and a good argument could be made that roof trusses as we know them today began their evolution with the cruck.

The early cruck builders relied on the earth as a buttress to prevent outward thrust, and ultimately, collapse. As the knowledge of structural design developed, along with the development of better steel to make tools and the ever-increasing knowledge of joinery design and function, framing systems that could adequately resist the effects of thrust began to develop. The earliest examples simply raised the cruck by placing it on top of a two vertical posts connected by a horizontal tie beam. The feet of the cruck blades were joined directly into the horizontal tie beam, effectively resisting thrust directly. The buttressing effect of the earthen berm no longer was a requirement to the structural integrity of the frame, and people could move above ground, at last. This development became know as a bent frame, the common structural pattern for timber framing to this day.

A timber frame house under construction in eastern Maine. Note wooden pegs securing the joints.

JOSEPH F. KENNEDY

MODERN TIMBER FRAME DESIGN

In using the term 'modern,' I include the period from 1400 to the present. Though the system of timber framing may have had a down time in the U.S. for nearly 100 years, the essential structural systems, methods and approach used by the common house builder in the 1860s, and the modern timber framer in 2001, are the same as those that were used in the 15th century.

Crucks are commonly equated with English and European building systems, but a similar evolution took place in Asia during the same period in time. And while there are many regional and national derivations in style and technique, the essential elements of traditional timber frames, east and west, are all based on the same basic structural principles: support posts, horizontal tie beams, rafters, and connecting plates, to which the enclosure system is attached. In nearly every example, from Europe throughout Asia, the wall enclosure was made up of clay mixed with a cellulose fiber, usually straw. While the basic structural elements of any timber frame remain constant, variations in the wall framing to accommodate the infill or enclosure method varied in some degree from region to region. Frames today can be designed to accommodate virtually any natural enclosure from straw bales, woodchip/clay to the traditional wattle and daub.

TOM LANDER

A non-slipping split beam detail in a Japanese timber frame.

One of the distinct benefits of timber framing as a structural system is that it acts as a structural skeleton, capable of carrying large clear-spans, and therefore, capable of creating more open living areas. This also allows great flexibility in how the structure is enclosed because the wall enclosure system is not load bearing.

In a typical frame, vertical support posts are spaced from 12 to 16 feet (3.6 to 5 meters) apart. A building 28 x 40 feet (8.5 x 12 meters) would require no more than ten vertical posts. Assuming that a common timber dimension for a post is 7 x 10 inches (18 x 25 centimeters), and the wall height is 8 feet (2.4 meters), the board footage of wood required to build the structural wall support system for a 28 x 40 foot timber frame would be less than 500 board feet (466 to be exact). Using a conventional 2 x 4 framing system, the same house would require nearly 2,500 board feet of wood (2,303 to be exact, for a wall with studs at 16 inches on center, using the common method of 2 studs per foot which compensates for double and triple studs at all openings and corners, double top plate and single bottom plate). If 2 x 6's were used (which is normally the case due to insulation requirements) the board footage would increase by 42 percent to 3,400 board feet. This is more than 7 times the amount of wood than that required for a structural timber frame wall system.

TIMBER FRAME AND POST AND BEAM SYSTEMS

The terms 'timber frame' and 'post and beam' are often interchanged, and with just cause. However, as construction language has evolved over the past generation or two, the two terms have come to define two variations of a structural system. 'Post and Beam' is a structural engineering term that simply means the supporting of a horizontal member (beam) by a column (post). To say that a 200-year-old Maine barn is post and beam is correct. It would also be correct to say that a modern pole barn, using no joinery, but fastened with steel plates is post and beam. But, to call the modern pole barn a 'timber frame' would be incorrect. The term 'timber frame' as it is used today, implies a timber structure that is connected using nothing but joinery — mortise and tenon secured with wooden pegs.

BENT FRAMING

The most common form of timber framing relies on a framework know as a 'bent.' A bent is a structural framework similar to a truss, made up at minimum of two posts, a tie beam and two rafters. These members are connected using a variety of joinery details to create a rigid framework. The design of the frame will determine the type and kind of joinery required, but there are relatively few joints that make up the basic vocabulary of joinery. Understanding the basic structural requirements of the timber frame bent is essential, but to the builder, increasing their vocabulary of joinery, and learning to execute it to the highest level of quality and craftsmanship is where the mystery and the art of timber framing come into play.

At minimum, a frame requires two bents, spaced anywhere from 8 to 16 feet (2.4 to 5 meters) apart, but a typical house frame usually has three or four. The common Cape house frame of New England usually consisted of four bents, spaced 12 feet (3.6 meters) apart, with each bent spanning 24 to 28 feet (7.2 to 8.5 meters). The bents were connected with a top plate at the eave line, with common purlins joined from rafter to rafter. These frames commonly used what is called an 'English tying joint' to make the critical connection of rafter, tie beam and post. In this design the rafters join directly to the top of the tie beam, having no contact with the posts. The post is also joined directly to the tie beam. Though the common name implies it is solely of English origin, a very similar joinery detail was used extensively in Japan. The beauty of this joinery detail is that it is a pure compression joint. As a rule, compression joints are better than tension joints because the complete cross section of the timber is resisting the force, whereas tension joints usually rely on a reduced cross section to resist forces.

TRADITIONAL BUILDING IS NATURAL BUILDING

One of the best ways to develop natural patterns of building is to study the traditional building patterns of the past. In so doing, we may also find that we gain a deeper understanding of the impact that fine craftsmanship has on our daily lives. Buildings of timber, straw, clay and stone have a rich history. If we wish to build houses naturally, then what better model is there to follow?

Steve Chappell is a master timber framer and author. He founded and runs the Fox Maple School of Traditional Building in Maine.

RESOURCES

Books

Benson, Tedd. *Building the Timber Frame House: The Revival of a Forgotten Craft.* Charles Scribner's Sons, 1980. Accessible introduction for the novice.

Chappell, Steve. *A Timber Framer's Workshop: Joinery, Design, and Construction of Traditional Timber Frames.* Fox Maple Press, 1998. An outstanding resource, not only for timber framers but for anyone who builds with wood. Excellent chapters on tools, structural considerations, comparing different wood species, builders' math and engineering, in addition to many different joinery details and framing and truss design.

Sobon, Jack. *Build a Classic Timber-Framed House.* Garden Way, 1994. Good hands-on information on design, layout, and basic-to-intermediate joinery.

Sobon, Jack, and Roger Schroeder. *Timber Frame Construction: All About Post-and-Beam Building.* Garden Way, 1984. Good basics, including history, simple joinery, and raising.

Periodicals

Joiner's Quarterly. Fox Maple School of Traditional Building (See "Organizations"). Excellent articles on all aspects of timber framing and natural building, especially for experienced builders, plus resources and networking.

Organizations

Fox Maple School of Traditional Building, P.O. Box 249, Corn Hill Road, Brownfield, ME 04010, U.S.A.; phone: 207-935-3720; email: foxmaple@foxmaple.com; website: www.foxmaple.com. Workshops in timber framing, thatching, and traditional enclosure techniques; plus books, information, and quarterly journal.

The Econest Building Company, P.O. Box 864, Tesuque, NM 87574, U.S.A.; phone: 505-989-1813; email: bakerlaporte@earthlink.net. Robert Laporte and crew offer workshops, consulting, and design/build services, focusing on timber framing, straw light-clay infill, earthen plasters, and floors.

The Timber Framers Guild of North America, P.O. Box 1046, Keene, NH 03431, U.S.A.; phone: 603-357-1706. A non-profit organization devoted to the advancement of timber framing.

Wattle and Daub

Joseph F. Kennedy

JOSEPH F. KENNEDY

WATTLE AND DAUB consists of a woven framework of thin, flexible sticks covered with plaster. It is likely the most ancient earth building technique, developed when an enterprising human first daubed mud upon a branch shelter to make it more weatherproof. Wattle and daub (also known as 'rab and dab,' *bajareque* in Central America, *quincha* in South America, and *Fachwerk* in Germany) was historically used in Europe, the Middle East, the Eastern U.S., Central America, and in Africa, where it is still in common use.

In medieval Europe, wattle and daub was used as infill in 'half-timbered' oak-framed houses. Oak staves would be placed vertically in each panel of the frame; then green twigs – usually of a flexible hardwood like ash, maple, hazel, or willow – would be woven horizontally between them. The wattle was often left unplastered where ventilation was needed. Over time, the technique evolved into the wood lath and plaster we are familiar with today.

In Africa and Central America, thin poles were lashed on either side of vertical posts, creating a cavity that was filled with mud or stones. The framework was then either plastered or left exposed. In Japan, bamboo (either narrow culms or split larger stalks) were used as wattle. In the Mississippean cultures of the Central U.S., researchers have conjectured that grass or reeds were used to create woven panels. Traditionally, in Argentina, straw-clay 'sausages' were draped over a horizontal framework between posts and then plastered.

However they are built, wattle panels are usually covered with a daub consisting of clay, cow dung, chopped straw, and/or horsehair, and then plastered with lime (if available). A high clay content makes the daub stick to the wattle, while fibers prevent excessive cracking. Pebbles can be pressed into the plaster to provide extra weather protection. A recent experiment used fibrous cement to replace the daub, with good results. (See "Paper Houses: Papercrete and Fidobe.")

Because of the thinness of the panels (generally 3 to 6 inches [7.5 to 15 centimeters]) traditional wattle and daub is not recommended for exterior walls in very cold or hot climates. Wattle and daub makes excellent interior walls or partitions that are thin yet strong. To increase thermal efficiency for exterior walls, two wattle 'forms' can be built, leaving a cavity between them which is insulated with light-clay or loose straw. (See "Regenerative Building: An Ecological Approach.")

Wattle and daub is fun and easy to build but is only appropriate where a large number of straight wattles can be ecologically obtained. The art of coppicing developed in many places where wattle and daub was traditional. Coppicing entails cutting down a suitable tree such as a willow or hazel, which then sprouts numerous thin shoots from the stump. These straight, flexible shoots are allowed to grow to the desired thickness and then cut for wattle, basketry, or other purposes. In heavily wooded areas, small saplings can be effectively harvested for wattle. Other alternatives include using flexible timber off-cuts, reeds, or bamboo.

Wattle and daub has been traditionally used to create infill panels in timber frame structures. This bamboo wattle in Japan awaits its daub.

RESOURCES

Books

Houben, Hugo, and Hubert Guillard. *Earth Construction: A Comprehensive Guide*. Intermediate Technology Publications, 1994. This detailed, well-illustrated technical guide to many forms of earthen building contains a brief discussion of wattle and daub and much information of general value.

Norton, John. *Building with Earth*. Intermediate Technology Publications, 1997. A good, brief introduction to general principles of earth building, including a brief discussion of wattle and daub.

Roofs for Natural Building

Joseph F. Kennedy

J UST AS A BUILDING needs a 'good pair of boots' (a foundation), it also needs a 'good hat' (a roof). Often the most complex part of a building, a roof must be designed and built carefully to ensure weatherproofness, insulative qualities, sturdiness, and esthetic consistency.

A roof has to:

- protect against rain, snow, wind, and excess light. A roof must be solid, strong, and water-proof. The more severe the weather a roof must withstand, the stouter and steeper it should be built. Thus, steep roofs are used in places with lots of snow, and shallow roofs in milder climates.

- prevent unwanted heat loss or gain. Since heat rises, most heat loss occurs through the roof. Roofs in temperate and cold climates must therefore be well insulated. Insulation and radiant barriers are also important in hot, arid climates, to avoid unwanted solar heat gain through the roof.

- withstand hurricanes, earthquakes, and high winds. This means the roof must be strongly constructed and well attached to the walls and foundation. Metal straps or hardware are usually used to connect the roof to the walls. When the walls are made of discrete units like straw bales, adobe blocks, or compressed earth bricks, a bond beam on top of the wall is very important to create a continuous strong surface to hold up the roof load.

- support its own weight and additional variable weights. The weight of the roof itself is called a 'dead load.' Weights that vary (snow, people) are called 'live loads.' A roof must be designed to avoid collapse from the greatest imaginable loading a building may incur.

- shed water away from the walls. This is achieved by overhangs, the parts of the roof that extend out beyond the edge of the wall. The greater the danger to the walls from weather, the bigger the overhang should be. Roof overhangs should also be designed to block the summer sun yet allow the winter sun in. (See "Designing with the Sun.")

- complement the esthetic qualities of the building. The shape and material of a roof is the often the most dominant esthetic feature of a building. Roof esthetics should be carefully considered early in the design stage.

ROOF SHAPES

Roofs come in several basic shapes. Simple buildings usually use one or another of the roof shapes described here. More complex structures may combine multiple roofs of different shapes, but be aware that with increased complexity comes increased construction time and cost.

Flat Roofs

Perhaps the easiest roof to build, a flat roof has a single surface with no peaks or valleys. Flat roofs are actually slightly sloped to let the water run off. However, because they do not shed water quickly, they are more likely to leak than steeper roofs, so they need to be absolutely waterproof and well maintained. They work best in areas that do not get much rain or snow.

Shed Roofs

Similar to flat roofs, the steeper slope of a shed roof removes water and snow quickly. Choosing a shed roof can make for awkward walls, however, as the walls must be built to different heights, and two of the walls must be sloped.

Gable Roofs

A gable roof is composed of two flat surfaces that meet at an apex (ridge) and slope away from each other. One advantage of a gable roof is that it can provide extra space for living or storage under the roof itself without increasing wall height. A building with this type of roof is more easily expanded than some other systems.

Earthen domed roofs of the Dar Al Islam Mosque in New Mexico, by Hassan Fathy.

JOSEPH F. KENNEDY

In a gable roof, the ridge beam is held up by the end walls or by posts. Rafters are attached to the ridge beam, with the ends of the rafters resting on the side walls. In order to keep the rafters from pushing out the side walls, horizontal tensile members (either boards or cables) are used to connect the rafters.

Trusses, which are triangulated structural components manufactured from small-dimension lumber, can be used instead of ridge beams and rafters. Because trusses are strong, yet relatively light, they are often used to cover large spans.

Hipped Roofs

Hipped roofs are sloped on all four sides, allowing the supporting walls to be all the same height. It is easy to build a bond beam across the level tops of the walls, making this a popular roof design for straw bale structures. The rafters must be supported, as in a gable roof, to keep them from pushing the walls apart.

Domes and Vaults

Domes and vaults are roofing systems common in dryer parts of the world, especially Africa and the Middle East. Unlike the roofs mentioned thus far, which require materials with tensile strength (usually wood), domes and vaults can be made with materials, such as bricks, concrete, stone, and earth, that are strong in compression. A vault is a single-curvature roof and is best used to cover a rectangular room. A 'double-curvature' dome can cover a square or round room. Combinations of vaults and domes can be infinitely varied and are extremely beautiful. (See "From the Nile to the Rio Grande.")

Earthen domes and vaults are not recommended for rainy climates, since they are difficult to waterproof, and if the roof gets soaked it can collapse. Another reason to use domes and vaults only in the driest climates is because they do not shed water away from the walls. However, recent experiments with straw bale vaults and earthbag domes seem to offer great promise. (See "Clay, Straw, and Permaculture" and "An Earthbag-Papercrete House.")

ROOF SYSTEMS

Nearly all roof systems have two general components: the structural component that determines the shape and strength of the roof and the protective component that covers and waterproofs the structure.

Roof Structure

Wood

Wood is still perhaps the most common material used to create roof structures, because it is easy to work, lightweight, and strong in tension and compression. Long spans in traditional framing can require lumber dimensions that are only achievable by milling large trees. However, small-dimension lumber trusses or engineered wood products can reduce pressure on our old-growth forests and are often more convenient. Truss systems are already engineered, and the pre-manufacturing process reduces the amount of labor necessary to install the roof.

Timber framing uses complex joinery techniques to create sophisticated integrated wall and roof structures. This option, while often expensive, can be viable in areas with sufficient wood resources. (See "Timber Framing: A Natural Building Form.")

Some natural builders are finding creative uses for abundant locally available timber that is unsuitable for milling. Homemade bentwood trusses can be made with flexible small-diameter trees, as has been demonstrated in Nova Scotia. Many builders use roundpole timber, which allows smaller trees to be used for the same structural strength as a similar sawn timber from a larger tree. Unmillable but beautifully curved trees can be used for unique custom roofs.

Bamboo

The largest of the grass family of plants, bamboo grows very quickly and provides a strong renewable material for building, tools, and utensils, as well as edible shoots. Common in the tropics, many species of bamboo grow in temperate climates as well. Strong and beautiful, bamboo has recently become popular with builders, especially for creating roof structures. Bamboo can replace wood and steel in many other situations as well. (See "Bamboo Construction.")

Metal

Though not recommended because of its high-embodied energy costs, metal structural members or trusses can be used, especially for long spans.

Waterproofing

Often a sheathing layer on top of the roof structure connects the structural elements, spreads loads, and provides an attachment surface for the water-proofing and protective layers. Highly toxic plywood is conventionally used for such sheathing, but many natural builders prefer to use natural boards, small-diameter saplings, or bamboo. Non-toxic manufactured board products are also becoming more available.

JOSEPH F. KENNEDY

Thatch is a common roofing material around the world. Palm leaves have been used for this pavilion in Alamos, Mexico. All the connections are lashed together with natural fiber.

Perhaps the most challenging aspect of natural roofs is the waterproofing layer. Our ancestors used layers of natural materials like birch bark, reed thatch, slate, and ceramic tiles. Today, these traditional methods tend to be expensive, labor intensive, or leaky. Conventional construction relies on tar, plastic, or rubber products for waterproofing membranes. A less toxic natural alternative is much needed.

Living Roofs

The living roof is really an update of the ancient sod roof of Europe. This type of roof has several advantages: it is beautiful, helps the house blend into its environment, and provides climatic stabilization.

A living roof is heavy and needs a very strong supporting structure. The waterproofing membrane (usually durable synthetic rubber) needs to be applied very carefully, as it is very difficult to locate leaks once the growing medium is in place.

The growing medium can be cut sod, rolled turf, loose topsoil, compost, or straw. It can be planted in ornamental or edible herbs and ground covers or allowed to grow naturally. In many climates, a living roof will need to be watered to stay green. (See "Green Roofs with Sod, Turf, or Straw.")

Thatch

The use of reeds, grasses, or palm fronds as a roofing material is still common in Europe and many less industrialized countries. Thatch is one of the only roof systems available that is entirely natural. Many builders are exploring its use to replace methods that rely on manufactured materials. Thatched roofs, if well built, can last up to 60 years or more and provide a beautiful complement to natural wall systems. Thatch 'breathes,' can use local materials, and is highly insulating and extremely attractive.

Thatching is a highly skilled and time-consuming craft, and very few professional thatchers are available in North America. Hence a thatched roof can be very expensive. If a thatched roof is not well built, it may leak and need to be replaced within a few years. Thatched roofs are vulnerable to fire, and they can also provide a home for undesirable pests. In many countries, thatching materials are increasingly rare and expensive.

Seaweed

Seaweed is a unique roofing material similar to thatch. In Denmark, certain species of seaweed are harvested and placed on roofs to provide long-lasting protection.

Shakes and Shingles

Shakes are overlapping pieces of wood used to shed water and snow. They are created by splitting a rot-resistant log into thin pieces, using a mallet and froe. Shingles are similar but are sawn instead of split. Cedar and redwood shakes and shingles used to be very common, but because they are made from old-growth trees, their use is no longer practical, except in certain rare circumstances. Although admittedly beautiful, a wood roof is also a potential fire hazard.

Metal

Although it is not really a natural material, many natural builders use metal for roofing. Relatively inexpensive compared to other systems, metal roofs are durable, long-lasting, easy to install, and lightweight (allowing the underlying roof structure to be lighter as well). They can last 50 to 100 years in a dry climate and are recyclable. Metal roofs can be used to collect rainwater, a very important consideration in dry areas. The mining of metal ore is, however, environmentally destructive, and the manufacture of metal is very energy intensive. Still, cost benefit analysis shows that metal is in many cases an appropriate roofing material for natural houses.

Other Roofing Materials

Other roofing materials exist; some natural, some man-made. Slate (a flat, sheetlike stone) can be attached to the underlying roof structure with nails and overlapped like shingles. Ceramic tiles are common in many countries and can be an easy and beautiful roof option. Slate and tile can be used to collect water. Both are extremely heavy, however, and need a very strong roof structure to hold them up. Some people have experimented with cutting up old tires and using them like tiles for roofing. Asphalt shingles and rolled roofing, although readily available and easy to use, have a relatively short life and are extremely toxic to dispose of. They are therefore avoided by most natural builders.

Resources

Books

Chappell, Steve. *A Timber Framer's Workshop: Joinery, Design and Construction of Traditional Timber Frames.* Fox Maple Press, 1998. Good chapter on engineering, design, and construction of timber frame trusses.

Clark, Sam. *The Real Goods Independent Builder: Designing and Building a House Your Own Way.* Chelsea Green, 1996. Contains helpful basic information for design and construction of conventional roofs.

Roy, Rob. *The Complete Book of Cordwood Masonry Housebuilding: The Earthwood Method.* Sterling, New York, 1992. Contains an interesting chapter on Roy's method of earth roof construction.

Smith, Michael. *The Cobber's Companion: How to Build Your Own Earthen Home.* 3rd ed. Cob Cottage Company, 2001. Explores the advantages and disadvantages of various natural roofing systems.

Steen, Athena Swentzell, Bill Steen, David Bainbridge, and David Eisenberg. *The Straw Bale House.* Chelsea Green, 1994. Useful chapter on roof design and options.

TOM LANDER

Various materials are used as a protective covering in roof structures. In this case, tile has been used on a house in Japan.

Green Roofs with Sod, Turf, or Straw

Paul Lacinski and Michel Bergeron

A GREEN COVER over your house can be a very attractive alternative to conventional roofing. You might choose a living roof for esthetic reasons; to help buffer the building from the heat of the summer sun; to grow flowers, herbs, or other edibles; or simply to blend the house with its environment. Covering a roof with soil may be the most natural way to conserve the earth removed by the imprint of a new house. Putting your local soil back on the roof is like a lung transplant for your environment. Sod- or turf-covered living roofs will last indefinitely if laid over a good-quality waterproofing membrane, and they will prolong the life of the membrane by protecting it from sunlight and weather.

CONSTRUCTION TECHNIQUES

Sod, turf, and other living roofs don't differ much in the way they are built and are quite simple to construct. Build a low-pitched roof frame, cover it with a solid deck, stick on a waterproofing membrane, and lay the organic material on top of the membrane. Little maintenance will be needed over the years to turn it into a rooftop garden or a long-lasting shaggy blanket.

Archibio developed another living roof system. A basic substrate made of second-quality straw bales, laid side by side with the twines cut to loosen the straw, is placed on top of the waterproof membrane. Then a thin coat of manure, compost, leaves, or any other organic material is spread over the surface and left to grow on its own, or planted with edibles and flowers. The only maintenance required, besides the usual gardening work, is to add more straw periodically as the original layer decomposes and becomes thinner.

ADVANTAGES

The temperature-moderating effect created by 5 to 6 inches (12 to 15 centimeters) of earth on the roof helps keep a house cooler in summer and warmer in winter, especially in extreme climates. Fourteen inches (35 centimeters) of decomposing straw will have the same effect, while adding some insulation for a while. Such roofs are therefore a prime choice for cold-climate houses built with a high degree of insulation for maximum comfort, though they shouldn't replace ceiling insulation. The wind and noise protection qualities of a living roof are also worth considering in specific environments. A city house built with bales and covered with an organic roof will become a peaceful retreat at any time of day, even in areas with dense traffic. On particularly windy sites, such a roof anchors the house to the ground physically as well as visually.

High-tech roofing membranes such as EPDM, Hypalon, neoprene, PVC, and modified bitumen are the best choice for low-pitched roofs. In conventional construction, these are left exposed to weather. Although they have some type of protective coating, they will nevertheless

212

slowly but surely degrade under ultraviolet light exposure, and some of them will also erode over time from continuous heavy rains and ice build-ups. In both cases the protective coat of organic matter will considerably enhance their life expectancy. Using a much lighter growing medium than soil, with enough volume for plant roots to stay healthy, was the origin of Archibio's straw bale concept. An interesting alternative to both of these heavy systems would be to lay down 4-inch-thick (10-centimeter-thick) flakes of straw. That wouldn't add more than 10 pounds per square foot (480 Pascals) to the whole structure, and it would still protect the membrane while offering the same natural look.

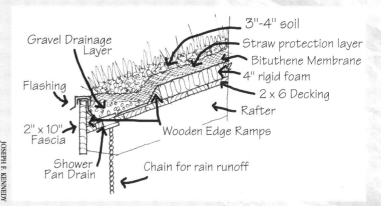

Gravel Drainage Layer

Flashing

2" x 10" Fascia

Shower Pan Drain

3"-4" soil
Straw protection layer
Bituthene Membrane
4" rigid foam
2 x 6 Decking
Rafter
Wooden Edge Ramps
Chain for rain runoff

JOSEPH F. KENNEDY

DISADVANTAGES

The main drawback of building a heavy roof is the additional 50 to 60 pounds per square foot (2.4 to 2.9 kiloPascals) that the structure will have to support. This might be too much on certain load-bearing walls and designs, so the bearing capacities will have to be thoroughly investigated. The need to shore up the structure would obviously increase the building costs, so that prospect should be cross-evaluated with the positive aspects of the roof. Although it may be reduced to a minimum, some seasonal maintenance will be required on a living roof. The type of maintenance will depend on the degree of refinement you want in the appearance of the roof. All the usual activities associated with gardening — weeding, watering, mulching — will be required if your roof is going to be some kind of garden. Otherwise you just need to keep a sufficient cover by periodically adding some material to the original layer. At worst, if no maintenance is done, the membrane might eventually become exposed, as it would have been if not covered at all.

Paul Lacinski is half-owner of GreenSpace Collaborative, a design and construction company based in Ashfield, MA, whose work emphasizes the synthesis of sustainable construction methods, energy systems, vernacular architecture, and ecological land use planning. He has been messing around with straw bales and related materials since 1991.

With a background in architecture and a degree in Industrial Design, Michel Bergeron's personal owner-builder, on-site experiences have led to professional consultancy, lectures, and workshops in Canada, the U.S., and Europe. With Clôde de Guise and Francois Tanguay, he founded Archibio in 1991, a non-profit group promoting sustainable architecture. Now specializing in straw bale construction, Michel has contributed innovations like form-worked straw bale concrete stemwalls, living roofs, and an owner-built composting toilet.

Thatching Comes to America

Deanne Bednar

INTEREST IN THATCHING is growing in North America as the natural building movement searches for roofing solutions, and people in general are responding to the beauty and soulful qualities of hand-built structures like those made by indigenous people throughout the world. Several European-trained master thatchers have brought their learning to this country, and there is a growing grassroots commitment to the exploration of thatched roofing in the United States.

Thatch allows us to create a roof without ecological compromise, and its harvest affords us connection to the natural world and the seasons. Warm in the winter and cool in the summer, thatched roofs provide responsive shelter from the elements that is soulfully and esthetically nurturing. A thatched roof offers a sustainable, insulating, non-polluting, and durable alternative to asphalt shingles; it provides creative scope to the builder and infinite charm to the dwelling.

My first encounter with thatch came during the 1996 Natural Building Colloquium at the Shenoa Retreat Center in California. In a gentle bowl of mountains, under a bright blue sky, Flemming Abrahamsson, master thatcher from Denmark, gave a delightful hands-on demonstration of Danish thatching techniques. I never imagined then that a year later I would be collaborating with the Cob Cottage Company to bring Flemming to Michigan to teach thatching. Out of that workshop grew a most incredible roof, for which, as I write these words, we are collecting the last reed bundles needed to complete it.

In July 1996, I joined with Carolyn Koch to begin work on a studio for a mutual friend, Fran Lee, on her rural land north of Detroit. Buoyed by a vision of a building that would express the spirit of its place, the three of us walked out to the site one day and designed a 650-'round foot' (60-square-meter) studio whose irregular and sculptural outlines are a response to the trees that surround and shape its site.

The studio is constructed of local materials. Stones for the foundation and log poles for the Dutch hip roof came from the site itself. We used straw bales from a nearby farm and plastered them with native earth to form the deep, sheltering walls. The sun comes freely in the south-facing windows onto the earthen floor, and the combination wood stove and heated-mass bench in the cozy nook radiates warmth when cold weather and snow come upon us in Michigan.

Reeds harvested by hand from a Michigan marsh. It required 1,700 bundles of this size to thatch Fran Lee's 1,500-square-foot (140-square-meter) roof.

DEANNE BEDNAR

In our process of design, we considered many different roof possibilities, but once we had pictured a thatch roof, we fell in love with it and there was no turning back! Turning vision into reality was no simple matter, however. You can't just flip through the Yellow Pages and call a local thatcher, as you might do in England. After contacting several American thatchers who gave us support and information, we chose Flemming Abrahamsson because of his willingness to work with students up on the roof!

To prepare for the workshop we needed reed — lots of reed. In fact, we needed to harvest 4 to 5 acres (1.6 to 2 hectares) of plants in order to cover our 1,500-square-foot (140-square-meter) roof. *Phragmites communis* (reed canary grass) is the best of all thatching materials. Roofs built of it are expected to last 50 to 75 years in Europe, when constructed by a master thatcher, with the ridge being replaced every 5 to 15 years. We knew that *Phragmites* grew in nearby private fields, in large state-owned marshes, as well as along the expressways.

COLLECTING AND STORING REED GRASS

In December 1997, with the permission of the Drain Commissioner and the Department of Natural Resources, we headed to the marshes of St. Clair County, about an hour east of our site. In this county, the reeds are invasive and are often cut or burned in an attempt to keep fields and vistas open. Finding reeds was not a problem: at first, every marsh appeared to be a vast resource, but we soon learned that only first- (preferably) or second-year reed grass is strong enough, straight enough, and small enough in diameter to make a good roof. Traditionally reed fields are cut on a one- or two-year rotation, to maintain optimum crops for thatching.

The use of straw as a thatching material would also have been worth considering. Specific older varieties of wheat, rye, and triticale have the long stalks required for thatching straw. Although grain straw has a shorter roof life than reed grass (20 to 25 versus 50 to 75 years), the grain constitutes another economic crop that can be grown locally and harvested with a mechanical binder or by hand. Use of grain straw can also avoid the potential ecological problems associated with reed grass, which is invasive in some areas.

We harvested *Phragmites* using both hand and mechanical methods, averaging about three bundles per person per hour. We found it most time effective to harvest with a gas-powered pole reciprocating hedge trimmer. It worked fine but can be dangerous to nearby legs and is quite noisy! We came to prefer hand harvesting with Japanese sickles because it is a quieter, more comfortable, and natural process.

It soon became apparent that we couldn't cut enough reed (1,500 bundles) by ourselves in time for the workshop, so we enlisted the help of some local folks, paying them US$2 per bundle

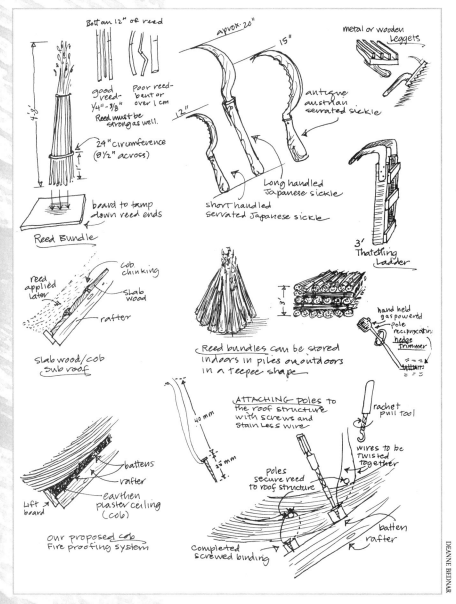

Details of the thatching process, including tools for harvesting and installing reed thatch, as well as preferred installation technique.

plus numerous bonus incentives based on the quantity of bundles cut. The first year, we were only able to get 1,200 bundles, and as the thatching progressed we realized we would need 500 more to finish the roof. We were able to complete two-thirds of the roof the first season but were forced to tarp the remainder of the building and wait until winter to collect enough reed to complete the project.

The second winter, we found ourselves confident and knowledgeable enough to collect 500 reed bundles on our own, with help from occasional volunteers. It's a great process to collect reed on a winter day, when the reeds have dried to a bamboo-like state, dropped their leaves, and wave feathery plumes under a vast sky.

Collected only during the winter, while the plants are dormant, reed bundles are traditionally 8-1/2 inches (21 centimeters) in diameter and 4 to 8 feet (1.2 to 2.4 meters) long. Ideally the ground is frozen during collection since the reed grows in areas that are often wet or under water.

After cutting, the reed is cleaned of weeds, bent stalks, and any remaining leaves, and tied twice: once just below the plumes and a second time about a foot (one-third of a meter) up from the cut end. The bundle is tamped down to give it a flat end and is then ready for the roof.

DEANNE BEDNAR

WORKING THE ROOF

In mid-April 1998 two master thatchers from Denmark — Flemming Abrahamsson and Ole Hans — arrived at the straw bale studio. The roof was prepared by the application of 2-by-2-inch purlins (battens) spaced at one-foot (one-third-meter) intervals, with a 2-by-6-inch 'lift' at the bottom, to put all the reed in a state of compression.

To apply the reed grass, bundles were taken up to the roof. We worked on scaffolding, full-length ladders, little roof-hanging ladders, and 4-by-4-inch beams attached by ropes to the purlins, which made a broad roof area accessible. Thatching tools were minimal: a 'leggett' — used to pound the reed at an angle, feathering in each row to attain an even surface texture; a screw with a long stainless wire attached for fastening down the reed bundles; a cordless drill with a driver bit extender; a manual 'pull, twist' tool that tightened the wires; and a long knife or similar piece of metal for holding the reed in place while working.

The reed bundles were applied to the roof cut end down, feather end up and held in place with long saplings $^1/2$ inch to 1-$^1/2$ inches (1.25 to 3.75 centimeters) in diameter. (Bamboo and rebar can also be used.) The saplings were attached to the roof structure and permanently hold each course of reed in place. The strings of each bundle were cut and the individual reeds blended together and feathered up at an angle by hand and with the leggett. The next overlapping row of bundles was applied, as with roof shingles; it, too, was held down, blended, and feathered in.

We found that it took quite some time to get a feel for the basic technique. The ridge treatment, chimney, roof valleys, etc. required variations on the basic method. As a first-time experiment, I would recommend thatching a very small building such as a doghouse or a garden or tool shed.

RESISTANCE TO RAIN, HEAT LOSS, AND FIRE

A thatched roof is able to shed water effectively only when the following criteria are met. First, the roof needs to be steep, with a minimum angle of 45 degrees. Second, the reeds need to be of good quality — strong and straight — so that when they are properly applied and lying tight together, rainwater will quickly transfer from the end of one reed to the next, without penetrating the roof more than about an inch (2.5 centimeters).

I have heard numerous insulation values quoted for a thatched roof. It clearly has a 10 to 12 inch (25 to 30 centimeter) thickness of trapped air spaces. The insulating quality of the reed is substantially increased when combined with a sub-roof or ceiling that inhibits air passage up through the reed. This is also an important factor in fireproofing the building. In Denmark, Flemming uses 'rock wool' for this air barrier. He also suggested the possible use of a slab wood ceiling, sealed up with cob. This understructure should be built before the thatching is done, if

DEANNE BEDNAR

Reed thatch is attached to the roof by wiring saplings that run horizontally on top of the reed bundles to the purlins underneath. Note the 'leggett' in center frame.

at all possible. Since we didn't know that at the time, we plan to experiment with applying a thick earthen plaster directly to the underside of the finished thatch.

Thatching is, from start to finish, an amazing process – and its natural beauty continues, over time, to bless the building it shelters and those who view it.

Deanne Bednar, construction coordinator and part of the Oxford (Michigan) Straw Bale Studio building team, has a background as an Art and Sustainable Futures middle school teacher. She illustrated The Cobber's Companion: How to Build Your Own Earthen Home.

RESOURCES
Books

Fearn, Jacqueline. *Thatch and Thatching.* Shire Books, 1978. Unfortunately out of print, this book is an overview, with lots of photos of different styles.

Hall, Nicholas. *Thatching: A Handbook.* Intermediate Technology Publications, 1988. General thatching information, including clear sketches of various techniques.

The Reed (Norfolk Reed). 2nd. ed. Norfolk Reed Growers' Association, 1972. A text on growing phragmites, reed grass, and marsh management. Lots of interesting facts about reed.

The Thatchers' Craft. Council for Small Industries in Rural Areas, 1981. The bible of English-style thatching.

Organizations

Cob Cottage Company, P.O. Box 123, Cottage Grove, OR 97424, U.S.A.; phone/fax: 541-942-2005; website: www.deatech.com/cobcottage/. Occasional thatching workshops.

Fox Maple School of Traditional Building, P.O. Box 249, Corn Hill Road, Brownfield, ME 04010, U.S.A.; phone: 207-935-3720; email: foxmaple@nxi.com; website: www.foxmaple.com Offers occasional thatching workshops.

Master Thatchers in the U.S.A.

William Cahill, P.O. Box 62054, Cincinnati, OH 45262, U.S.A.; phone: 513-772-4974; website: www.roofthatch.com.

Colin McGhee, P.O. Box 39, Crozet, VA 22932, U.S.A.; phone: 1-888-842-8241; website: www.thatching.com.

Websites

See www.thatching.org for extensive information from a European thatching organization and visit the Straw Bale Studio Project website at www.geocities.com.rainforest/vines/7729/.

Earth Plasters and Aliz

Carole Crews

CLAY SLIP, known to some as 'aliz,' can be applied to an earth-plastered wall almost like paint is used on other surfaces. The purpose is to seal and beautify the surface; after it has become soiled or damaged, another coat may easily be applied to renew its fresh look. Traditionally, aliz was applied in a very thin layer with a sheepskin (often the skin of a spring lamb that had been killed for food) as a part of spring cleaning after a winter of woodsmoke. In Taos, New Mexico, the favorite aliz material was a micaceous pearly-gray clay called *tierra blanca* found in a cave south of town. Finish work on adobe buildings was traditionally the women's domain, and many vintage photos portray this activity.

Although earthen architecture is common throughout most of the world, the accessibility of cement and cinder blocks is causing people to devalue traditional methods. They want to try out what they think is a more permanent, and therefore better, means of construction. This process is very apparent in Mexico where people associate mud dwellings with poverty. They prefer the status of concrete buildings despite their expense and failure to moderate temperatures.

Modernization has definitely affected the use of clay finishes here in Taos. Even at the Pueblo, some people are buying latex paint for their interior walls instead of using the old techniques. Wherever there is a leak, the paint peels off, revealing dark mud beneath. Paint keeps the wall from 'breathing' properly; it inhibits the wall's ability to transpire moisture. Clay slips on the interior and mud plasters on the exterior allow an earthen structure to absorb moisture and then dry out again without creating major moisture problems.

A big lesson was learned at the famous St. Francis de Assisi Church in Ranchos de Taos when it was coated with cement stucco in 1967. This plaster cracked and allowed moisture to penetrate deeply into the adobes, but the relatively impermeable stucco prevented the adobes from drying out again. Large sections of the buttresses had to be rebuilt. The community has

The yearly replastering of the St. Francis Church in Ranchos de Taos, New Mexico brings the whole community together in a tradition dating back more than 200 years.

NYGEL FUSELLA

now gone back to the annual renewal of the mud plaster, which not only keeps the church building in beautiful condition but strengthens neighborhood ties as well.

Before sharing the details of clay slips with you, I will briefly explain the basics of plastering the wall with mud. Clay is essential for stickiness, so first you must locate a supply. Do a shake test. Place your sifted earth in a jar of water to which salt has been added, and shake it up thoroughly. When it settles, clay will be the top layer, silt will be in the middle, and the heavier particles of sand will have sunk to the bottom. Plaster dirt should be at least 20 percent clay. Even at this percentage, you may wish to add manure or flour paste to make it stickier.

Applying earth plaster by hand is one of the most sensuous and satisfying parts of natural building.

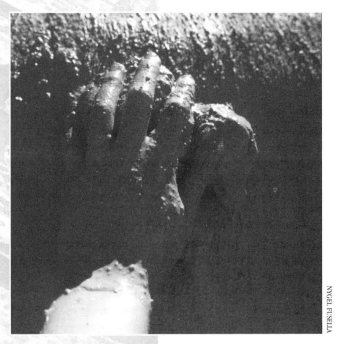

NYGEL FUSELLA

When plastering straw bales, I find it easiest to first spread on a thin layer of mud with a high clay content and no additional sand or straw. This locks in to the straw and provides a surface to which the next layer can adhere. If you use this technique on tight bales, you can avoid using stucco netting. You don't have to wait for this to dry before applying the thicker layer of plaster with straw added.

On rough cob or adobe and for the second layer on straw bales, I like to use a plaster with high clay content and lots of straw, mixed to a slippery, easily spreadable consistency. This can be applied with the hands to a dampened wall and is very good for filling in depressions. (It gets rid of your own depression, too, because it feels so good to sling that mud around.) The condition of your walls and the amount of shaping they need will determine whether to use long straw, chopped straw, or a combination. The thicker the layer needs to be, the more long straw it should have. Don't trowel this layer smooth; get it as flat as you can with your hands and let it dry out thoroughly. It will make lots of little cracks that provide a perfect surface for the next layer to adhere to.

Always try out an earth plaster you are not familiar with by making a test patch of several square feet (a square meter). Clays differ in their shrinkage rates, and if it cracks too much, then you need to add sand and more straw. I've seen some plasters dry into the sort of cracks you find on the bottom of a dry lakebed, and fall off the wall. This happens more often to a troweled surface than to a rough one, because there is less surface area available to release moisture.

If the dry plaster is very soft when you scratch it, then it has too much silt or sand and needs more clay, fresh manure, and/or flour paste. In India, the Middle East, and elsewhere, it was discovered long ago that old stinky mud works better than fresh mud, so it is mixed in a pit with animal manure and other wastes and left to 'ripen.' This causes the molecules of clay to line up as closely as they can, improving wet plasticity and dry toughness.

The next layer is the final coat before the aliz. If your walls are of rammed earth, pumicecrete, or straw-clay, then this is the only layer of plaster you may need. The clay should be sifted through a window screen-sized mesh and added to the water in whatever container you are mixing in. Let nature do the work, and it will soak up the water with no effort. Then add equal volumes of chopped straw and fine sand to the soupy clay and water mixture. These proportions may vary, according to the amount your particular clay shrinks and the texture of the plaster you prefer to use. Some people prefer twice as much sand as clay, and less straw. The plaster should be easily workable, sticky enough to adhere well to the dampened wall, and wet enough to trowel on easily but not so wet that it's hard to pick up. Robert Laporte recommends adding a small amount of cooking oil to the mixture to make it slide on more smoothly, and I find it does make a positive difference. A disk of plastic cut from the top of a coffee can or yogurt container is a useful tool for negotiating curves and 'bullnosing' around windows and doors.

If you have gathered a purer clay that is full of lumps, it's best to soak it and make a slip by stirring it into water. A paint-mixing tool attached to the end of a drill simplifies this job, as long as the lumps are not so big as to jar the tool. Add fine sand to the thick clay slip until it is the right consistency (up to 70 percent, depending on the clay), and then add the straw.

To apply this plaster in preparation for a clay slip, you need a trowel, a tile sponge, and a bucket of water. I prefer to work from a bucket of plaster rather than a hawk (a tray for holding plaster) so that I can use both hands and don't wear out my left arm holding the awkward hawk, though I know most professional plasterers would disagree. I wear rubber gloves, scoop some plaster onto the trowel, and apply it to the dampened wall like icing on a cake. I cover about a square yard (about a square meter) at a time, without worrying overmuch about smooth perfection. Then I go on to the next yard. When I finish that, I go back to the first yard, which has had time to set up a bit, and smooth it out with the sponge. The sponge leaves a perfect, fine-grained 'tooth' for the aliz to bind with. If it's still too wet to sponge smooth, then wait a little longer. If you want to leave the plaster without a clay slip, then you can trowel it hard and smooth at this point, spraying it lightly with a squirt bottle as you go.

A very fine finish plaster can also be made without straw to be applied in a thin layer to a wall that is quite flat already. If clay is hard for you to find, then you can purchase it at a pottery supply store. White kaolin that we use for slips can also be used for plasters. Ball clay of a gray color is very good in plaster because it has greater plasticity and dries harder than kaolin. Use it if you're less concerned about color or are planning to put a slip over it anyway. Either mix the fine dry sand (70 percent) and clay (30 percent) together first and then add water, or mix the clay and water into a slip first and then add the sand. Don't forget the splash of oil for workability. Proportions may vary somewhat depending upon your sand.

And now for my favorite part, the final clay slip or aliz. I use white kaolin and ground mica as major ingredients in a clay slip. Often I add a small amount of fine sand, especially to the first coat, to make it thicker and to fill in any small irregularities in the plaster surface. I use cooked flour paste as a binder in the proportion of 20 percent to 25 percent of the liquid.

Bill Steen, experimenting with a variety of earthen plaster mixes in Mexico. This kind of testing is essential, since soils vary from site to site.

CATHERINE WANEK

To cook the flour paste, set a two-thirds-full pot of water to boil on the stove. In a mixing bowl, whisk together equal parts cheap white flour and cold water. When the pot of water comes to a rolling boil, pour in the flour and water mixture and stir it well. It should thicken immediately and become somewhat translucent. Don't keep cooking it or it will scorch. The final proportion of water to flour is approximately four to one. I have substituted Elmer's glue on occasion to give the first coat of aliz more strength over a weak plaster. Wallpaper paste, an instant flour paste, also works well. Milk products also act as a binder, buttermilk being best.

To mix the aliz you will need a container at least as large as a 5-gallon (25-liter) bucket and a big whisk or a paint-mixing attachment on the end of a drill. Start with three parts water to one part cooked flour paste in the bucket until approximately three-fifths full. Use a saucepan or coffee can for a scoop and start adding the ingredients proportionally. Recipes vary according to the surface and whether people love mica or not, but generally I use three scoops of white kaolin, two scoops ground mica (or more), and one scoop (more or less) of fine sand. Sand is mainly for the first coat or if mica is not available. Be careful not to breathe in the fine particles of dust and mica; wear a dust mask while mixing.

Keep adding these ingredients until the mixture is the same thickness as heavy cream. You may have to add a bit more water to achieve this consistency. Sodium silicate is an ingredient used in slip casting to keep the particles of clay suspended in the water and is useful in this context as well. A very small amount is required. It will also thicken the mixture somewhat, as will powdered milk, which makes the final product a little tougher.

Colored clays or pigments may be added to aliz to create different colors. Colored clays would replace some or all of the white kaolin in the recipe, and pigments should be soaked in water or ground to prevent color spots from showing up. Earth pigments that are sold to color concrete are quite suitable. If mold might be a problem, then add a little dissolved borax powder. I love to add larger chips of mica to the mix, but they are not commercially available as far as I know. If it's easily available, mica makes a lovely addition to finish plasters as well as to clay slips. Bits of chopped straw are a popular addition to the aliz, too.

You will need a few tools to apply the aliz to your wall: a three- or four-inch-wide (8- or 10-centimeter-wide) brush, a one-inch (2.5-centimeter) brush for edges (natural bristles are best), two small buckets, and a fine-grained tile sponge. I wear rubber gloves for all the wet work.

Do not moisten the wall first. Make sure it is completely dry, because damp plaster will leave water stains. Start brushing at the top of the wall, so that you don't mess up your fresh work with drips. Cover the floor with dropcloths. If the wood of your window edges and lintels is rough, then tape it first to save yourself cleaning work. If it's smooth and painted, then the slip can be wiped off easily while it's still wet. Use the small brush for edges or mix some of the slip with extra sand in a small container and apply it to the edges with a palette knife. In small curvy areas, I sometimes mix the slip a bit thicker and apply it with my hands. At the bottom of walls, I will often use the sponge to dip out some slip and slide it up the wall, starting at the base.

Most walls require two coats. Make sure the first one is completely dry before applying the second one. When the second coat starts to dry and look mottled, becoming 'leather-hard,' take your sponge and a bucket of warm water and start to polish in circular strokes, using the squeezed-out sponge. Rinse and squeeze out your sponge often so that it will cleanly polish off the mica flakes and bits of straw. Polishing smoothes out the brush strokes and gives the surface a finer texture. You can even dry-polish it again later with a rag to get off any last bits of sand and to polish the mica to a greater sheen.

When you are finished with your job, save the leftovers as 'cookies,' by drying them on a tarp or plastic; these may be stored dry, then rehydrated and used to repair any minor damage.

I can't emphasize enough the need for trials and experimentation in this type of work. There are many variables in Mother Nature's materials, so never take them for granted. Happy mudding!

Carole Crews of Gourmet Adobe creates sculpted bas-reliefs and other artful earth plaster projects, and specializes in aliz. She loves adobe arches, domes, and flowers.

RESOURCES

BOOKS

Courtney-Clark, Margaret. *African Canvas: The Art of West African Women*. Rizzoli, 1990. Beautiful photographs highlight exquisite earthen plasters and natural finishes on hand-crafted earthen homes.

Elizabeth, Lynne, and Cassandra Adams, eds. *Alternative Construction: Contemporary Natural Building Methods*. John Wiley and Sons, 2000. Contains a detailed chapter on earthen finishes by Carole Crews.

Huyler, Stephen. *Painted Prayers: Women's Art in Village India*. Rizzoli, 1994. Inspirational, full-color photographs of natural finishes including decorative earthen murals.

McHenry, Paul. *Adobe and Rammed Earth Buildings: Design and Construction*. University of Arizona Press, 1989. Contains a chapter comparing various plaster and stucco options, including traditional earthen, gypsum, and cement.

Meagan, Keely. *Earth Plasters for Straw-bale Homes*. Self-published, 2000. A brief but very clear and practical overview of various earth plaster recipes and application techniques especially for straw bale walls. Available from the author at P.O. Box 5888, Santa Fe, NM 87502, U.S.A.; phone: 1-888-441-1632.

Organizations

Cob Cottage Company, P.O. Box 123, Cottage Grove, OR 97424, U.S.A.; phone/fax: 541-942-2005; website: www.deatech.com/cobcottage/. Occasional natural plaster workshops as well as cob and other techniques.

Gourmet Adobe, HC 78 Box 9811, Ranchos de Taos, NM 87557, U.S.A.; phone: 505-758-7251. Professional earthen finishes and workshops.

Proclay, P.O. Box 249, Brownfield, ME 04010, U.S.A.; phone: 207-935-3720; email: proclay@hotmail.com. Frank Andresen offers professional earth building and restoration, including fine clay finishes; also workshops.

The Canelo Project, HC1 Box 324, Elgin, AZ 85611, U.S.A.; phone: 520-455-5548; fax: 520-455-9360 email: absteen@dakotacom.net; website: www.caneloproject.com. Offers workshops on natural plasters in addition to straw bale and other techniques.

Materials Suppliers

Oglebay Norton, a division of Franklin Minerals, P.O. Box 130, Velarde, NM 87582, U.S.A.; phone: 505-852-2727. The only commercial source of ground mica in the U.S.A. Their 'V-115' is the largest grain currently available and gives a visible sparkle to the surface. The '1117' is the next-largest grade and has more sheen. 'Mica 200' is finely powdered and offers no sparkle at all but improves the texture of aliz.

Working with Lime

Barbara Jones

LIME HAS BEEN USED all over the world as a binding material and as a surface protector of buildings for thousands of years. Here in Europe, lime was used in building for hundreds of years before contemporary cement was invented. However, whereas cement is foolproof (in that any fool can use it), lime requires thought and an understanding of the processes involved in the slow carbonation back to limestone in order to use it successfully. The preparation and practice of lime work is simple, but variables in the materials themselves (the sand, the lime, and particularly in the weather during application and drying time) are crucial to the overall durability of the material.

Traditionally, knowledge about lime was passed down from one generation to the next and so built up a wealth of experience based on a sound knowledge of the material. Today, there are very few skilled craftsmen left living (I haven't found any women yet) who worked in those times, and we have to learn as best we can from what we have left. To some extent, that can lead us into an overly technical approach to what was essentially a practical and rather ad hoc building practice. We are trying to specify exact lime/sand mixes when most likely what happened on-site was fairly rough and ready, except for the most prestigious jobs.

LIMESTONE AND LIME BURNING

The raw material for lime mortars and renders is naturally occurring limestone, shells, or coral calcium carbonate (chemically $CaCO_3$). The process of making lime putty from the raw material is relatively simple. Traditionally, limestone is placed in a specially built kiln (sometimes a pit or a heap), layered with fuel such as coal or brush, and burnt for about 12 hours. At the end of the burning process, whitish lumps of calcium oxide are left, along with bits of burned and unburned fuel. Overburned limestone appears as black, glassy pieces, and these are removed and discarded.

The material needs to reach a temperature of 2,200 degrees Fahrenheit (1,200 degrees Celsius). At 1,650 degrees Fahrenheit

This lime-plastered cob house in the village of Haddington, England, is kept looking fresh by periodic applications of limewash.

CATHERINE WANEK

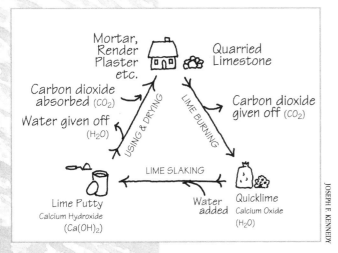

Mortar, Render Plaster etc.

Quarried Limestone

Carbon dioxide absorbed (CO_2)

Water given off (H_2O)

USING & DRYING

LIME BURNING

Carbon dioxide given off (CO_2)

LIME SLAKING

Lime Putty
Calcium Hydroxide ($Ca(OH)_2$)

Water added

Quicklime
Calcium Oxide (H_2O)

JOSEPH F. KENNEDY

The lime cycle.

(900 degrees Celsius), carbon dioxide (CO_2) is driven off, and 2,200 degrees Fahrenheit (1,200 degrees Celsius) is required for the heat to penetrate through to the center of the stone. As it heats up, steam (H_2O) is driven off, and a chemical change occurs. Heat acting upon calcium carbonate ($CaCO_3$) produces calcium oxide (CaO) plus carbon dioxide (CO_2). The chemical reaction is usually more complicated than this, due to other carbonates and silicates being present in the limestone, but it's important to understand the basic changes that are taking place at this stage.

Calcium oxide is very reactive and can be dangerous; it is called 'lump-lime' or 'quicklime' and may be left as lumps or ground down into powder. It must be kept dry, as it reacts very quickly with water — even the water in the air or the moisture in your skin — to form calcium hydroxide, which is the first step to reversing the process back to calcium carbonate. Just as making quicklime needed heat, the reverse process produces heat: calcium oxide (CaO) plus water (H_2O) produces calcium hydroxide ($Ca(OH)_2$) and heat. Quicklime added to water gives us lime putty!

HOW TO MAKE LIME PUTTY

Always add quicklime to water. Never do it the other way around. If you do it backward, it can explode!

Recipe: 1 part quicklime to 2 parts water, by volume. Great care must be taken in the making of lime putty. A mask, goggles, and gloves must be worn. The tremendous amount of heat that is generated produces steam and can spit lime.

The process of adding quicklime to water is called 'slaking.' In the method I use, only a portion of the water is used to begin with, followed by some of the quicklime. Two people are needed: one to pour the water and quicklime, and the other to rake and mix. First, water is poured into a metal tub. Care must be taken when placing the bath, as the heat generated can burn any grass or wood underneath it. Quicklime is gradually added to the water, which is immediately raked and mixed; a garden hoe is the best tool for the job. Care needs to be taken as the temperature soars and the whole mix starts to bubble and boil. Water is added as the mix progresses and until all of the quicklime has been mixed.

The purer the quicklime, the faster the hydration process occurs. Raking and mixing is carried out until the lumps have all broken down; the resulting putty (which feels like double cream at this point) is sieved through a $1/16$-inch (2-millimeter) grid to take out any pieces of unburned limestone, which will not react. These usually go back in the kiln for burning next time.

Slaked lime or lime putty is best stored for at least three months before use. This is to ensure that all the calcium oxide has hydrated, which can take time.

Do not expose lime putty to the air, or it will begin to carbonate before you can use it as a render or mortar. If it carbonates, then it will not bind with the sand when you mix it. Traditionally, lime putty was stored in a pit in the ground, where it would remain for several months or years before use. In fact, lime putty in pits would often be passed on from one generation to the next. The Romans forbade the use of any lime putty that was less than three years old, and all the old practitioners say that the older the lime is, the better.

MAKING LIME RENDER (STUCCO) AND LIME PLASTERS

There are two main ways to make a lime render or lime plaster.

1. **Lime putty mix.** Recipe: 1 part lime putty to 3 parts sand, by volume. Ideally, the sand should contain particle sizes ranging from very small (dust) to quite large ($3/8$ inch or 10 millimeters), and these should be angular, not rounded. The aim is to use only as much lime putty as necessary to fill the void spaces between the grains. The mix is almost always 3 to1 because the void spaces take up about 33 percent or one-third of the volume of most sands.

The only real difference between a plaster (for inside work) and a render (for outside work) is the fineness or coarseness of the sand used. Render may contain aggregate up to $3/8$ inches (10 millimeters) in size in areas that experience lots of wind-driven rain; usually people prefer a smoother finish on their inside walls, and so they would choose a sand with smaller grain sizes.

The longer a lime putty has matured, the more solid it becomes, and the better render it makes. It can be hard to work at first, but by pounding and beating it (in a large boat or on a sheet of plywood) with wooden mallets or posts, the putty soon becomes more plastic and can be worked into the sand. The process can be very labor intensive, but this beating part should not be left out. Because it's so hard to work, it may be easier to mix the sand with fresh lime putty, and then leave this mix to mature.

2. **Hot lime mix.** Recipe: 1 part quicklime powder to 3 parts sand, by volume. This is probably the most common method used traditionally in the U.K. In this method, the quicklime is added to damp sand and mixed with a shovel. It is raked and mixed continuously, and may not need any extra water depending on the dampness of the sand. Again, it should be left to mature for at least three months.

When the time comes to use a lime mortar or render, it should be beaten and worked to a stiff consistency, so sticky that it can be held upside-down on a trowel. It will generally become more

JOSEPH F. KENNEDY

Simon Pratt slaking powdered quicklime in England. Note protective clothing an eyewear.

plastic with lots of beating! There should be no need to add water to it, which would increase the risk of shrinkage cracks. Traditionally, it was a completely separate trade to be a lime render beater. These days, render can be knocked up in a paddle mill (used by potters) to save all that work by hand. Generally, a cement mixer won't do the job, as the mix stays in a lump and can knock the machine over; the tendency then is to add water to soften it, and the resulting mix will crack due to too much shrinkage.

HOW TO USE LIME RENDER AND PLASTER

For straw bale walls, my preference is to apply the first coat of lime by hand (with gloves!) because it's more fun, and because the straw tends to flick the stuff back at you otherwise. The lime needs to be well rubbed in to get a good bond between it and the straw. It's important to encourage the render to cure from the inside out, not to let the outside skin carbonate too fast. Therefore, keep the applied render or plaster moist (not wet). Here in England it takes two to three days before the render feels hard.

I apply the first coat thinly, leaving stubbly bits of straw sticking out. It is usually ready for the second coat the next day, unless there are pockets of thicker mix in places. Before putting on the second coat, I wait until the first is hard enough that you cannot push your thumb into it. I wet the walls down with a mister (not a hose) before putting the second coat on. I work the second coat in with hands or a wooden float. The render is kept damp by misting it, unless there is an English drizzle!

Over the next few days, protect the render from direct sunlight, rain, forceful wind, and frost. You can hang sacks from scaffolding and keeping them moist, creating a humid atmosphere close to the lime. Misting is not to add water to the render, but to make sure that carbon dioxide can be carried into the thickness of the layer. It's probable that lime renders on straw bale walls carbonate more quickly than on stonework, because the straw itself is breathable. Air thus has access to the back of the render as well as to the surface.

If the render cracks, I rework it (several times if necessary) before the surface hardens, to squeeze and compress the sand particles together. The aim is to compress all the render so that there are no air spaces left. Using a steel trowel on a lime render tends to close up the texture of the surface, preventing humid air from penetrating into the body of the render.

It's essential to understand the chemical change that starts to take place once the render is exposed to air, so as to know how best to care for it. Once render is on a wall, it begins to carbonate, a chemical process whereby carbon dioxide starts to change the calcium hydroxide back into the original limestone (calcium carbonate). Calcium hydroxide ($Ca(OH)_2$) plus carbon dioxide (CO_2) produces calcium carbonate ($CaCO_3$) and water.

The chemical change happens very slowly. Lime absorbs carbon dioxide from the air and only in the presence of moisture; too much water inhibits the process.

It can take a pure lime putty/sand mix several days to harden, which does not mean that all the lime is carbonated. Some of our renders are hundreds of years old, and still not all of the calcium hydroxide in them is carbonated. The ideal conditions for applying and curing a lime render are: high humidity and good ventilation.

PLASTERS

On the whole, it is a straightforward matter to use a lime render directly onto a mud plaster backing; this is traditionally what we did with our cob houses. However, there have been some failures, usually in the form of cracks developing around corners of buildings, and occasionally whole sheets of lime work falling off. There are two problems occurring here. The first has to do with different rates of expansion and contraction in the mud and the lime. Mud plasters generally have greater flexibility than those of lime, so in conditions that would cause expansion and contraction — such as significant changes in temperature or humidity — the backing coat (mud) may move more than the finish coat (lime), and cause the latter to crack. This problem would be accentuated at corners where the render coat is in tension.

Solutions would be to: 1) make corners curved rather than angled to reduce tension; 2) add lots of fiber (chopped straw) to the mud and hair to the lime, to increase their tensile strength; 3) make sure the mud coat is wet and sticky before applying the lime.

The problem of the lime coat dropping off in pieces from the mud is caused by a poor bond between the two materials. This can be solved by: 1) making sure the mud coat is wet and sticky; 2) leaving the mud coat rough to provide a good key for the lime; 3) alternatively or also, applying a coat of limewash to the walls before rendering; 4) rubbing the lime well in to the mud backing.

DRY HYDRATE LIME MIXES: TYPE N AND TYPE S

The bags of lime bought at a builder's supply store are almost always hydrated lime, which is quicklime that has been factory slaked only to the point that a powder is formed and not a putty. Hydrated lime is far less reactive and dangerous than quicklime and usually does not have the same properties as lime putty or hot lime mixes. In the U.K., our hydrated limes are made from quite pure limestone, otherwise known as high-calcium lime. In the U.S., due to differing geology, much of the limestone contains proportions of magnesium. It can still produce a good material.

Applying limewash in Santorini, Greece.

JOSEPH F. KENNEDY

Limes containing magnesium were often less favored when slaked outside of factory conditions, due to the fact that the magnesium component took longer to slake. However, this is no longer the case with Type S hydrates. Type S hydrates are auto-claved, ensuring that all the magnesium oxide has been slaked, as well as the calcium oxide. Although Type S dry hydrate can be used right out of the bag, it improves when made into a putty and gets better still if left to remain even longer in the putty stage. Type N hydrate is only partially hydrated; only the calcium portion of the lime is combined with water. Type N hydrate needs to be made up into a putty and aged before using to make sure that all the magnesium oxide has slaked.

When you buy powdered hydrated lime it is difficult to know anything about the lime. Usually you won't know what type of lime it is, how it was burnt, or how it was slaked. However, you may be able to find out how long it has been on the shelf and that, in the long run, may be the most important thing to know. If the dry hydrate has been in the bag too long, it may have already begun to absorb moisture from the air and begun to carbonate, thereby declining in quality. Some manufacturers date their bags. If not, you can always ask when a shipment arrived.

HOW TO MAKE LIME RENDERS FROM DRY HYDRATE

1. Always use fresh hydrated lime, less than one month old if possible. Look for the date of manufacture on the bag.

2. As far as possible, check the production process and buy from a reputable company — although this still doesn't guarantee the quality of the product!

3. Make up the hydrate into a lime putty by putting it into a bucket and adding water. Stir well, and only add enough water to make a very stiff mix. Leave it for 24 hours or longer, and then make up the render as described previously.

4. Use 1 part lime putty to 2-$^1/_2$ parts sand, by volume, to compensate for the extra aggregate if you think your dry hydrate is not quite pure calcium hydroxide. If you have reliable information that your hydrate is pure, then stick to the original 3-to-1 mix.

5. Once mixed up with sand, use in the same way as any other lime render.

CARE OF LIME RENDERS AND PLASTERS

With all lime renders, most problems such as cracking or powderiness can be solved by a coat or two of limewash. Limewash is basically a more dilute form of lime putty, often with small amounts of other substances, such as casein, added for greater durability. Lime renders have the capacity to 'self-heal' (that is, cracks tend to close up over time) because they are slowly carbonating. As long as a lime render is limewashed as needed, there should be no need for other maintenance, unless something else is causing problems (for example, a broken gutter or an overgrown garden).

Lime renders should be limewashed at least every five years — every two or three is better — and it may need to be once a year on the most exposed wall. We had a tradition in England of limewashing our houses on May Day each year. Limewash is much quicker to use than ordinary paint, because it's very watery. If you do need to patch in a section of render for any reason, the patch will adhere well to the rest of the render. Old render can be pounded up and used in addition to or instead of sand for aggregate in a new mix.

Barbara Jones has trained for over 20 years in carpentry, cob building, and limework in England and the U.K. She runs a (mostly!) free information and advice service, acts as consultant on large contracts, teaches on-site, and acts as an enabler for people to become involved in the building process themselves.

RESOURCES

Books

Holmes, Stafford, and Michael Wingate. *Building with Lime: A Practical Introduction.* Intermediate Technology Publications, 1997. This technical yet very readable book contains everything you ever wanted to know about lime, including classification, preparation, tools, use of lime mortars, washes, and especially plasters; and lots more.

Schofield, Jane. *Lime in Building: A Practical Guide.* Self-published, 1995. An easy-to-read booklet, including simple recipes and advice on preparation, application, materials, and equipment. Available in the U.S.A. from Taylor Publishing, P.O. Box 6985, Eureka, CA 95502, U.S.A.; phone: 1-888-441-1623; email: tms@northcoast.com. Jane Schofield, Lewdon Farm, Black Dog, Crediton, Devon EX17 4QQ, U.K.

Taylor, Charmaine. *All About Lime: A Basic Guide for Natural Building.* Elk River Press, 1999. This excellent booklet contains lots of useful information combed from other books and the Internet, with references. For the beginner, this may be all you need.

Periodicals

The Last Straw: The International Journal of Straw Bale and Natural Building. HC66 Box 119, Hillsboro, NM 88042, U.S.A.; phone: 505-895-5400; email: thelaststraw@strawhomes.com; website: www.strawhomes.com. Issue #29, Spring 2000 was dedicated entirely to lime plaster. Packs a lot of excellent information into 40 pages.

Organizations

National Lime Association, 200 Glebe Road, Suite 800, Arlington, VA, 22203 U.S.A.; phone: 703-243-5463; website: www.lime.org. This industry association offers technical booklets and information on products and applications.

OK OK OK Productions, 256 East 100 South, Moab, UT 84532, U.S.A.; phone/fax: 435-259-8378; email: okokok@lasal.net; website: www.ok-ok-ok.com. Kaki Hunter and Doni Kifmeyer offer lime application workshops and consulting, and supply high-calcium lime putty.

The Building Limes Forum, 82 The Street, Hindolveston, Dereham, Norfolk NR20 5DF, U.K.; phone/fax: 1263-860-257; email: michael.wingate@zetnet.co.uk. A voluntary organization established to promote the skillful use of lime in building. Many books available by mail order.

The Canelo Project, HC1 Box 324, Elgin, AZ 85611, U.S.A.; phone: 520-455-5548; fax: 520-455-9360 email: absteen@dakotacom.net; website: www.caneloproject.com. Workshops on lime plastering as well as straw bale and other natural building techniques. They also provide special harling trowels and limewash brushes by mail order.

Websites

Lime-Online, www.limeonline.it. An Italian site (in English) with many articles on using lime.

Natural Paints and Finishes

Joseph F. Kennedy

U NTIL THE EARLY PART of the 20th century, all paints were made with natural materials and were usually mixed directly from raw ingredients. As these traditional paints were somewhat unpredictable, modern 'plastic' paints were developed to meet decorators' demands for easier-to-apply, consistent, pre-mixed paints. Now there is a renewed interest in the older paints, based on esthetic and practical considerations. Traditional paints have softer, subtler colors, age longer and better than modern paints, and have been found to be less toxic. In contrast, our industrially produced modern paints, made with volatile organic compounds (VOCs), heavy metals, and bio-cides are some of the most toxic substances we bring into our homes. They are also impermeable, trapping moisture, which often leads to mildew and rot. Esthetically, these paints are uniform in color and texture, thus much less 'lively' than traditional paints.

Traditional paints, especially milk paints and limewash, are vapor-permeable, making them particularly appropriate for many of the building techniques described in this book. Traditional paints are perishable, however, and need to be used quickly once mixed. They also demand more skill to prepare and use than do modern paints, and often require specific tools and techniques to prepare surfaces and apply the paint.

Applying natural pigment by hand in an age-old tradition, a Mauritanian woman decorates the walls of her mud house.

Paint is used to protect, preserve, and decorate a surface. Paints are generally either water based or oil based, with different tools and materials used to prepare and paint different surfaces. Some surfaces need to be prepared for painting, by sanding and priming. The primer coat saves paint by reducing the absorbency of the surface. An undercoat provides a surface for the next coat to adhere to. One or more finishing coats provide the desired color and texture. Sometimes the finish coat is followed by a transparent overcoat, to protect and beautify the finish.

Traditional paints can be either simple or sophisticated. The simple paints were those made by everyday folks from whatever they had at hand. These paints were usually based on milk, lime, glue size, and earth pigments. Sophisticated paints were used by the well-to-do and included more use of expensive ground pigments, resins, and oils.

JOSEPH F KENNEDY

INGREDIENTS FOR PAINTS

Binders

A binder (also known as the medium or carrier) is anything that can hold the pigment together and adhere to a surface. The best binders are transparent; stick well; dry in a reasonable amount of time; are long lasting; and don't flake, dust, or crack. The choice of binder depends on the surface to be painted and the amount of paint needed. Binders come from several sources.

- **Casein.** Casein (milk protein) is derived from the curds of curdled milk. Skim milk is generally used if you are making your own casein. Casein achieves high binding power with the addition of an alkali (lime, ammonium, or borax) that 'hydrolizes' it. Casein can also be used as a glue or primer. Powdered casein for larger jobs is available from mail-order sources. (See "Suppliers" in the Resources section.)

- **Lime.** Burnt limestone that is slaked in water to produce lime putty is used to make limewash, and as an additive to casein paints. (See "Working with Lime.")

- **Egg Yolk.** Egg yolk is used as a binder in tempera painting.

- **Oils.** A 'drying' oil is generally used to make traditional oil paints. Linseed oil, which is pressed from flax seeds, is most common. It comes raw, boiled (better), or as 'stand' (best), which is linseed oil heated to 572 degrees Fahrenheit (300 degrees Celsius). Linseed oil from the hardware store contains chemical drying agents that may be toxic. Unfortunately, natural linseed oil is much more expensive. Other oils traditionally used were poppyseed oil, walnut oil, and peanut oil. 'Dryers' are often added to commercial oils to decrease drying time.

- **Size or Glue.** Simple glues (also known as size) can be made from gelatin or the hides of certain animals (rabbit is most common, but calf is used as well). Size is soaked in water, then heated. Pigments and other ingredients can be added to size to make opaque or transparent non-waterproof interior paints. Size was often used as a primer to save paint.

Pigments and Dyes

Pigments are powdered color, usually earth materials or minerals that are carried by the binder. The more finely the pigments are ground, the more uniform the paint will be. To avoid clumping, mix pigments with an appropriate solvent to disperse them, then add to the binder. Certain alkaline-resistant pigments are used in lime paints. Be careful of some mineral pigments that may contain toxic heavy metals.

Vegetable dyes can also be dissolved into the binder, but they are of variable permanence. (A good selection of different plant dyes are listed in *Better Basics for the Home.* See the "Resources" section.) A good way to extract plant dyes is to use an old percolator. Pigments or dyes can be added to a base white color (be careful as a little goes a long way) or to other colors. They can also be added to the final coat of plasters. (See "Earth Plasters and Aliz.")

Thinners/Solvents

Thinners are used to create a more flowing consistency for paints. They include water, turpentine, and alcohol. Non-toxic thinners are available by mail order.

Extenders

Extenders are added to paint to make it go farther. They include calcium carbonate lime, barium sulfate, kaolin clay, marble dust, chalk, and diatomaceous earth.

Preservatives

Most preservatives used in modern paints are extremely toxic. Natural alternatives include: borax, zinc oxide, salt, ammonia, and oils of clove or spike lavender.

KINDS OF TRADITIONAL PAINTS

Oil Paints

Oil paints are used mostly on woodwork, in areas that see a lot of wear, or in areas like kitchens or bathrooms that require a lot of wiping. They are generally stronger and more durable than water-based paints and are useful for protecting softwoods. Oils are mixed with a base color (usually titanium dioxide) and pigments to produce an opaque paint. When painting with oil paints, alternate 'thin' (less oil) layers with 'fat' (more oil) layers. Adding a small amount of pigment to oil makes a transparent glaze. Resin mixed with oil makes a hard gloss paint.

Water-Based Paints

Water-based paints are quick drying and easy to clean up but are not as strong as oil paints. They tend to deteriorate when scrubbed or washed. Water-based paints include those made from boiled flour paste, lime, casein, or glue (or combinations of the above). Two of the most popular with natural builders are milk paints and lime paints.

Milk Paint

Milk paints evolved from necessity. A staple for farm families, casein binder for the paint came from the milk of the family cow. Casein was mixed with lime and locally available pigments (iron oxide, raspberries, ox blood, to name a few) to make a serviceable paint that would protect vulnerable wood and plaster surfaces.

Milk paints are not made from raw milk but from the curds of sour milk. These curds contain the casein, or milk protein, which is extremely adhesive when mixed with an alkali. If milk is used straight, the paint will likely mold. Milk (usually skim or non-fat) can be left to sour naturally, or the process can be hastened by adding sour cream. The sour milk is then curdled by heating or by adding an acid such as lemon juice or vinegar. If you are adding lime to the casein paint, be sure to wash the curds of any residual acid, as it will react with the alkaline lime. Old recipes for milk paint often include whiting (chalk), but this is not recommended, as whiting will alter the chemical composition of the paint and lead to increased dusting.

Milk paint is quick, easy, and forgiving, with a finish that improves over time. Differential wear of milk paints results in subtle differences of shading that enliven a room or piece of furniture. The ingredients are simple: casein, lime, clay, and pigment; oil can be added as well. Although you can make your own casein, powdered casein, which is a much more potent binder, is readily available from several sources. (See the "Resources" section.)

Unlike modern paints that lie on the surface, milk paint absorbs into the porous substrate, either wood or plaster. It cannot be used over commercial paints, as it only binds to wood, plaster, or itself. Milk paint is perishable, so use it the same day it is made.

It is important to have a smooth, well-prepared surface when you are using milk paint, as it won't fill in small holes or mask blemishes. The procedure is to wet the surface (if wood) to raise the grain, sand it smooth, and then paint. The first coat will look uneven, but this will diminish with further coats; two or three are usually sufficient. A protective overcoat of 5 parts linseed oil to 1 part thinner can be painted on, then wiped off.

If milk paints are used outside, they are susceptible to water stains. If an antique look is what you're after, though, milk paints work well. Be sure to add lime for increased weatherproofness, or seal with an overcoat.

Natural paints can be made at home from simple non-toxic ingredients, using mineral pigments and clays for color.

CATHERINE WANEK

Lime Paints

Farm families also used lime paints, otherwise known as 'whitewash' or 'limewash.' A disinfectant, lime paint was used as part of spring cleaning every year, and excess paint was often diluted for use on wooden furniture.

For increased durability lime paint often includes casein and/or linseed oil. Eggwhites, fermented cactus juice, blood, and other materials are also used to enhance durability. Pigments are often used with lime paints, but they must be alkaline tolerant. (*Classic Paints and Faux Finishes* has a list of lime-tolerant pigments; see the "Resources" section.)

Lime paint must be applied over a permeable surface. Prepare the surface by removing loose particles, wet the wall, and brush the limewash in well. The 'sgraffito' technique involves painting a colored lime plaster with a limewash that is then scratched back to reveal patterns of underlying color.

Size Paints

An example of size paint is calcimine distemper, which made from water, whiting (chalk), size (glue), and pigments. The whiting and size must be properly proportioned to avoid dusting (too much whiting) or flaking (too much size). These paints can only be used for interior surfaces. As with milk and lime paints, they cannot go over modern paints. 'Oil-bound' size paints are only available commercially.

OTHER FINISHES

Other finishes include:

- **Shellac.** Shellac is insect secretions (lac) dissolved in thinner. It forms a delicate transparent finish and is used mostly for painted wood furniture.

- **Lacquer.** Lacquer is lac plus pigments dissolved in alcohol.

- **Wax.** Different waxes can be used as an overcoat or even a binder for pigment. Waxes include paraffin, beeswax (soft), and carnuba wax (hard). These are melted and often mixed with oil for application.

- **Varnish.** Varnish is mastic resin, beeswax, and linseed oil dissolved in alcohol or spirits. It creates a hard, glossy, but delicate finish.

- **Stains.** Stains are transparent washes of color, often used to enhance the grain of wood. They can be oil-, water- or alcohol-based.

- **Waterglass Paints.** 'Waterglass' is potassium silicate, which, when mixed with water, quartz dust, and mineral or earth pigments, is appropriate for use on lime, cement, or mud plasters.

The underlying plaster must contain silica sand, as the waterglass binds with this sand both chemically and mechanically.

Caulks, Putties, and Glues

Natural materials can be used to make the caulks, putties, and glues often needed in home construction and maintenance. A simple caulk can be made from whiting (chalk) mixed with linseed oil. Another caulk is made from corn starch and plaster of paris. Joint compound can be made from casein, water, and whiting, with borax added for its anti-fungal properties. A serviceable glue for wallpapering and other uses can be made from boiled flour paste.

RESOURCES

Books

Berthold-Bond, Annie. *Better Basics for the Home.* Three Rivers Press, 1999. An informative book that contains a very useful chapter on making your own paints, finishes, glues, and caulks. It also contains a plethora of non-toxic recipes for all your home needs.

Meyer, Ralph, and Steven Sheehan. *The Artist's Handbook of Materials and Techniques.* Viking Press, 1991. The standard artist's reference, with encyclopedic information on painting materials and techniques.

Sloan, Annie, and Kate Gwynn. *Classic Paints and Faux Finishes.* The Reader's Digest Association, 1993. This beautifully illustrated book makes you want to run out and make your own paint. Exceptional discussion of a wide range of painting techniques.

Suppliers

Building for Health Materials Center, P.O. Box 113, Carbondale, CO 81623, U.S.A.; phone: 1-800-292-4838; fax: 970- 963-3318; website: www.buildingforhealth.com. A supplier of a wide range of natural and non-toxic paints, pigments, and finishes. Also carries a wide range of environmentally sound building materials and appliances.

The Old Fashioned Milk Paint Co., Inc., 436 Main Street, Groton, MA 01450, U.S.A.; website: www.milkpaint.com. Check out their web page for lots of information about milk paint, and how to obtain pre-mixed milk paints made from traditional recipes.

Recovering from Waste: Using Recycled and Agricultural Materials

Dan Imhoff

IT IS EASY, given the scale of ecological threats such as biodiversity loss, global warming, and cumulative toxic pollution, to make too much of the collective act of recycling. The root causes of these problems won't be addressed through recycling, no matter how many tons of milk bottles we convert into sweaters or decking materials, or how much straw we use for paper or wall boards. Yet diverting 'waste' from landfills and incinerators can decrease the demand for deforested, mined, and harvested materials. In many cases, recycling can also conserve energy when compared to processing and manufacturing virgin resources. The good news is that the range and number of pre-consumer and post-consumer recycled materials entering the construction market is growing all the time. It now includes plastics, wood, newsprint, fly ash, blast furnace slag, styrofoam, steel, shipping pallets, paper pulp sludge, wood lignin, concrete, rubber, tire shreds, carpeting, glass, and agricultural residues, to name a few.

Rastra blocks are made of recycled styrofoam filled with cement. Marley Porter designed this rastra theater in Austin, Texas.

CATHERINE WANEK

RECLAIMED AND SALVAGED WOOD

With harvest rates outstripping growth rates in North America's private forests for at least two decades, the quality of wood available for building has been suffering a continual decline.[1] This has made the recycling of old-growth lumber from old warehouses, buildings, bridges, brewing tanks, and other structures more attractive than ever before. These reclaimed and salvaged timbers are frequently tightly grained old-growth wood. Having stood in the open air many years, reclaimed wood is dry and has a stable moisture content that will prevent warping and twisting.

CATHERINE WANEK

Logs are also being salvaged in urban woodlots and rural areas, where blow-downs, disease, insect infestations, or logger oversight present the opportunity to convert raw materials into lumber.

Other important and currently underutilized sources of wood include construction and demolition (nearly 15 percent of landfill volume is wood construction waste), and the urban waste stream (including some 300 million wooden pallets and unheard-of quantities of wood-based paper and packaging per year). These materials can be remanufactured into a diverse range of building components. (See "Paper Houses: Papercrete and Fidobe.")

'Waste' straw is packed in poly mesh to create straw 'wattles' for landscape and building use.

AGRICULTURAL FIBERS

Every harvest season, in fields across the continent, fibers are burned by the millions of tons, a practice that generates significant amounts of carbon dioxide. Currently underutilized crops, such as industrial hemp, kenaf, and flax, could provide significant amounts of fiber if grown in regular rotations and in accordance with the principles of sustainable agriculture. (See "Building with Hemp.")

Straw bale construction is currently leading the natural building revival. Yet many experts believe that straw's greatest contribution to the construction industry may eventually come in the form of manufactured panels. After at least a decade of experimentation, wheat, rice, and rye grass straw; bagasse; corn stalks; hemp; kenaf; rice hulls; and sunflower stalks and seed hulls are just a few of the many agricultural fibers finding their way into building and furniture manufacture. They are used in low-density insulation boards, medium density fiber boards, hard boards, particle boards, and as strengtheners for shingles and other composite products. According to the May/June 1995 issue of *Environmental Building News*, if we used just 25 per cent (35 million tons) of the annual U.S. straw harvest for the building industry (based on statistics from 1987 to 1994),

> *2.7 million 1,000-square-foot single-story houses could be built each year. If we turned that straw into structural compressed straw panels, they could provide the exterior walls, roofs, interior partition walls, and floors of 1 million 2,000-square-foot two-story houses per year. Or, that straw could be used to produce 22 billion square feet of ³/4-inch particle board, which is five times the current U.S. production of particle board and medium-density fiber board (all thicknesses).[2]*

THE WAY AHEAD

In the future, designing houses with a more cyclical view of buildings and construction materials could play an important role in minimizing waste. Rather than considering materials for a one-time use (with the ultimate destination being either the landfill or incinerator), all building components should have the potential for further use — if only as compost. For example, the posts and beams of a timber-framed house, because of their size, stand a far better chance of being remilled and reused than a two-by-four stud. In the same vein, steel framing, which is endlessly recyclable, could be viewed as a renewable resource.

The holy grail of building applications for agricultural fibers lies in the development of regional mills that can produce products such as oriented-strand straw board and structural insulated panels. Such mini-mills would be located close to farming areas and would serve, first and foremost, the surrounding regional markets. The rice-growing region of California's Sacramento Valley, the grain belt of the Midwest, and the sugar cane production corridors of the Southeast are all examples of areas with an ample supply of both raw materials and customers. In this way, the benefits of using straw would be available to many who don't have the time, luxury, or ability to construct their own straw bale home. Unfortunately, a number of early attempts to establish alternative structural fiber companies in the United States have faltered in the face of marketing and distribution challenges and high start-up costs.

Ultimately, many of us hope that our basic needs will be met primarily within our local communities and broader bioregions. But local resources will languish in the global economy as long

JOSEPH F. KENNEDY

Used aluminum cans are mortared together to make a lightweight dome.

as it is cheaper and more efficient to import virgin materials from elsewhere. The way ahead should be relatively clear: a new value system and policies aimed at making the most of those resources we choose to exploit, in order to relieve pressures on the already overburdened natural systems of the world that sustain us.

Dan Imhoff is an author and publisher living in Anderson Valley, California, who covers issues of agriculture, the environment, and design. The cofounder of SimpleLife Books and executive director of Watershed Media, Dan is currently working on a wood reduction trilogy series that includes The Simple Life Guide to Tree-free, Recycled and Certified Papers *(1999),* Building with Vision: Optimizing and Finding Alternatives to Wood *(2001), and* Unwrapping Packaging *(2001).*

NOTES

1. See Franklin Wayburn, et al., *Forest Carbon in the United States: Opportunities and Options for Private Lands.* (Pacific Trust, 2000), p.1.
2. See *Environmental Building News* Volume 4, No. 3 May/June 1995, p.8.

RESOURCES
Books

Chappell, Steve, ed. *Alternative Building Sourcebook: Traditional, Natural, and Sustainable Building Products and Sevices.* Fox Maple Press, 1998. A resource guide to professional builders and designers, educational centers, and products suppliers.

Edminster, Ann, and Sami Yassa. *Efficient Wood Use in Residential Construction: A Practical Guide to Saving Wood, Money, and Forests.* Natural Resources Defense Council, 1998. Good suggestions on how to reduce lumber use in conventional building.

Falk, Robert, ed. *The Use of Recycled Wood and Paper in Building Applications.* Forest Products Society, 1997.

Harris, B.J. *The Harris Directory: Recycled Content Building Materials.* B. J. Harris, 2001. Available from the author, P.O. Box 31133, Santa Fe, NM 87594, U.S.A.; phone: 505-983-2962; email: bjharris@igc.org; website: www.harrisdirectory.com.

——. *The Harris Directory of Pollution Prevention Products for Home, Office, and Garden.* Published since 1992 for the building and design professional as an electronic directory, *The Harris Directory* is licensed to design professionals, state, and regional agencies.

Hermannsson, James. *Green Building Resource Guide.* Taunton Press, 1997. A gold mine of information on environmentally friendly building materials.

Imhoff, Dan. *Building with Vision: Optimizing and Finding Alternatives to Wood.* Watershed Media, 2001. A comprehensive overview of alternatives to conventional construction.

Spiegel, Ross, and Dru Meadows. *Green Building Materials: A Guide to Products Selection and Specification.* John Wiley and Sons, 1999. An up-to-date resource guide.

Organizations

Wood Reduction Clearinghouse, 116 New Montgomery, STE 800, San Francisco, CA 94105, U.S.A.; phone: 415-896-1580. Provides information on wood reduction, recycled timbers, and alternative fibers.

CASE STUDIES

In designing the house, the first essential, naturally, was that it should be suited exactly to the requirements of the life to be lived in it; the second, that it should harmonize with its environment, and third, that it should be built, so far as possible, from the materials to be had right there on the ground and left as nearly as possible in the natural state.

Gustav Stickley, 1908

Building with The Sun: The Real Goods Solar Living Center

David Arkin

A LEADING MAIL-ORDER DISTRIBUTOR of products for renewable energy and sustainable lifestyles, the Real Goods Company likes to say, "Knowledge is our number one product." On Summer Solstice, 1996 they opened their new 12-acre (5-hectare) Solar Living Center (SLC) in Hopland, California, the centerpiece of which is the new 5,000-square-foot (475-square-meter) retail store, designed by Sim Van der Ryn and Associates. Showcasing environmentally responsible architectural and landscape design, this project was the culmination of several years of integrative work by many individuals.

The collaborative design and construction process reinforced the five primary goals of the Solar Living Center. I have outlined these goals, and related a few vignettes from the process of designing and building the Center.

The Real Goods Solar Living Center in Hopland, California.

CATHERINE WANEK

GOAL 1: CREATE A CLIMATE-RESPONSIVE BUILDING (SOLUTIONS GROW FROM PLACE)

Creating a climate-responsive building meant coordinating all aspects of the design, from landscape to details, toward this goal. Wall and roof systems were selected specifically for their climate-appropriate performance. The straw-bale walls with 3 to 4 inches (8 to 10 centimeters) of concrete gunnite and soil-cement finish achieve a calculated insulating value of R-65 (a typical 2-by-6 wood stud wall with fiberglass insulation is R-19.) The roof features 12 inches (30 centimeters) of cellulose insulation below a radiant barrier, which by itself is R-10. A 1-1/2-inch (4 centimeter) air space above the barrier ventilates the roof for any solar gain that gets beyond the white 'Hypalon' membrane roof, which reflects 90 percent of the solar radiation it sees. Warm air is drawn out of the building by the chimney effect (hot air rises) and by the Bernoulli effect (low pressure created by breezes passing over the roof). The operable clerestory windows along the stepping roofs aid in night flushing.

There is a great lesson in the simplicity and effectiveness of the SLC's passive solar design. Without fancy motors or heat exchangers, or really much of anything other than careful attention to the sun, this building lights, heats, and cools itself. At the grand opening, several thousand people walked through the building, radiating 500 BTUs each, while the temperature outside hit triple digits. Inside, the temperature never topped 86 degrees Fahrenheit (30 degrees Celsius), passing its ultimate performance test.

I recall a conversation my father and I had during the design process. He installs heating, ventilating, and air-conditioning system controls. I was telling him about this cool

The design and execution of the Solar Living Center reflects the philosophy of this environmentally minded company.

new building we were designing, and he wanted to know all about the mechanical systems. I explained that the building was designed to shade the windows during the summer months, and that each night high clerestory windows were opened and the building is flushed with cool night air, storing up this 'coolth' in the walls and floor. The next morning the windows are closed so the building remains cool all day. "So, what senses the temperature and opens or closes the windows?" he asked. "The store staff," I replied. "Well ... what's so innovative about that?" he exclaimed.

That's just it — it's not innovative in that it features the latest techno-gadget. It's quite fundamental and very graspable in how it works. And the staff is not denied the opportunity to interact with their workplace. This is perhaps our most important success: the people that work here are very proud of the building and truly enjoy working in it and interacting with it.

Project manager Jeff Oldham's favorite anecdote took place shortly after the grand opening, on a July day when temperatures hit 100-plus degrees Fahrenheit (37-plus degrees Celsius). A woman entered the store and reprimanded the staff for wasting energy by having the air-conditioning system turned down too low. She was impressed to learn we had no air conditioner and that she was experiencing the triumph of mass and passive design over the elements.

GOAL 2: CREATE AN EDUCATIVE ENVIRONMENT (MAKE NATURE VISIBLE)

Our intention at the outset was to create a place that at every turn — or even at a glance from a passing car — could teach you something. From an entry drive that passes constructed wetlands and restored riparian areas, to a parking lot with electric vehicle charging stations; from the approach along a hillside of tracking photovoltaic panels, to the PV Equipment Room which displays the storage and inversion of electrical energy; from the cool, green oasis to the myriad of reused and recycled materials in the restrooms, this place is relentless in its education.

Another expression of education was a decision we made to be honest about our use of materials. Almost brutally honest. Jeff and I were discussing finishes and, after going around with non-toxic versus low-toxic and such, concluded that the best finish may well be none at all. In other words, select materials that by their own nature are suited to the task at hand. This thinking guided our process.

GOAL 3: DESIGN FOR LOW-IMPACT CONSTRUCTION (ECOLOGICAL ACCOUNTING INFORMS DESIGN)

We sought to minimize the energy and resources the showroom would be using on an ongoing basis; we also sought to minimize the impacts of its construction. We acknowledged that any building activity was going to have impacts, but we believed that by studying and monitoring these impacts, we might lessen them to some degree.

Take concrete, for example. The manufacture of Portland cement requires huge amounts of energy and generates both extensive greenhouse gases and particulate pollution. Project engineer Bruce King suggested that we substitute fly ash (the waste product from coal-fired power plants) for one-quarter of the cement in our concrete mix. That choice lessened the amount of cement used and made productive use of a waste material. We also, with tongues firmly in cheek, displaced some of the concrete volume in the thick wall footings with 'consumer flotsam and jetsam' (my favorite example being an old 8-track tape deck) donated to the project by Real Goods' shareholders.

Visit the 'weird' restrooms and you'll find a cornucopia of reused and recycled materials. A band of 'Meadowood' trim encircles the room. This finish board is manufactured out of rye grass straw in Oregon. The sinks came from a used-building-material yard in the Bay Area, and the countertops are made of recycled bottle glass by Counter Productions of Berkeley. The glass is poured into a mold and then ground to a smooth finish in a process similar to that used for finishing stone.

We also designed several elements of the project to use construction waste during later phases of the project. For example, we were able to reuse concrete formwork for framing overhangs, light shelves, and the handful of wood stud walls. All of the redwood in the project was reclaimed from dismantled lumber mills and beer and wine tanks.

The careful passive design of the Center was augmented by the straw bale construction of the walls. Straw bale construction is a most appropriate building material for California; it can even bear resemblance to the historic adobe and the mission structures of California's past. And, unlike wood, we certainly don't have any shortage of it. Here in California we grow close to 500,000 acres (200,000 hectares) of rice each year. Each acre produces 4-$\frac{1}{4}$ tons (4 metric tons) of rice and enough straw for around 80 bales. A typical 1,500-square-foot (140-square-meter) house will need about 200 straw bales. That's one house for every 2-$\frac{1}{2}$ acres (1 hectare) of rice, or 200,000 homes we could be building of straw every year!

A typical 1,500-square-foot (140-square-meter) wood home will consume around 5,000 board feet of

lumber for its walls, another 5,000 for the roof, and yet another 5,000 if it has a wood floor. According to the Institute for Sustainable Forestry, a typical acre of Douglas fir, growing in medium soils in Northern California, will yield around 800 board feet of lumber per year. This means that the same wood house needing about 12 acres (5 hectares) of trees can be built with only 2-$\frac{1}{2}$ acres (1 hectare) of straw and 6 acres (2.5 hectares) of wood (to frame the roof). I'm not suggesting that we replant our forests with rice, but I will say that we can build the same number of homes — better homes, using half the amount of wood we currently use.

When we did use wood at the Center, we exposed it wherever possible, treating it as the precious resource that it is. In the showroom, the exposed glu-lam beams reveal both their structure and beauty. The Douglas fir we used was grown and certified sustainably harvested, milled, and manufactured into beams, all within 40 miles (65 kilometers) of Hopland.

GOAL 4: INVOLVE EVERYONE AND HAVE FUN
(EVERYONE IS A DESIGNER)

My greatest joy through the entire design and construction of the building was my role, which was somewhat like that of a team captain. It was my job to synthesize and coordinate all of the professionals, building systems and subcontractors; to facilitate communication; and to resolve

Sophisticated design lets natural light penetrate while minimizing heat gain; minimal cooling is needed even on the hottest days.

CATHERINE WANEK

differences. Unlimited credit goes to John Schaeffer and Real Goods for pushing us as much as we pushed them in setting and achieving the goals of this project. The process is just as important as the product, and this project proved that the two are not mutually exclusive; in fact, they are mutually beneficial.

One of the greatest lessons we learned from designing and building the Solar Living Center is the importance of collaboration in the creation of integrated ecological design. As project architect, I experienced this collaboration throughout the project, from the first visit Sim Van der Ryn and I made to the site, to the design of the sculpture at the center of the oasis fountain. The traditional boundaries between design and construction disappeared.

The whole process was also a great deal of fun. One morning during construction, Tom Myers, the general contractor, remarked that some friends had asked him how construction was going. He had told them that he was having fun. "They didn't believe me," Tom said. "I'd forgotten how much fun it is to build."

GOAL 5: FEEDBACK: MEASURE SUCCESSES AND FAILURES (DESIGN WITH NATURE)

All natural systems have a feedback mechanism that is continuously tuning and refining in response to changing conditions. As a branch grows in search of sunlight, so too did our design evolve to fit its climate and setting. During design we paid great attention to what was happening at and near our site. We took note of the climate and culture and kept tabs on locally produced and locally available materials, etc. This information became the launching point for a design process that revisited each element in turn, and adapted itself accordingly.

David Arkin was the project architect for the Solar Living Center while with Sim Van der Ryn and Associates. He and wife, Anni Tilt, have since founded Arkin Tilt Architects in Albany, California, specializing in ecological planning and design. David is a founding member of the California Straw Building Association (CASBA).

RESOURCES
Books

Schaeffer, John, et al. *A Place in the Sun: The Evolution of the Real Goods Solar Living Center.* Chelsea Green, 1997. The story of how the Real Goods Solar Living Center came to be.

Van der Ryn, Sim, and Stuart Cowan. *Ecological Design.* Island Press, 1995. This book describes how the living world and the human world can be reconnected by taking ecology as the basis for design — adapting and integrating human design with natural processes. Van der Ryn Architects, Sausalito, CA; 45-332-5806; www.vanderryn.com

From the Nile to the Rio Grande

Dick Doughty

WHEN DANIEL CAMACHO bought a diminutive plot of land in the town of Ojinaga, Chihuahua, along the U.S.-Mexico border, in 1994, he had never heard of Hassan Fathy. (See "Elegant Solutions: The Work of Hassan Fathy.") Like others in town, Camacho did daily battle against a local unemployment rate just shy of 50 percent, working when he could as a field hand or laborer and at odd jobs. He figured it would take a few years to save enough cash to build the walls of a two- or three-room home made of cinder blocks. Later, he hoped, he would find a way to buy vigas (unmilled timber rafters) to hold up a roof of corrugated metal.

One evening late that year, there was a neighborhood meeting at which a woman from 'the other side' — the United States — showed pictures of adobe houses. She claimed they could be more comfortable, more spacious, and yet less expensive than the cinder-block-and-sheet-metal houses ubiquitous in the poor sections of Ojinaga. She also claimed that the adobe homes might not need expensive air conditioning, even through the fierce Chihuahan summer.

Camacho was intrigued. Adobe was nothing new to him, of course: it had lent architecture in northern Mexico and the Southwestern U.S. a distinctive look for nearly 500 years — until the cinder block came along in the 1950s, tagged as a 'modern material.' But the catenary vaulted ceilings that used no wood and didn't even require wooden forms to construct made these adobe houses different from what he had seen. Although it had never appeared in the Western Hemisphere, Camacho learned, the design and the technique of building it were more than 8,000 years old. They came from the Middle East, having been revived recently by Hassan Fathy.

Afterward, Camacho approached the presenter, Simone Swan, and told her, "I have some land. I need a house, but I don't have a steady job. If you'll give me the materials, I'll help build the house. Then you'll have a prototype, and you can have people visit it whenever you want." Swan agreed to design Camacho's home, and on this project began training her mason, Maria Jesus Jimenez, how to build adobe vaults and domes.

In November 1995, after building for eight months under the tutelage of Swan and Jimenez, Camacho moved into his new house. Since then, he's hosted dozens of visitors from around the town and, indeed, the world. The four-room-home's plan is L-shaped, and two courtyard walls complete a rectangular compound.

Inside, on a hot May afternoon, it is comfortable. It smells of earth. Camacho says he doesn't have an air conditioner, because the heavy walls and ceiling absorb heat in the daytime and radiate it at night, moderating indoor temperatures, much like a small cave. Although the kitchen

Daniel Camacho making adobes from his local soil.

Elegant Solutions: The Work of Hassan Fathy

Simone Swan

In 1926, with his University of Cairo degree fresh in hand, Hassan Fathy's first job was to build a village school in the Nile Delta, on land owned by his father. There, he was revolted by the ugliness of the village and the poverty of its residents. Fathy felt "… terribly responsible. Nothing had been done out of consideration for the human beings who spent their lives there; we had been content to live in ignorance of the peasant's sickening misery. I decided I must do something."[1] Thus began his quest for a means of rebuilding communities that would allow people to live with self-respect despite their exclusion from the consumer economy. He never turned away from this goal, and the economically dispossessed were to be Fathy's constant preoccupation.

As Fathy realized that people who possess no cash can hardly become an architect's clients in the usual sense, and that they cannot be simply integrated on command into a cash economy, he set to work devising techniques of producing low-cost energy-efficient houses. Using concrete, so much in vogue in Egypt at that time, was out of the question: It required skilled labor, expensive equipment, and industrial materials produced abroad, all of which put it well out of reach of the budget of the Egyptian peasant (fellah). Worse, in hot climates concrete traps and holds high temperatures unbearably, exactly the opposite of traditional earthen interiors, which remain cool during the day and release warmth at night.

Fathy's solution was to turn to sun-dried bricks made of mud and reinforced with straw:

➤ CONTINUED ON PAGE 251

measures only a bit more than 10 feet by 10 feet (3 by 3 meters), its domed adobe ceiling not only increases the sensation of space but also gracefully transforms the room into a simple shrine to the rituals of food. His vaulted living room, though narrower than a railroad car, is also deceptively spacious. Its three cushion-covered sofas, coffee table, and bookshelves are all built-in, made of the same plastered adobe as the walls. They make the room appear hewn from stone.

Only a few hundred meters away lies an assembly-line row of government-sponsored cinder-block homes, sobering reminders of how innovative Camacho's house really is. Each is half the size of his 500 square feet (50 square meters) but costs roughly three times the US $5,000 that Camacho's did. However, the buyers of these homes benefited from government-backed, low-interest credit, something not generally available. Without such arrangements, lending rates in Mexico can run to 48 percent, and it is this that has so far prevented some 50 families who have expressed interest in Camacho's design from building.

As Camacho treads straw and mud to make adobe bricks, he can look north across the Rio Bravo — called the Rio Grande in the U.S. — to what from his distance appears as no more than a smudge on a scrubby hill. This is the region's second Fathy-style home. Camacho supplied 18,000 bricks for it, and the mason who taught him, Maria Jesus Jimenez, is working there now.

The home's owner and resident is Simone Swan, whose presentation to Camacho's neighborhood group was an early program of the Swan Group. The Swan Group is dedicated to introducing both Fathy's philosophy and — as applicable — his techniques to the Rio Grande/Rio Bravo valley. A self-taught architect and lifelong student of the arts, Swan spent three years in Cairo as an assistant and student of Fathy's.

On an early summer afternoon, with the thermometer pushing 106 degrees Fahrenheit (41 degrees Celsius), Simone Swan's kitchen is pleasantly warm. Above, a vaulted ceiling traces the catenary arch that peaks at 14-1/2 feet (4.4 meters), giving the 10-by-25-foot (3-by-8-meter) room the feel of an old Middle Eastern market. But this ceiling is disconcerting to an eye accustomed to the plumb verticality of Roman and Gothic vaults.

The parallel courses of bricks, which Swan has left unplastered to reveal the technique in use, list off-plumb like a less-than-full shelf of books leaned casually against a bookend. The effect imparts a sense of motion that belies physics, like a string of dominoes frozen in mid-fall. On the other side of the H-shaped house, the vaults over her bedroom and the guestroom are much the same. Yet all of them, like their countless millennia-old archetypes in Nubia, will likely long outlive the masons who raised them.

Building catenary vaults is "something you get a feel for," says master builder Mauro Rodriguez, who joined Jimenez in the task. "Each vault goes up just a little different, each course is a little different, and that's okay so long as it stays even over the full length. Even each adobe [brick] can be a little different, too. Have you ever looked at a wasp's nest?" he asks. "They build their nests just the way we make these vaults. I think that's where [the Nubians] must have first learned this."

In 1997, Swan built her home, which she coolly calls 'Prototype Two,' some 10 miles (15 kilometers) outside Presidio on a rolling, cactus-strewn mesa of 430 acres (175 hectares) that she hopes, someday, to develop with more homes built on Fathy's principles. But her sights are set first on local, low-income adobe housing. Even when her crew labored on her house, she labored in her office opposite the kitchen, sketching plans, sending reports, soliciting testimonials from engineers, and seeking contact with micro-credit lenders and philanthropic foundations. She hopes to convince the Rural Housing Agency (RHA) of the U.S. Department of Agriculture to give the

adobe. He engaged the advice of structural engineers and soil-mechanics specialists to ascertain the maximum strength and durability of adobe under different conditions. After this research, in the early 1940s, he began to design dwellings that demonstrated an unprecedented degree of harmony with the natural environment, climate, and local culture and the spiritual tradition of Islam. With inspiration from the very soil of Egypt, he aimed to help the poor build for themselves.

Roofing remained a problem. In rural Egypt, the *fellahin* could afford neither wood nor corrugated galvanized metal for roofs, nor could they even buy the wood needed to make forms to shape vaulted adobe roofs. Fathy's early attempts at building adobe vaulting without wooden forms — the only economically sensible solution — resulted in a series of discouraging collapses. This was particularly maddening because it was clear from his visits to Upper Egypt that just such form-less vaulting had been used for millennia to build ordinary houses, tombs, and even royal buildings.

Fathy feared that the secret had been lost, but in 1941, in the Nubian village of Abu al-Riche, he found village masons building catenary vaults of mud brick that could measure two stories high, up to 10-1/2 feet (3 meters) wide and of any desired length, without forms. The technique, he was exhilarated to learn, was simple enough to teach to any willing person.

Henceforth, adobe became Fathy's technological passion, and he remained loyal to it not only because of its durability over millennia — some adobe structures in Egypt are more than 3,000 years old — but also because of its thermal properties: in many desert climates it maintains comfortable temperatures within a

► CONTINUED ON PAGE 252

range of five to seven degrees Fahrenheit (three to four degrees Celsius) over a 24-hour cycle. Furthermore, it is plentiful: approximately two-thirds of the world's people already live in houses made of earth. Finally, the flexibility of a material for which right angles and straight lines are not always essential nourishes architectural creativity. Under Fathy's control, adobe led to simple captivating beauty.

Today there are two centers in France inspired by Fathy. Both work with owner-builders in West Africa and the Middle East: CRATerre (Centre de Recherches en Architectures de Terre) of Grenoble and the Development Workshop of Lauzerte have helped introduce the Nubian technique of mud-brick dome and vault construction among villagers in Mali, Niger, and Iran. In Egypt, Fathy's ideas can be found in the work of architects, planners, and cultural developers in numerous institutions. In the United States, I have spent much of the past decade among architects, architectural conservationists, and soil engineers dedicated to continuing his work in the desert climates of the Americas. Since 1994, my resolution to carry on Fathy's work has led me to form the Swan Group, part of the tax-exempt corporation Adobe Alliance, in the border cities of Presidio, Texas and Ojinaga, Chihuahua.

As our global population continues to rise, the number of people without dignified, healthy, safe housing has soared far beyond what it was 30 years ago when Fathy wrote Architecture for the Poor. *Fathy's designs, ideas, principles, and character promise to grow only more relevant with time.*

Nubian vault a federal stamp of approval, and this may allow Presidio residents to receive low-interest mortgages to build all-adobe homes.

"Not many engineers have studied adobe," says Demetrio Jimenez, director of the non-profit Greater El Paso Housing Development Corporation, who has helped Swan navigate the channels of the RHA. "Even fewer have heard of Hassan Fathy or these parabolic vaults." And low-income people, he explains, can't get government-backed loans without an engineer's approval of the house design. "When that engineer signs off, he has some big liabilities if anything goes wrong. They don't sign on something they don't know," he explains. "But from my experience along the border, there's a lot of families building their own homes anyway; that's just the way people do it here." Swan's ideas thus "lend themselves excellently" to existing local practices.

Swan has now built four structures in the Ojinaga/Presidio area, with hopes for many more. She is also engaged in extensive research regarding plastering these homes with lime, a difficult feat in such a hot climate, and sealing them with a traditional Mexican recipe of soap and alum.

Swan's home was finished in 1999. She added a freestanding square guest room with an elegant dome and a utility shed to house the batteries that power the home. The batteries are recharged daily by a photovoltaic array and a windmill. "Now that the house is finished," Swan says, "and we have prototypes on both sides, I can really concentrate on the low-income aspect, which of course is the heart of all this."

Although progress is slow, Swan takes some comfort in recalling the official resistance Fathy faced so consistently for a half-century. "If he could be here right now," she says, "I'd ask him first, 'Hassan Bey, do you find this architecture that I have built to be truly harmonious with the culture, with the environment, and the climate?'" She pauses to look about with a self-critical eye. "I hope he would agree. I really hope he would."

But as for community-building and her role as a 'barefoot architect,' Swan says, "I know what he would say about that! He would say, 'Simone, you've already created a community link with your mason, plasterer, and helper, with Daniel [Camacho] and many others. It takes time for the rest to come. To be authentic, to have real change, it takes a lot of time.'"

And over on the other side of the river, as he beats earth, water, and straw each morning with his feet, Daniel Camacho is learning the same lesson.

Dick Doughty once spent much of a year carrying bricks and mixing mortar for a West Virginia chimney mason. He is now assistant editor of Saudi Aramco World *magazine.*

NOTES

1. See Hassan Fathy, *Architecture for the Poor: An Experiment in Rural Egypt* (University of Chicago Press, 1973), p.4.

RESOURCES

Books

Fathy, Hassan. *Architecture for the Poor: An Experiment in Rural Egypt.* University of Chicago Press, 1973. Documents Fathy's experiment in constructing the village of New Gourna by teaching poor people to build their own homes out of mud brick. Includes details of training, organization, construction techniques, and cost analysis.

———. *Natural Energy and Venacular Architecture: Principles and Examples With Reference to Hot Arid Climates.* University of Chicago Press, 1986. This book is filled with valuable technical details of natural housing technologies.

Khalili, Nader. *Ceramic Houses and Earth Architecture.* Cal-Earth Press, 1996. This book has excellent technical information on adobe construction, including vaults and domes; as well as Khalili's inspiring story of how he rediscovered the value of his ancient architectural heritage.

Steele, James. *An Architecture for People: The Complete Works of Hassan Fathy.* Whitney Library of Design, 1997. Amply illustrated with plans and beautiful photographs, this professional biography shows Fathy to be an idealist, an innovative designer, and an ingenious thinker.

Organizations

Swan Group, P.O. Box 1915 Presidio, TX 79845, U.S.A.; phone/fax: 915-229-4425; email: adobesim@brooksdata.net. Simone Swan's not-for-profit organization and the building arm of Adobe Alliance (www.AdobeAlliance.org.) Working to bring Fathy's ideas to the border communities of South Texas/North Mexico and elsewhere.

An Earthbag-Papercrete House

Kelly Hart

IN 1997 I was researching natural building techniques for a video program I produced, called *A Sampler of Alternative Homes: Approaching Sustainable Architecture*. As I explored various ways of building, I began to imagine the sort of house that I would like for my wife Rosana and me.

Domed structures eliminate much of the need for tensile roof materials, such as wood and steel. Since I wanted to avoid these materials for environmental reasons, the pictures in my mind were taking rounded shapes. I remembered seeing domes built of polypropylene bags filled with soil. I had seen people using crushed volcanic rock as sub-floor insulation. Why not fill bags with crushed volcanic rock and build the house with insulation?

Other earthbag buildings that I had seen were plastered with either adobe or concrete stucco. Earth plasters tend to erode over time and require ongoing maintenance, especially on domes; concrete stucco uses a lot of Portland cement and doesn't breathe very well. Then I remembered that a small amount of Portland cement could be added to a slurry of paper fiber to create a cured material (papercrete) with some very interesting properties. (See "Paper Houses: Papercrete and Fidobe.") Perhaps this material would make a good covering for my domed home.

An exterior view showing papercrete plaster.

CATHERINE WANEK

To test this theory, we began a small experimental dome (14 feet [4.3 meters] interior diameter), filling the bags with local volcanic scoria, and it held together beautifully. As with Nader Khalili's experiments, we placed two strands of four-point barbed wire between each two courses of bags to help hold them together. (*See* "Building with Earthbags.") We also tied polypropylene baling twine around the bags to help unify the entire wall.

We covered the outside of this little dome with papercrete, made in a simple barrel mixer. We were even able to imbed thermal pane glass (surplus units from the local glass shops) into the papercrete, covering the circular culvert couplers we used to form the windows.

Our building site is a south-facing sand dune that we dug into to provide berming on the north side. We dug down about 1 foot (0.3 meters) below our eventual floor level to leave room for a pad of 6 to 8 inches (15 to 20 centimeters) of scoria and then a poured adobe floor. There was no other foundation; the bags were placed directly upon the pad of scoria. With our dry climate and sandy soil there was little danger of poor drainage or frost heave.

The first big challenge with the bedroom dome (16-foot [5-meter] interior diameter) was the 6-foot (2-meter) arched entryway. On the experimental dome we had created a simple semicircular arch spanning 3 feet (1 meter), using a single row of sewn bags placed over a wooden form. When I tried the same technique for the larger span, I was rewarded with a lesson in physics and a spectacular collapse. I went back to the kit of miniature sand bags we had made to play with building concepts. I eventually came up with a double-bag pattern, which, along with increasing the height of the arch to create a pointed, gothic shape, produced a very strong self-supporting arch.

CATHERINE WANEK

Kelly and Rosana Hart in front of their earthbag and papercrete home.

As with the first dome, we found that putting in a loft with joists that are supported by the bags themselves is a good idea. Not only does it provide more usable space inside, but it also makes the whole structure more rigid as it is being built and provides a platform for the higher work.

The next part of the house that we tackled was the large, elliptical dome that would become our kitchen and living area. I thought an ellipse would provide plenty of space for south-facing glass and make for a pleasantly rounded but not monotonous shape. I soon discovered that an ellipse, especially the rather large 20-by-30-foot (6-by-9-meter) one that we were attempting, is not nearly as stable as a circular dome. I ultimately had to create a permanent wooden framework above loft level to stack the bags against and to keep the shape I wanted. So now we have a combination of a compressive and a tensile structure.

On the north side, off the kitchen, is a completely bermed circular pantry that leans up against the large dome. In this case I placed several layers of 6-mil polyethylene over the entire pantry before backfilling it. This has worked well to seal out moisture and burrowing insects.

The large and the small domes are connected by a space that serves as bathroom, greenhouse, spa room, and utility room, with an upstairs office. I had a notion that I could make a bag wall with the shape of a partial section of a sphere that would lean on the two domes from the north side. This would then be supported in place on the south side by a planar wood-framed roof section above a wood-framed greenhouse bay. I wanted a flat roof section facing south to support both photovoltaic and water-heating solar panels. There were a few scary moments when I prematurely removed some temporary braces and the back wall began to shift, but I persevered, and the whole thing has worked out well.

An interior view of the Harts' house. Note the roundwood poles used to support the earthbags.

CATHERINE WANEK

The last piece of architecture to enclose the house was a vaulted mudroom entryway, with a bell tower and bell for visitors to ring. Though the space is only about 8 feet (2.4 meters) square on the inside, it required a massive double-bag wall to be self-supporting without buttresses.

Once all of the major elements of the house were in place, I was able to put the final coat of papercrete stucco (with sand added) on the whole thing to strengthen and unify the building. The entire building is 'breathable,' with the exception of those areas that are underground (where I used either polyethylene sheets or asphalt to keep the moisture out).

One of the more interesting properties of papercrete is that it is extremely water-absorbent. The papercrete does not swell or contract in this process, or with temperature variations. Since we live in a very dry climate, and nothing in the wall is adversely affected by moisture, I was willing to experiment with such a system. So far it has worked well; we have had no moisture enter the house through the walls, even when there were huge cracks in the initial covering of papercrete.

The first coat of plaster on the interior was a thin splattering of pure papercrete. The final plaster inside the large dome was a combination of lime, silica sand, and a trace of white Portland cement, that was troweled into place. In most of the rest of the house, I just troweled papercrete stucco mix into a fairly smooth but irregular surface and then stained it with latex paint mixed maybe 1 part to 20 with water.

The floors are a combination of adobe, flagstone, cement mortar, papercrete, and tile. I allowed the adobe to shrink and crack, then filled the cracks with damp adobe, leaving a groove to resemble grout in stonework.

To make sure that there was plenty of thermal mass in the house to moderate the temperatures, I used sand in some of the lower bags, insulating them from the berm or the atmosphere outside. At night during the cold season, we use thermal curtains over the windows to help keep the heat inside. Since most of the windows do not open, we provided ventilation with a system of large pipes in strategic places, which are closed by inserting rubber tether balls inflated to just the right size.

As far as costs go, the house has been quite economical. The footprint of the house encompasses a little less that 1,000 square feet (91 square meters) of interior space, with a total square footage of about 1,250 square feet (114 square meters) if the lofts are included. If you add in the 150 square feet of the little prototype dome, the total enclosed space is about 1,400 square feet (130 square meters). The total for all of this was US$22,740, or about US$16 per square foot (US$1.44 per square meter). This, of course, excludes our labor and that of several friends who have helped out during the three years of construction.

So far I am very pleased with how the design is working, in terms of function and comfort. The outside temperature can get down to freezing at night and we need no additional heat. During the summer, it is usually cooler inside than out on warm days. It will be interesting to see how the concept performs over the years. It could be extremely durable. Certainly the scoria will not degrade; the durability of the papercrete and polypropylene are unknown. We do not live in a seismically active region, but should the ground shake, the tests that Nader Khalili has done at Cal-Earth would suggest that things should be fine.

Kelly Hart is a professional video producer, who, along with his wife Rosana, operates Hartworks, Inc.

RESOURCES
Organizations

Hartworks, P.O. Box 632, Crestone, CO 81131, U.S.A.; phone: 719-256-4278; website: www.hartworks.com. Information and images pertaining to our house and products.

Clay, Straw, and Permaculture: Natural Building at P.I.N.C.

Toby Hemenway

The cob office at P.I.N.C. Note rainwater collection from the steel roof into the duck pond at lower left.

Penny Livingston's route to natural building was circuitous. Her 1-acre (0.4-hectare) lot in Point Reyes Station, the home of the Permaculture Institute of Northern California (P.I.N.C.), hosts a cob office with a north wall of straw light-clay, a load-bearing straw bale cottage, and an innovative vaulted straw bale guest house. "When I started," Penny says, "I was just trying to figure out what to do with the dirt from our pond." She then reflects for a moment. "No, that's beginning in the middle. It began with sheet mulch."

JANINE BJÖRNSEN

Like many of us, Penny returned from her first permaculture design course enthralled with sheet mulch and set about smothering her yard in compostable debris. The huge bolus of organic matter proved a fertile home for insect life, not all of it beneficial. "It was a bug feeding frenzy out there," she reports. "I decided to use ducks to control them, knowing that I'd rather change duck-water than kill bugs." The downside of this approach was that she had to schlep heavy buckets of water around the yard for the Mallard flock. "So I thought, I'd rather sit by a pond than carry water," she says. Thus the first of a series of ponds was born, fed by household graywater and rooftop runoff. The topsoil from the excavation of this deep, roughly 8-by-12-foot (2.5-by-4-meter) pond went to the garden, but the subsoil lay in a pile awaiting its proper function.

The inspiration for the subsoil's ideal role came when Penny visited Aprovecho Research Center in Cottage Grove, Oregon. There she saw a cob building and was entranced. She drafted a design for a cob office for P.I.N.C. Soon after that, Ianto Evans and Michael G. Smith of the Cob

258

Cottage Company arrived to run a workshop. By the end of the class, the pond's subsoil had been mixed with sand and straw and packed into cob walls about six feet (two meters) tall. Plenty of work remained, but with the help of friends, interns, and Penny's husband James Stark, the building inched its way to completion.

It's now a comfortable office, lined with books and holding a large table in each of its two sunny, south-facing alcoves. These sun-spaces quickly warm the building on cool days. Cob enthusiasts often tout the benefits of the thermal mass provided by their buildings' foot-thick (0.3-meter-thick) earthen walls, and these claims have been borne out by the P.I.N.C. office. A local architect ran an energy study of Penny's building, comparing it to a conventional structure built for energy efficiency. The software he used found that the cob office uses only one-fourth the energy of a comparable conventional building.

The pond that provided the office's soil eventually grew into a network of four, fed by a gray-water treatment marsh. It was this system that first led Penny to approach Bill Mollison. "When we dug the pond," she says, "the ducks just jumped right in, like little inspectors telling us we were doing a good job." But with the addition of graywater to the pond, the ducks shunned it. Shortly thereafter, Penny took a permaculture course from Bill in Texas. She asked him about the pond-avoiding ducks. "And he said, 'It's because they'll sink.' Bill told me that the soaps — the surfactants in the graywater — strip the oils off the ducks' feathers so they can't float." Penny, ever the permaculturist, notes that this was a solution to another problem. Vegetation in the nearby graywater marsh couldn't get established because the ducks were gobbling it up. But the high soap levels barred the ducks from the marsh long enough to let the plants take root. Soon the plants were wringing the soaps and other potential nutrients from the graywater, converting them to greenery. The ducks returned to the clean water of the pond system. The mallards are sensitive biological indicators that all is well (a pond test kit also confirmed that nitrate, phosphate, and other pollutant levels were suitably low).

The pond system is densely connected to the cob office. Not only did the pond excavation yield the office walls, but rainwater sluicing from the office roof tops up the ponds. Also, the office sits on the north side of the ponds, basking in light reflected from the water. "It's not just that the office is brighter than it would be without the ponds," Penny explains. "The effect is magical: reflected light bounces and shimmers off the walls and ceiling. It creates a sacred place to work." Nearby plants also benefit from the pond. A dwarf nectarine, washed by light sparkling from the pond, ripens far earlier than its companions placed elsewhere.

Another element deepens this web of connection. Beside the pond and office is a grape arbor, underlaid with flagstones and set with benches. The arbor has become an extension of the office, where, on the many fine days that Marin County's climate offers at any time of year, Institute staff do paperwork or meet with clients. Even on a cool winter day, the light reflected from the pond and the heat gathered by the stonework create a bright, cozy outdoor room.

BUILDING THE COB OFFICE

The cob office began with the digging of a roughly 12-by-16-foot (4-by-5-meter) foundation pit. In this, Penny, James, and company set a pond liner and layered it with straw for insulation. Around the pit's perimeter they built the building's footings of stone. The crew then filled the pit with tamped sand and gravel road base. Then began the cob wall building, much of which was completed in a Cob Cottage Company workshop. During a separate workshop, P.I.N.C. and friends built the north wall from light-clay (straw wetted with a thin clay-and-water mix and tamped between forms). This is an ideal material for office walls because it accepts screws for shelving with no backing or toggle bolts.

The walls are plastered with earth and covered with aliz (from the Spanish *alisar*, to polish), a thin mix of clay that in this case contains sand, mica, and wheat flour paste. The floor is poured adobe that holds piping for radiant heat.

A bank of six arched windows and a French door let in plenty of light on the south side. Two skylights further brighten the office. The ceiling is of Meadowood panels, a product from Albany, Oregon, formed of compressed rye grass bonded with non-toxic resins from Germany. Salvaged 1-inch (2.5-centimeter) redwood forms the rafters. These have straw-clay insulation stuffed between them and support green-enameled metal roofing. The gutters, 4-inch (10-centimeter) flexible black drainage pipe, slit on one side and snapped onto the roofing's edge, are the brainchild of Brock Dolman of the Occidental Arts and Ecology Center. The gutters have a flowing organic sinuousness that mates well with the cob's curves. Holes drilled at intervals in the pipe guide rainwater down chains, into a drain, and to the pond system.

The outside is covered with what's normally an interior plaster: earth, sand, clay, and rice hulls (this last is an abundant agricultural by-product in California). It contains no lime or cement, which normally give plaster its weather resistance. The plaster has held up well where it is protected by the roof overhang, but where it's exposed to rain, it is slowly wearing away.

On the east side, a cob oven shaped like a dragon's head thrusts from the wall, an abalone shell for an eye. A long cob bench, molded to form the dragon's tail, extends from the back wall. Workers in the office are truly in the belly of the beast.

VAULTING WITH STRAW

A second innovative structure has sprung from another corner of the P.I.N.C. property: a vaulted straw bale guest house. The architectural vault, two walls that lean together and meet at the top to form a pointed arch, is an ancient concept. Bay Area architects Bob Theis and Dan Smith consulted with Penny to build the first permanent straw bale vault at P.I.N.C. The construction began much the same as that of the office: a pit, pond liner, and tamped sand and road base. But instead of stone stemwalls, the foundation consists of several tiers of polypropylene feedbags filled with gravel and well compacted.

Next, the builders drove short lengths of rebar every three feet (one meter) into the ground just inside and outside of the gravel bags. To these they fastened long bamboo poles, each arched to meet its opposite number across the foundation. This created an inner and outer vault. Each inner pole was then tied at intervals to the outer pole just across the gravel bags from it. Next, the crew placed wooden wedges (2-foot-long [60-centimeter-long] 2-by-4s cut diagonally) on the foundation bags and upon them laid the first row of straw bales. The wedges tilted the bales inward at the angle needed to lean the vault walls inward. They pinned the bales in place using bamboo and occasionally rebar. (Penny remarks that driving in bamboo pins is tough work.)

Putting the walls up only took a couple of days, but plastering and finishing them was time-consuming and grueling. For those who eschew cob because it is slow going, Penny relates that "Cob may not be that much more labor intensive than straw bale. With cob, though, there's more work at the front end; when the walls are up, you're done. The utilities are in, and you don't even have to plaster the outside if you don't want to. Straw seems fast because the walls just go zip, right up. But with bales, then you have to go back and fill in all the gaps with straw. Then there's all the stuccoing and layers of plaster, and finishing around the doors and windows. All that detailing takes a lot of time. We left the plaster pretty rough in places, but even so, it was a tremendous amount of work. Six hundred hours. So, having built both, I'd say that cob and straw bale may be about even in terms of labor."

With the walls-cum-ceilings up, next came plastering. Penny had vowed to avoid cement-based plasters, as cement is perhaps the most energy-consuming construction material on Earth, but the architects insisted that it was necessary for seismic stability (Penny's land is barely a mile [1.6 kilometers] from the San Andreas fault). Some architects believe that cement should be added for moisture resistance, but in this case, the roof overhang is so ample that even a mud-based plaster would have been protected from rain.

The front wall of the guest house — the narrow wings that flank the French doors — is made of cob set on a stone foundation and stuccoed with earthen plaster. It is finished with an aliz of porcelain clay mixed with flour and water and colored bright orange with ferrous sulfate, a natural, non-toxic pigment.

Inside, the plaster contains gypsum. "We did that because of the leaning walls," Penny explains. "Walls that aren't plumb are very difficult to plaster, and here the exposed bamboo poles compound the problem. Adding gypsum to the plaster makes the difference between plastering with whipping cream and with mashed potatoes, which is what earthen plasters without gypsum are like. A gypsum plaster adheres to the bales, and is very moldable. Plus there's plenty of gypsum on the planet."

The white gypsum walls and the banks of small windows that pierce them give the room a soft, luminous glow. A big double bed, covered by a fluffy down comforter, fills the cottage. It's a pillowy, enveloping space that muffles the outside world, with the comforting feel of being covered in a thick blanket of snow.

The French doors open onto a flagstone patio and another pond that is backed with a row of pear trees woven into a Belgian fence. The trees, tightly interlaced, have begun to graft together into a single being. Again we see a synergy, where buildings, patio, pond, Belgian fence, and other garden sites meld to offer far more than a single element ever could. Binding separate buildings and spaces together to create a dwelling space is reminiscent of the 'house compounds' of Bali and works well in California's often sub-tropical climate.

Next to the vaulted cottage is a second straw bale building, which adds a living room to the bedroom supplied by the straw bale vault. Of the three natural buildings at P.I.N.C., this straw bale living room is the closest to a conventional design. It forms a simple square in plan, a plain cube in shape. But even this structure holds its surprises. It is load-bearing straw — the bales themselves support the roof. Many straw bale buildings are held up by timber frames, with the straw serving merely as insulating infill between wood posts. But Penny loves to surf out toward the margins of what is known, bringing back data from these far reaches. 'Cutting edge' is a phrase she uses often, and her work nearly always resides there. So it is no surprise that her ever-evolving home contains three structures — of hybridized cob and light-clay, of vaulted straw, and of load-bearing straw — that individually have challenged their designers at nearly every turn, and that collectively form one of the most diverse assortments of natural building techniques in the region.

Toby Hemenway is associate editor of The Permaculture Activist *and the author of* Gaia's Garden: Guide to Home-Scale Permaculture *(Chelsea Green, 2001). He teaches and consults throughout the continent and lives on an evolving ten-acre permaculture landscape in southern Oregon.*

The Earth Sweet Home Institute

Juliet Cuming and David Shaw

JULIET CUMING AND DAVID SHAW are filmmakers who believe that only by working with nature can humans create homes that are more nurturing and less destructive to our planet and ourselves. They founded Earth Sweet Home to promote sustainable methods of building through hands-on experimentation and assessment of natural and alternative technologies, with the goal to encourage and empower others by example. David and Juliet wanted not only to teach about these ideas through their filmmaking and video-production skills but wanted a project of their own. It would

The Earth Sweet Home Institute. A straw bale home/office, with photovoltaic panels in the foreground.

be imbued spirtitually, as well as enviromentally — partly as a real-life experiment, partly as a subject for their films, but most of all to provide a 'home,' not just a 'house' for their family.

The Earth Sweet Home house, located in Southern Vermont, puts principles of ecological design into action in one of the most challenging building climates in the United States. With a special emphasis on design for good indoor air quality, because of Juliet's chemical sensitivity, they planned their home as a model of the potential for low-embod-

DAVID SHAW

ied-energy, full-cycle-sustainable design and building. Created almost entirely with locally produced (within a 30-mile [48-kilometer] radius) materials, it uses nearly no concrete. It has a dry-laid stone foundation, heavy-timber frame, cedar shingle roof, and passive and active solar strategies and equipment. *Feng shui* and permaculture principles were used throughout the site and during the building design process. Built with straw bale walls, it also uses cellulose roof insulation and has 'breathable,' natural wall finishes. Although built nearly entirely of natural materials, the Earth Sweet Home house is an elegant, comfortable home with all the modern conveniences.

Adhering to the principles of using local materials and supporting local businesses was easier than expected — even the super-efficient windows were made locally. Some 'imported' materials include the super-energy-efficient appliances: a Sunfrost refrigerator, Asko washer and dishwasher, and O/S natural stains and finishing products. The solar and wind systems enable the entire building to be powered by locally produced renewable energy. Sixteen Solarex solar panels, a Zomeworks tracker and a 1.5-kilowatt wind turbine have provided electricity throughout the entire construction of the house and for all workshops held on-site.

The library at Earth Sweet Home.

The Earth Sweet Home house is one of the first straw bale houses in the Northeast to get homeowner's insurance. Another first: In accordance with the newly revised State of Vermont environmental codes, project engineer Jane Morano created a constructed wetland for the treatment of the Earth Sweet Home house's residential wastewater. Through wise planning and serendipity, they were able to meet their environmental and health criteria without incurring extra expense. Now five years old, the house is doing fine.

The Earth Sweet Home project is of particular interest because so much information about so many aspects of sustainable design has been collected in one compact area. Housing both the offices of Earth Sweet Home and a real live family, the building is being tested every day for performance and durability.

Filmmakers Juliet Cuming and David Shaw promote sustainable building methods through information and workshops offered by the Earth Sweet Home Institute.

A view of the bathroom at Earth Sweet Home.

DAVID SHAW

DAVID SHAW

Evolving a Village Vernacular: The Earthaven Experiment

Chuck Marsh

EARTHAVEN, AN EVOLVING ECOVILLAGE, is very much a work in progress. Seven years into our story and much experimentation later, we have learned a few things about housing ourselves and about building with locally available natural materials. We still have much to discover about what it means to 'reinhabit' a place and about how to create a village culture, a culture of connection that supports both the needs of the natural world and of its human inhabitants. As a community, Earthaven members have chosen to educate ourselves about permaculture, natural building, appropriate technology, self-governance, and village-based economics, and to apply what we learn to our settlement's design and development. We are also committed to sharing the fruits of our learning with others.

Our land is a mid-slope complex of ridges and valleys on the Blue Ridge front range near Black Mountain, North Carolina. The land was abandoned during the 1930s and 1940s after being abused by the previous white settlers, so we inherited a young recovering forest landscape and one rotting log cabin. Since there were no decent structures on the land when we bought it, and since we chose to take responsibility for housing ourselves, we became builders and designers from necessity. And natural builders by choice and ethic.

We were interested in evolving a new vernacular architecture appropriate to the climate and available natural materials of our Southern Appalachian bioregion. We wanted a strategy responsive to our needs for energy conservation that was reasonably low cost and relatively easy to construct and replicate. We were interested in building techniques and architectural designs that met the above criteria and lent themselves to amateur

A circle within a circle. A ceremonial circle after the first post is raised for the council hall at Earthaven.

CHUCK MARSH

builders, as none of us was a professional builder when we began. So we went out and learned all the natural building techniques that we could find teachers for: cob, straw bale, straw light-clay, and timber framing. We taught ourselves other techniques through experiment and practice, including wattle and daub, earth-coupled floors, earthen plasters, and gravel bag foundations. We are continuing our experimental approach with new work and are learning about living roofs, geopolymers, and earthship techniques.

Our practice has been to learn and apply various techniques, then comparatively evaluate them for durability in our climate, esthetics, ease of construction, labor requirements, materials availability and processing needs, construction costs, maintenance needs, energy conservation, and insulative values. We began by building small structures, practicing an experimental learning process that involved making small mistakes and correcting from what was learned. We wanted to make inexpensive mistakes on small structures, so that when it became time to build larger buildings and dwellings, we wouldn't make large and costly mistakes that we would pay for forever through ongoing maintenance or energy costs.

Thus evolved the 'hut hamlet' near the center of the land. Members built small homes with footprints under 300 square feet (28 square meters) and at near urban densities as initial dwelling places on the land. This hut hamlet was intended to be the place where we learned natural building and how to live together and share common facilities (kitchen, composting toilets, bathing facilities, and gardens). The lessons we have learned here have been numerous, ongoing, difficult at times, and quite valuable to our village's development.

Earthaven is located in the great eastern forest, so wood is a major natural and renewable building material for us. To access this resource, we purchased a simple and portable band saw sawmill early on in our development. It proved to be an invaluable liberating technology. We could provide for our own lumber needs from the land and free ourselves from dependence on the rapacious global timber industry. Then, about four years into Earthaven's development, the Earthaven Forestry Co-op arose. It helps support the village's needs for ecologically based forest management; provides a village-based economy (that is,

Brandi points out an orchard bee colony on an unplastered section of cob wall. An unintended benefit of this natural building was the creation of habitat for this very beneficial pollinator.

CHUCK MARSH

jobs on the land); and helps with designing and building community members' homes, community and neighborhood buildings, and business buildings. The Forestry Co-op is a Mondragon-style worker-owned cooperative business that employs about eight village members; it is vertically integrated to cover timber harvesting, sawmilling, and building construction.

The Forestry Co-op has helped to further evolve our village vernacular architecture. It has developed a wood-based building system that incorporates innovative timber framing techniques. By using small-diameter posts and beams and a wrap-around wall truss system, wood otherwise wasted in conventional sawmilling gets put to good use. This system is also designed for natural insulative infills and a lath-and-clay/lime plaster system for interior and exterior wall finishes.

Interior framing of the Night Owl Café. Note the wall system with exterior lath in place.

The Co-op has also developed a simple, standard design for an easy-to-construct basic building. Easily expandable, these buildings provide a good primary structure for home or business. The basic building plan offers an option for the Forestry Co-op to mill the lumber and erect the building's foundation, frame, and roof. The owners then finish the building themselves with the help of their families, friends, and neighbors. Builders who choose this option often host cooperative work parties to do the remaining labor-intensive pieces like earth plastering and earthen floors. We have found that working together like this is a great way to celebrate our true interdependence and build deep community connections.

And so we grow and learn and build our village's vernacular architecture along with our lives. Slowly, with practice and with consideration for what we have learned along the way, we are redesigning our way home. Earthaven will continue to co-evolve the natural building systems that work for us as we further elaborate bioregionally appropriate, permaculture-based settlement patterns for the Southern Appalachians. We welcome others who want to join us in this work.

Chuck Marsh is a cofounder of Earthaven Ecovillage, a permaculture teacher and designer, an amateur natural builder, a cultural re-evolutionary, and a rascal in training.

RESOURCES
Organizations

Earthaven Ecovillage, email: chuck@earthaven.org; website: www.earthaven.org.

Building with the Earth at Auroville

Satprem Maini

A compressed earth block office at Auroville.

This huge solar collector provides enough heat for this compressed earth block kitchen to produce meals for hundreds of people a day.

AUROVILLE, THE "CITY OF DAWN," is an international city under construction, located near Pondicherry in southern India. Auroville aims to harmonize the material with the spiritual, based on the work and inspiration of Sri Aurobindo and "The Mother." During the foundation ceremony in 1968, representatives of 124 nations and 24 Indian states dropped a handful of soil from their country into an urn, as a testimony of human unity. Presently around 1,500 people of about 30 different nationalities are living in Auroville.

The first Aurovilians settled in a red desert, as the dry tropical evergreen forests had been cut down long before. For about 30 years, their main occupation was to give life again to the eroded plateau. More than two million trees were planted, and now Auroville is again a wonderful lush green landscape.

Building the city really started in the 1960's. The Auroville Building Centre/Earth Unit was created in 1989 as a training and research center in earth architecture. Since that time, Auroville architects have been instrumental in developing earthen architecture for the Indian subcontinent and elsewhere. In particular, they have taken compressed earth block architecture to a very high degree of beauty and sophistication, building numerous residential and business structures with blocks from a press of their own design, the Auram. The AVBC/Earth Unit workshops deal with the production of compressed earth blocks (CEB), masonry with CEB, various composite technologies based on stabilized earth, stabilized rammed earth for foundations and walls, and building arches, vaults, and domes.

Satprem Maini is an architect at AVBC/Earth Unit and UNESCO Chair of Earth Architecture.

268

Natural Building — A European Tradition

Catherine Wanek

YOU HAVE ONLY to get off the beaten track in Europe to discover a deep tradition of handsome buildings of stone, timber, earth and straw finished with lime plasters and thatched roofs. Unfortunately, this picturesque landscape is succumbing to a modern urban fate, with pre-fabricated steel and concrete mini-malls and neon-colored fast-food shops intruding into historic villages. Traditions are crumbling as urban populations push city boundaries, and techniques used to construct many buildings that have lasted centuries have nearly been lost to history.

Fortunately, some visionaries are revisiting the age-old building technologies. Appreciating more than historic value, many modern Europeans are attracted by the same things that motivate U.S. natural builders: affordability, concern for their ecological footprint, the desire for a healthy home, and esthetics — simply the beauty of natural materials.

The spectrum of inspiring people, places, and buildings might first be sampled at open-air folk museums across the continent. In nearly every country, historic structures have been saved from the bulldozer, restored in 'villages,' and finished with authentic furniture and tools, often accompanied by recreations of traditional crafts and cooking. Three outstanding folk museums are in Stockholm, Sweden; Oslo, Norway; and Kiev, Ukraine, but smaller open-air museums in Germany, The Netherlands, Belgium, England and elsewhere, offer an experience of how life was lived and how homes were constructed without modern tools and with completely natural materials.

In the Nordic countries, wooden structures predominate, with the living space often built up on 'legs' — for safety and to keep above snow levels in the winter. The magnificent Norwegian stave church might be the culmination of the woodworker's art and craft. Sod or 'green' roofs are common, as are straw and reed thatch. Elsewhere in Europe, historic buildings are primarily stone

This stave church in Oslo, Norway is well over 100 feet (30 meters) tall, with elaborate wood carvings inside.

CATHERINE WANEK

The walls of traditional English cob buildings were often over three feet (one meter) thick, as seen in this cottage in Devon, England.

or oak timber frame structures. In Germany, these are infilled with wattle and daub (*fachwerk*), straw-clay (*leichtlehm*), and, in more recent eras, with fired bricks that have been plastered with lime. In parts of England and Wales, cob homes with thick mono-lithic earthen walls predominate, typically thatched with reeds.

Interestingly, a relatively rapid deterioration of the centuries-old timber frames has been caused by the replacement of lime with a cement-based plaster during the restoration of historic buildings. This is traced to moisture retention inside the walls, due to cement's vapor impermeability. Natural builder and permaculturist Harald Wedig is currently overseeing the re-restoration of an open-air museum in Germany. His crew is replacing the infill material with more authentic wattle and daub, and the cement stucco with lime plaster.

Careful research helped recreate Shakespeare's Globe Theatre on the bank of the Thames River in London, faithful to the materials and craftsmanship of the original. With concessions to modern codes and fire safety hidden within its lime-plastered walls, the Globe once again proudly offers timeless natural building techniques along with world-class performances. Set on a brick plinth wall, 20 huge oak timbers form the three-story structural framework of the new Globe, connected with mortise and tenon joinery by master carpenter Peter McCurdy and crew. Oak staves support strips of oak lath, which are plastered with a traditional mix of sand, slaked lime, and animal hair to form its walls.

Reeds for the thatched roof were gathered from far afield, as modern London no longer has local marshland. The thick thatch sheds rain outside — and inside — the oval structure, leaving the 'groundlings' (the ones with the 'cheap seats') standing in the center, exposed to the weather. In Shakespeare's day, a barrel buried in the center of the sloped interior yard caught rainwater and channeled it underneath and away from the structure via wooden drainage pipes made from hollowed-out tree trunks.

Historic rammed-earth or pisé buildings in eastern France were an inspiration to young architects from Grenoble, who in 1979 founded CRATerre, the Centre for Research and Applications of

Earth Building. Establishing their center in Villefontaine, near Lyon, CRATerre has since acquired international renown through its affordable housing initiatives, publications, research, and teaching. In 1985, they completed an innovative rammed-earth rental housing development called *Le Domaine de la Terre* — creating comfortable, modern dwellings from age-old techniques. Today there is a long list of people waiting for an opening. In the mid-1970s, the founders of the Centre for Alternative Technology in Wales took up the challenge to convert a derelict slate quarry into a self-sustaining community. Over 25 years, CAT has evolved into an ecological demonstration center and a fun place to visit, with interactive technology displays, permaculture gardens, as well as a straw bale theater.

At Le Domaine de la Terre, France, architects from CRATerre combined rammed earth walls with energy-efficient bioclimatic greenhouses and ventilated conservatory roofs.

The Folkecenter for Renewable Energy near the north tip of Denmark is a place of windswept beauty and serious scientific study. Visitors see full-scale functioning photovoltaic systems and wind technology — in a region that many days can produce 150 percent of its electricity needs from wind power. The Folkecenter's forays into natural building include an earth-bermed conference center with a living roof and a straw bale home for long-term interns.

Denmark is also the birthplace of co-housing and the Global Ecovillage Network (GEN) — brainchildren of Ross and Hildur Jackson. After successfully experimenting with co-housing, the Jacksons envisioned a type of community that would combine this cooperative spirit with ecological and spiritual consciousness. They envisioned the 'ecovillage' as a positive example of how humans might live in harmony into a sustainable future. In the mid-1990s they contacted ten existing communities and formed the Global Ecovillage Network, which to date has expanded into dozens of ecovillages worldwide. Many such as the Findhorn Community in Scotland, founded more than 30 years ago, have developed educational programs and invite visitors to learn about sustainability by going and living it. (*See* "Ecovillages and Sustainable Communities.")

CATHERINE WANEK

The Danish organization "Happy and Mortgage Free" enjoy breakfast at Steen Møller's inspiring self-built natural home.

In the same cooperative spirit that fuels ecovillages, a vibrant group of Danish youth recently formed an organization called "Happy and Mortgage Free." Inspired by the creative natural buildings of Steen Møller, they plan to help each other build their own homes, free from debt.

Steen, a former farmer, achieved national fame as the subject of a Danish TV documentary, in which he built a low-cost straw bale cottage for a well-known actress. The cozy cottage incorporates natural materials in nearly every aspect of construction, from its foundation insulated with shells to its straw bale walls, living roof, earthen and lime plasters, cob stove, and straw bale furniture. Total cost of materials was under US$2,000. Steen himself lives in a majestic, self-built rammed earth, timber framed structure that is earth-plastered and incorporates straw bale and a thatched roof. He gives frequent tours of his home and lectures about sustainable living. Other bale builders with conviction are a group of women builders in Amsterdam:, Stro & Co., led by Cai van Hoboken and Jolien van der Maaden. Working with those on the economic fringe, they lead workshops about building with bales and found materials. Fabricating window frames and roof trusses from wood scraps, and shingles from a roll of plastic material found in a dumpster, they are helping to inspire a vibrant urban building scene. Stro & Co. got their inspiration at a workshop led by Barbara Jones, of Amazon Nails in England. Empowering women and trying experimental techniques like rammed tire foundations, Barbara has helped build more natural structures in the challenging climate of the U.K. than anyone else in recent times.

Members of the Austrian Straw Bale Network have organized workshops, conducted surveys, published reports and books, initiated testing, and attracted government funding for a straw bale demonstration building. Natural builders from all over France have banded together as the *Association pour la Construction en Fibres Végétales,* including a multilingual couple, Andre and Coralie de Bouter, who offer building workshops and tours of their straw bale home in the Cognac region. The French owner-builders seem to infuse an eclectic personal creativity into their natural homes.

In Belarus, the former Soviet state that received the bulk of radioactive fallout from Chernobyl, the people face a hard lesson of the nuclear age: since 1986 they have lived in a land that will be radioactive for centuries to come. In this shadow, life goes on. Evgeny Shirokov, president of the Belarussian Division of the International Academy of Ecology, is on a personal crusade to bring issues of sustainability into a country that is still fundamentally communist. He has been the catalyst for successful initiatives, from installing pollution-control stacks on power generating stations, to instigating a government program that has built an estimated 60 straw bale homes for families displaced by Chernobyl fallout. This program, "Straw Bale Homes for Chernobyl Settlers," recently won the Green Globe award at World Sustainable Energy Day 2000. The Belarussian village of Drushnaja ('Friendship') is being built atop a battlefield from World War I. For three years it was the front line between the Russians and the Germans. Now this remote field has become home to a new community of Chernobyl settlers, led by Valentin Jarmoltschik. His was the first family to move in, and he now supervises the construction of three to five homes built there every year.

Jarmoltschik's group first builds a wooden frame, then infills the walls with a straw/clay or woodchip/clay mix. They seal the interior walls with earthen plaster and finish the exterior with a traditional decorative wood plank siding. Although most of their funding comes from a German non-governmental organization (NGO), the families put sweat equity into the homes they will occupy. Every time they dig a foundation, they unearth shrapnel, bullets, and bones. But their colorful houses and neat gardens, and the young children playing within them, are indicators that hope does 'spring eternal.'

CATHERINE WANEK

Evgeny Shirokov (L) and Valentin Jarmolschik at the first straw-clay home in the Belarussian settlement called Friendship, populated by families displaced by the Chernobyl nuclear accident.

Many European natural builders are working in isolation, figuring things out as they go without benefit of a network. That's where the European Straw Building Network (ESBN), comes in. A network of natural builders motivated by concerns of global warming and our cumulative ecological footprint, ESBN members give lectures, lead workshops, and lobby governments to promote affordable sustainable building. The continent-wide network functions through annual meetings and a rapidly expanding Internet-based discussion group, which connects anyone with a modem, irrespective of national boundaries. Fortunately for us here in North America, we can listen in, too, as the most common language on the ESBN list-serve is English.

Ironically, it may be computer technology that allows a worldwide natural building network to emerge, creating the prophesied Global Village among like-minded visionaries. Meanwhile, in

CATHERINE WANEK

Shakespeare's Globe Theatre, recently recreated on the banks of the Thames River, is the first thatched building in London since the great fire of 1699.

actual villages throughout Europe, traditional technologies are gaining new respect as examples of low-impact building. It does seem fitting that we look to what has proven itself in the past as we seek equitable, sustainable shelter for the century in front of us.

Catherine Wanek has traveled from Orange County to Red Square, learning about and documenting natural buildings. The best part of every trip has been the hospitality of friends made along the way. She considers it a privilege to share some of the work of this diverse community that is connected by their deep environmental convictions and their passion for the art of natural building.

Resources

Books
Eco-logic Books, 19 Maple Grove, Bath BA2 2AF, England; phone: 01225 484472; email: books@eco-logic.demon.co.uk.

Periodicals
Baling Out. Newsletter for Straw Bale Building Association for Wales, Ireland, Scotland, and England — SBBA (WISE). (See "Organizations" for address.)

EcoDesign. Journal of the Ecological Design Association. Glochester, U.K.; website: www.salvo.co.uk/mags/EcoDesign.htm.

Ecovillage Living. Journal for the Global Ecovillage Network. (See "Organizations" for address.)

Sustainable Energy News. Newsletter for INFORSE, the International Network for Sustainable Energy, Gl. Kirkevej 56, DK 8530, Hjortshoej, Denmark.

The Real Green Building Book – A Directory of Members. Association for Environment Conscious Building members in the U.K. and Ireland. (See "Organizations" for address.)

Organizations
Association for Environment Conscious Building (AECB), Nant-y-Garreg, Saron, Llandysul, Carmarthenshire SA44 5EJ, U.K.; phone: +44 0 1559 370908; email: admin@aecb.net; website: www.aecb.net.

Association pour la Construction en Fibre Végétales (ACFV), Contact: Lorenzo Robles, Le Bourg, 86110 Mazeuil, France; email: lorobles55@hotmail.com

Austrian Straw Building Network (ASBN), Contact: Herbert Gruber, A – 3720 Baierdorf 6, Austria; email: asbn@aon.at; website: www.baubiologie.at.

European Straw Building Network (ESBN), Contact: Martin Oehlmann, email: martin.oehlmann@wxs.nl; listserve: strawbale-l@eyfa.org.

Global Ecovillage Network, GEN International, Skodsborgvej 189, 2850 Naerum, Denmark; phone: 45 45 56 01 30; email: gen@gaia.org; website: www.gaia.org.

Happy & Mortgage Free, Contact: Lars Keller, Blabjergvej 2, 7280 Sdr. Felding, Denmark; phone: +45 2024 0505; email: larskeller@livinghouses.net.

Society for the Protection of Ancient Buildings, 37 Spital Square, London, England E16DY.

Straw Bale Building Association for Wales, Ireland, Scotland, and England — SBBA (WISE), Contact: Barbara Jones, Hollinroyd Farm, Todmorden OL 14 8RJ U.K.; phone: +44 01 70 681 4696; email:

barbara@strawbalefutures.org; website: www.strawbale-futures.org.uk.

The Norwegian Straw and Earth Building Organisation (NJH), Contact: Arild Berg Wærnjus, N — 1540, Vestby, Norway; phone: 47 22 67 05 95; email: arild.berg3@chello.no.

CATHERINE WANEK

In Holland, farmer Johan Beukeboom built a post-and-beam-and-bale barn big enough for 50 cows.

Centers

Centre For Alternative Technology (CAT), Canolfany Dechnoleg Amgen, Machynlleth, Powys SY20 9AZ U.K.; phone: 01654 702400; email: info@cat.org.uk; website: www.cat.org.uk; catalog of publications: pubs@cat.org.uk.

CRATerre – Centre de Recherces en Architecture de Terre, Parc Fallavier, Rue du Lac, B.P. 53, F-38092 Villefontaine, Cedex France; phone: +33 (4) 74 95 43 91; email: craterre@clubinternet.fr; website: www.craterre.archi.fr.

Folkecenter for Renewable Energy, Kammersgaardsvej 16, Sdr. Ydby, P.O. Box 208, DK-7760 Hurup Thy, Denmark; phone: 45 9795 6600; email: energy@folkecenter.dk; website: www.folkecenter.dk.

Shakespeare's Globe Theatre, New Globe Walk, Bankside, Southwark, London SE1 9ED England; phone: +44 (0) 207 902-1500 (Tours), +44 (0) 207 401-9919 (Performances); website: www.shakespeares-globe.org.

VIBA (Association Integral Bio-logical Architecture), P.O. Box 772, 5201 AT Den Bosch, The Netherlands; email: info@viba-expo.nl.

Workshops

Andre and Coralie De Bouter, La Maison En Paille, Le Trezidoux Champmillon, Charente, France 16290; phone: +33 0 5 45 66 27 68; email: sim.plicity@laposte.net; website: www.la-maison-en-paille.com.

Cai van Hoboken and Jolien van der Maaden, Stichting Stro & Co, p/a Monnikendammerplantsoen 11, Amsterdam 1023 EL, The Netherlands, 31 (0)20 6365390, email: <caistrobv@dds.nl> <jostro@dds.nl>.

Helen and Kevin Ireland, Deanburn Cottage, Hayford, Buckfastleigh, Devon U.K. TQ11 0JQ; phone: +44 01 36 464 3267; email: hkireland@aol.com.

Martin Oehlmann, Sportlaan 336, Den Haag, The Netherlands NL-2566LN; email: martin.oehlmann@wxs.nl.

Harald and Margit Wedig, Sualmana Permaculture Gardens, Kerkebroekweg 46, NL-6071 GL Swalmen, The Netherlands; phone: 31 0 475 600-555; email: avantgarden@wxs.nl.

RESOURCES

Desert Island Books

An annotated list of the editors' favorite books on natural building and ecological design.

Imagine you are marooned on a deserted island with your family and friends. There is plenty of fresh water and wild food but absolutely no human-built infrastructure and no hope of rescue. For your community to stay healthy and comfortable, you will need to build a settlement. On a hunch, you brought some books along to help you with everything from how to design a sustainable, integrated community to how to plaster your house. Which books would you choose?

Following is the editors' selection of desert island books. Even if you aren't stranded on a remote island, we think they would still make an excellent startup library for anyone seriously interested in natural building and ecological design. Buying books can be an expensive habit. We encourage you to start a natural building association or study group and share books, or ask your local public library to purchase them.

Books

Alexander, Christopher, et al. *A Pattern Language.* **Oxford University Press, 1977.**

Together with its companion volume, *A Timeless Way of Building*, this book may do no less than change the entire way you view the built environment. Considering the environment as a 'language,' the authors have identified 'patterns' that range in scale from an entire region to the size of trim, that support the highest human potential. While it is a thick book, full of information and recommendations, it is organized in such a way to enable that information to be easily accessed, so that you may either skim or delve deeply into a given topic.

Baker-Laporte, Paula, et al. *Prescriptions for a Healthy House.* **New Society Publishers, 2001.**

The best of the 'Healthy Housing' books, Baker-Laporte and her fellow authors have created a graphically stunning and exceptionally well-organized overview of this often-confusing field. Filled with useful tips, products, and explanations of natural and 'green' building systems.

Barnett, Dianna Lopez, William D. Browning, et al. *A Primer on Sustainable Building.* **Rocky Mountain Institute, 1995.**

This book is a simple but thorough treatise on the design and building process that leads to a sustainable building. Filled with useful charts, graphs, sketches and resources, this book is of particular interest to people seeking a mainstream process of creating an ecological home.

Bourgeois, Jean-Louis, and Carollee Pelos. *Spectacular Vernacular: The Adobe Tradition.* **Aperture Foundation, 1989.**

Through outstanding color photographs and poetic text, this book celebrates both the sensual beauty and the elegant functionality of adobe architecture in desert regions, especially Western Africa and Afghanistan. It makes a passionate plea for the respect due to vernacular building traditions which have evolved over thousands of years to meet human needs for comfort, protection, and artistic expression, then brings it back home to reflect on the eroding adobe tradition in the Southwestern United States. The photos provide endless inspiration for hand-sculpted earthen walls and plasters.

Chappell, Steve. *A Timber Framer's Workshop: Joinery, Design, and Construction of Traditional Timber Frames.* **Fox Maple Press, 1998.**

There are a lot of books on timber framing out there, perhaps more than on any other technique described in this book. This one stands out as an excellent practical guide for timber framers. Builder and workshop leader Steve Chappell does a particularly fine job of describing where and how to use a very broad range of different joints, and contrasting the properties of many different timber species. There's also a refreshingly accessible treatment of the thorny subjects of math and engineering for builders.

Easton, David. *The Rammed Earth House.* **Chelsea Green, 1996.**

The book to get on rammed earth construction, describing both ancient and modern techniques, including Easton's innovation, P.I.S.E. (Pneumatically Impacted Stabilized Earth). Easton has been tireless in his efforts to bring natural building to the mainstream, and he shares his hard-won knowledge here. Excellent chapters on design issues that would be applicable to any building system. Profusely illustrated with drawings and Cynthia Wright's excellent photography.

Elizabeth, Lynne, and Cassandra Adams, eds. *Alternative Construction: Contemporary Natural Building Methods.* **John Wiley and Sons, 2000.**

This large, scholarly work contains more technical information on a wide variety of natural building systems than any other book. There are long, informative chapters on eight different techniques written by leading practitioners, as well as a good discussion of building code issues, structural considerations, and natural conditioning; and several excellent case studies. *Alternative Construction* is bound to impress skeptics with its authority and thoroughness and should be considered an essential part of the libraries of all serious students of natural building, especially professional designers and contractors.

Fathy, Hassan. *Natural Energy and Vernacular Architecture.* **University of Chicago Press, Chicago, 1986.**

Although Fathy's book *Architecture for the Poor* is justly famous, this lesser-known book is more useful. A technical description of timeless techniques developed in the Middle East to provide a comfortable climate using humble materials in a beautiful way in some of the harshest conditions on earth. Highly recommended, especially for those in hot, dry climates.

Kahn, Lloyd. *Shelter.* **Shelter Publications, 1973.**

A cult classic from the heyday of teach-ins and VWs, this large-format book may have inspired more owner-builders to build crazy structures than any other. Organized like a big scrapbook, it seamlessly blends vernacular building traditions from all over the world with far-out American hippie shelters, including geodesic domes, gypsy wagons, tree houses, windmills, and bizarre ferrocement living sculptures. The great photos and drawings, interviews with builders, historical research, and wacky anecdotes are still just as entertaining 30 years later.

Khalili, Nader. *Ceramic Houses and Earth Architecture.* **Cal-Earth Press, 1996.**

Although this book is one of the better technical books on adobe construction, it is even more recommended for the incredible story of rediscovery of traditional architecture that threads its way through the narrative. Khalili's poetic style, influenced by the Persian poet Rumi, makes this much more than your usual how-to book. This is most evident in Khalili's discussion of the 'geltaftan' method of firing earthen homes into ceramic. Filled with photos and clear drawings, this book also has a great chapter on creating your own clay house models, and even an inspiring discussion of building in outer space!

King, Bruce. *Buildings of Earth and Straw.* **Chelsea Green Publishers, 1996.**

An engineer's take on modern applications of the oldest building materials. Gives hard structural data unavailable anywhere else on straw bale and rammed earth construction. Very useful for designers, builders, and when meeting with your building inspector.

Komatsu, Yoshio. *Living on Earth.* **Fukuinkan-Shoten Publishers, 1999.**

Unparalleled in its full-color celebration of the kaleidoscopic range of human creativity, this may be the definitive photographic record of the world's vernacular building traditions. It is the fruit of years of travel and visits to traditional people in nearly 60 countries, documenting the way they live and build. Although the minimal text is entirely in Japanese, it really doesn't matter since the photos speak for themselves and maps help identify the location of each.

Magwood, Chris, and Peter Mack. *Straw Bale Building: How to Plan, Design, and Build with Straw.* **New Society Publishers, 2000.**

This clear step-by-step guide is especially useful during the planning process, whether you intend to build your own straw bale home or hire a contractor. Good information on permitting, budgeting, designing, drawing up plans, and shopping for materials.

Mollison, Bill, and Reny Mia Slay. *Introduction to Permaculture.* **Tagari Publications, 1991.**

If your interest in sustainability goes beyond the house, then this book is for you. It provides both a theoretical framework and practical strategies for understanding natural patterns of energy and material cycles and applying them to site design, integrating structures, gardens, orchards, and livestock in the most synergistic ways. There are even guidelines for sustainable urban, community, and financial development. Serious students of permaculture should consider buying Bill's big book, *Permaculture: A Practical Guide for a Sustainable Future* (Island Press, 1990), which covers roughly the same material in far greater detail, with specific strategies for various climate zones.

Mumma, Tracy, ed. *Guide to Resource Efficient Building Elements.* **6th ed. Center for Resourceful Building Technology, 1997.**

This book is one of the simplest, yet most useful of the numerous guides to green building materials. Regularly updated.

Myhrman, Matts, and S.O. MacDonald. *Build It With Bales: A Step-by-Step Guide to Straw-Bale Construction* (**Version Two**). **Out on Bale, 1997.**

While there are an increasing number of books on straw bale construction, none does a better job of explaining the basic steps and various building options than this classic how-to guide. Its simple language, clear diagrams, and down-home wisdom make BIWB2 indispensable for any straw bale builder.

Pearson, David. *Earth to Spirit: In Search of Natural Architecture.* **Chronicle Books, 1994.**

David Pearson's follow-up to *The Natural House* (also highly recommended) is a beautiful and poetic journey through some of the most marvelous examples of natural building anywhere. Illustrated with Pearson's exquisite photography, this is the book to give someone to explain the power and appeal of natural building.

Potts, Michael. *The New Independent Home.* **Chelsea Green, 1999.**

The only book you need for a good sense of what it takes to create a home that can provide its own energy, water, and waste treatment. Particularly entertaining are interviews with numerous pioneers who have lived happily 'off the grid.'

Roy, Rob. *Complete Book of Cordwood Masonry Housebuilding: The Earthwood Method.* **Sterling, 1992.**

This is the best book in print on cordwood building, describing several different building techniques and multiple design considerations. A lot of the book is dedicated to case studies, especially the author's own work at the Earthwood Building school in New York. Rob Roy is not only one of the most knowledgeable cordwood builders in North America, he's also one of the best writers in the field of natural building. All of his many books are highly entertaining, filled with gentle humor and hard-won wisdom.

Rudofsky, Bernard. *Architecture Without Architects.* **University of New Mexico Press, 1987.**

One of the books that inspired the natural building renaissance. Rudofsky has done us all the immeasurable service of finding obscure photos and placing them in a context that helps us marvel at the ingenuity of our forbears. With brief but useful text, this is a wonderful book to flip through.

Smith, Michael G. *The Cobber's Companion: How to Build Your Own Earthen Home.* **3rd ed. Cob Cottage Company, 2001.**

Michael is too modest to say how wonderful his own book is so I (Joe) will do it for him. If you pick up this book, I guarantee you will feel capable and inspired to build your own natural house. Extremely clear, assisted by the excellent drawings by Deanne Bednar, *The Cobber's Companion* is the book to have on cob construction. However, it is about to be superseded by a much longer and more thorough work. Look for *The Hand-Sculpted House: A Philosophical & Practical Guide to Building a Cob Cottage,* by Ianto Evans, Linda Smiley, & Michael G. Smith. Chelsea Green, 2002.

Steen, Athena Swentzell, Bill Steen, David Bainbridge, and David Eisenberg. *The Straw Bale House.* **Chelsea Green, 1994.**

The 100,000-copy bestseller, with good reason. This book is one of the reasons why so many people now know about natural building. Great info on straw bale of course, but also provides useful information on other natural building topics such as finishes and floors.

Stulz, Roland, and Kiran Mukerji. *Appropriate Building Materials: A Catalogue of Potential Solutions.* **SKAT Publications, 1993.**

This book gives technical information on the widest range of natural building materials systems imaginable. While it is slightly dated, nothing else out there comes close to giving as thorough an overview of natural and 'appropriate' building materials. Organized by system (foundations, walls, roofs, etc.), this book is filled with sketches and resources.

Taylor, John. *A Shelter Sketchbook.* **Chelsea Green, 1997.**

This slim volume is filled with the author's sketches of shelter ideas from many regions and historical eras. The simple yet evocative drawings are organized into logical sections for easy reference and contain a wealth of detail. This book is a wonderful source for musing and dreaming about your natural house.

Todd, John, and Nancy Jack Todd. *From Ecocities to Living Machines.* **North Atlantic Books, 1994.**

A wonderfully inspiring book on ecological design, from pioneers in the field. Discusses how to apply nature's design principles to everything from urban agriculture to building remodels.

van Lengen, Johan. *Manual of the Barefoot Architect* *(Manual del Arquitecto Descalzo).* **Editorial Concepto, 1980.**

Although this hard-to-find book is in Spanish, it is an incredibly useful exploration of natural, appropriate building techniques, especially for the 'two-thirds' world that most needs housing. As it is filled with clear drawings, knowledge of Spanish is almost unnecessary to derive benefit from the range of techniques and ideas presented here. Seek it out.

Periodicals

If there were mail delivery to your deserted island, we would encourage you to scrape together enough sea shells and dried fruit to trade for subscriptions to the following magazines and journals. In a rapidly evolving field like natural building, periodicals are the best way to keep up with the latest technical developments and current learning opportunities, as well as to network with natural builders on other islands. Like books, magazine subscriptions can easily be shared by a group of people or even the whole community, through a public library.

Environmental Building News

(122 Birge Street, Brattleboro, VT, 05301, U.S.A.; phone: 802-257-7300; fax: 802-257-7304; website: www.BuildingGreen.com). Each month, this newsletter is filled with insightful articles about the green building industry and independent assessments of ecological building products. The outstanding research and updates are particularly useful to professional designers and builders wishing to use healthier, less environmentally damaging methods and materials. You can download a sample issue from their website.

The Last Straw: The International Journal of Straw Bale and Natural Building

(HC 66, Box 119, Hillsboro, NM 88042, U.S.A.; phone: 505-895-5400; website: www.strawhomes.com). This quarterly journal serves multiple functions in the natural building movement. First, it is the primary networking and communication tool for straw bale builders around the world, including constant updates on new technical developments and innovative straw bale projects. In addition, frequent special issues collect difficult-to-find information of interest to all natural builders, such as the recent issues focused on lime plaster and small houses. Excellent resources, reviews, and workshop calendars. Email: thelaststraw@strawhomes.com.

The Permaculture Activist

(P.O. Box 1209, Black Mountain, NC 28711, U.S.A.; phone: 828-669-6336; email: peter@PermacultureActivist.net; website: www.permacultureactivist.net). The natural building and permaculture movements overlap to a large degree. In fact, natural building can be considered a subset of permaculture, which concerns itself with all aspects of creating a sustainable culture. This quarterly journal is filled with news from around the world on how people are doing just that. Each issue focuses on a specific topic, such as natural building, earthworks and energy, medicine and health, useful plants. Excellent reviews and workshop calendar.

Joiner's Quarterly: The Journal of Timber Framing and Traditional Building

(P.O. Box 249, Snowville Road, Brownfield, ME 04010, U.S.A.; phone: 207-935-3720; email: foxmaple@foxmaple.com; website: www.foxmaple.com). This glossy, professional quarterly does for timber framers what *The Last Straw* does for straw balers. Articles range from highly technical descriptions of timber framing tools, techniques, and design considerations to overviews of contemporary and historical earth building methods.

Selected Learning Centers

Artisan Earth

P.O. Box 5888, Santa Fe, NM 87502, U.S.A.; phone: 505-421 3788; email: keelymeagan@hotmail.com.Workshops and consulting in earth plaster and cob.

Bear Mountain Outdoor School

US 250, Hightown, VA 24444, U.S.A.; phone: 540-468-2700; fax:540-468 2703; email: bearmtn@bfw.com; website: www.reston.com/bmos/bmos.html. Provides educational hands-on seminars, workshops, and retreats with emphasis on utilizing natural materials in an ecological/sustainable manner and promotes energy efficiency and alternative energy systems.

Builders without Borders

119 Main Street, Kingston, NM 88042, U.S.A.; phone: 505-895-5400; email: mail@builderswithoutborders.org; website: www.builderswithoutborders.org. Courses and hands-on projects to serve the underhoused. Focuses on ecological building in cross-cultural contexts.

California Earth Art and Architecture Institute (Cal-Earth)

10376 Shangri La Avenue, Hesperia, CA 92345, U.S.A.; phone: 760-244-0614; fax: 760-244-2201; website: www.calearth.org. Research and teaching center focusing on earthbag construction, adobe, and brick domes and vaults.

The Canelo Project

HC1 Box 324, Elgin, AZ 85611, U.S.A.; phone: 520-455-5548; fax: 520-455-9360; email: absteen@dakotacom.net; website: www.caneloproject.com. Athena and Bill Steen's non-profit educational organization offers workshops on straw bale construction, earthen floors, earth and lime plasters, work-study tours to Mexico, and more.

Cob Cottage Company

P.O. Box 123, Cottage Grove, OR 97424, U.S.A.; phone/fax: 541-942-2005; website: www.deatech.com/cobcottage/. Workshops, consulting, mail order books and videos, networking and information on cob and other natural building systems. Also workshops in Mexico on traditional building, permaculture, and international development.

CRATerre

Maison Levrat, Rue de Lac B.P. 53, F-38092 Villefontaine Cedex, France; phone: 33-474-954391; fax: 33-474-956421; email: craterre@club-internet.fr; website: www.craterre.archi.fr. Professional school of earth architecture, engineering, and construction, especially for developing nations; excellent technical publications.

Development Center for Appropriate Technology

P.O. Box 27513, Tucson, AZ 85726, U.S.A.; phone: 520-624-6628; email: david@dcat.net; website: www.dcat.net. Consulting, seminars, workshops, and slide shows on straw bale and other natural building systems. Works to create building codes for natural building.

Earthaven Ecovillage

P.O. Box 1107, Black Mountain, NC 28711, U.S.A.; phone: 828-669-3937; email: info@earthaven.org; website:www.earthaven.org. Workshops on permaculture, natural building, consensus decision making, and other topics related to ecovillage development.

Earth Sweet Home Institute

98 Falk Road, East Dummerston, VT 05346, U.S.A.; phone: 802-254-7674; email: earthswt@sover.net; website: www.enviroweb.org/earthsweet/INSTITUTE. Information and workshops on healthy building technologies.

Earthwood Building School

366 Murtagh Hill Road, West Chazy, NY 12992, U.S.A.; phone: 518-493-7744; website: www.cordwodmasonry.com. Offers workshops, mail-order books and videos, and consulting on cordwood masonry, earth-sheltered construction, mortgage freedom, and stone circles.

The Ecological Building Network

Bruce King, P.E. (Director), 209 Caledonia Street, Sausalito, CA 94965, U.S.A.; phone: 415-331-7630; fax: 415-332-4072; email: ecobruce@sbcglobal.net; website: www.ecobuildnet.org. A growing and international association of builders, engineers, architects, academics, and developers committed to promoting intelligent building methods and materials for a sustainable future. Sponsors the International Conference on Building Structure.

The Econest Building Company

P.O. Box 864, Tesuque, NM 87574, U.S.A.; phone: 505-984-2928 or 505-989-1813; fax: 505-989-1814; email: info@econests.com. Workshops on straw light-clay and timber framing as well as professional design/build services.

Ecovillage Training Center

The Farm, P.O. Box 90. Summertown, TN 38483, U.S.A.; phone: 931-964-4324; fax: 931-964-2200; email: ecovillage@the-farm.org; website: www.thefarm.org/etc. Workshops on ecovillage design, natural building, solar energy and related topics for sustainable culture.

Fox Maple School of Traditional Building

P.O. Box 249, Corn Hill Road, Brownfield, ME 04010, U.S.A.; phone: 207-935-3720; email: foxmaple@foxmaple.com website: www.foxmaple.com. Workshops on timber framing and traditional enclosure techniques, including light-clay and thatching.

Gourmet Adobe

HC 78 Box 9811, Ranchos de Taos, NM 87557, U.S.A.; phone: 505-758-7251; email: seacrews@taosnet.com. Professional earthen finishes and workshops.

Groundworks

P.O. Box 381, Murphy, OR 97533, U.S.A.; phone: 541-471-3470; website: www.cpros.com/-sequoia/workshop.html. Information, books, and workshops on cob, especially for women.

Heartwood School

Johnson Hill Road, Washington, MA 01233, U.S.A.; phone: 413-623-6677; fax: 413-623-0227; email: info@heartwoodschool.com; website: www.heartwoodschool.com. Timber framing and conventional construction.

International Institute for Bau-Biologie and Ecology

P.O. Box 387, Clearwater, FL 33757, U.S.A.; phone: 727-461-4371; email: baubiologie@earthlink.net; website: www.bau-biologieusa.com. Correspondence course, seminars, literature, and consulting on building biology and healthy housing.

OK OK OK Productions

256 East 100 South, Moab, UT 84532, U.S.A.; phone/fax: 435-259-8378; email: okokok@lasal.net; website: www.ok-ok-ok.com. Workshops on earthbags, earth and lime plasters.

Out on Bale (un)Ltd.

2509 N. Campbell Avenue #292, Tucson, AZ 85719, U.S.A.; phone: 520-622-6896. Public presentations on straw bale and global citizenship, design consulting, customized workshops, and wall-raisings.

Rammed Earth Works

101 S. Coombs, Suite N, Napa, CA 94559, U.S.A.; phone: 707-224-2532; email: rew@interx.com. Consultation, referrals, and workshops on rammed earth.

Real Goods Institute for Solar Living

P.O. Box 836, Hopland, CA 95449, U.S.A.; phone: 800-762-7325 or 707-744-2017; email: isl@rgisl.org. Frequent workshops on alternative energy, straw bale building and other natural building techniques, permaculture, and more.

Solar Energy International

P.O. Box 715, Carbondale, CO 81623, U.S.A.; phone: 970-963-8855; fax: 970-963-8866; email: sei@solarenergy.org; website: www.solarenergy.org. Workshops on solar and alternative energy as well as natural building.

Southwest Solaradobe School

P.O. Box 153, Bosque, NM 87006, U.S.A.; phone: 505-861-1255; fax: 505-861-1304; website: www.adobebuilder.com. Adobe and rammed earth construction.

Sustainable Systems Support

P.O. Box 318, Bisbee, AZ 85603, U.S.A.; phone: 520-432-4292; email: sssalive@earthlink.net; website: www.bisbeenet.com/buildnatural/. Straw bale workshops, training, consulting, engineered building plans, building services, tours, and mail-order resources.

Women Builders

P.O. Box 4114, Tucson, AZ 85717, U.S.A.; phone: 520-206-8000; email: womenbuilders@theriver.com. Workshops on straw bale, natural, and conventional building for women.

Yestermorrow Design/Build School

RR Box 97-5, Warren, VT 05674, U.S.A.; phone: 802-496-5545; fax: 802-496-5540; email: ymschool@aol.com. Yestermorrow teaches a series of both layperson and professional design/build courses, in both conventional and natural techniques.

PERMISSIONS

1. "The Earth She Laughed" by Robert Francis Johnson appeared originally in *The CobWeb*, Issue #4, Spring 1997.

2. "The Case for Natural Building" by Michael G. Smith appeared originally in a longer version in *Sustainable Living News*, #15, March 1997.

3. "The Importance of Housing Ourselves" by Ianto Evans was adapted from *The Cob Cottage: A Philosophical and Practical Guide to Building an Ecstatic House*. © 2002 Chelsea Green.

4. "Building As If the Future Matters" by Ted Butchart was adapted from an article that appeared originally in two parts in *Talking Leaves*, Fall 1998 and Winter 1999.

5. "Vernacular Architecture of the Desert" by Jean-Louis Bourgeois was adapted from *Spectacular Vernacular*. © 1989 Aperture.

6. "A Case For Caring Craftsmanship" by Duncan McMaster was adapted from an article that originally appeared in *Joiners Quarterly* #30, Spring 1996.

7. "Eighteen Design Principles to Make Square Feet Work Harder" by Robert Gay appeared originally in *The Last Straw* #30, Summer 2000.

8. "Combining Natural Materials for Energy Efficiency" by Catherine Wanek appeared in a different version in *Permaculture Drylands Journal* #32, Summer 1999.

9. "R-Value Comparison Chart" appeared originally in *House of Straw*, U.S. Department of Energy, Energy Efficiency and Renewable Energy, April 1995.

10. "Siting a Natural Building" by Michael G. Smith was adapted from chapter two of *The Cobber's Companion*. © 2001 Cob Cottage Company.

11. "Regenerative Building" by Michael G. Smith appeared in a longer version in *The CobWeb* #7, Fall 1998.

12. "Rubble Trench Foundations" by Rob Tom appeared originally in *The Last Straw* #16, Fall 1996.

13. "Earthen Floors" by Athena and Bill Steen was adapted from their booklet *Earthen Floors*. © 1997 The Canelo Project.

14. "A Tamped Road Base Floor" by Frank Meyer appeared originally in *The Last Straw* #17, Winter 1997.

15. "Bamboo Construction" by Darrel DeBoer appeared originally in *Building Standards Magazine*, 1999.

16. "Earthships: An Ecocentric Model" by Jack Ehrhardt appeared originally in *Building Standards Magazine*, 1999.

17. "Digging In for Comfort" by Kelly Hart appeared originally in *The Crestone Eagle*, September 2000.

18. "Light-Clay: An Introduction to German Clay Building Techniques" by Frank Andresen was adapted from three articles that appeared originally in *Joiner's Quarterly* magazine between 1992 and 1997: 'Loam Instead of Foam,' 'Oh Muddy Clay. O Clayish Loam,' and 'Building with Wood Chip and Light-Clay Infill Systems: An Introduction.'

19. "Paper Houses: Papercrete and Fidobe" by Gordon Solberg appeared originally in *Back Home* #47, Nov/Dec 2000.

20. "Rammed Earth: From Pisé to P.I.S.E." by Scott Grometer appeared originally in *Arcade Magazine*, January/February 1993.

21. "Green Roofs with Sod, Turf, or Straw" by Paul Lacinski and Michel Bergeron appeared originally in *Serious Straw Bale: A Home Construction Guide for All Climates*. © 2000 Chelsea Green.

22. "Thatching Comes to America" by Deanne Bednar appeared originally in *Permaculture Activist* #41, May 1999.

23. "Working with Lime" by Barbara Jones appeared originally in *The Last Straw* #26, Summer 1999.

24. "Building with the Sun: The Real Goods Solar Living Center" by David Arkin was adapted from an article that appeared originally in *The Last Straw* #19, Summer 1997.

25. "From the Nile to the Rio Grande" by Dick Doughty appeared originally in a slightly different version in *Saudi Aramco World*, July/August 1999.

26. "Elegant Solutions: The Work of Hassan Fathy" by Simone Swan appeared originally in a slightly different version in *Saudi Aramco World*, July/August 1999.

27. "Clay, Straw, and Permaculture: Natural Building at P.I.N.C." by Toby Hemenway appeared originally as "A Laboratory for Natural Building" in *Permaculture Activist* #41, May 1999.

CONTRIBUTORS

Frank Andresen
Proclay
Kiefernstrasse 25
Dusseldorf 40233 Germany
email:
franka@proclay-international.com

David Arkin
Arkin Tilt Architects
phone: 510-528-9830
email: info@arkintilt.com
website: www.arkintilt.com

David Bainbridge
Environmental Studies Coordinator
GLS Department,
Alliant International University,
10455 Pomerado Road,
San Diego, CA 92131, U.S.A.
phone: 858-635-4616
fax: 858-635-4730

Paula Baker-Laporte
P.O. Box 864,
Tesuque, NM 87574, U.S.A.
phone: 505-989-1813
email: bakerlaporte@earthlink.net

Peter Bane
Permaculture Activist
P.O. Box 1209,
Black Mountain, NC 28711, U.S.A.
phone: 828-669-6336
email:
Peter@PermacultureActivist.net
website:
www.PermacultureActivist.net

Albert Bates
The Farm Ecovillage Training
Center
P.O. Box 90, Summertown, TN
38483-0090, U.S.A.
phone: 931-964-4474
email: ecovillage@thefarm.org

Alfred von Bachmayr
1406 Bishops Lodge Road,
Santa Fe, NM 87501, U.S.A.
phone: 505-989-7000
email:
bachmayr@compuserve.com

Deanne Bednar
2641 Warner,
Orchard Lake, MI 48324, U.S.A.
phone: 248-363-1756
email: ecoartdb@aol.com

Michel Bergeron
6282 de St. Vallier,
Montreal, Quebec H2S 2P5, Canada
phone: 514-271-8684
email: bergeron@dsuper.net

Darrel DeBoer
1835 Pacific Avenue
Alameda, CA 94501, U.S.A.
phone: 510-865-3669
email: DdarrelD@aol.com

Robert Bolman
888 Almaden Street,
Eugene, OR 97402, U.S.A.
phone: 541-344-7196
email: robtb@efn.org
website: www.efn.org/~robtb

Jean-Louis Bourgeois
P.O. Box 526,
El Prado, NM 87529, U.S.A.
phone: 505-751-1282
email: jeanlouisbour@yahoo.com

Andre de Bouter
La Maison en Paille
Le Trezidoux, Champmillon,
Charente, France 16290
phone: +33 0 5 45 66 27 68
email: sim.plicity@laposte.net
website: la-maison-en-paille.com

Ted Butchart
842 NE 67th,
Seattle, WA 98115, U.S.A.
phone: 206-985-2334
email: greenfire@igc.org

Steve Chappell
Fox Maple School
of Traditional Building
P.O. Box 249, Corn Hill Road,
Brownfield, ME 04010, U.S.A.
phone: 207-935-3720
email: foxmaple@foxmaple.com
website:
www.foxmaple.com

Carole Crews
Gourmet Adobe
HC78 Box 9811,
Ranchos de Taos, NM 87557,
U.S.A.
phone: 505-758-7251
email: seacrews@taosnet.com

Dick Doughty
Saudi Aramco World Magazine
P.O. Box 2106,
Houston, TX 77252-2106, U.S.A.
phone: 713-432-4000
email:
dick.doughty@aramcoservices.com

Jack Ehrhardt
2170 Northern Ave., Ste. B,
Kingman, AZ 86401, U.S.A.
phone: 928-757-4202
email: cerbatnp@citlink.net
website: ecolifetours.com

David Eisenberg
Development Center
for Appropriate Technology
P.O. Box 27513,
Tucson, AZ 85726-7513, U.S.A.
phone: 520-624-6628
email: david@dcat.net
website: dcat.net

Ianto Evans
Cob Cottage Company
P.O. Box 123,
Cottage Grove, OR 97424, U.S.A.
phone: 541-942-2005
website:
www.deatech.com/cobcottage

Robert Castle Gay
Radius Associates
8220 North Rancho Catalina
Avenue,
Tucson, AZ 85704, U.S.A.
phone: 520-575-8239
email: valleymind@earthlink.net
website: www.radiusassociates.com

Scott Grometer
62 Sierra Ave.
Mountain View, CA 94041
phone: 650-961-7366
email: scott@skillful-means.com

Susie Harrington
P.O. Box 264,
Moab, UT 84532, U.S.A.
phone: 435-259-7073
email: wgaia@lasal.net

Kelly Hart
Hartworks
Box 632, Crestone, CO
81131, U.S.A.
phone: 719-256-4278
email: kelly@hartworks.com

Toby Hemenway
1500 Wildflower Lane,
Oakland, OR 97462, U.S.A.
phone: 541-459-0966
email: hemenway@jeffnet.org

Dan Imhoff
Watershed Media
556 Matheson Street,
Healdsburg, CA95448, U.S.A.
phone: 707-895-3490
email: danimhoff@pacific.net
website: watershedmedia.org

Barbara Jones
Amazon Nails
Hollinroyd Farm
Todmorden, 0L148RJ
England
phone/fax: 44 1706 814696
email:
barbara@strawbalefutures.org.uk
website:
www.strawbalefutures.org.uk

Joseph F. Kennedy
6364 Starr Road,
Windsor, CA 95492
phone: 707-837-8138
email: livingearth62@hotmail.com

Paul Lacinski
Greenspace Collaborative
P.O. Box 107
Ashfield, MA 01330
phone: 413-628-3800

Duncan MacMaster
P.O. Box 1174,
Fairfield, IA 52556, U.S.A.
phone: 641-472-6812
fax: 641-472-6882

Chuck Marsh
1025 Camp Elliott Road,
Black Mountain, NC 28711, U.S.A.
phone: 828-669-1759
email: chuck@earthaven.org

Paul McHenry
5928 Guadalupe Trail Northwest
Albuquerque, NM 87107, U.S.A.
phone: 505-345-2613
email: mchenry@unm.edu
website: www.unm.edu/~mchenry

Frank Meyer
904 E. Monroe,
Austin, TX 78704, U.S.A.
phone: 512-282-2341
email: thangmaker@aol.com

Wayne Nelson
Construction and
Environment Resources
Habitat for Humanity International,
121 Habitat Street,
Americus, GA 31709, U.S.A.
phone: 229-924-6935
email: wnelson@hfhi.org
website: www.habitat.org

Rob Roy
Earthwood Building School
366 Murtagh Hill Road,
West Chazy, NY 12992, U.S.A.
phone: 518-493-7744
website: robandjaki@aol.com

David Shaw and Juliet Cuming
Earth Sweet Home
98 Falk Road,
East Dummerston, VT 05346,
U.S.A.
phone: 802-254-7674
email: earthswt@sover.net
website:
www.envirolink.org/orgs/earth-
sweet

Linda Smiley
Cob Cottage Company
P.O. Box 123,
Cottage Grove, OR 97424, U.S.A.
phone: 541-942-2005
website:
www.deatech.com/cobcottage

Michael G. Smith
P.O. Box 764,
Boonville, CA 95415, U.S.A.
email: lorax@ap.net

Gordon Solberg
Papercrete News
Box 23-B,
Radium Springs, NM 88054, U.S.A.
website: www.zianet.com/paper-
crete

Bill and Athena Steen
The Canelo Project
HC1 Box 324,
Elgin, AZ 85611, U.S.A.
phone: 520-455-5548
fax: 520-455-9360
email: absteen@dakotacom.net
website: www.caneloproject.com

Simone Swan
Swan Group
P.O. Box 1915,
Presidio, TX 79845, U.S.A.
phone/fax: 915-229-4425
email: adobesim@brooksdata.net.

Rob Tom
C/o Erehwon Design Group
43 Grierson Lane
RR 1, Kanata, Ontario K2W 1A6,
Canada
email:
RobTom@ErehwonDesignGroup.in
tranets.com

Carol Venolia
P.O. Box 4417,
Santa Rosa, CA 95402, U.S.A.
phone: 707-579-2201
email: cvenolia@compuserve.com

Catherine Wanek
Black Range Films/
Natural Building Resources
Star Rt. 2, Box 119,
Kingston, NM 88042, U.S.A.
phone: 505-895-5652
email: blackrange@zianet.com
website:
www.StrawBaleCentral.com

Tom Woolley
Centre for Green Building Research
School of Architecture,
Queens University,
Belfast 2 Lennoxvale,
Belfast BT9 5BY,
Northern Ireland, U.K.
phone/fax: 0044 28 90 335466
email: t.woolley@qub.ac.uk

INDEX

Page numbers in *italics*
reference photographs.

A

About Building Cordwood, 148
Abrahamsson, Flemming, 214, 215, 217
Ackerman, Dianne, 42
Adams, Cassandra, 10, 32, 65, 153, 168, 224, 277
adobe, 120–124
   case study of, 249–253
Adobe Alliance, 252
Adobe and Rammed Earth Buildings, 124, 224
Adobe: Build it Yourself, 124
Adobe Builder, The, 124
Adventist Development Relief Agency (ADRA), 194–195
African Canvas, 224
air quality, 8, 39–40
Alexander, Christopher, 58, 164, 277
aliz, 219–224
All About Lime, 232
Alternative Building Colloquium, 3
Alternative Building Sourcebook, The, 10, 242
Alternative Construction, 10, 32, 65, 153, 168, 224, 277
Alternative Housebuilding, 160
American Bamboo Society Newsletter, 131
American Institute of Architects, 51
Anasazi architecture, 26, *159*
Anatomy of the Spirit, 43
Anderson, Bruce, 65
Andresen, Frank, 285
   on light clay building, 165–168
Appropriate Building Materials, 101, 279
Archibio, 212, 213
Architectural Resource Guide, 130
Architecture for People, A, 253
Architecture for the Poor, 253
Architecture Without Architects, 25, 279
Arkin, David, 285
   on the Real Goods Solar Living Center, 244–248

Artisan Earth, 281
Artist's Handbook of Materials and Techniques, The, 238
Association for Environment Conscious Building, 274
Association pour la Construction en Fibres Végétales, 272, 274
Aujames, Francis, 164
Aurobindo, Sri, 268
Auroville Building Centre, *140*, 142, 268
Austrian Straw Bale Network, 272, 274

B

Bachelard, Gaston, 21
Bachmayr, Alfred von, 285
   on mechanizing straw-clay production, 169–170
Backyard Stonebuilder, The, 188
Baggs, Sydney and Joan, 52
Bailing Out, 274
Bainbridge, David A., 117, 196, 211, 279, 285
   on home life cycle costs, 31–32
Baker-Laporte, Paula, 277, 285
   on healthy houses, 49–52
bamboo, 97, 125–131
Bamboo: A Grower & Builder's Reference Manual, 131
Bamboo as a Building Material, 131
Bamboo Technologies, 130
Bamboo World, 131
Bane, Peter, 75–82, 285
Banta, John, 52
Barnett, Diana Lopez, 277
Basic Cordwood Masonry Techniques (video), 148
Bates, Albert, 87, 285, xi
Bau-biologie, 50–51
Bear Mountain Outdoor School, 281
Beauty of Straw Bale Homes, The, 195
Bednar, Deanne, 285
   on thatcthing, 214–218
Bee, Becky, 137
Bell, Michael, 131
Benson, Tedd, 203
Bergeron, Michel, 195, 285
   on green roofs, 212–213

Berthold-Bond, Annie, 238
binders, 234
bioregional building, 86
Bioshelters, Ocean Arks, City Farming, 82
Blue Evening Star, teepee hand-made by, *36*
Bolman, Robert, 285
   house built by, *107*
   on natural building and social justice, 14–15
Book of Bamboo, The, 131
Bourgeois, Jean-Louis, 277, 285
   on desert architecture, 21–25
Bouter, Andre de, *268*, 272, 275, 285
Bouter, Coralie de, 272, 275
Bower, John, 52
brick, 96
Browning, William D., 277
Build a Classic Timber-Framed House, 203
Build Here Now workshop, 65
Build it with Bales, 195, 279
Builders Without Borders, 281
Building for Health Materials Center, 52, 238
Building Less Waste, 130
Building Limes Forum, 164, 232
"Building Revolution, A", 30
building sizes, 14–15, 17–18, 56, 76–77
Building Standards, 30
Building the Timber Frame House, 203
Building with Bamboo, 131
Building with Earth, 124, 137, 142, 205
Building with Earth: A Guide to Flexible Form Earthbag Construction, 153
Building with Earth: Oregon's Cob Cottage Company (video), 137
Building with Lime, 232
Building with Nature, 41
Building with Papercrete and Paper Adobe (video), 176
Building with Stone, 188
Building with Straw (videos), 196
Building with Vision, 242

Buildings of Earth and Straw, 278
Butchart, Ted, 285
   on building for the future, 16–20

C

Cahill, William, 218
Cal-Earth, 2–3, 149, 150, 152, 153, 281
California Straw Builders Association (CASBA), 196
Camacho, Daniel, 249–250, 253
Campbell, Stu, 160
Canelo Project, The, 117, 196, 224, 232, 281, 286
Cannon, Carol, house built by, 133
Carpenter, Ralph, 163, 164
   hemp house of, *162*
Carter, Mike, house built by, 133
Casas Que Cantan (Houses that Sing), 194
CEB (compressed earth blocks), 138–142
cellulose, 103
Center for Environmentally Responsible Building Alternatives (CERBAT), 157
Center for Maximum Building Potential, *28*
Centre for Alternative Technology (CAT), 271, 275
Ceramic Houses and Earth Architecture, 124, 253, 278
Chanvriere de L'Aube, La, 164
Chappell, Steve, 10, 211, 242, 277, 285
   on timber framing, 196–203
Chenevotte-Habitat, 164
Chiras, Daniel, 10, 74, 148, 157
Clark, Sam, 211
Classic Paints and Faux Finishes, 238
clay, 96, 165–168, 169–170
   slip, 219–224
Cline, Ann, 61
cloth, 99
cob, 132–137
   case study of, 258–262
Cob Builder's Handbook, The, 137
Cob Cottage Company, 2, 3, 9, 13, 134, 135–136, 137, 218, 224, 281
Cob Cottage, The, 13, 48, 74, 137
Cob Reader, A, 137

Cobber's Companion, The, 137, 211, 279

CobWeb, The, 137

Communities Directory: A Guide to Intentional Communities and Cooperative Living, 91

Complete Book of Cordwood Masonry Housebuilding, The, 148, 211, 279

Complete Book of Underground Housing, 160

compressed earth blocks (CEB), 138–142

concrete & cement, 24, 100
    in foundations, 107–108

Connell, John, 58

Corbett, Judy and Michael, 91

Cordwood Construction, 148

Cordwood Homes (video), 148

cordwood masonry, 143–148

cork, 103

Courtney-Clark, Margaret, 224

Cowan, Stuart, 244

Cradle to Cradle, 20

craftsmanship, caring, 33–34

CRATerre, 142, 178, 252, 271, 275, 281

CREST Straw Bale listserve, 196

Crews, Carole, *115*, 285
    on earth plasters and aliz, 219–224

Crystal Waters (video), 92

Cuming, Juliet, 263–264, 286

Cusack, Victor, 131

D

Dan Smith and Associates, house designed by, *38*

Dancey, Chris, 162, 164

Dar Al Islam Mosque, *207*

Dawson, Jim, 42

Day, Christopher, 48
    house designed by, *68*

DeBoer, Darrel, 285
    on bamboo construction, 125–131

desert architecture, 21–25

design and designing
    of ecovillages, 87–91
    for energy efficiency, 62–65
    for health, 49–52
    integrating home with site,

53–58, 68–74
    intuitive, 43–48
    for optimal use of space, 59–61
    permaculture houses, 75–82
    for regenerative building, 83–86
    with the sun, 66–67, 244–248
    for vitality, 36–42

Designing Sustainable Communities, 91

Dethier, Jean, 25

Development Center for Appropriate Technology (DCAT), 29, 30, 281, 285

Development Workshop of Lauzerte, 252

Devon Earth Builder's Association, 137

Directory of Ecovillages in Europe, 91

Dolman, Brock, 260

Domaine de la Terre, Le, *90*, 178, 271

Doughty, Dick, 285
    on adobe construction case studies, 249–253

Down to Earth, 25

drainage, 106–107, 114

Drengson, Alan, 86

Dwellings: The House Across the World, 25

dyes, 234–235

E

earth, 95. *see also* adobe; clay; cob
    compressed blocks, 138–142, 268
    and earthbags, 109–110, 149–153, 254–257
    and earthships, 154–157
    floors of, 113–117
    in foundations, 109–110
    insulation of, 62, 64
    plasters, 219–224
    rammed, 177–181
    sheltered houses, 154–157, 158–160

Earth Building Foundation, 124

Earth Construction: A Comprehensive Guide, 142, 205

Earth, Hands & Houses, 153

Earth Plasters for Straw-Bale Houses, 224

Earth Quarterly and Papercrete News, 176

"Earth She Laughed, The", x

Earth-Sheltered House, The, 160

Earth Sweet Home Institute, 52, *71*, *108*, 263–264, 282, 286

Earth to Spirit, 48, 279

Earthaven Ecovillage, *88*, *103*, 265–267, 282

earthbags, 109–110, 149–153
    case study of, 254–257

Earthbuilder's Encyclopedia, The, 124

Earthen Floors, 117

Earthship, 157

Earthship Biotecture, 157

Earthship Global Operations, 157

Earthwood Building School, 2, *144*, 148, 282, 286

Easson, Lindsay, 164

Easton, David, 3, 179–180, 277
    home of, *178*

Eaton, S. Boyd, 42

Eco-logic Books, 274

EcoDesign, 274

Ecoforestry, 86

Ecological Building Network, 282

Ecological Design, 244

Econest Building Company, 52, 168, 203, 282

Ecovillage Audit Document (website), 92

Ecovillage Living, 274

Ecovillage Network of the Americas, 91

Ecovillage Training Center, 91, 282

ecovillages, 87–91
    case study of, 265–267

Ecovillages and Communities Directory: Australia and New Zealand, 91

Edminster, Ann, 242

Efficient Wood Use in Residential Construction, 242

Ehrhardt, Jack, 285
    on earthships, 154–157

Ehrhardt, Sharon, 154, 156

Eisenberg, David, 26–30, 117, 196, 211, 279, 285

Elliot, Erica, 52

empowerment, 8–9, 11–13

Empress Hotel, conservatory in, *41*

energy, embodied, 6–7, 79

Environmental Building News, 101, 280

Erewhon Design Group, 286

Escott, Carol, 150, 196

European Straw Building Network (ESBN), 273, 274

Evans, Ianto, 2, 46–47, 48, 74, 134, 137, 147, 258, 285
    on importance of natural building, 11–13

F

Falk, Robert, 242

Farelly, David, 131

Farm Ecovillage Training Center, 285

Fathy, Hassan, 249, 250–252, 253, 278
    mosque designed by, *207*

Fearn, Jacqueline, 218

fiberglass, 103–104

fibers, 98, 161–164, 240

fidobe, 98, 171–176

Fifty Dollar and Up Underground House Book, The, 160

Findhorn Community School, 271–272

Finding and Buying Your Place in the Country, 74

finishes, 233–238

Fisk, Pliny, 28

Flatau, Richard, 148

floors
    earth, 113–117
    tamped road base, 118–119

Folkecenter for Renewable Energy, 271, 275

foundations, 105–110, 111–112

Fox Maple School of Traditional Building, 168, 203, 218, 282, 285

framing, timber, 197–203

From Ecocities to Living Machines, 280

future, considerations of, 16–20

G

Gardener's Guide to Growing Temperate Bamboos, The, 131

Gay, Robert, 285
    on designing for optimal use of space, 59–61

Gentle Architecture, 58
glass, 100
Glassford, John, 193
Global Ecovillage Network (GEN), 87, 91, 92, 271, 274
Good Life, The, 13
Gourmet Adobe, 224, 282
gravel, 95
Gray, Virginia, 124
Great Mosque of Djenne, *21*
Green Building Handbook, 101
Green Building Materials, 242
Green Building Resource Guide, 242
Green Nature, Human Nature, 42
green roofs, 209–210, 212–213
GreenFire Institute, 20, 282
GreenSpace Collaborative, 213
Grometer, Scott, 285
    on rammed earth construction, 177–181
Groundworks, 137, 282
Grow Your Own House, 131
Gruber, Herbert, 274
Gudie, Clôde de, 213
Guide to Resource Efficient Building Elements, 278
Guillaud, Hubert, 142, 205
Gwynn, Kate, 238

H
Habitat II conference model home, *139*
Habitat Revolution, The (video), 92
Hans, Ole, 217
Happy & Mortgage Free, 275
Harrington, Susie, 285
    on designing with the sun, 66–67
    on integrating spirit and vision in design, 53–58
Harris, B.J., 42
Harris Directories, 242
Harrison, Lea, 75
Hart, Kelly, 10, 152, 153, 285
    on earth-sheltered houses, 158–160
Hart, Kelly and Rosana
    earthbag-papercrete house of, 254–257
Hartworks, 257
Healing Environments, 41, 42

health, 8, 37–42, 49–52
Healthy House Institute, 52
Healthy House, The: Creating a Safe, Healthy, and Environmentally Friendly Home, 52
Healthy House, The: How to Buy One, How to Cure a Sick One, How to Build One, 52
Heart House, *46*, 46–47, *53*
Heartwood School, 283
Hemenway, Toby, 285
    on the P.I.N.C., 258–262
hemp, 98, 161–164
Hemp Horizons, 164
Hemp Pages, 164
Hempline, 164
Henstridge, Jack, 148
Hermannsson, James, 242
Heschong, Lisa, 39, 42
Hildago, Oscar, 131
Hoboken, Cai van, 272
Hobson, John, 164
Holmes, Stafford, 232
Holmgren, David, 75
Homing Instinct, 58
Honen, Giles, 178
Houben, Hugo, 142, 205
How to Build Your Elegant Home with Straw Bales (video), 196
Howard, Alfred, 134
Hubbell, James, 35
Huff and Puff Productions, 193
Huggins, Geoff, 146
Hunter, Kaki, 153
Hut of One's Own, A, 61
Huyler, Stephen, 224

I
ICBO Evaluations Services, Inc., 130
Imhoff, Dan, 285
    on recycled materials, 239–242
Institute for Lightweight Structures, 131
insulation, 62–65, 66
intentional communities, 87–91
    case study of, 265–267
International Institute for Bau-Biologie and Ecology, 52, 283
International Raw Earth Institute, 178
Introduction to Permaculture, 82,

278
intuitive design, 43–48
Ireland, Helen and Kevin, 275
Isochanvre method, *162*

J
Jackson, Hildur, 271
Jackson, Ross, 87, 271
Jannsen, Jules, 130, 131
Jarmoltschik, Valentin, 273
JB Plant Fibres, 164
Jimenez, Demitrio, 252
Jimenez, Maria Jesus, 249, 250
Johnson, Robert Francis, x
Joiner's Quarterly, 281
Jones, Barbara, 272, 275, 286
    on working with lime, 225–232
journal writing, 44–45

K
Kachadorian, James, 65
Kahn, Lloyd, 13, 278
Keller, Lars, 275
Kemble, Steve, 150, 196
Kennedy, Joseph F., 286, *xii*
    on building with earthbags, 149–153
    on ecovillages, 87–92
    on natural insulation, 102–104
    on natural paints and finishes, 233–238
    overview of natural building materials by, 94–101
    on roofs for natural building, 206–211
    on wattle and daub building, 204–205
Kern, Ken, 2, 13, 108, 188
Khalili, Nader, 2, 124, 149, 150, 253, 257, 278
Kifmeyer, Doni, 153
Kimmens, Sam, 101
King, Bruce, 246, 278
Kiva structure, *159*
Knox, Judy, 2, 194, 196
    home built by, *195*
Koch, Carolyn, *214*
Komatsu, Yoshio, 25, 278
Kramer, Karl, 131

L
Lacinski, Paul, 195
    on green roofs, 212–213

Lama Foundation, *63*, 65
Lamballais, Loik, 164
Laporte, Robert, 2, 52, 168, 203, 221
Last Straw, The, 110, 196, 232, 280
Lawlor, Anthony, 48
Leadership in Energy and Environmental Design (LEED), 29
leaves, 98
Lee, Fran, *214*
Lebmwickelstaken and *Lehmwellerbau*, 165–168
Lengen, Johan van, 101, 280
Lenssen, Nicholas, 30
Lerner, Kelly, 194
Lewis, Charles A., 42
Liberman, Jacob, 42
life cycle costs, 31–32
light-clay, 165–168
Light: Medicine of the Future, 42
lime, 99, 225–232
Lime in Building, 232
Lime-Online (website), 232
Living on Earth, 25, 278
living roofs, 209–210, 212–213
Living the Good Life, 2, 188
Livingston, Penny, 258–262
Long, Charles, 188
Loos, Adolf, 20, 93
Lyle, John Tillman, 58
Lynne, Elizabeth, 10, 32, 65, 153, 168, 224, 277

M
Maaden, Jolien van der, 272
MacDonald, S.O., 195, 279
Mack, Peter, 195, 278
MacMaster, Duncan, 33–34, 286
Macrae, Alan, 124
Magers, Steve, 188
Magwood, Chris, 195, 278
Maini, Satprem, 268
Manual de Construcción con Bambú (Bamboo Construction Manual), 131
Manual del Arquitecto Descalzo (Manual of the Barefoot Architect), 101, 280
manure, 99
Marsh, Chuck, 286

on Earthhaven, 265–267
masonry
    cordwood, 143–148
    stone, 182–188
Mazer, Susan, 42
McCabe, Kevin, 134
McCain, Mike, 171
McCall, Wayne, 124
McClintock, Mike, 160
McCurdy, Peter, 270
McDonough, William, 20
McGhee, Colin, 218
McGrady, John, 164
McHenry, Paul G., 120–124, 224, 286
McRaven, Charles, 188
Meadows, Dru, 242
Meagan, Keely, 224
meditation, 44–45
Metz, Don, 160
Meyer, Frank, 286
    on tamped road base floors, 118–119
Meyer, Ralph, 238
Mid-Atlantic Straw Bale Association (MASBA), 196
milk paints, 235–236
Mindell, Arnold, 44, 48
Modece Architects, 164
model-making, 45–46
Møller, Steen, 147, 272
Mollison, Bill, 74, 75, 82, 259, 278
Mooseprints: A Holistic Home Building Guide, 168
Morano, Jane, 264
Mud, Space, and Spirit, 124
Mukerji, Kiran, 101, 279
Mumma, Tracy, 278
Myers, Tom, 248
Myrhman, Matts, 2, 194, 279
    home built by, *195*
Myss, Caroline, 43

N

National Association of Home Builders, 51
National Lime Association, 232
natural building. *see also specific building materials and techniques (e.g., adobe, cob, etc.)*
    and building codes, 26–30
and caring craftmanship, 33–34
and considerations of the future, 16–20
designing for. *see* design and designing
and empowerment, 8–9, 11–13
in Europe, 269–275
foundations and, 105–110, 111–112
historical overview of, 1–4
insulation for, 102–104
and life cycle costs, 31–32
overview of benefits, 6–10
overview of materials for, 94–101
paints and finishes in, 233–238
recycled materials in, 239–242
roofs for, 206–211
and site selection, 68–74, 77–78
and social justice, 14–15
Natural Building Colloquia, 3, 65
natural cycles, 37–38
Natural Energy and Vernacular Architecture, 253, 278
Natural History of the Senses, A, 42
Natural House, The, 10, 148, 157
Ndebele houses, *24*
Nearing, Helen and Scott, 2, 13, 108, 188
Nelson, Wayne, 286
    on compressed earth blocks, 138–142
New Independent Home, The, 279
Newsletter of the Pacific Northwest Chapter of the ABS, 131
Norton, John, 124, 137, 142, 205
Norwegian Straw and Earth Building Association, 275
Not So Big House, The, 61

O

Oehlmann, Martin, 274, 275
Oeler, Mike, 159, 160
Oglebay Norton, 224
OK OK OK Productions, 153, 232, 283
Old Fashioned Milk Paint Co., Inc., 238
Oldham, Jeff, 245, 246
Oliver, Paul, 25
oregon cob, 134–136
organic additives, 99
Ornament and Crime, 20
Out on Bale (un)Ltd., 2, 196, 283
Owner Builder's Guide to Stone Masonry, The, 188
Owner-Built Home, The, 2, 13

P

Painted Prayers, 224
paints, 233–238
Paleolithic Prescription, The, 42
paper, 98
papercrete, 98, 171–176
    case study of, 254–257
Papercrete News, 176, 286
Passive Solar Energy, 65
Passive Solar House, The, 65
Pattern Language, A, 58, 277
Patterson, Eric, 171
Pearson, David, 48, 279
Pelos, Carollee, 25, 277
Penfield, Lou, 188
perlite, 104
permaculture, 75–82
    case study of, 258–262
Permaculture: A Designer's Manual, 74
Permaculture: A Practical Guide for a Sustainable Future, 82
Permaculture Activist, The, 82, 280, 285
Permaculture Institute of Northern California (P.I.N.C.), 258–262
Perry, Susan, 42
pigments, 234–235
Pilarski, Michael, 86
pise (accent) and P.I.S.E., 177–181
Place in the Sun, A, 248
Places of the Soul, 48
plasters
    earth, 219–224
    lime, 225–232
plastic foams, 104
Porter, Marley
    house designed by, *69*
    theater designed by, *239*
Potts, Michael, 279
Pratt, Simon, *228*
Prescriptions for a Healthy House, 52, 277
Primer on Sustainable Building, A, 277
Proclay, 168, 224, 283, 285
Prodigious Builders, 25
pumice, 104

R

R-Value comparison chart, 64
Radius Associates, 285
rammed earth, 177–181
Rammed Earth House, The, 277
Rammed Earth Works, 179, 181, 283
Real Goods Independent Builder, The, 211
Real Goods Solar Living Center, 244–248, 283
Real Green Building Book: A Directory of Members, 274
recycled materials, 100, 239–242
Reed, The, 218
reeds, 98, 214–218
regenerative building, 83–86
Regenerative Design for Sustainable Development, 58
Reiss, Gary, 44
Rennick, Jennifer, 32
Restoration Forestry, 86
Reynolds, Michael, 3, 154, 156, 157
    office of, *155*
Robles, Lorenzo, 274
Rodriguez, Mauro, 251
Roodman, David Malin, 30
roofs, 206–211
    green, 209–210, 212–213
    thatched, 214–218
Roulac, John, 164
Roy, Jaki, 2, 144, 147
Roy, Rob, 2, 160, 211, 279, 286
    on cordwood masonry, 143–148
rubble trench foundations, 111–112
Rudofsky, Bernard, 25, 279

S

Sampler of Alternative Homes, A, 10
sand, 96
Sands, David, 130
Sands, Sean, papercrete home of, *172*
Sandy Bar Ranch, *147*
Save the Children office building, *2, 62*

Schaeffer, John, 248
Scher, Les and Carol, 74
Schofield, Jane, 232
Schroeder, Roger, 203
scoria, 104
Secrets our Body Clocks Reveal, The, 42
self-reliance, 11–13
Serious Straw Bale, 195
Shakespeare's Globe Theatre, 275
Shaw, David, 263–264, 286
Sheehan, Steven, 238
shells, 99
Shelter, 13, 278
Shelter Sketchbook, A, 280
Shirokov, Evgeny, 272–273
Sim Van der Ryn and Associates, building designed by, 244–248
site selection, 68–74, 77–78
    and design of home, 53–58
Slay, Reny Mia, 82, 278
Sloan, Annie, 238
Smiley, Linda, 2, 13, 74, 134, 137, 147, 286
    on intuitive design, 43–48
Smith and Associates, 194
Smith, Dallas, 42
Smith, Dan, 194, 261
Smith, Michael G., 13, 48, 117, 211, 258, 279, 286, *xii*
    on cob building, 132–137
    on foundations for natural buildings, 105–110
    on natural building, 1–4, 6–10
    on natural insulation, 102–104
    on regenerative building, 83–86
    on siting natural buildings, 68–74
    on stone masonry, 182–188
Snyder, Phillip, 87
Sobon, Jack, 203
social justice, 14–15
Society for the Protection of Ancient Buildings, 275
sod, 97
solar design and construction, 55, 66–67, 69
    case study of, 244–248
    and life cycle costs, 31–32
Solar Energy International, 283
Solar Survival Architecture, 154

Solberg, Gordon, 286
    on papercrete and fidobe, 171–176
Sorvig, Kim, 58
Sound Choices, 42
Southwest Solaradobe School, 283
Spectacular Vernacular, 25, 277
Spiegel, Ross, 242
square feet, making optimal use of, 59–61
St. Francis de Assisi Church (NM), *219*
Stabilized Earth Structures, 178
steel, 100
Steele, James, 253
Steen, Bill, *221*
Steen, Bill and Athena, 193, 194, 195, 196, 211, 279, 281, 286
    building designed by, *2, 62*
    on earthen floors, 113–117
Stern, Ana, 11
Stickley, Gustav, 243
stone, 95
    as foundation, 108
    insulation of, 62
    masonry, 182–188
story-telling, 46
straw, 97
    and clay, 165–168, 169–170
    insulating properties of, 103
straw bale building, 189–196
Straw Bale Building, 195, 278
straw bale building
    case study of, 261–262, 263–264
    insulation of, 62, 64
    and life cycle costs, 31–32
Straw Bale Building Association for Wales, Ireland, Scotland, and England, 275
Straw Bale House, The, 30, 117, 196, 211, 279
Straw Bale Solution, The (video), 196
Stro & Co., 272
Stultz, Roland, 101, 279
Sturmann, Jan
    cob cottage designed by, *136*
Surfin' Strawbale (website), 196
Susanka, Sarah, 61
sustainable communities, 87–91
Sustainable Energy News, 274

Sustainable Landscape Construction, 58
Sustainable Systems Support, 196, 283
Swan Group, 253, 286
Swan, Simone, 249–253, 286

T
tamped road base floors, 118–119
Tanguay, Francois, 213
Taos Pueblo, *12, 122*
Taylor, Charmaine, 232
Taylor, Duncan, 86
Taylor, John, 280
Temperate Bamboo Quarterly, The, 131
Temple in the House, The, 48
Thatch and Thatching, 218
thatched roofs, 214–218
Thatchers' Craft, The, 218
Thatching: A Handbook, 218
Theis, Bob, 194, 261
Thermal Delight in Architecture, 39, 42
thermal mass, 62–65, 66–67, 78
Thierry Dronet workshop/stable, *xi*
Thompson, J. William, 58
Thoreau, Henry David, 5, 13
Tibbets, Joseph, 124
tile, 96
Tilt, Anni, 248
Timber Frame Construction, 203
Timber Framers Guild of North America, 203
Timber Framer's Workshop, A, 203, 211, 277
timber framing, 197–203
Tiny Book of Tiny Houses, The, 61
tires, rammed, 110
Todd, Nancy Jack and John, 82, 280
Tom, Rob, 286
    on rubble trench foundations, 111–112
Trudeau, Jeffree, 130

U
Underground House Book, The, 160
U.S. Green Building Council (USGBC), 29
Use of Recycled Wood and Paper in Building Applications, The, 242

V
Van der Ryn, Sim, 244, 248

Vélez, Simon, 129, 131
    house designed by, *125, 127*
Venolia, Carol, 286
    on designing for vitality, 36–42
vermiculite, 104
VIBA (Association Integral Bio-logical Architecture), 275
vitality, designing for, 36–42
voluntary simplicity, 15

W
Waernjus, Arild Berg (squish a & e), 275
Walden, 13
Walker, Lester, 61
Wanek, Catherine, 286, *xii*
    on European tradition of natural building, 269–275
    on natural materials and energy efficiency, 62–65
    on straw bale building, 189–196
Watershed Media, 285
wattle and daub building, 204–205
Weaver, Dennis, 3
Wedig, Harold, 270, 275
Wedig, Margit, 275
Wells, Malcolm, 58, 65, 160
Wilkinson, Merv, 19
Wimberley House of Healing, *69*
Wingate, Michael, 164, 232
Wojciechowska, Paulina, 153
Women Build Houses, 283
wood, 97
    and cordwood masonry, 143–148
    as foundation, 108–109
Wood Reduction Clearinghouse, 242
wool, 102
Woolley, Tom, 101, 286
    on building with hemp, 161–164
Working on Yourself Alone, 48
Wright, Cynthia, home of, *178*
Wright, Frank Lloyd, 46

Y
Yassa, Sami, 242
Yestermorrow Design/Build School, 283

Z
Zuker, Gary, house of, *170*

If you have enjoyed The Art of Natural Building you might also enjoy other

Books to Build a New Society

Our books provide positive solutions for people who want to make a difference. We specialize in:

Sustainable Living • Ecological Design and Planning • Natural Building & Appropriate Technology
New Forestry • Environment and Justice • Conscientious Commerce • Progressive Leadership
Educational and Parenting Resources • Resistance and Community • Nonviolence

For a full list of NSP's titles, please call 1-800-567-6772 or check out our web site at:
www.newsociety.com

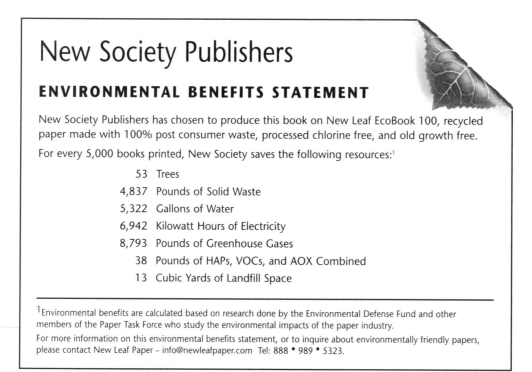

New Society Publishers

ENVIRONMENTAL BENEFITS STATEMENT

New Society Publishers has chosen to produce this book on New Leaf EcoBook 100, recycled paper made with 100% post consumer waste, processed chlorine free, and old growth free.

For every 5,000 books printed, New Society saves the following resources:[1]

53	Trees
4,837	Pounds of Solid Waste
5,322	Gallons of Water
6,942	Kilowatt Hours of Electricity
8,793	Pounds of Greenhouse Gases
38	Pounds of HAPs, VOCs, and AOX Combined
13	Cubic Yards of Landfill Space

[1]Environmental benefits are calculated based on research done by the Environmental Defense Fund and other members of the Paper Task Force who study the environmental impacts of the paper industry.

For more information on this environmental benefits statement, or to inquire about environmentally friendly papers, please contact New Leaf Paper – info@newleafpaper.com Tel: 888 • 989 • 5323.

New Society Publishers